THE THAI ECONOMY
IN TRANSITION

TRADE AND DEVELOPMENT

A series of books on international economic relations and economic issues in development

Edited from the National Centre for Development Studies, Australian National University, by Helen Hughes

Advisory editors
Juergen Donges, *Kiel Institute of World Economics*
Peter Lloyd, *Department of Economics, University of Melbourne*
Gustav Ranis, *Department of Economics, Yale University*
David Wall, *Department of Economics, University of Sussex*

Executive Editor
Maree Tait, *National Centre for Development Studies,
  Australian National University*

Other titles in the series
Helen Hughes (ed.), *Achieving Industrialization in East Asia*
Yun-Wing Sung, *The China–Hong Kong Connection: The Key to
  China's Open Door Policy*
Kym Anderson (ed.), *New Silk Roads: East Asia and World Textile
  Markets*
Rod Tyers and Kym Anderson, *Disarray in World Food Markets:
  A Quantitative Assessment*
Enzo R. Grilli, *The European Community and the Developing
  Countries*

THE THAI ECONOMY IN TRANSITION

Edited by PETER G. WARR

John Crawford Professor of Agricultural Economics
Australian National University

CAMBRIDGE
UNIVERSITY PRESS

Dedicated to Dr Puey Ungphakorn who helped lay the institutional foundations for Thailand's economic transition

Published by the Press Syndicate of the University of Cambridge
The Pitt Building, Trumpington Street, Cambridge CB2 1RP, UK
40 West 20th Street, New York, NY 10011-4211, USA
10 Stamford Road, Oakleigh, Melbourne 3166, Australia

© Cambridge University Press 1993
First published 1993

Printed in Hong Kong by Colorcraft

National Library of Australia cataloguing in publication data
The Thai economy in transition.
  Includes bibliographies and index.
  ISBN 0 521 38186 X.
  1. Thailand—Economic conditions. 2. Thailand—Economic policy.
  3. Thailand—Industries. I. Warr, P.G. (Peter George). (Series:
  Trade and development).
330.9593

Library of Congress cataloguing in publication data
The Thai economy in transition/edited by Peter G. Warr.
—(Trade and development)
  Includes bibliographical references and index.
  ISBN 0 521 38186 X.
  1. Thailand—Economic conditions. 2. Thailand—Economic policy.
  I. Warr, Peter G. II. Series: Trade and development (Cambridge,
  England)
HC445.T397 1993
338.9593—dc20   93-19011
                                                                      CIP

A catalogue record for this book is available from the British Library.

ISBN 0 521 38186 X hardback

Contents

List of Figures and Tables

Tables

List of Contributors

PETER G. WARR, PhD, Stanford University, is John Crawford Professor of Agricultural Economics in the Department of Economics, Research School of Pacific Studies, the Australian National University, Canberra. In 1986–87 he was Visiting Professor in the Faculty of Economics, Thammasat University, Bangkok.

AMMAR SIAMWALLA, PhD, Harvard University, is President of the Thailand Development Research Institute, Bangkok, and formerly Professor of Economics, Faculty of Economics, Thammasat University, Bangkok.

SUTHAD SETBOONSARNG, PhD, University of Hawaii, is Associate Professor of Economics at the Asian Institute of Technology, Bangkok, and formerly Research Associate at the Thailand Development Research Institute, Bangkok.

DIREK PATAMASIRIWAT, PhD, University of Georgia, is Associate Professor of Economics, Naresuan University, Phitsanuloke, Thailand, and formerly Research Fellow at the Thailand Development Research Institute, Bangkok.

SOMSAK TAMBUNLERTCHAI, PhD, Duke University, is Associate Professor, Faculty of Economics, Thammasat University, Bangkok, and presently Coordinator of International Trade and Regional Cooperation Program at the Asian and Pacific Development Centre, Kuala Lumpur, Malaysia.

PASUK PHONGPAICHIT, PhD, Cambridge University, is Associate Professor, Faculty of Economics, Chulalongkorn University, Bangkok.

SAMART CHIASAKUL, MA, Thammasat University, is Associate Professor, Faculty of Economics, Chulalongkorn University, Bangkok.

BHANUPONG NIDHIPRABHA, PhD, Johns Hopkins University, is Assistant Professor, Faculty of Economics, Thammasat University, Bangkok, and Research Fellow at the Thailand Development Research Institute, Bangkok.

CHAIPAT SAHASAKUL, PhD, University of Rochester, is Research Economist with the Securities Exchange of Thailand, Bangkok, and formerly Research Fellow at the Thailand Development Research Institute, Bangkok.

NARIS CHAIYASOOT, PhD, University of Hawaii, is Associate Professor, Faculty of Economics, Thammasat University, Bangkok.

KRAIYUDHT DHIRATAYAKINANT, PhD, University of California, Los Angeles, is Professor of Economics, Faculty of Economics, Chulalongkorn University, Bangkok.

PRAIPOL KOOMSUP, PhD, Yale University, is Associate Professor, Faculty of Economics, Thammasat University, Bangkok. He is the current President of the Economic Society of Thailand.

SIRILAKSANA KHOMAN, PhD, University of Hawaii, is Associate Professor, Faculty of Economics, Thammasat University, Bangkok.

CHALONGPHOB SUSSANGKARN, PhD, Cambridge University, is Program Director of the Human Resource Program at the Thailand Development Research Institute, Bangkok.

MEDHI KRONGKAEW, PhD, Michigan State University, is Associate Professor, Faculty of Economics, Thammasat University, Bangkok, and currently Senior Research Fellow at the Department of Economics, Research School of Pacific Studies, the Australian National University, Canberra.

Editorial Preface

Thailand is the 'flavour of the decade'. Not only have Thai restaurants proliferated throughout the Western world, but interest in Thailand itself and its economy is greater than ever before. Thailand's economy is booming. Its volumes of exports and imports and the level of foreign investment in Thailand itself have reached unprecedented levels. Along with its Southeast Asian neighbours, Malaysia and Indonesia, Thailand is one of what Schlossstein (1991) has called 'Asia's new little dragons', and is well advanced towards joining East Asia's exclusive, if imaginary, club of Newly Industrializing Countries (NICs), presently consisting of Korea, Taiwan, Hong Kong and Singapore. The rest of the world needs to learn about Thailand and its economy, and learn it quickly, if it is to do business successfully with this booming neo-NIC. Scholars too are anxious to learn whatever lessons may be gleaned from Thailand's experience of rapid economic growth.

Learning about Thailand is not easy. Thai scholars have generally preferred to write in Thai—a beautiful but difficult tonal language with its own Sanskrit-based script. Partly because of the language problem, the English language literature on Thailand is thin. A non-Thai looking for an accessible, in-depth but comprehensive account of the contemporary Thai economy looks in vain. Hence the present offering.

This book aims to help bridge the gulf between Thai and non-Thai audiences. It brings together the work of some of Thailand's leading economic researchers. Each was asked to focus on an aspect of the Thai economy in which he or she is expert. The aim was to provide Thai and non-Thai readers with an authoritative yet accessible overview of the Thai economy.

As editor, I wish to acknowledge the cooperation, patience and professionalism of the Thai scholars who contributed to this book. Working with them was a pleasurable, as well as an educational experience.

The financial support of the Australian National University's National Centre for Development Studies made the enterprise possible. The encouragement and assistance of Helen Hughes, Maree Tait and D.P. Chaudhri is gratefully acknowledged. Bandid Nijathaworn was an invaluable colleague during the early planning of the book. Editorial assistance was provided by Anne Dunbar–Nobes, Carol Kavanagh and Monique Lumb. My wife, Suthida, assisted generously at all stages of the task and the assembly of the bibliography was largely her work.

Completion of this enterprise was a labour of love, in several respects. If the resulting product encourages more non-Thais to take a serious interest in this fascinating but little-understood country and its people, it will have been worth the effort.

Peter G. Warr

Notes on Referencing and Tables

Referencing

Much of the literature on the Thai economy has appeared only in the Thai language, but few non-Thais are able to read it. We have thus separated Thai language and English language references in the bibliography. The two are also distinguished in the text. English language references appear as Ingram (1971). Thai language references are identified with a superscript 'T', as in Ammar (1978[T]).

The Western custom of citing authors by their family names is awkward in the case of Thais in that Thai custom is to identify individuals by their first names. Thai family names tend to be long and the use of family names at all is a relatively recent innovation in Thai history. We have thus followed the Thai custom of referring to Thai authors by their first names. These are shorter than family names and are in any case the names by which Thais are most readily recognized within Thailand and abroad. Thus, for example, the 1978 paper of Supote Chunanunthatham is cited as Supote (1978) rather than Chunanunthatham (1978).

Tables

The following symbols are used:
- .. not available
- — zero or insignificant
- n.a. not applicable

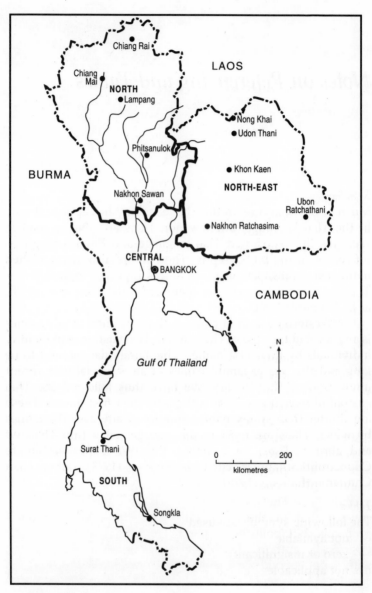

Thailand and its regions

1

The Thai Economy

PETER G. WARR

In 1950, after a century of zero growth of output per head of population, Thailand was one of the poorest countries in the world.[1] In the following four decades, the economy was transformed. Rapid and sustained growth of output was achieved simultaneously with low inflation and only moderate growth of external debt. The incidence of poverty fell dramatically. Despite the international turmoil caused by the two oil price shocks of the 1970s, Thailand did not experience a single year of negative growth, even in per capita terms— an achievement unmatched by any other oil-importing developing country. Over the four years to 1990, the Thai economy was the fastest growing in the world. Manufactured exports surged, and investment from both domestic and foreign sources increased dramatically.

The structure of the Thai economy, and its trade with the rest of the world, is changing rapidly—from that of a relatively backward exporter of agricultural products to that of an economically progressive state with exports dominated by manufactured goods and services. Thailand is truly an economy in transition. The growth of the urban middle class, heavily concentrated in the capital, Bangkok, has led to political problems. But political trouble is nothing new for Thailand. Historically, authoritarian military governments have alternated with brief periods of democracy or semi-democracy, all combined with repeated coups, attempted coups and political violence. The paradox is that after a long period of economic stagnation, economic progress has occurred in an extraordinarily rapid and stable manner, and in spite of apparent political turmoil.

How did this puzzling combination of events happen? Can

Thailand's economic progress be sustained? What lessons, if any, might other countries learn from Thailand's experience? The first place to look for answers is obviously the literature written by Thais themselves. Unfortunately, while Thailand has many outstanding economists, much of their written output has appeared only in the Thai language, making it inaccessible to all but a handful of Westerners.[2] Moreover, the Thai literature has reflected an understandable preoccupation with the country's own immediate economic problems. Consequently, this literature has usually been narrowly focused and has tended to lack an international perspective.[3] Other countries have experienced problems similar to most of those identified in the Thai literature, and their experience is presumably relevant for an understanding of Thailand's problems and successes.

Very little discussion in the Thai literature has addressed the reasons for Thailand's comparatively good aggregate economic performance. The Thai authors have focused instead on the structural problems of their economy, including those that are products of the growth process itself, and the problems of the social groups that have so far been by-passed by economic growth. These are important matters, especially within the Thai context, but the outsider finds little explanation in this literature of why Thailand has apparently done so well relative to other developing countries.

The foreign literature on the Thai economy has included much scholarly and useful work, but a high proportion of it has fallen into two ideological and predictable forms of discussion.[4] They are each so different from the Thai literature, and from one another, that at times it seems doubtful that the same country is being discussed by all three. One group of foreigners casually attributes Thailand's good aggregate economic performance to what are taken to be its liberal domestic trading environment, open international trade policies, conservative macroeconomic policies, and dynamic private sector. This group ignores almost all of the problems that the Thais themselves stress to be important. Rather than describing the triumph of market forces, the Thai authors are more likely to describe the growth-inhibiting effects of existing interventions, bureaucratic slowness and corruption, and problems of equity.

A second group of foreigners seems preoccupied with pointing to the evils of capitalism as such and this has coloured its perspective on Thailand. This group finds very little that is positive in Thailand's rapid economic growth. It focuses on environmental despoilment caused by ill-planned development, enormous income gaps between the urban rich and the rural poor, cultural changes (presumed to be unfavourable) induced by economic development, especially from tourism, and more recently, the genuine and terrible prospect of an AIDS epidemic. The Thais themselves discuss all these issues, but in a less apocalyptic manner; after all, they have a greater stake in finding workable solutions.

The book aims to help bridge the gulf between the Thai and non-Thai audiences. It brings together the work of some of Thailand's leading economic researchers. Each was asked to focus on an aspect of the Thai economy in which he or she is expert. The aim is to provide Thai and non-Thai readers with an authoritative yet accessible overview of the Thai economy.

This chapter attempts to provide the background for this discussion. It is intended to complement the specialized chapters which follow by providing an overview of the Thai economy as a whole. The following chapters each take an important aspect of the Thai economy and discuss it in depth. The present chapter begins with a brief profile of Thai social and economic data. It is followed by a summary of Thai political history since the founding of Bangkok two centuries ago. This discussion is meant to provide some of the historical background within which Thailand's remarkable post-war economic growth has occurred. The following sections then survey the present structure of Thailand's product markets, labour markets and financial markets; the role and structure of the public sector; Thailand's economic performance, both over the long term and then, in more depth, over the period since 1970; and finally some of Thailand's environmental issues.

Social and political profile

Population

In mid-1990, Thailand's population was 55.8 million and, in the decade prior to that, had been growing at an average annual rate of 1.8 per cent, down from 2.7 per cent over the decade before. Population density was 107 persons per square kilometre of total area and 275 persons per square kilometre of cultivable land. In 1990, the urban population was 23 per cent of the total, compared with 13 per cent in 1965. In 1990, 70 per cent of the population worked in agriculture, compared with 6 per cent in industry and 24 per cent in services (Table 1.1). The corresponding data for 1965 were: agriculture 82 per cent, industry 5 per cent and services 13 per cent. For countries in Thailand's income group, its degree of urbanization is unusually low and the importance of agriculture in total employment is high. For example, in the Philippines in 1990, urbanization was 43 per cent and the 1990 distribution of employment in agriculture, industry and services was 41, 10 and 49 per cent, respectively. Even more unusual is the degree to which the urban population is concentrated in a single city, Bangkok. For countries of Thailand's size, the concentration of the urban population in the capital city is surely unique.

In 1990, some 60 per cent of the population were of working age (15–64 years) compared with 50 per cent in 1965. Life expectancy at birth was 63 years for males and 67 years for females, an increase for both of about nine years since 1965. The crude birth rate and crude death rates in 1990 were 22 and 7 per thousand, respectively, compared with 43 and 12 per thousand, respectively, in 1965.

The majority of the Thai population is Buddhist, with Islam an important force in the southern provinces. There is a large population of Chinese origin, concentrated in Bangkok, which dominates Thailand's domestic commerce. Ethnic and religious conflicts have occurred but are of minor importance by international standards, including the standards of most of Thailand's Southeast Asian neighbours.

Government

Thailand's government is nominally a constitutional monarchy with an elected parliament. In practice, the military plays a significant role in Thai politics and heavy military involvement in government affairs has traditionally been tolerated. In the last two decades, the role of the military in public affairs has become increasingly contentious. The growth of an urban, educated middle class has led to increasing demands for democratic reform and for a reduced role for the military, in economic affairs as well as in political life. An important example has been the traditional role of senior military figures in controlling Thailand's public enterprises (see Chapter 8). Critics have attributed much of the corruption and inefficiency associated with Thailand's public enterprises to military domination of their controlling boards. Recent political history has been characterized by a succession of military coups and attempted coups, sometimes followed by relatively democratic periods (as at present), sometimes not.

The present king is His Majesty King Bhumibol Adulyadej who has reigned since 1946 and whose popularity clearly transcends that of any political figure. The degree of public reverence accorded to the present king is astounding to any non-Thai who witnesses it.

Social indicators

Table 1.1 provides comparative social data for Thailand and several other Asian countries. Thailand's expenditure on education as a proportion of GDP is normal for countries at its income level (the exceptional case is Indonesia); its adult literacy rate in 1990 was 93 per cent. However, the pattern of expenditures on education was skewed heavily towards the tertiary level, as Sirilaksana Khoman describes in Chapter 10. In 1989, the percentage of persons in the relevant age groups who were enrolled in formal education were: primary school 86, secondary school 28, and higher education 16. The low participation rate at the secondary school level is especially significant—the comparable statistic for the Philippines was more than twice this at 73 per cent. In 1965, the participation rates in Thailand were (per cent): primary school 78, secondary school 14, and higher education 2. It is clear that educational investment has been concentrated at the higher level, at the relative expense of secondary school education.

Thailand's infant mortality rate was 27 per thousand live births in 1990, compared with 90 per thousand in 1965. Comparable data for the Philippines were 41 per thousand and 73 per thousand, respectively. Data on income distribution are available for 1988. The percentage share of household income by quintiles, beginning with the lowest, was: 4.0, 8.1, 12.5, 20.5 and 54.9. The

Table 1.1: Basic indicators: Thailand and other selected East Asian countries

	Average annual growth of population (%) 1980-90	GNP per capita US$ 1990	Average annual growth of real GNP per capita (%) 1965-90	Average annual rate of inflation (%) 1965-90	Life expectancy at birth (years) 1990	Employment % total (1986-89) Agriculture	Industry	Services
Thailand	1.8	1,420	4.4	5.1	69	70	6	24
China	1.4	370	5.8	2.1	70	74	14	13
Indonesia	1.8	570	4.5	24.7	62	54	8	38
Philippines	2.4	730	1.3	12.8	64	42	10	49
Malaysia	2.6	2,320	4.0	3.6	70	42	19	39
Korea, Republic	1.1	5,400	7.1	13.1	71	18	27	56
India	2.1	350	1.9	7.2	59	63	11	27

	Expenditure on education as % GNP (1989)	Secondary school enrolment (% age group) (1988–89)	Urban population as % total (1990)	Per cent urban population in largest city (1980)	Income distribution lowest 20% total share of (%) year	Gini coefficient	Poverty per cent population below poverty line (1980–89) Total	Rural
Thailand	3.2	38	23	69	4.0 (1988)	0.47	30	34
China	2.4	44	33	6	..	..	..	..
Indonesia	0.9	47	31	23	8.8 (1987)	0.31	39	44
Philippines	2.9	73	43	30	5.5 (1985)	0.45	58	64
Malaysia	5.6	87	72	41	4.6 (1987)	0.48	27	38
Korea, Republic	3.6	87	72	41	n.a.	0.36	16	11
India	3.2	43	27	6	8.1 (1983)	0.42	48	51

·· not available
Source: World Bank, *World Development Report*, 1992.

percentage share of the highest 10 per cent was 34.8. Comparable data for the Philippines (relating to 1985) were: 5.2, 8.9, 13.2, 20.2 and 52.5, with the highest 10 per cent, 37.0. These data suggest a marginally more unequal distribution in Thailand than the Philippines. The Gini coefficients reported in Table 1.1 also suggest this conclusion (the higher the Gini coefficient, the more unequal the distribution). Thai data for 1981 suggest a somewhat less unequal distribution than the above Philippine data or the 1988 Thai data. Income inequality in Thailand appears to be widening (Figure 1.1). The data in Table 1.1 also show that, as in most Asian countries, poverty in Thailand is particularly concentrated in rural areas.

Figure 1.1 Income shares by population quintile, 1975–76 and 1988

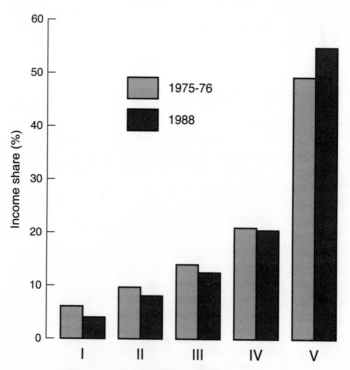

Note: Quintile I is the poorest, quintile V the richest.

Sources: Suganya and Somchai (1988) and National Statistical Office (1988), *Report of the 1988 Household Socio-economic Survey: Whole Kingdom*, Bangkok, Thailand.

Political history

The principal focus in this book is on economics, rather than politics, but the two cannot really be divorced. This section provides a brief outline of the political and historical context within which Thailand's economic transition has occurred.

The Bangkok period, 1782 to the present

The destruction of the Thai capital of Ayuthaya by Burmese forces in 1767 led to the relocation of the capital to Bangkok in 1782. The latter event coincided with the founding of the Chakri dynasty, which has reigned since. The present king is the ninth of the dynasty (thus known as Rama IX). Appreciation of the importance of these historical events is crucial to understanding the dominant role Bangkok continues to play in Thai public life and in the Thai imagination. Bangkok's central importance extends well beyond its being merely the national capital. Partly because of this history, the concentration of Thailand's economic activity in this one city is unmatched among countries of Thailand's size.

The relocation of the capital from Ayuthaya to Bangkok was apparently motivated by military considerations, but it had an important economic consequence. Whereas Ayuthaya is located far up-river, Bangkok is a maritime city adjacent to the Gulf of Thailand. This fact was later to facilitate commerce and international communication in a way that might not have been possible if the capital had remained at Ayuthaya.

Avoidance of colonization

In the nineteenth century, Thailand avoided colonization by European powers by successfully playing off the British (in Burma and India to the west and in Malaya to the south) against the French (in Indo-China to the east and in Laos to the north). Major territorial concessions were made to the British (including what is now Penang in Malaysia) and the French (including much of present Cambodia and Laos) to preserve the independence of Thailand's Central Plains—particularly Bangkok.

The Bowring Treaty, signed between King Mongkut (Rama IV) and Great Britain in 1855, required Thailand to adopt relatively free trade economic policies. But, unlike similar treaties signed at around the same time with China and Japan, Thailand entered into the agreement relatively voluntarily, perhaps in anticipation of the alternatives the British might have otherwise imposed (Ingram 1971).

In the Thai historical accounts, King Chulalongkorn, the fifth king of the Chakri dynasty (Rama V) reigning from 1868 to 1910, is given great credit for avoiding colonization, establishing the Thai civil service and abolishing slavery. Recent historical accounts have attributed Thailand's non-colonization more to a convenient compromise between the British and French (Wyatt 1984), but it is clear that King Chulalongkorn perceived the importance of internal financial stability in keeping the European colonizers at bay. Any sign of Thai financial instability, it was feared, might have been used as a pretext for the European gunboats to attack Bangkok. The King engaged a British financial adviser from the Bank of England to advise on economic matters. Predictably, the advice was conservative. The position of British Financial Adviser was influential and was not finally abolished until the late 1950s. More importantly, the Bank of England became the conservative model for the establishment and operation of the Bank of Thailand following World War II.

Free trade policies promoted the expansion of agricultural exports but did not produce rapid economic growth per head of population. In the century following the Bowring Treaty, Thai economic growth barely kept pace with population growth (Sompop 1989), and there was virtually no structural change. Agricultural exports were the main source of both foreign exchange and government revenue. The agricultural growth was not driven by improved productivity but by expansion of the cultivated land area, a point discussed in depth by Ammar Siamwalla, Suthad Setboonsarng and Direk Patamasiriwat in Chapter 2. Cultivable land remained abundant until the 1960s.

Constitutional monarchy, 1932 to present

The period of absolute monarchy ended in 1932 with a *coup d'etat* against King Prajadhipok, the seventh king of the Chakri dynasty (Rama VII). The coup occurred while the King was on a seaside holiday near Bangkok. He agreed to return to the capital and support a constitutional monarchy. Although the coup seems to have lacked public support almost entirely, it was successfully portrayed as a 'revolution' (Wright 1991). A succession of military-dominated governments followed.

Thailand allied itself with Japan during World War II, once invasion by Japanese forces became imminent. The Japanese enforced a fixed exchange rate between the baht and yen, and Thailand consequently shared in the Japanese hyperinflation towards the end of the war. This inflation continued for several years after the war and constituted the country's sole experience of sustained rapid inflation. It immediately preceded the founding of the central bank, the Bank of Thailand, which has rigorously pursued anti-inflationary monetary policies ever since—not unlike those of the Bank of England, on which it was modelled.

Conservative military-controlled governments followed World War II. The decade after the war was dominated politically by Phibul Songkhram, prime minister from 1948 to 1957—when a coup, motivated by charges of election-rigging, forced him into exile. The military strongman Field Marshal Sarit Thanarat installed two consecutive prime ministers, first diplomat Phote Sarasin and then General Thanom Kittikachorn, until assuming the premiership himself in 1958. Sarit's government began with the arrest of scores of suspected communists and the dissolution of parliament. The subsequent period has become known as the period of 'Despotic Paternalism'.

An event with unusual significance for subsequent Thai economic history was a World Bank advisory mission in 1957 (Suehiro 1989). The report of this mission (International Bank for Reconstruction and Development 1959) influenced Thai economic policy in two important ways. First, the report recommended a fundamental shift in the nature of public sector involvement in the economy—away from direct production, via the extensive and highly inefficient public enterprise sector that existed at that time, and towards concentration on investment in the public infrastructure required for economic development (roads, ports, electricity supply, telecommunications and so forth). Second, the report recommended a change in the government's method of promoting private sector investment.

The report found a receptive audience in the government of the time and significant changes in economic policy followed. There was a new surge of public investment in infrastructure and the newly formed National Economic and Social Development Board (NESDB) began to produce regular five-year development plans to guide these investments. Although most of the public enterprises then in existence remained, they became relatively less significant as private sector economic activity in manufacturing grew. Also, a Board of Investment (BOI) was created in 1958 to render assistance to private investors.

The Thanom military government, 1963–73

With Sarit's death in December 1963, power shifted to a new military alliance headed by General Thanom Kittikachorn and General Prapas Charusathien. Thanom became the prime minister and Prapas assumed the powerful posts of commander-in-chief of the army and minister of the interior. The new government was less rigid than its predecessor but continued to ban political parties and political gatherings. The administration was preoccupied with the security problems associated with the growing communist threat.

A new constitution was promulgated in June 1968 and an election was held in February 1969. Thanom continued as prime minister. The new government's main weakness was its inability to control the large number of independent MPs. In November 1971, a plan to defeat the government in a vote of no confidence by the opposition was discovered and prompted Thanom to stage a coup against his own government. The constitution and the Political Parties Act were abrogated and the country was brought under the management of the National Executive Council headed by Thanom. In December, an interim constitution gave sweeping power to the government and Thanom continued as prime minister.

The government became increasingly unpopular, partly because of its unwillingness to return to democratic rule. The military was also becoming wary of Thanom and Prapas, who had built up lucrative networks in business and dominated the succession in the army. In October 1973, a number of students and former MPs were arrested on a charge of inciting public unrest while distributing leaflets calling for democracy. The arrest prompted a student protest at Thammasat University which gained momentum and led to the downfall of the government when a bloody confrontation broke out between students and soldiers. Many students were killed and the King personally intervened by asking Thanom and Prapas to leave the country. Under pressure from other members of the military, the two went into exile.

Civilian government, 1973–76

The King appointed Sanya Dhammasak, Rector of Thammasat University, as the new prime minister. The Sanya government prepared the way for a period of democracy and civilian government. The absence of Thanom and Prapas weakened the military and provided an opportunity for experimentation with civilian-based politics. A new constitution was promulgated in October 1974. Unlike the previous constitutions, the 1974 constitution featured most of the basic elements of British-style parliamentary democracy. The Political Parties Act was liberalized, although the Communist Party remained illegal. There were 43 political parties registered for the general election held in January 1975.

The election returned to the House of Representatives some 269 MPs belonging to 22 political parties. The Democrats headed the list with 72 elected MPs and managed to form a minority government headed by Seni Pramoj, who became Thailand's first elected prime minister. The new government was defeated in a vote of no confidence in March 1975 and the premiership went to Kukrit Pramoj, leader of the Social Action Party, who had engineered the Democrats' defeat.

Some interesting policy initiatives were introduced under Kukrit's government. These could be seen as reflecting Kukrit's attempts to accommodate conflicting interests in Thai society. Thailand renormalized diplomatic relations with China, closed American military bases in the country, and introduced several welfare programs and measures that later became basic elements of policies other governments were to follow. The rice price support program, the Tambon (district) development funds, and the policy for free medical care for the poor, were examples. Kukrit's main problem was the hostility of the army, a problem which later democratic governments were to share. The military became increasingly impatient with public demands for social change and the growing influence of left-leaning ideologies among students and the labour movement. The in-fighting among government MPs for cabinet portfolios was another of Kukrit's problems. Under pressure from the military, Kukrit reshuffled cabinet members and finally dissolved parliament in January 1976 when a motion to oust him through a vote of no confidence was about to be launched.

The election of April 1976 was unusually violent. A number of farmers, students and labour leaders who supported liberal political parties were killed. The Democrats again returned the largest number of MPs to the House of Representatives, with 114 elected. Kukrit's Social Action Party won 56 seats but he himself failed to be re-elected. The Democrats formed a four-party coalition government under the premiership of Seni Pramoj.

The new coalition government was divided when former prime minister Thanom Kittikachorn returned from exile as a Buddhist monk. Students mobilized in protest against the return of the former dictator. It seemed to many that the return of Thanom was a provocation to disorder. The situation became uncontrollable when civilian mobs and police stormed Thammasat University to silence the student protest. On the morning of Sunday 6 October 1976, many students were killed and many more arrested. The Seni government was unable to keep order. That same evening, the military staged a coup, dissolved parliament and abandoned the constitution. This coup, ending three years of civilian government marked by perpetual political turmoil and student unrest, put the premiership and the control of government back in the hands of the military.

The brief years of civilian government had coincided with significant economic changes. New interest groups had emerged and new policies initiated and implemented. An important new development was the involvement of the business class in politics. A number of bankers and well-known business people obtained ministerial portfolios and were able to influence the direction of economic policies. This was a radical departure from the previous periods when control over policy was shared only by the military and the bureaucracy.

Military rule, 1976–79

The new military strongman was Admiral Sangad Chaloryu who headed the coup under the banner of the National Administrative Reform Council. The new government, backed by the military, was headed by an ultra-conservative lawyer, Thanin Kraivichien. Thanin's strong anti-communist stand and nationalistic attitude led him to adopt extreme policies which alienated his government from the bureaucracy, the press, foreign allies, and factions in the army, particularly the army's young field commanders. The emphasis of the administration had shifted back towards national security and law and order, ignoring the country's basic social problems. The military became increasingly embarrassed by Thanin's conservative vision. In October 1977, the military staged a coup to dismiss the man they had put into power.

Although no major change in economic policy was evident, one important policy implemented by Thanin during his one year of tenure was the decision to empower the Ministry of Finance to borrow from abroad. This, for the first time, provided the public sector with direct access to foreign funds. It is not clear whether the decision was made to please the military or to facilitate expansion of public investment, but it led to a surge in both public expenditure and the country's foreign debt.

The 1977 coup was again led by Admiral Sangad, who headed the National Revolutionary Council that took power. Nevertheless, the premiership was offered to an army general, Kriangsak Chamanand, whose soft diplomacy during the Thanin period had made him popular among many sections of the Thai community. The premiership, which was granted under an interim constitution, was to be limited to one year during which Kriangsak was to prepare for national elections and civilian rule.

The military had been divided over the choice of the premiership succeeding Thanin. Kriangsak's leadership was known to have the backing of the young field commanders in the army and was favoured by Washington and Peking to ease tensions in the region. His immediate task was to consolidate power within the military and to ease tensions that had accumulated during the Thanin period. To achieve this, he personally sponsored an amnesty bill pardoning all those arrested in the incident of 6 October in the previous year.

Censorship of the press was lifted. He concurrently made himself defence minister and reshuffled the military to consolidate his power base. One of his major appointments was that of General Prem Tinsulanonda as the army commander-in-chief.

A new constitution was promulgated in November 1978. Under it, the parliament was made up of an elected House of Representatives and an appointed Senate. The constitution gave limited power to the elected house and preserved military influence in the parliament through the appointed Senate. The leader of the Senate, who was also leader of parliament, was to nominate candidates for the premiership for a vote in a joint sitting. This tacitly brought the prime ministership under the influence of the military and the bureaucracy, which dominated the Senate. The constitution was thus seen by many as a perpetuation of military rule.

Quasi-civilian government, 1979–91

In April 1979, a general election was held under the new constitution. No single party obtained a majority and the Senate selected Kriangsak to continue the premiership by leading a coalition government made up largely of pro-Kriangsak independents. The composition of the Kriangsak cabinet was a focal point for attack by the opposition because it reduced the role of elected MPs in government. The downfall of the government came in February 1980 when the government announced a string of oil price increases, which promptly met with strong public protest. The parliamentary opposition united over the issue and submitted a motion calling for a vote of no confidence. A number of government MPs openly supported the no-confidence motion. Unable to control the situation, Kriangsak resigned one day before the scheduled motion was to be debated in parliament.

The prime ministership was offered to General Prem Tinsulanonda, a respected army general, who was favoured by the military and the main political parties. Prem became prime minister in March 1980. He was not an elected member of parliament—a constitutional possibility that was to produce havoc a decade later. The Prem government's main feature was an accommodation or a sharing of power between the political parties, the military and the bureaucracy. Through the appointed

Senate, the military and the bureaucracy controlled the premiership and screened important policies. The prime minister maintained the influence of the bureaucracy in government by controlling the appointment of three important cabinet portfolios: defence, finance and interior. The other portfolios were shared among the coalition parties. Although there were several political crises during the Prem administration which led to cabinet reshuffles, attempted coups and elections, the basic arrangement of power sharing described above remained undisturbed for eight years. Threats of a vote of no confidence, and of embarrassing revelations regarding Prem himself, led to Prem's resignation in 1988.

The resulting election in July 1988 led to the selection of Chatichai Choonhavan as prime minister, the first elected member of parliament to become prime minister since Seni Pramoj in 1976. The Chatichai government presided over the period of most rapid economic growth in Thai history, but the government itself was widely regarded as corrupt, even by Thailand's generous standards. Civilians were appointed to key economic posts which the military leadership had regarded as its own, leading to serious tensions.

The 1991 military coup

In February 1991 the military leadership staged a sudden coup against Chatichai, installing a National Peace Keeping Council to run the country and abolishing the 1978 constitution. The coup leaders, General Suchinda Kraprayoon and General Sunthorn Kongsompong cited the corruption of the Chatichai government as the reason for the coup. Close observers regarded corruption itself as a less significant reason than that the Chatichai government had acted to exclude the top military leaders from its benefits.

The coup leaders installed a widely respected businessman, Anand Panyarachun, as prime minister. Elections were held in early 1992 and parties supporting the military won control of the parliament. General Suchinda became prime minister even though he was not himself an elected member of parliament and had publicly promised not to claim the prime ministership for himself. Public uproar by pro-democracy demonstrators followed. The demonstrators were led by the former Governor of Bangkok, Major-General Chamlong Srimuang, who staged a public hunger strike in protest at Suchinda's actions. The composition of the protesters reflected the rapid socio-economic change occurring in Thailand. Unlike the youthful student demonstrators of 1973 and 1976, the 1992 demonstrators included a high proportion of affluent, middle-aged, middle-class professionals—many reportedly carrying mobile telephones and driving to the demonstrations after work in Volvos and BMWs—but a significant number of these were themselves veterans of the student demonstrations of the 1970s.

The chaos led, in mid-May, to a massacre of demonstrators by soldiers apparently acting under the orders of Suchinda himself. Suchinda was forced from office in disgrace. Further conflict was avoided when the King intervened by re-appointing Anand Panyarachun to the prime ministership to prepare for fresh elections, subsequently held in September.

Political stability?

The above summary of recent Thai political history would hardly lead one to predict stability of either economic policy or performance. But that is exactly what happened. How can it be explained? The facts are indeed puzzling, but four points can be mentioned in partial explanation.

First, Thailand's political history has not been as turbulent as it may seem. Although power has often changed hands through violence, or the threat of violence, the various contending forces have had a great deal in common. Political leaders must in general be acceptable to the military or at least to some powerful factions within it. Most potential political leaders either are or have recently been senior military men. The degree of military involvement in political affairs in Thailand surprises many foreign observers, as does its wide public tolerance within Thailand where it has been seen as a normal state of affairs for most of Thailand's history. Strong military connections are indispensable for aspiring political leaders. This means that politicians espousing views that conflict strongly with the conservative outlook shared by most Thai military men can expect trouble.

Second, partly because of the military factor, Thailand's political life is not characterized by wide ideological differences. Thai politics is highly competitive but the major parties share acceptance of the importance of preserving Thai traditions and institutions, and especially a loyalty to the present monarch, King Bhumibol. In these respects, the fact that Thailand was not colonized by European powers is clearly very important. Thai traditions and institutions were not trampled upon or discredited by the militarily superior Europeans in the way that they were in most former colonies. The Thai intelligentsia have little difficulty in identifying with their country's past.

Third, since the 1960s, most political leaders in Thailand have perceived a military threat from communist Vietnam. This has had a unifying effect and encouraged caution in domestic and foreign policy.

The fourth and final point relates to the Thai bureaucracy. The above three points apply at least as much to the bureaucrats as to the politicians, and Thailand's conservative bureaucracy exhibits a surprising degree of independence from political control. For our purposes, the most interesting example is the central bank, the Bank of Thailand. The bank has a reputation for striving to preserve its independence from political control and for using that independence to pursue conservative monetary policies, almost regardless of the government of the day.

Market structure

Macroeconomic overview

Before describing Thailand's product, labour, finance and capital markets in detail, I shall provide a simplified description of the macroeconomic environment operating in the Thai economy. Thailand has followed a fixed exchange rate policy since the end of World War II. The baht has been pegged to the US dollar. The trading system is relatively open, but the capital account is less so. Movements of foreign exchange and Thai currency out of Thailand are regulated, although some of these regulations have recently been relaxed. Large conversions of Thai currency into foreign exchange, for the purpose of capital export, require Bank of Thailand approval.

Interest rates within Thailand are regulated by ceilings set by the Bank of Thailand. These apply to both borrowing and lending rates. Throughout most of Thailand's recent economic history, interest rates have remained at these ceiling levels.

Wages within Thailand are officially subject to minimum wage controls, but these controls are effective only within the public sector and among large business enterprises. Elsewhere—in agriculture, small industrial enterprises and in much of the service sector—the minimum wages cannot be enforced. The minimum wages, in any case, seem to follow market forces, remaining somewhat above wages seen in the small private manufacturing enterprises.

Thailand's macroeconomic policies have been conservative for most of the last century and for all of the post-war period. Maintenance of a stable exchange rate backed by secure international reserves and, most especially, avoidance of domestic inflation have been central policy objectives. The post-war Thai policy environment has also been characterized by the relative independence of the central bank, the Bank of Thailand.

A central issue in understanding the Thai macroeconomic experience relates to the combined implications of its fixed exchange rate, partially controlled capital account and domestic interest rate controls. These variables determine the extent to which the domestic money supply can be controlled by the Bank of Thailand versus international capital flows. Monetary and fiscal policies both appear to have been counter-cyclical and stabilizing in the past (see Chapters 5 and 6), suggesting that capital flows are not fully free. But recent capital account reforms will enhance capital mobility and hence reduce the Bank of Thailand's ability to exercise this stabilizing role.

Product markets

As with most low- and middle-income developing countries, Thailand's product market policies imply taxation of agriculture and subsidization of industry. Export taxes have historically been applied to several agricultural export commodities, but have been slowly phased out. Rubber is now the only commodity subject to an export tax. Tariffs and quantitative import restrictions are used to protect part of the manufacturing sector. The production of these commodities is highly competitive, with a couple of exceptions mentioned below.

Rice is by far the most important agricultural commodity and a major export revenue earner for Thailand. Until recently, rice exports were taxed by a combination of instruments: the rice premium (a specific export tax); an export duty (an ad valorem export tax); and a reserve requirement (equivalent to an ad valorem export tax). The effect was to keep both consumer prices and prices received by farmers well below international prices. Chirmsak (1984) calculated that the combined effect of these policies was equivalent to a 31 per cent export tax in 1970, using the f.o.b. export price as a base, a 67 per cent export tax in 1973–74 (years of very high international prices), which then declined to 13 per cent by 1984. The rice premium was suspended in early 1986 in response to the low international prices for rice, and has not been reinstated.

In addition to these policies, the government assigns export quotas to individual export agents, the effect of which is to introduce a non-competitive element into the rice export market. The government annually announces target prices for paddy, but this is generally understood to be cosmetic. Some farmers are able to sell at support prices above current market prices with funds derived from the Farmer Aid Fund, the funds originating earlier from the proceeds of the rice premium. The majority of farmers derive no benefit from this provision. The major exception to the general story of taxation of smallholder agriculture for the benefit of urban consumers occurs in the case of sugar. Domestic sugar prices are held above international prices. In the mid-1980s, domestic prices were at least three times as high as international prices. The sugar industry is characterized by some large farmers and a greater number of smaller ones. The small farmers are dependent on the larger ones for their markets because the large farmers typically hold supplier contracts with the small number of large sugar mills. These large farmers and the mill owners act jointly to form a powerful political lobby.

Parts of the manufacturing sector are highly protected and inefficient, but the manufacturing sector is generally competitive and less highly regulated than the manufacturing sectors of some of Thailand's Southeast Asian neighbours.

Labour markets

Thailand's labour markets can be divided into four major sectors: the civil service, the public enterprises, large private firms and small private firms. Average wages are higher in the first two sectors, but so too are the educational requirements for jobs in those sectors. The data on wages in Thailand are very unreliable. Under the Labour Relations Act of 1975, trade unions are not permitted in the civil service but are legal elsewhere in the economy. In practice, trade unions are strong only in the public enterprises, which have a long history of labour organization. These firms generally enjoy monopolies in their industries and commonly have only a single large plant, located in Bangkok. These features make it relatively easy for unions to organize the workforce. Large private firms have a history of opposing the formation and operation of unions. In this, the firms have generally received government support. A variety of tactics, including physical intimidation, have been used against workers attempting to organize unions (Mabry 1984; Hewison 1989). The unions cannot expect much help from the government.

Small private firms—which make up almost all of the agricultural sector most of manufacturing and almost all of the service sector—obviously employ the bulk of the workforce. The employees are not organized because the cost of organizing workers in scattered small firms would be very high. Labour markets in this, the dominant part of economy, are generally competitive, and wages appear to be flexible in response to variations in labour supply and demand (Bertrand and Squire 1980).

The evidence presented by Bertrand and Squire does not support the 'dual economy' hypothesis in regard to Thailand's labour markets. Minimum wage legislation exists, but is effective only within the public sector and some, but not all, of the large private firms. The legislated minimum wages tend to be marginally above the wages paid by small private firms. The discrepancy is greatest among the youngest, least skilled employees.

There is considerable geographical mobility of labour. In recent decades, this has largely meant migration to Bangkok where the new jobs have been heavily concentrated. Nevertheless, as Chalongphob Sussangkarn points out in Chapter 11, seasonal migration among agricultural regions is also important. Official statistics on unemployment rates are very unreliable; nevertheless, open unemployment seems to be a rare phenomenon in Thailand, except among the most highly educated. Chalong-phob's chapter provides a valuable discussion of the reasons for high rates of open unemployment among university graduates.

Financial markets

As with many other developing countries, Thailand's financial markets include both substantial organized and unorganized sectors. The organized sector can be broadly defined to include all legally registered institutions. The unorganized sector refers to financial transactions which do not go through organized financial institutions, of which the most prevalent forms are borrowing and lending among individuals and the rotating credit societies.

Thailand's organized financial markets are made up of seven main financial institutions: commercial banks; finance, securities, and credit companies; specialized banks; development finance corporations; insurance companies; savings cooperatives; and other mortgage institutions. The commercial banks comprise the largest component in terms of total assets, credit extended, and savings mobilized. The second largest is the finance companies which began operating in 1969. There are three specialized banks, the Government Saving Bank (GSB), the Bank of Agriculture and Agricultural Cooperatives (BAAC) and the Government Housing Bank (GHB), and two development finance corporations, the Industrial Finance Corporation of Thailand (IFCT), and the Small Industries Finance Office (SIFO). These specialized institutions are either owned or partly owned by the government.

The financial market is dominated by the activities of commercial banks, which absorb roughly three-quarters of all deposits placed with financial institutions. They are, therefore, the central actors in Thailand's financial system, and they are discussed in detail by Naris Chaiyasoot in Chapter 7. The current structure consists of 16 local (Thai-owned) banks and 14 foreign banks, with the role of foreign banks being very limited. The 1962 Commercial Banking Act restricted entry to the banking business by requiring licensing permits—and the last permit was granted in 1965. Of the 16 local commercial banks, one is a state enterprise (Krung Thai Bank), one is owned by the

Crown Property Bureau (Siam Commercial Bank), another is partly owned by the government (Sayam Bank) and one is primarily owned by military personnel (Thai Military Bank).

A significant feature of the commercial banking industry in Thailand is the high degree of concentration in ownership, as Naris describes. Ownership is dominated by 16 families of Chinese origin. This feature is considered by the Thai monetary authorities to be a problem, and attempts have been made in the past to diversify bank ownership by means of special legislation to limit the concentration of shareholding. The Stock Exchange has been used as a main venue for ownership transfer, by limiting the number of shares a person may hold. The legislation appears to be ineffective, however, as banks have not been able to meet the deadlines for ownership diversification and the deadlines have to be extended repeatedly.

The Thai commercial banking industry has a cartel-like structure with the 16 banks organized loosely under the Thai Bankers Association, whereby they collectively set the standard rates of service charges and loan rates. This oligopolistic practice makes interest rates (loans and deposits) respond relatively slowly to market conditions as it takes time for all banks to agree on the same adjustment, particularly in the downward direction. An important corollary of this is that collectively the Thai bankers possess substantial power in dictating the cost and the allocation of domestic credit and in influencing the effectiveness of monetary policies.

A number of important government regulations affect the financial market, especially the banking industry. Their main features are the stipulation of interest rate ceilings for loans and deposits, control of new entry, agricultural credit policy, and compulsory bond holding for branch expansion. The Bank of Thailand adjusts the ceiling rates to keep the domestic rates in line with foreign rates, to smooth out liquidity problems, or as deliberate instruments of monetary policy. Another important control is the stipulation of a compulsory minimum to the banks' capital fund to risky assets ratio. This measure is designed to prevent excessive expansion of bank credit and thereby to ensure the soundness of the banking system. In some years, this measure has acted as a major restraint on banks' abilities to reduce excess liquidity through loan expansion. Chapter 5, by Bhanupong Nidhiprabha, discusses these issues in depth.

A novel feature of monetary policy which is administered through the banking system is the use of rediscount facilities. The basic idea has been to assist priority sectors by providing low-cost funds. The use of the rediscount facility, which first appeared in 1960 to finance rice exports, has been extended throughout industry, agriculture and construction.

Private foreign borrowing is relatively free. Although a withholding tax on foreign borrowing exists, it plays little role in influencing the inflow of international credit. From the mid-1970s, local commercial banks and large companies have used foreign borrowing as a means of adjusting their liquidity positions. This feature makes local liquidity highly responsive to changes in foreign interest rates and the exchange rate. What has been observed is that when the foreign interest rate was high and/or when there was speculation of a baht devaluation, there would be a slowdown in capital inflow. Capital outflows, while officially requiring Bank of Thailand approval, occur through quasi-legal channels such as transfer pricing. Domestic interest rates, constrained by the ceilings set by the Bank of Thailand, do not rise correspondingly. This results in tight liquidity in the domestic money market. The reverse is observed at times of low foreign interest rate and/or a strong baht.

An important implication of the above structure is that Thailand's financial system is prone to excess liquidity when the world interest rate declines, and this excess liquidity problem is prolonged. This occurs because local commercial banks have a rather limited portfolio choice as the country's capital markets are not well developed and capital outflow, in the form of investing in foreign assets, is tightly regulated. Most banks therefore hold substantial amounts of government bonds and investment in short-term money markets such as treasury bills and bonds in repurchase markets. Another factor prolonging excess liquidity is the rigidity in interest rate adjustment as noted earlier.

Capital markets

Capital markets are a recent phenomenon in Thailand. The Securities Exchange of Thailand (SET) began operation only in 1975 as a way of offering savers alternative means of investment, including common and preferred stocks, straight bonds, debentures and unit trusts. The market—as measured in terms of the number of listed companies and securities, types of securities, trading volume, and market value—remains relatively thin by international standards.

Since the establishment of the SET, the stock market has grown steadily. The market has recovered from a crash in 1979 and the ratio of market capitalization to GDP has increased from less than 4 per cent in 1980 to 29 per cent in 1990 (Robinson et al. 1991: 22). Confidence in the market was increased by reforms instituted in 1984 to prohibit all insider-trading activities and to improve the supervisory and regulatory framework.

The public sector

Compared with most other developing countries, the role historically perceived for the public sector in Thailand was strictly limited. This view had roots in the traditional conservatism of Thai ruling elites. The Thai aristocracy of the nineteenth and early twentieth centuries held a virtual monopoly of government affairs. Avoidance of domination by the European colonial powers and maintenance of the existing social order domestically were given overriding priority, and the maintenance of financial stability at home was seen as a necessary condition for both of these ends. Accordingly, the domestic role of government was severely constrained by these attitudes, which continued well into the twentieth century.

By the 1980s, the influence of the public sector—particularly the core agencies of macroeconomic policy—had increased as the government became more active in economic affairs. This was partly the result of a change in political leadership, and partly due to the perceived macroeconomic difficulties facing the economy. There were increasing demands from the educated public for the government to be more active in initiating and coordinating economic development.

This section reviews the role of the public sector in Thailand. It discusses its current structure and its modes of intervention in the economy. The latter takes a variety of forms that are often used in combination. After describing the institutional background, I then discuss the methods of intervention—fiscal measures, sectoral interventions, regulation, public provision of infrastructure and the public enterprises.

The institutional framework

The basis for the current system of administration was laid over a century ago in the reign of King Chulalongkorn (Rama V). The system, which was modelled along British lines, modified the traditional functions of the court into a hierarchical system of government agencies, with administrative power assumed principally by the central government, reflecting the highly centralized political structure then prevailing. This administrative centralization has survived, surprisingly without radical modification, to this day.

The system of government is organized at three levels—the central government, the local governments, and the state enterprises.

Central government

By far the largest public sector body is the central government. It is made up of twelve ministries, the Office of the Prime Minister, the Office of University Affairs, and seven independent government agencies including the Parliament and the Bureau of Crown Property. Apart from supervising the work of departments, offices and publicly funded agencies directly under them, the central government also supervises the work of local governments and state enterprises.

The finance of central government rests on the distinction between budgetary and non-budgetary transactions. The national budget requires approval of the parliament. Its expenditure is supported by incomes from six main sources: (1) tax revenue, (2) contributions from state enterprises, (3) fines, fees and proceeds from sales of goods, (4) domestic borrowings, (5) issue of new coins, and (6) use of treasury cash balance. Items (1) to (3) are budgetary revenues whereas items (4) to (6) involve the financing of budgetary deficits. Note the absence of foreign borrowing as a source of budgetary finance. It is prohibited by the Budget Control Act of 1959.

Non-budgetary transactions occur outside the annual budget. They take two basic forms: (1) expenditure financed by external grants and loans; and (2) expenditure financed by advances from the state treasury deposits. The latter is a special case and is possible only with the approval of the parliament, in the form of a special Act. Being non-budgetary, expenditure financed by foreign borrowings does not require approval of the parliament. It was through this channel of expenditure that the growth in public sector spending of the early 1980s occurred.

Three regulations governing central government expenditure are notable. First, in any fiscal year, the amount of budgetary deficit may not exceed 25 per cent of the expected revenue. Second, direct foreign borrowing by the Ministry of Finance in any fiscal year (1 October to 30 September) must be within 10 per cent of the expenditure budget. And third, foreign loans for state enterprises which are guaranteed by the Ministry of Finance in any year must not exceed 10 per cent of the expenditure budget.

Local governments

Local governments are the administrative arms of the central government in the provinces. Their administration is the responsibility of the Ministry of Interior, through the Local Government Department (LGD). At present, local governments consist of 126 municipalities, 795 sanitary districts, 72 Changwat (provincial) Administrative Organizations (CAOs), the Bangkok Metropolitan Administration, and the Pattaya City Administration. The main administrative power rests with the CAOs whose heads, with the exception of the cities of Bangkok and Pattaya, are elected. Provincial governors are civil servants appointed by the Ministry of Interior. This direct line of command means that local government administration is closely controlled by the central government.

Local government finance has a relatively small weight in overall public sector finance—less than 5 per cent in terms of expenditure. Its main source of income is revenues from local taxes, revenue from shared tax with the central government, own income from property, fines, fees and permits, contributions from the central government, and domestic borrowings. Foreign borrowing by local governments is legally possible but must be organized on its behalf by the Ministry of Interior. To date, no such borrowing has occurred.

The core agencies of economic policy

Within Thailand's system of government, decision-making on macroeconomic policy issues is in the domain of ministers. Policy decisions at the ministerial level, either made individually by a minister or by ministers acting collectively, usually as a cabinet, rely a great deal on information and analyses made available to them by the departments concerned and the core agencies. The latter includes the National Economic and Social Development Board (NESDB), the government's major economic planning agency, the Fiscal Policy Office (FPO) of the Ministry of Finance, the Bank of Thailand (BOT), and the Bureau of the Budget (BOB). The directors of these core agencies sit permanently in the Council of Economic Ministers.

Prior to discussion at the ministerial level, policy options are formulated through coordination and consultation between departments and experts from the core agencies. In recent years, the role and the influence of the core agencies have increased significantly as the government has become increasingly reliant on them for opinions and analyses. The heads of these core agencies are the central actors in formulating Thailand's economic policies.

The development plans

Planning for economic development became a formal process of the Thai government in 1959 when the National Economic Development Board (NEDB)—now the NESDB—was established. Since then, seven national development plans have been implemented. The underlying philosophy of economic planning in Thailand is a commitment to a market economy. Planning has been directed mainly towards securing a smooth functioning of markets with minimum direct government intervention or controls.

It would be easy to overstate the importance of the development plans in Thailand's economic policy formulation. Circumstances change quickly, and plans made five years or more in advance must always be modified. The plans are almost never implemented in the form described in the plan documents, and often not at all. The plans are more useful as indicators of the policy directions that the government viewed as appropriate at the time the plans were drawn up. In reviewing the plans, it is helpful to relate them to the economic outcomes that were actually experienced over the plan periods.

The First Plan (1961–66) was essentially a public expenditure program, accounting to a moderate degree for the source of revenue and the outlays of the Thai government. The main objective was to encourage economic growth in the private sector through the provision of basic infrastructure facilities in transport, communications, power, social and public services, and agriculture.

Economic growth achieved during the First Plan period was both rapid and broadly based. The real annual GDP growth rate averaged 8.1 per cent. In sectoral terms, infrastructure and construction recorded the highest average annual rates of increase at 22.3 and 17.8 per cent, respectively. Agricultural output expanded at an average rate of 6.2 per cent. These rates were impressive by international standards. Much of this achievement was due to favourable world market demand for Thai products. Military spending by the United States in the country also did much to support the plan. Capital expenditure increased markedly at an average annual growth rate of 18 per cent while inflation was low. Despite an accelerated population growth rate of 3.5 per cent per year, per capita income rose on average by 4.8 per cent per year.

The Second Plan (1967-71) was still largely a public expenditure program. It incorporated manpower planning but with no attempt at directing resource allocation among sectors. The Second Plan continued the First Plan's task of building infrastructure, particularly in those areas considered conducive to development. The pattern of public expenditure under this Plan revealed the government's increased emphasis on the slower growth areas, especially the rural sector.

The growth of GDP during the Second Plan was less impressive than that during the First. The average GDP growth rate was 7.5 per cent. High expansion of output continued in infrastructure and services while industry grew at 10.1 per cent. The slowdown in overall growth reflected the slowdown in foreign investment and US military spending, and the disappointing performance of agriculture, which grew at only 4.5 per cent. The decline in the growth of agriculture was due partly to the droughts of 1967 and 1968, and partly to the fluctuation in world prices of major export commodities.

The Third Plan (1972-76) reflected a moderate shift of emphasis in development thinking. While still aiming for higher growth, the Third Plan set specific priorities of reducing the increasing disparities between urban and rural areas, and between sectors. This shift reflected a growing awareness amongst NESDB planners of the increasing problems of regional disparity and poverty in the rural areas. The emphasis of the Plan was placed not only on the improvement of public infrastructure and the maintenance of economic stability but also on achieving a more equitable distribution of income and social services.

Achievements in the Third Plan period were disappointing, reflecting the 1973-74 oil crisis, the resultant world economic slump, and the continued decline in US military spending. Real GDP growth averaged 6.2 per cent. Again, this aggregate slowdown was partly attributable to the performance of agriculture, which grew at only 3.9 per cent. The increase in capital investment by the government continued the momentum of infrastructure investment. In spite of the expansion in industrial production (about 8.6 per cent per year), it was evident that industry was not oriented towards employment. Migration from rural areas to the capital city, Bangkok, was rapid and clearly visible. It was widely thought that the benefits of industrial expansion were not reaching the majority of the population. It was also realized that the achievement of rapid growth since the First Plan had been at the expense of deteriorating land, forest, water and marine resources.

Against this background, the Fourth Plan (1977-81) was intended to restructure the national economy. Its immediate objective was recovery from the effects of world economic recession and implementation of desired structural adjustments. Compared with the previous plans, the Fourth stressed investment projects. The plan document summarized its objectives in terms of eight development issues: (1) development and conservation of economic resources and the environment, (2) diversification and increased efficiency of production in rural areas, (3) development of industry, (4) promotion of tourism, (5) development of principal cities and the improvement of Bangkok, (6) dispersion of basic services, (7) dispersion of social services, and (8) social development. The essence of the plan was the attempt to switch from a growth orientation approach towards one reflecting greater social awareness and promoting economic readjustment.

The performance of the economy during the Fourth Plan was again affected by the rapidly changing world economic conditions, particularly the rising price of oil (especially the second oil price shock of 1979-80), high interest rates (especially after 1980), and declining demand and prices for commodity exports. In spite of the unfavourable external conditions, the economy did expand satisfactorily. Growth of output averaged 7.1 per cent per year over the plan period. This achievement resulted partly from expanding public investment despite a drastic deterioration in domestic savings. The enlarged domestic investment-saving gap was reflected in a serious trade imbalance, and as income from other sources failed to compensate for this deficit, the economy suffered balance of payments deficits and growing foreign debt throughout the Fourth Plan period.

The Fifth Plan (1982-86) continued to give high priority to economic restructuring, the maintenance of financial stability and the welfare of the rural poor. These goals were meant to be achieved by placing more emphasis on the quality of growth rather than its rate. In the process, reform of the public development administration system was to be carried out. Growth was thought to lie with industrial development—its share of output was projected to reach that of agriculture by the end of the planning period. Industrial policy was to promote export-oriented industries and the dispersion of manufacturing industries to provincial areas. Such a dispersion was seen as a way of achieving a balance of growth between urban and rural areas. The ambitious Eastern Seaboard Development Scheme, to be located close to the seaside resort of Pattaya, was to have been a central component of this policy.

The years 1982-86 coincided with slowed growth as a result of the world recession of the early 1980s. Largely as a result of the international oil price increases of the 1970s and early 1980s, Thailand suffered a severe deterioration in its terms of trade—from an index of 100 in 1973 to 51 in 1985 and 56 in 1987. Although it had avoided the economic collapse that these external events had produced in other developing countries—including its near neighbour, the Philippines—by 1985 Thailand was experiencing serious macroeconomic problems. These macroeconomic imbalances can be summarized as:

• A persistent and unsustainable balance of payments deficit on current account equivalent in 1985 to 5 per cent of GDP.
• An investment-savings gap of a similar magnitude. This represented mainly a decline in savings as a proportion of GDP from 20-22 per cent in the late 1970s to 16-17 per cent in 1985.

- Foreign exchange reserves had fallen, as a proportion of GDP, from 12 per cent in 1970 to 3 per cent in 1985. This required a US$500 million IMF standby loan in mid-1985. Its renewal was negotiated a year later.
- External debt had risen to US$16 billion by 1985, equivalent to 40 per cent of GDP and 146 per cent of exports. US$12 billion of this was long-term debt, of which US$8 billion was public or publicly guaranteed. An additional US$4 billion of short-term debt was held mainly in the private sector. The debt service ratio in 1985 was around 26 per cent, up from 17 per cent in 1980.
- The government's budget deficit had remained at over 5 per cent of GDP over the previous five years. Total public expenditure, comprising central and local governments and state enterprises, was around 40 per cent of GDP. The central government just managed to finance its current expenditures from its revenues. Virtually all capital expenditures were financed by borrowing. General government savings had fallen from 3.7 per cent of GDP (average of 1970–77 period) to less than 1 per cent in 1985.
- The overall rate of growth of GDP in real terms was lower in the 1970s than the 1960s, and lower still in the first half of the 1980s. Growth in the years 1985 and 1986 was the lowest of any two consecutive years since the 1950s; but this was a decline from a long-term real rate of growth of almost 7 per cent to 'only' 5 per cent.

The Sixth Plan (1987–91) was drafted in response to the above problems. Its objectives were:
- To increase the economic growth rate to over 5 per cent per year.
- To improve the administrative structure of the government and review its role. The private sector was to play a greater role, thereby reducing the burden on the government.
- To increase the mobilization of domestic saving from both private and public sectors from the target of 18.2 per cent under the previous plan to 23.7 per cent.
- Continuation of the privatization process and improvement of the administrative efficiency of the state enterprises. The proportion of their foreign borrowing was also to be reduced.
- To use fiscal and monetary measures to support economic growth and to reduce the deficit in the trade and current

accounts. One fiscal measure was the restructuring of the taxation system to increase government revenues and to attract foreign investment.

From 1986 onwards, Thai macroeconomic policy was adjusted sharply to counter the imbalances described above. The adjustments included a striking fiscal contraction. The fiscal deficit described above was transformed into a surplus equivalent to 1.3 per cent of GDP in fiscal year 1988 and 4.9 per cent in 1990. Cuts in public investment expenditure were a major source of this adjustment. Public sector fixed capital formation declined by three percentage points of GDP from fiscal years 1985 to 1988 (to 5.8 per cent of GDP). Simultaneously, Thailand was experiencing an export boom, concentrated in manufactures.

The boom appears to have been a consequence of two mutually reinforcing events, neither of which can reasonably be attributed to deliberate acts of policy on the part of the Thai government. The first was a 30 per cent depreciation of Thailand's real effective exchange rate from 1986 to 1990 resulting from the baht being pegged to a depreciating US dollar. The second was the international relocation of light manufacturing industries from Taiwan, Hong Kong, Korea and Singapore, where labour costs were rising rapidly, to lower wage countries like Thailand, Malaysia, Indonesia and the south-eastern corner of China. The magnitude of the boom was as much a surprise to the Thai economic planners as to anyone else. But the reduction in expenditure on basic infrastructure (roads, ports, telecommunications, and so on) threatened the medium-term sustainability of the boom because these facilities were becoming badly congested.

The tax system

Responsibility for planning and managing taxation policy rests with the Ministry of Finance, specifically its Fiscal Policy Office (FPO). The overall tax system includes both central government and local government tax, but the former is dominant. In 1990, the tax revenue (central and local) to GDP ratio was 20 per cent, which is low by international comparison. The composition of tax revenues has changed markedly since the 1960s (described in detail by Chaipat Sahasakul in Chapter 6).

The relative importance of international trade taxes (import and export taxes) has declined, both in relation to GDP and as a share of total taxes (from 30 per cent of total tax revenue in 1970 to 22 per cent in 1990), a result of a reduction in the reliance on export taxes and the reduced average import taxes. This has been balanced by increases in the relative importance of income-based and consumption taxes. The decline in the relative importance of international trade taxes has made the present tax system more dependent on indirect domestic taxes. Despite the increasing importance of income-based taxes (personal and corporate), direct tax revenues are of limited importance by international standards.

The main features of the current tax system include:

- A high proportion of indirect taxes which are inelastic with respect to GDP and have a small tax base. This feature tends to reduce the average tax rate automatically as GDP increases.
- The personal income tax is progressive and is the only tax which has an income elasticity greater than unity. The progressive tax schedule has limited effects on the top income earners; however, many types of income—including income from bequests and income from interest on bank deposits— are exempt from taxation. As a result, the ratio of tax to assessable income is not steeply progressive.
- Corporate income tax is losing its relative importance as close to half of all corporations declare losses for tax purposes. In 1990, less than 1 per cent of all corporations paid three-quarters of corporate tax revenues. Without substantial improvements in collection, corporate income tax will become an increasingly unreliable revenue measure.
- Domestic consumption tax (business and excise taxes) has a regressive structure and the tax base is relatively small. At present, state enterprises do not have to pay business tax and the excise tax covers only nine commodities. This feature makes revenue mobilization costly to the general public as tax rates frequently require adjustment upwards for revenue purposes. The tax burden is therefore passed on to all consumers regardless of their income positions.
- Despite the reduced relative importance of international trade taxes there exists a large diversity in the tariff rates, ranging between 5 and 60 per cent ad valorem.
- Direct transfer payments by the government play a small role

in Thailand's fiscal structure. No welfare system exists. Most of the transfers are between public sector agencies and not between households and the government.

In January 1992 the government introduced a new value-added tax (VAT) system. The new tax was designed to overcome some of the problems identified above. The cascading effect of the existing business tax system—the fact that the rate of the tax effectively increases along the chain of production—was stressed as a motivation for implementing the VAT system. The rate of VAT was set at 7 per cent, with some industries being exempt. The latter included all of agriculture and industries producing inputs for direct use in agriculture, such as fertilizer, animal feeds and pesticides. Businesses with total revenues less than 600,000 baht (approximately US$24,000) were also exempt. Exporters were entitled to a refund of VAT on proof of export of goods having been completed.

In summary, despite the VAT reform, the existing tax system remains handicapped by a structure which hinders effective revenue mobilization. The government needs to continue to reform the existing tax system so that additional revenue can be raised without seriously distorting private incentives and without creating further inequality in the distribution of income.

Sectoral interventions

Until the late 1960s, the role of the public sector was limited largely to tax collection, direct production through the public enterprises, and public provision. As the economy expanded, the price system came increasingly to be seen within the bureaucracy as distorted and as an unreliable guide to resource allocation. This perception resulted in more direct interventions by the public sector. Some of the interventions were designed to modify the pattern of resource utilization to keep it in line with overall economic policy, but clearly many had more to do with the generation of economic rents benefiting particular interest groups. In this section, I briefly discuss government interventions in three important areas: agriculture, industry and trade.

Interventions in agriculture
The main impetus of Thailand's economic growth in the 1960s and the 1970s had been the growth of agriculture. The

momentum of agricultural growth was lost in the late 1970s as the land frontier was exhausted and the relative importance of agriculture in production declined. Nonetheless, agriculture remains the largest source of employment and the largest provider of income for the majority of the population. Moreover, Thailand's poorest citizens are disproportionately concentrated in the agricultural sector.

Although growth in agriculture has come mainly from private initiative, government interventions in agriculture, particularly in the pricing system, have had considerable impact. The most important intervention, and the one with the longest history, was the taxation of rice exports. The *rice export tax*, which was set in place immediately after the end of World War II as a way of raising government revenue, was suspended in 1986. While in operation, this heavy export tax on rice had depressed rural incomes by reducing the farm-gate prices of paddy and rural wages. It also impeded technological change by altering the price–cost ratio in the rice sector. Rubber remains subject to an export tax (15 per cent of the f.o.b. price).

The *compulsory rice reserve scheme* had a similar effect. The scheme came into effect in 1973 (a period of rice shortage) and ended in 1982. Under the scheme, exporters were required to sell a proportion of their rice to the government at a price set lower than the domestic price. The quantity of these compulsory sales was fixed in relation to the amount of rice exported. The policy was intended to enable the government to obtain cheap rice for resale to the general public. It was thus similar to an ad valorem export tax, and further depressed farm-gate prices for paddy.

The government has occasionally imposed periodic *export quotas* on agricultural products. In the past, both rice and maize were occasionally subject to such controls. At present, only cassava is affected by this policy, due to the government decision to restrict its cassava exports to the EC. The allocation of export quotas is under the responsibility of the Ministry of Commerce. It is said that the quota allocation system is often politically motivated.

Apart from rice, maize, cassava and rubber, other agricultural products such as swine, castor oil seeds and tobacco are subject to government regulation. In most of these cases, government regulations have introduced monopolistic elements into the markets, resulting in inefficiency. For example, the Animal Slaughtering and Meat Sale Control Act of 1960 requires a transfer of property rights on land and buildings to the local government as a condition for setting up a private slaughterhouse. This is tantamount to handing monopoly power to public slaughterhouses managed by local governments.

Intervention in industry

The main feature of government intervention in industry has been the promotion of private investment administered through the Board of Investment (BOI). The BOI, established in 1959, uses a combination of various investment promotion schemes, tariff policies, tax regimes, and trade and price controls to direct the pattern of private investment. During the 1960s and early 1970s, industrial policies strongly favoured import substitution. Import tariffs were raised significantly to protect local industries, with incentives being strongest for production of final products based on imported intermediate and capital goods. The emphasis of industrial promotion policy was shifted towards exports with the passage of the Investment Promotion Act of 1972.

To earn a BOI promotion certificate, prospective investors apply for privileges according to the BOI's regulations. A list of industries eligible for promotion privileges is drawn up by the BOI using the national development plan as a broad framework. The incentives offered typically include tax and tariff exemptions, guarantee of government protection from nationalization and from direct competition by state enterprises, and guarantees of rights of profit and capital repatriation. The range of incentives differs between industries, reflecting priority rankings in the promotion policy. The main criticism of the promotion policy is that policy measures are frequently changed and the BOI often exercises discretionary powers in the granting of promotional privileges and the extent of incentives given. It has been observed that the incentives offered differ among firms within the same industry.

In addition to the BOI, the Ministries of Industry, Commerce, and Finance, and the Bank of Thailand also formulate and administer policies which directly affect industrial development. The Fiscal Policy Office of the Ministry of Finance operates a comprehensive tax refund system for all taxes incurred in the production of goods for export. The Bank of Thailand provides a rediscount facility at subsidized interest rates to export-oriented firms. The Ministry of Commerce provides technical assistance through its Export Service Centre.

Important regulations administered by the Ministry of Industry are the controls on establishing and expanding factories and production plants, and the regulation on the use of local contents in production. At present, there are 23 categories of industry which are subject to factory control and four industries subject to local content requirements (i.e. motor vehicle assembly, motor cycle production, electric wire and cable, and steel production).

Protection policy
Apart from tariffs and export taxes, the trade regime in Thailand includes a number of restrictive measures such as quantitative import and export controls. Currently, there is an import ban on 18 commodities, and special permission is required to import another 30. The Ministry of Commerce imposes and supervises import controls. Commodities under control include those produced in the socialist countries, weapons and strategic firearms, rice and sugar. The controls on rice and sugar are to prevent re-importing after the products have been exported. Export controls are placed on 38 commodities, 16 of which are outright bans. The export controls are meant to ensure domestic supplies for local consumption at low prices. Items such as paper, pesticide, flat iron sheets, polyfibre and cement are regulated to ensure local supplies.

Besides direct controls on imports and exports, the Ministry of Commerce also administers price controls on 'essential products'. This has been possible with the passage of the Price Setting and Anti-Monopoly Act of 1979. In 1986 there were 34 commodities under price control. Such control has helped to keep down the cost of living but at the expense of shortages of these products in retail stores.

Thailand does not practise free trade, but its protection levels are moderate and relatively stable. Since the 1960s, empirical studies of effective rates of protection (ERPs) in Thailand have used different sets of data, different product definitions, as well as different methodologies. For example, some studies use the official tariff rates, while others use tariff rates estimated from customs duty collections or from price comparisons. It is thus difficult to compare the results of these studies over time. Nevertheless, the effective rate of protection studies show the same pattern over the past three decades. The protective system has been biased against the agri-based industries and towards the manufacturing sector, both import competing and non-import competing goods. This is the typical pattern of protection found in developing countries. Tables 1.2 and 1.3 summarize the results of these studies.

Trairong (1970) studied Thailand's ERPs in 23 manufacturing industries in 1964 using input coefficients from Belgium and the Netherlands data derived from Balassa's standardized input–output table. Using official tariffs and the 1962 Investment Promotion Act as measures of the protective system, his results showed that the system of protection was biased towards consumption goods, followed by intermediate goods, and biased against capital goods (Juanjai et al. 1986).

Narongchai (1973, 1977) estimated ERPs of 58 industries for 1969, and 80 industries for 1971 and 1974 using input–output coefficients obtained from industrial surveys. When tariffs were used as the main instrument of trade policy and industries were classified by trade orientation, his results showed that over the period studied the import competing and non-import competing industries received highest protection. When the industries were classified by end use and level of fabrication, the effective protection system was favoured towards beverages and tobacco and processed food, followed by transport equipment and consumer goods.

Pairote (1975) estimated the ERPs of 58 industries for 1964, and of 82 industries for 1971 and 1974 using the input–output coefficients obtained from industrial surveys. The results showed that the protection system over the period of study was inward-looking, favouring firms selling on domestic markets. Import competing and non-import competing industries received greatest protection. The structure of protection was biased against export industries. When industries were classified by end uses and levels of fabrication, the incentive effects were strongly in favour of consumer goods, especially beverages and tobacco, and transport equipment, followed by consumer goods (Juanjai et al. 1986).

Paitoon et al. (1989) estimated ERPs in Thailand's manufacturing sector for 1981, 1984 and 1987 using input coefficients from the 180-sector input–output tables of 1982 and 1985. The

Table 1.2: Effective protection of industry groups by levels of fabrication and end uses, 1964 to 1984 (per cent)

Industry Group	1964	1969	1974	1984
Processed food	47.47	-32.6	-19.41	7.93
Beverages and tobacco	215.45	241.3	2,280.55	26.50
Construction materials	. .	47.4	46.91	17.38
Intermediate goods I	82.02	2.8	15.91	17.63
Intermediate goods II	60.09	79.1	48.53	241.84
Consumer non-durable goods	70.95	32.5	90.63	23.84
Consumer durable goods	63.87	69.1	200.62	19.29
Machinery	37.48	30.6	30.02	32.40
Transport equipment	118.00	34.9	353.88	45.70

Sources: ERPs for 1964 and 1969 were obtained from Juanjai (1986). The ERPs for 1974 and 1984 were obtained from Narongchai (1977) and Paitoon et al. (1989), respectively. The weights used to aggregate products for 1974 and 1984 were value added at market prices of 1975 and 1985, respectively, obtained from the Thai input-output tables.

Table 1.3: Effective rates of protection of the manufacturing sector classified by trade oriented group, 1969 to 1987 (per cent)

Sector	1969	1974	1984	1987
Export group	-43	-35	2	4
Import competing group	54 [a] (648)[b]	63	21	39
Non-import competing group	187	77 [c] (812)[d]	53	55

[a] Tyres and tubes are excluded.
[b] Tyres and tubes are included.
[c] Cigarettes and soft drinks are excluded.
[d] Cigarettes and soft drinks are included.

Products are classified into three groups based on Narongchai's studies (1973, 1977): export oriented, import competing and non-import competing, according to their trade orientation. A product is classified as export if its export level is greater than 10 per cent of its domestic production and its net export is positive. It is import competing if its import is greater than 10 per cent of its total consumption and if its net import is positive. The rest are classified as non-import competing. The 1975 data on value added at market prices of each industry are used as weights to estimate the aggregate ERP of each product group of all years.
Sources: 1969 calculated from Narongchai (1973); 1974: calculated from Narongchai (1977); 1984 and 1987: calculated from Paitoon et al. (1989).

protective instruments covered in the study were mainly tariffs, import surcharges, export taxes, tax rebates and refunds, and royalties. When industries were classified by trade orientation, the results showed that the effective protection was biased against export industries. The non-import competing industries received the highest protection, followed by the import competing industries.

From Table 1.3 it may be concluded that over the period 1969–87 the export industries received the lowest effective protection, followed by the import competing industries, while the non-importing industries received the highest effective protection.

In 1969 and 1974, most of the export industries were agri-based, such as rice milling, frozen seafood and canned fruit, which use agricultural products as raw materials. From 1980 onwards, there have been more diversified export industries. The new export industries, in addition to the traditional agri-based ones, have been canned fish and crustaceans, garments, rubber sheets and rubber products, wood products, jewellery and footwear. A dominant characteristic of the new export industries is that they are labour-intensive industries, such as garments and footwear. But these have generally *not* been the industries favoured by the system of protection. The protected industries, as well as those favoured by the BOI's promotion policies, have in general continued to perform poorly.

Exchange rate policy
Since 1955, when the multiple exchange rate system was abolished, until the devaluations of 1981, the baht was maintained virtually at a fixed parity with the US dollar (between 20 and 21 baht per US dollar). The main argument for the peg with the dollar was the stability and confidence it was believed to provide. Between 1955 and 1977, the dollar depreciated in relation to other currencies and the baht–dollar rate was adjusted slightly five times to maintain parity with the depreciated dollar (Supote 1978[T].)

The volatility of the dollar and the enlarged trade deficits in the late 1970s following the second oil shock (1979–80) led to a reconsideration of exchange rate policy. Although much of Thailand's trade is denominated in US dollars, less than 20 per cent of exports and imports are with the United States.

The over-valued dollar in the late 1970s had worked to increase the country's balance of payments deficits. In March 1978, the Bank of Thailand announced that the baht would no longer be tied to the dollar but would be linked to a basket of currencies in which the dollar would be a major component. The new system was short-lived. In November 1978, a system of daily fixing was introduced, in effect putting the baht back in parity with the dollar at 19.8 baht per dollar. There have been four devaluations since, as summarized in Table 1.4.

The announced objectives of the 1981 and 1984 devaluations were to reduce the existing current account deficits. The devaluations relative to the US dollar of 1981 and 1984 were small relative to the exogenous movements in Thailand's effective exchange rate induced by movements in other countries' exchange rates relative to the dollar. Thus, even taking the devaluations into account, Thai exchange rate policy since 1955 was essentially that of fixity relative to the US dollar.

Devaluations have been avoided whenever possible because they undermine the Bank of Thailand's central objective of controlling inflation. They also have unpopular political consequences. They create hardships for those who depend on imported raw materials as well as those holding debts denominated in foreign currencies. In Thailand, devaluations are usually employed only after other methods of coping with trading imbalances have already been used. These other means include raising import tariffs, contractionary fiscal and monetary policies, and credit controls.

An example of such a policy response was the limit on commercial banks' credit growth which began in 1984. This was a major shift in monetary policy since it was the first time that

Table 1.4: Dates and magnitudes of devaluations

Date	Rate of devaluation (per cent)
May 1981	1.1
July 1981	8.7
November 1984	14.9
December 1985	1.9

Source: Bank of Thailand, *Annual Reports*, 1981 to 1985.

a quantity control was imposed together with a price control (i.e. the interest ceiling). The shift in policy stance was attributed to the conditions set by the IMF for the standby arrangement loans negotiated in 1984. The Bank of Thailand, alarmed by the huge deficits in the balance of trade in 1983, decided to take this drastic measure against the expansion of imports. The commercial banks were subject to the maximum credit expansion at 18 per cent of the 1983 level of credit.

Devaluations can be costly for the politicians who implement them. The 1981 devaluation led to political attacks from opposition parties as well as some members of the governing coalition. Fear of inflation was one of their major concerns. However, some members' opposition to devaluation stemmed from a lack of understanding. The record of the parliament in July 1981 indicated that some MPs expressed the fear that the budget would be invalid because the value of the baht had been eroded by 8.7 per cent. Others suggested alternative policies such as totally banning imports, increasing tariffs, or asking the Bank of Thailand to assume a monopoly role of foreign exchange dealer. Other MPs even regarded the devaluation as equivalent to *lèse-majesté*, since the value of the bank notes bearing the King's picture had been reduced. There was also strong opposition from the press. The deputy finance minister, Paichitr Uathavikul, pictured as the main culprit, resigned.

While the 1981 devaluation was opposed mainly by politicians, the 1984 devaluation produced a confrontation between the prime minister and the commander-in-chief of the army. The army commander, in a public broadcast, called for the cancellation of the devaluation and a reshuffling of the cabinet. The latter implied the removal of the finance minister, who was responsible for the devaluation. The finance minister had also angered the military by opposing the airforce plan to purchase new tactical fighters, pointing out that it would substantially increase Thailand's external public debt. Devaluation was seen as a threat to the plan to modernize the Thai military since the jet fighters would now cost 14.9 per cent more. Prime Minister Prem satisfied the military by promising to find the three billion baht needed to shield the cost of the aircraft from the impact of devaluation. The government also introduced new controls on the price of petroleum and some other necessities, so as to placate the opposition to devaluation. Five days later, the army commander backed away from his opposition, announcing that the dispute had been a 'misunderstanding'.

After the 1984 devaluation the fixed exchange rate system was officially replaced by a 'flexible exchange rate system'. Under this, the baht is theoretically tied to a basket of currencies to provide greater flexibility in the management of foreign exchange. In fact, the close relationship to the US dollar has been maintained, in spite of the dollar's realignment relative to other currencies. Clearly, the 'basket' of currencies is dominated by the US dollar.

Public provision of infrastructure

Provision of infrastructure has been a central theme of the development plans. During the first two plans, public investment was concentrated on roads, irrigation, power and telecommunications. The expansion of the road network in the 1960s, which was tacitly linked to an American-supported counter-insurgency program, had a considerable impact on agricultural development and overall economic growth. It provided farmers with direct access to external markets, which significantly increased farm-gate prices for cash crops as well as access to vast uncultivated land. The extension of the land frontier was instrumental in agricultural growth in the 1960s and 1970s.

Investment in irrigation took the form of building large dams and waterways. Irrigation investment, which provided a source of power supplies, also provided a basis for investment in power, telecommunications and electrification. There were also significant developments in airports and harbours. The security risks associated with the Vietnam War partly motivated these developments. From very poor infrastructure facilities of the 1950s, Thailand came to possess a basic infrastructure that compared favourably with most other developing countries by the middle of the 1970s.

The provision of basic infrastructure in the 1960s provided a stimulus for private investment and economic growth. The main drawback was considered to be the unequal distribution of benefits. The irrigation system was concentrated in the regions of the Central Plains and the Lower North, and lacked a proper feeder system. The main beneficiaries were large farmers in close proximity to the irrigation sites. Similar problems were observed in the distribution of power, telecommunications and electricity.

In the Third Plan (1972–76), the pattern of public expenditure was slightly modified to give greater emphasis to the distribution problem. This shift was partly influenced by the change in the political mood in 1974. As noted earlier, this was a period of representative government. More emphasis was given to the rural areas, with programs which included electrification, rural health centres and family planning. Between 1974 and 1976, the share of public expenditure on health, education and agriculture rose considerably.

In the Fourth Plan (1977–81), there was a noticeable shift in the composition of public expenditure: the shares of public expenditure in agriculture, health and education declined while the shares of industry, energy, transport, defence and administration increased. This change was influenced by a number of economic and political developments. The military coup of 1976 placed control of the economy's finances back under the direct influence of the military and the bureaucrats. In 1977, a special decree was announced, increasing the public sector's access to foreign borrowings. For the first time, the state enterprises were able to borrow directly from abroad with government guarantees to finance their capital investment. The passage of this decree led to a dramatic expansion in defence expenditure and in the role of state enterprises. Between 1978 and 1983, there was a steady increase in expenditure by the state enterprises, financed in particular by foreign borrowing. The bulk of this was spent on energy-related activities, intended to develop an alternative local energy source and reduce dependence on imported energy.

There was no definitive policy on the management of public debt when the decision to liberalize the public sector's foreign borrowing was made in 1977. Regulations on foreign debt merely limited the amount each state enterprise could borrow but not the aggregate for the public sector. The enlarged foreign debt commitment became a serious policy problem in the early 1980s as the economy went into a recession following a slump in primary commodity exports. The current account deficit reached 7 per cent of GDP in 1983 and the debt-service ratio reached 23 per cent and was still rising. This development, which was considered to be a threat to the country's financial stability, prompted the government to revise its foreign borrowing policy and led to the establishment of the National Debt Reform Committee and new policy guidelines on foreign borrowing were announced. The guidelines set annual limits on the public sector's foreign borrowing. Although this decision was welcomed on financial grounds, it affected the economy's long-term growth potential. Several of the large development projects being planned, most of which relied on foreign funds, were either scaled down or postponed due to lack of foreign exchange.

By the early 1990s, the export-led boom of the late 1980s had left Thailand's infrastructural facilities severely congested. Ports, roads and telecommunications were all in need of upgrading if the growth was to be sustained. In particular, the heavy concentration of economic activity in Bangkok made improvement of road transport extremely difficult.

Public enterprises

Public enterprises play an important role in the Thai economy as in many other LDCs. As Kraiyudht Dhiratayakinant describes in Chapter 8, the activities of state enterprises in Thailand stretch into many areas of business. This includes infrastructure, manufacturing, transport, hotels, services, trade and finance. The central bank, the Bank of Thailand (BOT), is also a state enterprise, as is the national air carrier, Thai International. At present, there are 68 state enterprises, 17 of which operate as infrastructural enterprises. Most state enterprises began as special projects under central government departments with their own staff and financial accounts, then slowly graduated to the status of state enterprises when their activities enlarged.

History

Until the end of absolute monarchy in 1932, royal monopolies of trade in a small number of luxury commodities and provision of basic utilities had been the major form of state business ventures. This situation essentially continued until the beginning of World War II, but during the war Thai nationalists were successful in expanding the role of state trading companies. This expansion had its origin in resentment of Chinese domination of domestic commerce and was seen as an instrument for reasserting Thai control of domestic trade (Silcock 1967: 260).

After the war, public enterprises became increasingly important in other sectors of the Thai economy. This growth was largely due to the role of these enterprises as sources of income for military officials and civilian politicians, a state of affairs which continues today. By 1957, when a World Bank mission visited Thailand to assess the state of the national economy, a large part of the country's industrial capacity was controlled by public enterprises. The industries concerned included tobacco, paper, sugar, gunny bags, timber, tin, metal cabinets, pharmaceuticals, batteries, tanneries, textiles, cement, spirits, glass, rubber footwear, alum and shoe polish (IBRD 1959: 90–1).

The growth of the public enterprises had been haphazard. Not only was there little economic rationale for the choice of industries dominated by the public enterprises, but the enterprises had become uncontrolled in their operational, financial and investment behaviour. The practice of public enterprises lending public funds to one another made their accounts difficult to interpret, as Kraiyudht points out. The public enterprises had become major vehicles for the purchase of political patronage (and they remain so today). This was especially important for those Chinese businessmen whose interests were directly threatened by the public enterprises, but the political importance of the public enterprises went well beyond this. The looser budgetary and operational control over public enterprises, in comparison with the central government, facilitated their political patronage function.

The management of a state enterprise comes under the jurisdiction of its parent ministry, making its chairman a political appointee. Increased numbers of civilian politicians taking on ministerial portfolios also led to increased political influence in state enterprises. By 1986, 56 of the 68 chairmen of state enterprises were affiliated members of political parties. This meant that political parties, through their control of state enterprises, had gained a widening influence in economic decision-making. Previously, the chairmanships of state enterprises had been dominated by senior bureaucrats and military officers.

Trading profits/losses and pricing policy

The Thai public's perception of public enterprises is that they incur huge losses. As Kraiyudht shows, this is only partially correct. It is true that some important public enterprises regularly lose large sums. The main examples are in the transport sector, notably the Bangkok Mass Transit Organization (losing an average of US$30 million each year) and the State Railways of Thailand (losing about US$23 million each year). Nevertheless, in most years, the public enterprises' aggregate revenues exceed their aggregate expenditures. The problem here is that calculations of the expenditures of the state enterprises do not include proper allowance for a return on the public sector's capital investment in them. In any case, some of the state enterprises included in these statistics operate as profit-maximizing monopolists and generate large operating surpluses. Examples are the Thailand Tobacco Monopoly and the State Lottery Bureau.

Each public enterprise has a board of control and is under the supervision of a government ministry. Generally, the board has responsibility for setting prices, but the supervising ministry may also play a role. The more important the enterprise, the greater the role of the ministry. A few of the most important enterprises must have any changes in their prices approved by the cabinet. This makes it politically difficult to raise prices in key public enterprises. In addition to the transport sector mentioned above, this applies to the water, electricity and telephone utilities. The cabinet also approves the price structure of all petroleum-related products. For these key public enterprises, the redistributive effects of changes in prices, and the political implications of these effects, dominate discussions of tariff rates. Decisions to change prices are made only rarely— long after economic circumstances have changed. This slowness to adjust prices, combined with inefficiency, largely accounts for the losses of the key public enterprises.

Investment behaviour and foreign debt

Capital expenditure by state enterprises accounts for over 70 per cent of total public sector expenditure (consolidated). Their capital budgets are subjected to review and approval by the National Committee on State Enterprises (NCSE) whose secretariat function is shared by the National Economic and

Social Development Board (NESDB), the Budget Bureau (BOB), and the Fiscal Policy Office (FPO). It is at this stage that the investment plans of state enterprises are scrutinized in detail. This practice allows the NESDB to tailor the proposed investment plans in line with the priorities laid down in the National Development Plan. Once approved, the projects which seek budgetary support in the form of a contribution from the central government receive further review by the BOB. Such support, if granted, becomes part of central government's expenditure budget.

For projects which require foreign loans, the National Debt Policy Committee (NDPC), which reports to the cabinet, conducts an additional review. This committee is chaired by the finance minister, and its main responsibility is to ensure that the conduct of foreign borrowing by the public sector is within the framework set by the cabinet. Two important regulations stand out at present. First, total debt service must not exceed 9 per cent of expected export earning; and second, total new borrowings in any year must fall within the limit set by the cabinet. The present limit is set arbitrarily at 1,000 million baht. Technically, it is at this stage that foreign loan proposals of all public sector agencies are compared and given priority ranking—and here that political lobbying for foreign loan quotas is most intense.

Public enterprises account for about two-thirds of the public sector's foreign debt outstanding. Servicing this debt absorbs roughly half the total debt servicing burden of the public sector. In recent years, recognition of this problem has caused the investment plans of all public enterprises—especially the foreign debt implications—to come under close scrutiny from the NESDB. Not only are public enterprises now required to have foreign and domestic borrowing plans examined by the National Debt Policy Committee, but all such loans are then negotiated and signed by the Finance Ministry's Fiscal Policy Office.

Economic performance

Economic growth

Long-term changes in Thai real income can be estimated from data provided by Sompop (1989). These estimates are of real

GDP per capita in baht for the period 1870 to 1950, expressed in 1950 prices (Table 1.5). These data imply that annual growth over this 80-year period was a mere 0.2 per cent. Growth since World War II can be estimated more readily. Figure 1.2 shows this information for the period 1951 to 1991, calculated from national income data provided by NESDB. Unlike the previous hundred years, growth per capita for this period has been impressive. The average annual rate of growth of measured real GDP per capita was 4.3 per cent.

Thai national income data before 1970 are considered to be questionable and the NESDB has released a revised national income series for the period since 1970. Thailand's annual rate of GNP growth from 1971 to 1991 calculated from this new series is shown in Figure 1.3. A more comprehensive statistical summary of Thailand's macroeconomic performance from 1970 to 1991 is provided in Table 1.6. The annual fluctuations around the average rate of growth of real GDP of 7.1 per cent were mainly caused by external phenomena. Domestic political events have had remarkably little apparent effect on aggregate economic performance. Thailand experienced an export commodity boom from 1972 to 1974. This boom affected Thailand mainly through the price of rice. Exports surged and economic growth rose sharply in 1973. This event was quickly followed by the first OPEC-induced international oil price increases of 1973–74 (known as OPEC I). Since Thailand is a substantial petroleum importer, the rise in oil prices slowed Thai growth in 1974 and 1975. Recovery occurred from 1976 to 1978, but the second round of oil price increases of 1979–80 (OPEC II) slowed growth again.

Other oil-importing countries, including the Philippines, were devastated by these petroleum price increases, but Thailand experienced only a 'growth recession'—from approximately 9 per cent to 6 per cent. Having borrowed internationally to finance the increased cost of petroleum imports during the mid to late 1970s, Thailand suffered again from the high international interest rates of the early 1980s. By 1985, serious macroeconomic problems were evident, as described above.

The boom which began in 1987 surprised Thai observers as much as outsiders. It was argued above that the boom was driven by two forces:
• the depreciation of the US dollar relative to other currencies

Table 1.5: Gross domestic product per capita, 1870 to 1950 (at constant 1950 prices)

Year	Agriculture (million baht)	Manufacture (million baht)	Services (million baht)	GDP (million baht)	Population	GDP per capita (baht)
1870	2,417	678	2,524	5,619	5,775,000	973
1890	2,959	828	3,035	6,822	6,670,000	1,023
1900	3,222	883	3,274	7,379	7,320,000	1,008
1913	4,459	1,245	4,281	9,985	8,689,000	1,149
1929	5,735	1,603	5,749	13,087	12,058,000	1,085
1938	7,490	2,091	7,337	16,918	14,980,000	1,129
1950	10,196	2,794	9,559	22,549	19,817,000	1,138

Source: Calculated from data provided in Sompop (1989)

Figure 1.2 Per capita GDP at constant 1972 prices, 1951 to 1991
(selected years)

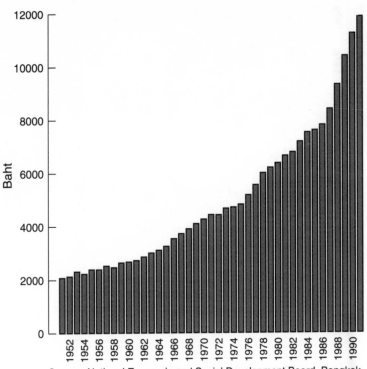

Source: National Economic and Social Development Board, Bangkok.

(the baht being pegged to it made Thai exports more competitive internationally); and

• foreign investment, especially from the present NICs, Taiwan and Hong Kong, motivated by the desire to avoid rising labour costs in their own countries.

In explaining Thailand's remarkable growth boom of the late 1980s, it would be easy to give too much weight to Thai-specific causes. Similar foreign investment-led booms were occurring in Malaysia and Indonesia, and even more significantly, in the south-eastern corner of China, adjacent to Hong Kong and Taiwan. The foreign investment did not flow to the Philippines. Its unreliable infrastructure, labour unrest and high level of political uncertainty were enough to discourage that.

Table 1.6: Macroeconomic summary, 1970 to 1991

Variable	Units	1970	1971	1972	1973	1974	1975	1976	1977	1978	1979	1980
GNP, real	% growth rate	7.4	4.6	5.4	9.1	4.1	5.0	8.9	9.8	9.3	5.9	6.2
Exports	% growth rate	0.3	10.7	26.6	33.2	44.9	-7.8	24.9	14.9	21.7	29.4	27.0
Imports	% growth rate	4.0	1.2	13.8	36.1	49.2	3.8	12.2	30.3	15.9	38.4	23.2
Terms of trade	export unit value/import unit value	100	101	111	155	130	116	107	101	102	105.0	100.0
Inflation	% growth rate	0.8	0.4	4.8	15.6	24.3	5.3	4.2	7.1	8.4	9.9	19.7
Current account balance/GDP	%	-3.8	-2.5	-0.6	-0.5	-0.7	-4.1	-2.7	-5.7	-1.5	-7.7	-6.2
Money supply (M1) real	% growth rate	9.7	11.0	17.7	17.9	13.0	11.0	12.4	9.0	17.1	17.0	13.8
Total debt/ GDP	%	16.6	17.2	16.8	14.3	13.2	15.5	13.1	14.8	18.5	20.2	25.7
Total debt service/ exports	%	17.1	18.9	17.4	15.3	14.8	15.1	12.8	16.7	17.4	19.1	14.5
Exchange rate	Baht/US$	20.80	20.80	20.80	20.40	20.00	20.00	20.00	20.00	20.34	20.42	20.48

Variable	Units	1981	1982	1983	1984	1985	1986	1987	1988	1989	1990	1991
GNP, real	% growth rate	5.2	4.8	7.1	6.3	3.0	4.6	9.7	13.3	12.4	10.3[a]	7.4[b]
Exports	% growth rate	14.1	6.0	-4.6	14.1	10.5	20.7	28.8	33.9	27.7	14.4	23.6[a]
Imports	% growth rate	14.3	-9.6	20.1	3.8	4.6	-3.0	39.0	46.1	29.8	28.5	16.6[a]
Terms of trade	export unit value/import unit value	87.0	79.0	85.0	83.0	80.0	89.0	89.0	86.0	83.0	81.0	80.0[a]
Inflation	% growth rate	12.7	5.2	3.8	0.9	2.4	1.9	2.5	3.8	5.4	6.0	5.7
Current account balance/GDP	%	-7.1	-2.7	-7.3	-5.1	-4.1	0.6	-0.7	-2.7	-3.6	-4.9	-4.9[b]
Money supply (M1) real	% growth rate	6.5	12.0	10.3	5.4	8.4	18.2	24.9	8.0	11.7	8.5	..
Total debt/GDP	%	31.0	34.2	35.0	36.4	46.9	44.6	35.9	30.1	28.2	31.3	31.6[b]
Total debt service/exports	%	14.4	16.0	19.1	21.5	25.3	25.4	17.1	13.7	12.4	9.8	15.2[b]
Exchange rate	Baht/US$	21.82	23.0	23.0	23.64	27.13	26.3	25.7	25.3	25.8	25.6	25.6

[a] Preliminary, from Bank of Thailand, *Quarterly Bulletin*, December 1991.
[b] Forecast, from Asian Development Bank, *Asian Development Outlook*, 1991. The 1991 real GNP growth rate estimate relates to GDP

Sources: Bank of Thailand, *Quarterly Bulletin*, various issues; World Bank, *World Development Report*, various issues; Asian Development Bank, *Asian Development Outlook*, 1991.

Figure 1.3 Real GNP growth rate, 1971 to 1991

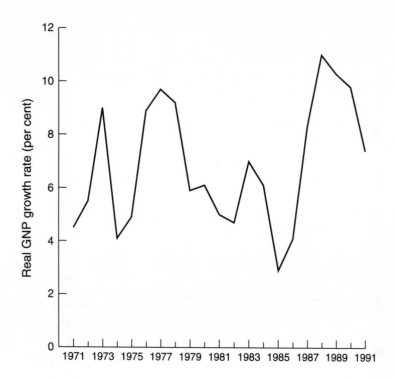

External events seem to explain most short-term fluctuations in Thailand's growth rate, but what about the long-term rate? To what extent can Thai economic growth be explained by the growth of conventional factors of production, capital and labour, or alternatively, by other factors, such as technological change and external price movements? The standard techniques of growth accounting are applied to Thai data below to attempt to answer this question.

The methodology of total factor productivity growth estimation is set out at the end of this chapter in an appendix. The results are summarized in Table 1.7, where the annual results are averaged over four periods: 1961 to 1972 (the period before Shock I); 1973 to 1979 (capturing the impact of Shock I); 1980 to 1985 (capturing the impact of Shock II); and 1986 to 1989 (capturing the impact of Shock III). The results are striking. The impacts of the two negative terms of trade shocks caused by OPEC I and II are clearly evident by comparing the results for 1973–79 (Shock I) and 1980–85 (Shock II) with the other two periods—before and after the two oil price shocks, respectively. Total factor productivity (TFP) growth was significantly reduced by the two oil price shocks. From an annual rate of TFP growth of 1.7 per cent prior to Shock I, this rate fell to –0.9 and –0.7 per cent during Shocks I and II, respectively. As the terms of trade recovered, during Shock III, TFP growth rose to a startling 5.2 per cent yer year.

The TFP growth contribution to overall growth from 1986 to 1989 can be interpreted to mean that the growth of conventional factors of production does not adequately explain this period of economic expansion. External forces seem to have been important, but the causes of this remarkable boom are still not sufficiently well-understood.

Table 1.7: Growth accounting for Thailand, 1961 to 1989 (per cent per year)

Variable	1961–72	1973–79	1980–85	1986–89
Growth in GDP	11.3	7.7	5.5	10.0
Growth of labour force	2.6	4.1	2.9	3.3
Growth of capital stock	8.7	8.8	7.0	4.2
Contribution from capital to overall growth	76.0	92.9	95.1	35.9
Contribution from labour to overall growth	8.5	18.4	18.0	12.2
Contribution of TFP to overall growth	15.5	-11.3	-13.1	51.9
TFP growth	1.7	-0.9	-0.7	5.2

Source: Author's calculations, as described in text, with data drawn from World Bank, *World Tables*, various issues.

Structural change

Figures 1.4, 1.5 and 1.6 compare the long-term patterns of structural change in Thailand with those observed in Korea and Indonesia. Korea is, of course, ahead of Thailand in the process of economic growth and structural transformation, while Indonesia is somewhat behind. The data show the GDP shares (at constant prices) of agriculture and manufacturing, and also the share of the agricultural labour force in total employment.

Manufacturing overtook agriculture as a share of GDP in 1985 in Thailand and in 1974 in Korea. The same transition seems likely in 1992 in Indonesia. Agriculture's share of the total labour force is also declining in all three countries, but lags well behind agriculture's declining share of national income. These issues are further brought out by Figures 1.7 and 1.8, which compare

Figure 1.4 Agriculture's shares in GDP and labour force, and manufacturing's share in GDP: Thailand, 1960 to 1990

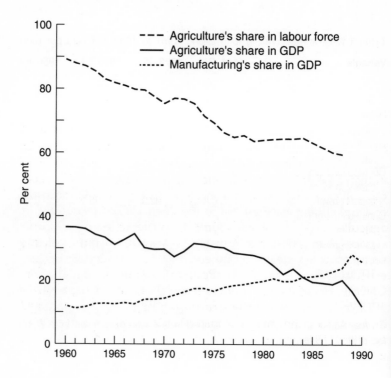

Figure 1.5 Agriculture's shares in GDP and labour force, and manufacturing's share in GDP: Korea, 1953 to 1990

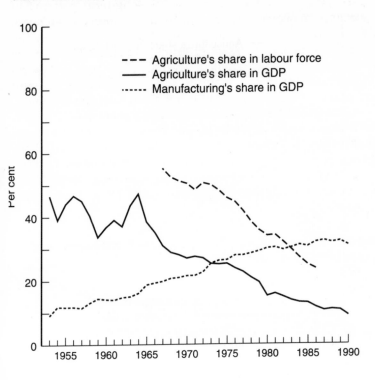

Thailand's GDP shares and labour force shares in 1965 with the latest available data. From Figure 1.7, the decline of agriculture's share of GDP coincided with an expansion of industry's GDP share. The share of services barely changed, but still exceeded industry's share. But turning to the structure of employment in Figure 1.8, the (much slower) decline in agriculture's share of employment was matched by a rise in services share, not that of industry. Clearly, although the services sector is widely neglected by economists, it is very significant, especially for employment. Pasuk Phongpaichit and Samart Chiasakul examine the services sector in detail in Chapter 4.

Table 1.8 shows that the structural change that has occurred in Thailand is not atypical insofar as it involves a decline of agriculture's share of GDP (Martin and Warr 1990ᵀ). What is unusual is the high share of services in GDP.

Figure 1.6 Agriculture's shares in GDP and labour force, and manufacturing's share in GDP: Indonesia, 1960 to 1990

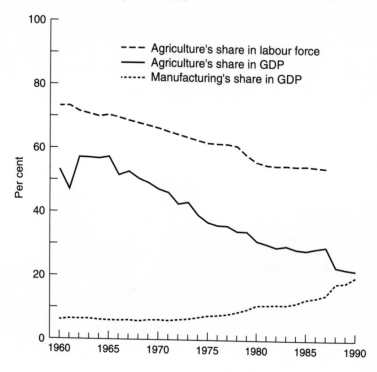

Exports and the terms of trade

From Table 1.9 it is clear that the growth rate of Thailand's merchandise exports accelerated through the 1980s. The composition of these exports moved away from primary commodities and towards manufactured goods. By 1990, total exports of manufactured goods exceeded those of primary goods, and exports of textiles and clothing alone exceeded that of rice, Thailand's traditional export commodity. These issues are discussed in detail by Somsak Tambunlertchai in Chapter 3.

Thailand's external terms of trade (the ratio of the average international prices of its exports to those of its imports) are shown in Figure 1.9. Two points can be noted. First, the terms

Figure 1.7 Sectoral GDP shares, 1965 and 1990 (per cent, current prices)

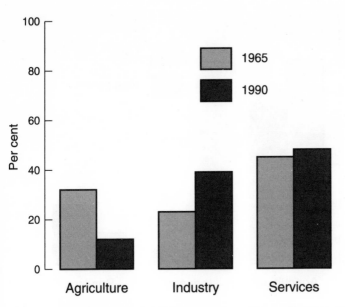

Source: World Bank, *World Development Report 1992*, Oxford University
          Press, 1992.

of trade have declined over the long term, from an index of
100 in 1965 to an index of 65 in 1990. Second, the terms of
trade surged upwards following the 1973 commodity price boom
and then fell with each of the two OPEC petroleum price shocks
(1973–74 and 1979–80).

Inflation

Thai economic policy has been characterized by a strong
aversion to inflation. This is especially true of the monetary
policies implemented by the Bank of Thailand since World War
II. How well has this goal been achieved? Figure 1.10 shows
the annual rate of inflation for the period since 1940. From 1940
to 1948 the data are based on rice prices. Since 1948, cost of
living surveys have been conducted and these data are used
in the construction of Figure 1.10.

Figure 1.8 Sectoral labour force shares, 1965 and 1986–89

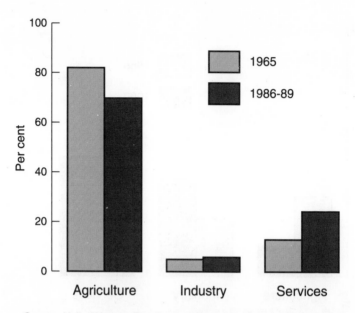

Source: United Nations Development Program, *Human Development Report 1992*, Oxford University Press, 1992.

The data show a rapid inflation during and shortly after World War II, as described in the earlier 'Political history' section. Since then, inflation has been below 5 per cent except for two brief surges associated with each of the two OPEC petroleum price increases of 1973–74 and 1979–80. It is notable that after each of these episodes, inflation was quickly brought under control by stringent monetary contractions. It is well understood in Thai financial circles that the Bank of Thailand will contract monetary policy whenever inflation rises above 6 per cent, and persist with this policy until the rate falls below 6 per cent. Monetary policy thereby has credibility. Inflationary expectations do not become a serious obstacle to the achievement of the goal of low inflation. The outcome is a superb record of monetary management.

Table 1.8: Structure of production: distribution of gross domestic product, 1965 to 1990 (per cent)

	Agriculture		Industry		Manufacturing[a]		Services	
	1965	1990	1965	1990	1965	1990	1965	1990
Thailand	32	12	23	39	14	26	45	48
China	44	27	39	42	31	38	17	31
Indonesia	56	22	13	40	8	20	31	38
Philippines	26	22	28	35	20	25	46	43
Malaysia	28	19	25	42	9	32	47	39
Korea, Republic	38	9	25	45	18	31	37	46
India	44	31	22	29	16	19	34	40

[a] Manufacturing is a component of industry. Except for rounding errors the shares of agriculture, industry and services should sum to 100.
Source: World Bank, *World Development Report*, 1992.

Table 1.9: Growth and structure of merchandise trade, 1965 to 1990

| | Annual growth rate of exports | | Percentage share of merchandise exports | | | | | | | | | |
	1965-80	1980-90	Fuels, minerals, metals 1965	1990	Other primary commodities 1965	1990	Machinery, transport, equipment 1965	1990	Other manufacturing 1965	1990	Textiles, clothing 1965	1990
Thailand	8.6	13.2	11	2	86	43	0	20	3	44	0	16
China	..	11.0	15	10	20	16	9	17	56	56	29	27
Indonesia	9.6	2.8	43	48	53	16	3	1	1	34	0	11
Philippines	4.6	2.5	11	12	84	26	0	10	6	52	1	7
Malaysia	4.6	10.3	34	19	60	37	2	27	4	17	0	5
Korea, Republic	27.2	12.8	15	2	25	5	3	37	56	57	27	22
India	3.0	6.5	10	8	41	19	1	7	47	66	36	23

Source: World Bank, *World Development Report,* 1992.

Figure 1.9 Terms of trade index, 1965 to 1989 (1971=100)

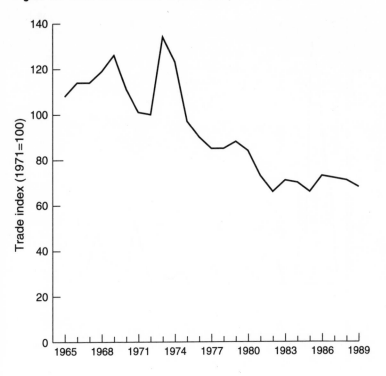

External debt

Thailand largely avoided the 'debt crises' experienced by many developing countries in the 1980s, but by Thailand's conservative standards its levels of debt were a problem. Table 1.10 shows that in 1990 total debt service as a proportion of exports of goods and services was moderately high by East Asian standards. The stock of debt relative to GDP and the annual volume of exports were large, but manageable, because of the high volume of exports. Nevertheless, the level of debt means that Thailand now could not afford a significant decline in the value of exports.

Thailand's adjustments to the oil price shocks of the 1970s, and the high interest rates of the early 1980s were financed to a large extent by foreign borrowing. This is sustainable, so

Figure 1.10 Inflation rate, 1940 to 1990

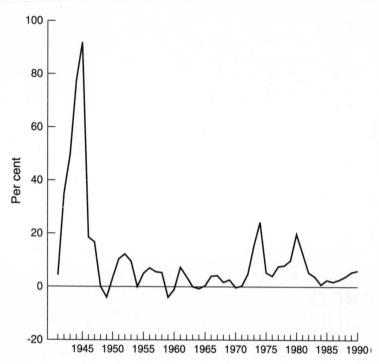

long as the borrowed funds are invested wisely, enabling the loans to be repaid. The major difference between Thailand and the Philippines in this respect is that in the Philippines the borrowed funds were not invested well. Indonesia is more heavily indebted than either of these two countries but appears to have used the borrowed funds in productive ways.

Balance of payments

As with all countries operating with fixed exchange rates, discussions on Thai economic policy are dominated by concern about the balance of payments. This preoccupation is almost certainly excessive, but it does act as a restraint on policies which would imply unsustainable external deficits. Thailand's international reserves are satisfactory, relative to its level of

Table 1.10: Total external debt and total external debt ratios, 1980 to 1990

| | Total external debt (millions of US dollars) | | Total external debt as % of | | | | Total debt services as % of exports of goods and services | |
| | | | Export of goods and services | | GNP | | | |
	1980	1990	1980	1990	1980	1990	1980	1990
Thailand	8,257	25,868	96.3	82.0	25.9	32.6	18.7	17.2
China	7,972	52,555	22.1	77.4	1.5	14.4	4.6	10.3
Indonesia	20,888	67,908	94.2	229.4	28.0	66.4	13.9	30.9
Philippines	17,386	30,456	212.5	229.2	49.5	69.3	26.5	21.2
Malaysia	5,195	19,502	44.6	55.9	28.0	48.0	6.3	11.7
Korea, Republic	29,749	34,014	130.6	44.0	48.7	14.4	19.7	10.7
India	20,560	70,115	136.0	282.4	11.9	25.0	9.3	28.8

Source: World Bank, World Development Report, various issues.

imports and GDP (Table 1.11). In 1990, these reserves were equivalent to 4.4 months of import coverage, compared with 1.5 months for the Philippines, 3.2 months for Indonesia and 1.9 months for India. For many African countries, reserves are equivalent to less than one month's import coverage.

Foreign investment

In the late 1980s, Thailand became a major recipient of direct foreign investment. The magnitude of this foreign investment boom is shown by Figure 1.11, which shows net private foreign investment in Thailand each year from 1971 to 1991. Table 1.12 shows data on net inflows of direct foreign investment over the 1980s. By 1991, the composition of this foreign investment had shifted away from Thailand's traditional sources (Japan, USA and Europe) and towards the Northeast Asian countries. In 1990, Northeast Asia accounted for 60 per cent of the US$2 billion total net direct foreign investment in Thailand, while ASEAN accounted for 13 per cent, Europe 10 per cent and the United States 12 per cent. But Japan alone represented only 30 per cent compared with 44 per cent in 1986. The change was the new importance of Hong Kong (23 per cent), Taiwan (6 per cent) and Singapore (13 per cent). These three sources together accounted for 40 per cent of the total, well exceeding Japan's investment.

Established NICs were looking for new places to invest. Labour-intensive manufacturing industries were becoming less profitable in the old NICs because of rising labour costs. Thailand was seen as an attractive host. The importance of this source of investment for Thailand is indicated by the fact that in 1990 total foreign investment (direct plus portfolio) accounted for 41 per cent of Thailand's total net private investment.[5]

Income distribution and poverty

Considering the intrinsic importance of the subject, the literature on the distribution of income and the incidence of poverty in Thailand has been disappointing. A single, deeply flawed and incomplete data set—the periodic Socio-economic Surveys (SES) conducted by the National Statistical Office (NSO)—has been the source for virtually all serious research on this subject. The

Table 1.11: Balance of payments and reserves, 1970 to 1990

| | Current account balance (millions of US dollars) | | | | Gross international reserves (millions of dollars) | |
| | After official transfers | | Before official transfers | | | |
	1970	1990	1970	1990	1970	1990
Thailand	-250	-7,053	-296	-7,235	911	14,258
China	-81	12,000	-81	11,935	..	34,476
Indonesia	-310	-2,369	-376	-2,430	160	8,657
Philippines	-48	-2,695	-138	-3,052	255	2,036
Malaysia	8	-1,672	2	-1,733	677	10,659
Korea, Republic	-623	-2,172	-706	-2,181	610	14,916
India	-385	-9,304	-591	-9,828	1,023	5,637

Source: World Bank, *World Development Report*, 1992.

Table 1.12: Direct foreign investment into Thailand (net flows), 1980 to 1991 (millions of US dollars)

	1980–85 (average per year)	1986	1987	1988	1989	1990	1991
Northeast Asia	103	159	188	831	1,160	1,683	1,179
ASEAN	14	14	21	65	109	252	253
Europe	45	30	67	111	196	198	196
North America	84	51	71	128	209	232	237
Other	22	9	5	4	97	77	130
Total	268	263	352	1,139	1,771	2,442	1,995

Source: Bank of Thailand.

Figure 1.11 Net private foreign direct investment in Thailand, 1971 to 1991 (selected years)

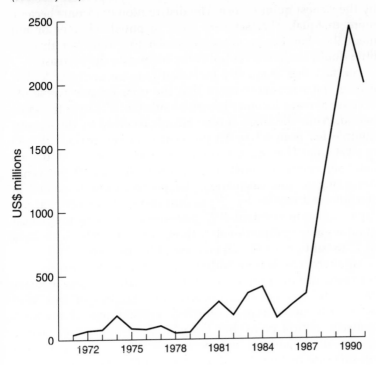

difficulty of making comparisons across time when the sampling procedures and definitions used by the NSO have repeatedly changed has necessarily dominated this literature. These measurement issues are reviewed in detail by Medhi Krongkaew in Chapter 12. What broad conclusions, if any, can be drawn about the changing distribution of income in Thailand?

Figure 1.1 above summarizes the SES data on the distribution of income for 1975–76 and 1988. We shall concentrate on this period because the NSO statistical definitions have been reasonably constant during it. The figure divides the population into five groups of equal population, arranged with the poorest one-fifth of the population (Quintile I) separated from the next poorest one-fifth (Quintile II), up to the richest one-fifth (Quintile V). The vertical axis then shows the proportion of total income received by each quintile. The data show that the proportion of total income received by the poorest one-fifth of the population fell over this period, while the proportion received by the richest quintile rose. The distribution of income became more unequal. Thai scholars have disputed whether or not inequality has increased at an accelerating rate, but there is little doubt about the central point: inequality did increase.

The fact that inequality increased may be undesirable, but it does not necessarily mean that the poor became worse off, because average incomes increased substantially over the same period. While the share of total income received by the poorest quintile fell from 6.1 to 4.5 per cent over the period 1975–76 to 1988, total Thai income rose in real terms from 5,200 to 9,500 baht per capita in constant 1972 prices (i.e. by 83 per cent). According to this calculation, the poorest quintile gained in absolute real income by 35 per cent (from 317 to 428 baht per capita, again in constant 1972 prices), even though the richest quintile gained proportionately three times as much—from 2,564 to 5,216 baht per capita, an increase of 103 per cent.

An alternative way of addressing issues of absolute poverty is to measure the proportion of the population whose incomes fall below a designated poverty line. Studies of this kind necessarily suffer from the intrinsic arbitrariness of any such 'poverty' cut-off point, but the change in poverty incidence, so measured, may not be especially sensitive to the particular cut-off point that is selected. Table 1.13 shows data on this issue, drawn from the studies of Suganya and Somchai (1988) and Medhi, Pranee and Suphat (1991). The data confirm that absolute poverty in Thailand is principally a rural phenomenon, especially concentrated in the Northeast region.

What about changes in poverty incidence over time? While the limitations of the underlying SES data must be stressed, a clear picture does emerge. Over the period 1975–76 to 1988, poverty incidence seems first to have declined until the early 1980s, then to have worsened until the mid-1980s, then to have declined again. What could explain this pattern of apparently fluctuating poverty incidence?

The final row of the table shows the average annual growth rate of real GNP over the period between the years shown, for which survey results are available. In the case of the 1975–76 column the data show average real GNP growth from 1970 to 1975. To the extent that the data can be trusted, the results are clear. Rapid growth from 1976 to 1981 coincided with declining poverty incidence. Reduced growth caused by the world recession in the early to mid-1980s coincided with worsening poverty incidence to 1986. The economic boom of the late 1980s coincided with markedly reduced poverty incidence. It would obviously be too simplistic to say that the answer to poverty is rapid growth and nothing more, but these data provide no support for the claim that economic growth is bad for the poor.

The environment

Passengers flying from capitalist Thailand to the neighbouring socialist or quasi-socialist states of Myanmar (Burma), Laos or

Table 1.13: Poverty incidence and economic growth, 1975–76 to 1988

	1975–76	1981	1986	1988
Poverty lines (baht per capita per year, constant prices)				
Urban	2,961	5,151	5,834	6,203
Rural	1,981	3,454	3,823	4,076
Poverty incidence (%)				
By community type:				
All municipal areas	12.5	7.5	5.9	6.1
All sanitary areas	14.8	13.5	18.6	12.2
All villages	36.2	27.3	35.8	26.3
By Region:				
North	33.2	21.5	25.5	19.9
Northeast	44.9	35.9	48.2	34.6
Central	13.0	13.6	15.6	12.9
South	30.7	20.4	27.2	19.4
Bangkok and vicinities	7.8	3.9	3.5	3.5
Whole Kingdom	30.0	23.0	29.5	21.2
Average growth rate of real GNP over preceding period (per cent per year)	5.9	7.5	5.2	11.5

Note: In both studies cited below, poverty incidence was calculated by applying the rural poverty lines to sanitary areas.
Sources: The poverty incidence data for 1975–76, 1981, 1986, are from Suganya and Somchai (1988) and for 1988 from Medhi, Pranee and Suphat (1991). The GDP growth rates are calculated from Table 1.6.

Kampuchea witness a sudden transformation in the terrain below. From the air they see the red, partly exposed soils of Thailand give way to the green, densely forested landscape of the neighbouring countries. There is no need to enquire where the border is located; even from a height of 8000 metres the national boundaries could hardly be clearer. Thailand has been extensively deforested. As the plane approaches its destination in Yangon (Rangoon), Vientiane or Phnom Penh another striking difference is apparent. Compared with booming, suffocating Bangkok the neighbouring capitals enjoy relatively unpolluted air.

Our travellers have scarcely left the airport before an equally dramatic difference becomes obvious. Compared with the Thais, the vast majority of their Burmese, Lao and Kampuchean neighbours live in poverty. Clothing is shabby, food is poor, transport is inadequate and housing rudimentary at best. Life is a constant struggle for survival. Thailand's economic development has been achieved at the expense of exploiting its natural resources. The rate of exploitation may well have been excessive and its pattern may have been inefficient, but the Thai people have benefited materially from this process in ways that are obvious to any fair-minded observer.

Since World War II, Thailand's agricultural growth has been achieved primarily by expansion of the cultivated area, through deforestation, rather than through improvements in yields. Chapter 2, by Ammar, Suthad and Direk, provides an excellent description of this process. The rapid rate at which land clearance has occurred is largely explained by two factors. First, the use of tractors facilitated the process of land clearance and increased the amount of land that could be profitably cultivated by a single family, relative to the area manageable with draught animals. Second, this technical change greatly exacerbated the effects of Thailand's inadequate system of land titling, an issue also discussed in depth by Ammar, Suthad and Direk.

Much of the newly deforested land is formally claimed by the Royal Forestry Department, based on legislation dating to the end of the last century. Under this law, the Department has legal claim to about half the total land area of the country, but this legal claim cannot be policed. As a result, no one has effective legal claim to this land. Loggers and transient squatters cannot be excluded, but when they occupy the land they cannot obtain legal title. The consequences are serious. When the land does come under cultivation the fact that the cultivators lack legal title has the common effect that the land is not properly maintained and protected from erosion. Moreover, since the land cannot be used as legal collateral for long-term loans the pattern of resource use on it has been inefficient. Farmers in this position have frequently been unable to obtain the credit required for investment in land productivity enhancement or even maintenance, or for purchase of yield-improving equipment.

The rainforests which covered much of Thailand only twenty years ago supported lush vegetation, but their nutrient cycles were fragile (Anat et al. 1988). Once burned and cleared, they supported much less plant growth. These shallow soils were then vulnerable to erosion, especially in sloping terrain. The resulting silt found its way partly to the bottoms of streams and reservoirs, partly to the alluvial plains downstream, and partly to the Gulf of Thailand. The upstream land was irreparably damaged. It is too easy to blame the process on 'development' or 'capitalism'. The problem is capitalist development combined with an inadequate system of property rights.

A similar story can be told of Thailand's fishery resources. Changes in fishing technology made it possible for a single fishing vessel to 'mine' huge areas of coastal fishing waters. Competition for fishing sites became increasingly intense and because individual fishermen lacked legal claim to any particular area of the sea, there was no private incentive to individual fishermen to conserve the stock of fish. Over-fishing resulted. As the Thai fishing fleet ventured further abroad, neighbouring countries were encouraged to establish exclusive economic zones (EEZs) to shut them out. Thai fishermen became increasingly desperate, conflict resulted and the incidence of piracy in the Gulf of Thailand rose alarmingly.

The situation regarding energy supplies is less bleak. Thailand remains an energy importer but, as Praipol Koomsup describes in Chapter 9, its dependence on imported petroleum has declined in the last decade. Although Thailand was adversely affected by OPEC's massive petroleum price increases of 1973–74 and 1979–80, its production of crude oil, and more particularly natural gas, through the 1980s reduced dependence on imported energy to about half its total energy requirements.

Like Venice, Bangkok is slowly sinking. Flooding is becoming increasingly serious during the rainy season. When it happens, the Bangkok Metropolitan Administration is usually blamed, but there is a 'deeper' problem: land subsidence caused by the over-pumping of groundwater (Anat et al. 1988). In 1968, the water table lay 12 metres under the surface of central Bangkok and 4 metres under the eastern suburbs. By 1979, the corresponding depths were 45 and 54 metres. A study by the Army Survey Department suggests that in the past 60 years the surface of central Bangkok has subsided by approximately 0.5 metres. In the areas of heaviest groundwater pumping, rates of land subsidence exceed 10 centimetres a year. The area surrounding Ramkhamghaeng University is now below mean sea level and is protected from massive flooding from the sea only by the fact that surrounding areas are still somewhat above sea level. Meanwhile, Bangkok's construction boom continues ever upwards. The tops of Bangkok's buildings are rising faster than the land is sinking, but this is little consolation to those residing at ground level.

Conclusions: Thailand's economic future

The Thai economy is growing very rapidly. Although the rate has recently accelerated dramatically, the high growth performance has been sustained over a long period. Rapid economic growth leads to structural transformation and, in Thailand, agriculture's share of national income has decreased very significantly since 1960. Agriculture's share in total employment has also declined, but not by as much; it seems to lag behind the changes in the structure of production. The difference between these two sets of facts gives us a good starting point for understanding the persistence of rural poverty in Thailand in spite of rapid economic growth.

There are two structural issues that must be distinguished. The first is how rapidly the adjustment of output and employment from agriculture to non-agriculture will occur, and the second is where the expanding non-agricultural economic activities will be located. It is important not to identify rural areas with agriculture. The production occurring in rural areas includes agricultural activities but also manufacturing and services. Where non-agricultural economic activities will be located depends partly on government policies, including the provision of economic infrastructure and provision of education and health facilities in rural and urban areas.

Until now, Thailand has managed reasonably well the transition from a slow-growing agricultural exporter to a rapidly growing industrializing NIC. Social tensions have resulted from the rapid change, however, and these could threaten the sustainability of the growth process. The possibility of continued political conflict—between the pro-democracy, urbanized and Westernized middle class versus the traditional, authoritarian military elite—remains real.

Education policy is critical for Thailand. For economic growth to be sustained, the education system must generate the educated workforce required for constantly upgrading the composition of output towards more skill-intensive economic activities, generating higher value added. The most worrying point is the low school enrolment rate at the secondary level. The drop-out rate at the primary level is particularly high. This phenomenon is especially significant in Thailand's rural areas. Further reductions in rural poverty are principally dependent on providing rural people with opportunities outside agriculture. On the supply side of education, there is a well-known bias on the part of government expenditure, including education expenditure, in favour of urban areas and against rural areas.[6] On the demand side of education, there is the difficulty for rural people of financing secondary education. Secondary education can be more costly for them than for urban people because rural children must often relocate to urban areas, away from their families, in order to attend secondary schools. Even more important is the fact that secondary education is perceived as being of low economic value to rural people. The latter is partly a consequence of the uniform and somewhat archaic curriculum imposed by the Thai Ministry of Education.

Infrastructure policy is also very important when the economy is changing rapidly. But Thailand's infrastructure facilities in existing urban areas are already heavily congested. This is especially true of roads, ports and telecommunications; Bangkok's traffic jams are world-famous. The problem of congested infrastructure is made more serious by the fact that since 1986 public investment in infrastructure has been contracting rather than expanding as required; privatization has occurred but has been insufficient to take up the slack. It is desirable that the movement of labour out of agriculture, which is inevitable, should not consist entirely of migration from rural to urban areas. This is especially important in a country like Thailand where 'urban areas' essentially means one city— Bangkok. For the foreseeable future, sustained economic growth in Thailand will continue to be concentrated in Bangkok. It is urgent that its over-burdened public infrastructure be upgraded.

Appendix

Estimation of total factor productivity growth

The derivation of the estimating equation is as follows. Let the aggregate production function be

$$Y = f(K,L,t), \tag{1}$$

where Y is GDP at constant prices, K is the aggregate capital shock at constant prices, L is the aggregate labour force and t denotes time. Now

$$\frac{dlnY}{dt} = \alpha_K \frac{dlnK}{dt} + \alpha_L \frac{dlnL}{dt} + \alpha_o, \tag{2}$$

where $\alpha_K = f_K(K/Y)$ and $\alpha_L = f_L(L/Y)$, the elasticities of output with respect to K and L respectively, and α_0 is constant.

An attempt to estimate the parameters of this equation is made using annual data for Thailand for 1961 to 1989, drawn from the World Bank's *World Tables*. The Cochrane-Orcutt autoregression technique was used to correct for autocorrelation. Constant returns to scale was imposed and the estimating equation was

$$\frac{dln(Y/L)}{dt} = \alpha_0 + \alpha_1 \frac{dln(K/L)}{dt}, \tag{3}$$

where the variables are formed by

$$\frac{dln(Y/L)}{dt} \equiv ln(Y/L)_t - ln\,(Y/L)_{t-1}, \tag{4}$$

etc.

The estimated parameters and relevant diagnostics (t-statistics in parentheses) were

$$\frac{dln(Y/L)}{dt} = 0.024 + 0.682 \frac{dln(K/L)}{dt} \qquad (5)$$
$$\phantom{\frac{dln(Y/L)}{dt} =} (2.40) \quad (25.73)$$
$$\overline{R}^2 = 0.96; \; DW = 1.93$$

These estimated parameters are related to the parameters of (2) by

$$\alpha_K = \alpha_1 \text{ and } \alpha_L = 1 - \alpha_1. \qquad (6)$$

Using these estimated parameters it is now possible to study total factor productivity growth on an annual basis by applying the equation

$$F_t = \frac{dlnY}{dt} - \alpha_K \frac{dlnK}{dt} - \alpha_L \frac{dlnL}{dt}, \qquad (7)$$

where F_t denotes estimated rate of total factor productivity growth in year t.

Notes to Chapter I

[1] Sompop (1989) has provided estimates of Thailand's GDP at constant prices and population for 1870 and 1950. When the GDP estimates are converted to per capita terms, the result implies virtually zero growth per capita over this period.

[2] For a recent survey in English of the economic literature which has appeared in the Thai language, see Warr and Bandid (1987).

[3] There are many exceptions. An excellent example is a recent study of Thai agricultural pricing policies (Ammar and Suthad 1989) which provides an insightful and analytical approach. Another is a recent study of Thai environmental issues (Anat et al. 1988), conducted by the prestigious Thailand Development Research Institute (TDRI). See also Sompop (1989) for a valuable account of Thai economic history, written from a Thai perspective.

[4] Again, there are exceptions. The classics are Ingram's superb account of Thai economic history (Ingram 1971) and the excellent collection of essays in Silcock (1967). Both are now badly dated.

Ingram's book, which first appeared in 1959 and was then partially revised for the 1971 edition, has remained the single most important source on the Thai economy until today!

[5] Source: Bank of Thailand, *Quarterly Bulletin*, December 1991.

[6] See Sirilaksana Khoman's insightful discussion of these issues in Chapter 10. If the transformation in Thailand's employment structure does continue to coincide with urban expansion, then the lower utilization of educational facilities in urban areas compared with rural areas described by Sirilaksana may cease. Empty schools in the countryside and crowded schools in Bangkok may become the norm.

2

Agriculture

AMMAR SIAMWALLA
SUTHAD SETBOONSARNG
DIREK PATAMASIRIWAT

Agriculture was the leading sector in the Thai economy during its crucial two decades of growth in the 1960s and the 1970s. That role was taken over by manufacturing during the 1980s, and developments in agriculture now appear less significant for the country's macroeconomic performance. Nevertheless, there are two reasons why it is important to look closely at the agricultural sector. First, the agricultural sector still employs the majority of the Thai people (some 60–65 per cent of the labour force). Second, an understanding of the historical growth of Thai agriculture is necessary in order to understand the impact of its dynamics on the industrialization process, particularly as the sector begins to shed much of its labour force.

The discussion below is divided into three parts. The first reviews the basic economic forces driving the agricultural sector, with emphasis on Thailand's comparative advantage in this sector and its various components. The second part discusses the institutional framework of the sector while the third outlines the effects of government policies upon it.

Output and inputs

Output mix

The growth of Thai agricultural output has been rapid by international standards. The annual rate of growth was 1.9 per cent between 1951 and 1958, 5.4 per cent between 1958 and 1973, and 3.9 per cent between 1973 and 1984. Much of this growth was made possible by the presence of large areas of unused land.

Within the agricultural sector, the crop subsector accounts for about three-quarters of the total agricultural value added, and the livestock subsector in turn accounts for about half of the remainder. Both these shares have been approximately constant since 1960. The fisheries subsector gained ground rapidly until 1980, rising from less than 4 per cent in the early 1960s to 10 per cent in the latter half of the 1970s. The share of the forestry sector, on the other hand, has steadily declined since 1960. It is interesting to note from a comparison of figures for the early 1980s and the late 1970s that value added in both these natural resource intensive sectors declined absolutely.

A recurrent theme in what follows is the past dependence of Thai agriculture on the exploitation and, in some cases, even the mining of natural resources. The expansion of the crop subsector was made possible by the clearance of forests with clearly observable results not only on the amount of forest cover, but also on the output from the forestry sector. As these natural resources were exhausted, attempts were made to shift from capture to culture, with varying degrees of success, as discussed below.

Crops

Crop production remains the core of Thai agriculture. Its expansion has been extremely rapid, peaking in the 1960s. Between 1958 and 1973, when the burst of road-building opened up vast new areas, the growth rate averaged 5.0 per cent per year. From 1973, the growth rate slackened to 3.9 per cent, with much of the decline occurring in the early 1980s.

Figures 2.1 and 2.2 show the distribution of the crops grown in Thailand using two different classifications. Figure 2.1 categorizes the crops according to plant types: paddy, upland field crops, tree crops, vegetables and other crops; Figure 2.2 categorizes the crops according to the nature of their markets: paddy, export, import-competing and non-traded crops.

There is considerable overlap between the categories of upland and export crops. The dramatic expansions of these two categories tell different parts of the same story. The new land areas that were opened up are well-suited to growing upland crops such as maize (as in the early 1960s), kenaf (in the mid-1960s), cassava (in the 1970s), and sugar-cane (in the 1960s and 1970s). Most of these are exported. The trigger for the rapid

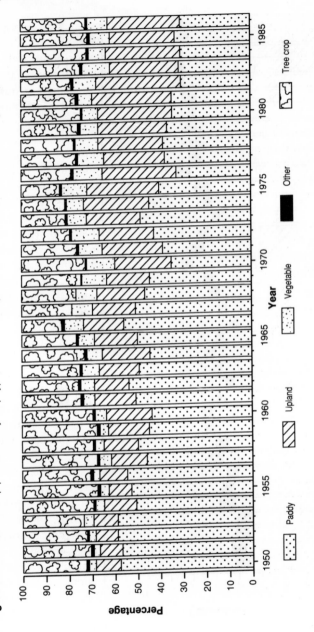

Figure 2.1 Structure of crop production by crop type, 1950 to 1986 (share of value added at current market prices)

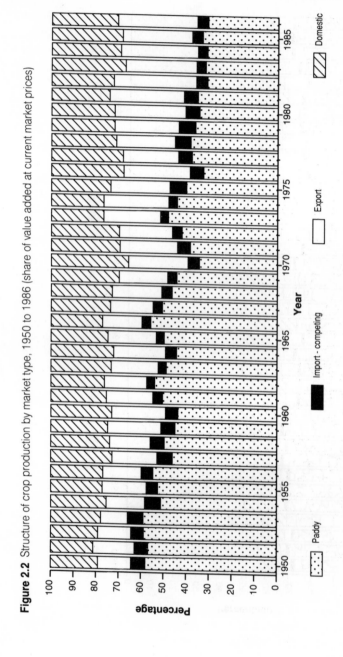

Figure 2.2 Structure of crop production by market type, 1950 to 1986 (share of value added at current market prices)

expansion of each of these crops has been different: for maize it was the introduction of the Guatemala variety which turned out to be particularly well-suited to Thai conditions; for kenaf it was the failure of the jute crop in what was then East Pakistan; and for cassava it was the demand arising from the peculiar system of protection within the European Community. The case of sugar-cane is slightly different and its origins must be traced to the import substitution policies followed from the 1950s and the continued protection even after sugar began to be exported (Phitsanes 1977).

Regardless of what triggered the boom in each of these crops, the availability of land allowed their rapid expansion, seldom at the expense of other crops. The relative decline of the paddy sector indicates the relative scarcity of paddy land. Even here, Thailand's performance has again been an exception among Asian countries in that land expansion rather than yield increases explains the greater part of the growth of production (Barker, Herdt and Rose 1985: 46–50).

Among the other crops, the surprising thing to note is the constant share of the non-traded items within the crop subsector, indicating that their share in total GNP has declined. This part of agriculture is dominated by fruits and vegetables, which are expected to be income-elastic. The slow increase in their production would suggest that there is now considerable scope for investment in this subsector to serve the domestic market.

Livestock
Dramatic shifts have occurred within the livestock sector. In the post-war period, animal-drawn ploughs were progressively replaced by tractors. The upland areas have been using tractors ever since they were first opened up. But more recently, from about 1970 and coinciding with the introduction of double-cropping in the Chao Phraya delta, paddy lands have begun to be ploughed by two-wheeled and four-wheeled power tillers. Because the stock of buffalo and cattle was reduced as a result of these changes, the total value added of this form of livestock production grew only slowly (Table 2.1). Only recently has the high income elasticity of demand for beef begun to make an impact on domestic beef production.

Table 2.1: Composition of livestock production, 1960 to 1986 (millions of baht at 1972 prices)

	Cattle and buffalo		Pigs		Hens, ducks and other poultry		Eggs		Dairy products		Others	
	Value	(%)	Value	(%)	Value	(%)	Value	(%)	Value	(%)	Value	(%)
1960-64	1,393	35.46	1,038	26.43	952	24.24	524	13.33	7	0.17	15	0.37
1965-69	1,577	33.68	1,376	29.39	1,111	23.74	588	12.55	8	0.17	22	0.48
1970-74	1,714	20.06	1,321	22.38	1,684	28.55	1,141	19.33	12	0.20	28	0.48
1975-79	1,995	24.60	1,848	22.79	2,293	28.28	1,925	23.74	21	0.26	26	0.32
1980-86	2,067	20.06	1,901	18.46	3,171	30.78	2,950	28.64	49	0.47	163	1.58

Source: National Account Division, NESDB; compiled by Agriculture and Rural Development Program, Thailand Development Research Institute (TDRI).

Dietary changes have had a more noticeable impact on the demand for poultry products—and should have had a similar impact on pig production. Poultry production has become a highly successful component of Thai livestock production. The introduction of modern breeds of poultry and advanced methods of raising them have been facilitated by large agri-businesses which first pioneered contract farming methods in the early 1970s. These innovations and low feed prices (Thailand has a surplus of carbohydrate feeds) have been responsible for the real decline in poultry prices and have increased the importance of poultry products in Thai diets at the expense of the traditional fish. Present consumption stands at about 6.6 kg per capita per year (Suthad et al. 1989: 190). In recent years increasing amounts of poultry have been exported, mostly to Japan. Consumption of pork stands at 4.7 kg per capita per year (Suthad et al. 1989: 130). Its role in the Thai diet could have been much larger had it not been for restrictive policies affecting the slaughtering industry (policies which have also adversely affected beef consumption).

Fisheries

The marine fisheries industry expanded rapidly in the 1960s. With the trawler revolution, Thailand became a major ocean-fishing nation almost overnight. Demersal (sea-bed) fishing grew rapidly. The motorization of fishing boats in the 1950s and 1960s and the replacement of the bamboo-stake by the purse-seine technique also led to an expansion of pelagic capture (Anat et al. 1988). These intensive methods of capture naturally led to the progressive exhaustion of the resources. As those close at hand were wiped out, Thai fishermen ranged further afield. The increase in oil prices and the introduction of 200-mile exclusive economic zones in the 1970s ended the rapid growth of the Thai marine fishing industry.

The case of inland fisheries is similar, although here the impact of population pressure has been more important. A recent response to the exhaustion of naturally available resources has been the shift to aquaculture. Fresh-water aquaculture, particularly of catfish, experienced a boom in the latter part of the 1970s but this ended in the early 1980s as a result of a severe epidemic of what was apparently a viral disease. There has since been an aquaculture revival but this time with a concentration on the cultivation of fresh water shrimp. Marine aquaculture is also enjoying a boom following the introduction of Taiwanese technology in the raising of tiger prawns. Major investments have been made in the mangrove forest areas along the coast for tiger prawn aquaculture.

Much of the output of the marine fishery industry is exported. The value of fisheries exports in 1988 (excluding canned fish, much of which is tuna brought in by foreign ships) was US$989 million—a marked increase from US$544 million in 1986.

Forestry

The depletion of Thai forests is a particularly serious problem and is the counterpart to the rapid growth of crop production. Much of the country's timber requirements are now met by imports. The movement away from capture to culture is also evident in this sector. The Royal Forestry Department has in recent years been promoting plantations of eucalyptus (*E. calmandulensis*) to produce wood-pulp. Although the alleged reasons for the promotion are to replenish forest reserves that have been lost to the plough and to produce the pulp as an import substitute, an important motive for the Forestry Department is to take back land from farmers who have occupied it illegally.

Inputs

Land

No other aspect of Thai agriculture is as emotion-laden as the expansion of cultivable land and its complement, the decrease in forested land. Over the four decades since World War II, the total area of farmland has been steadily expanding at the expense of the forest (Table 2.2). Until the latter half of the 1970s, the amount of land cultivated per agricultural worker was actually increasing. The period of fastest expansion was in the 1960s, when more kilometres of road were constructed than in probably any comparable period of Thai history. Another factor that made the post-war expansion qualitatively different from the earlier times was the growing availability of tractors. This has had two influences. It made the process of land clearance much easier (Moerman 1968, particularly Chapter 8), and it made the areas cultivable by each family farm much larger than if the farmer had depended on draught animals. This lifting of the constraint on the amount of land able to be cultivated by each farmer speeded up the pace of land clearance.

Did farmers overdo it? The rapid decline in forest land as a result of expanding cultivation has been much debated in recent years, and the adverse environmental impact of deforestation has become a major item on the political agenda. Much of the land that has supposedly been 'deforested' by farmers is in areas that are claimed by the Forestry Department, relying on an old law of 1897. Under this law, the Department could lay claim to half of the total land area of the Kingdom. The claim is grossly unrealistic in administrative and policing terms, and could hardly be justified even from an environmental perspective. The result is that the Department is unable to protect from loggers even those lands that are environmentally fragile (for example, watershed areas), while farmers in perfectly good agricultural lands are prevented from acquiring title to these lands—with adverse economic and social consequences. Some mapping studies by the World Bank in 1982 appear to indicate that farmers do not encroach on environmentally fragile lands—the overwhelming proportion of the land onto which they have moved is suited to agriculture.

Labour

The availability of land for clearance and cultivation has enabled the agricultural sector to absorb the rapidly increasing labour force. According to the population censuses, the annual growth rate of the aggregate labour force was 1.7 per cent between 1960 and 1970, and 3.8 per cent between 1970 and 1980. The marked increase in the 1970s is partly explained by the high birth rates in the late 1950s and the 1960s, and partly by the increase in female labour force participation.

The three censuses indicate that the agricultural labour force has been declining as a proportion of the total from 82 per cent in 1960 to 78 per cent in 1970 and 71 per cent in 1980. These figures are high by international standards (Figure 2.3). The availability of land may have kept more labour in agriculture than would otherwise have been the case, but the census data drawn from asking respondents their primary occupation are biased upward to some extent.

Table 2.2: Land utilization, 1950 to 1988 (million hectares)

	1950	1955	1960	1965	1970	1975	1980	1982	1984	1986	1988
Forest land	31.71	29.73	28.19	26.23	23.27	20.92	16.55	15.58	15.15	14.66	14.38
Farm holding land	8.27	9.03	10.00	12.76	15.04	17.95	19.04	19.77	20.05	20.78	23.65
Housing area	:	:	:	:	:	0.45	0.40	0.41	0.44	0.49	0.53
Paddy land	5.40	5.77	6.20	6.64	9.37	11.40	11.77	11.72	11.83	11.88	11.87
Field crops	0.73	0.76	1.11	1.98	2.25	3.19	4.12	4.69	4.81	5.13	5.72
Tree crops	0.77	0.83	0.93	1.54	1.46	1.67	1.78	1.90	1.93	2.23	3.13
Vegetables and flowers	—	—	—	—	—	0.06	0.05	0.05	0.07	0.09	0.13
Pasture land	—	—	—	—	—	0.06	0.05	0.05	0.12	0.15	0.76
Idle land	0.85	0.85	0.84	0.79	0.66	0.73	0.49	0.62	0.58	0.57	1.23
Others	0.51	0.83	0.92	1.81	1.30	0.38	0.34	0.26	0.28	0.25	0.28
Unclassified	:	:	:	:	:	12.44	15.72	15.88	16.11	15.87	13.28

Sources: 1950–74: *Land utilization in Thailand 1950/51–1977/78*, Office of Agricultural Economics, Ministry of Agriculture and Cooperatives; 1975–82: *Agricultural Statistics of Thailand*, Office of Agricultural Economics, Ministry of Agriculture and Cooperatives; 1983–90: *Statistical Handbook of Thailand*.

The bulk of Thai agriculture is rainfed and therefore does not provide year-round employment for farmers and their families. Data from the Labour Force Surveys, which are conducted in two rounds every year (Table 2.3), show that not only do many people leave the labour force altogether during the dry season, but that agriculture's share of those who do stay in the labour force also drops. A study of rural off-farm employment (Narongchai et al. 1983) indicates that among rural households in the North and Northeast, farm income provides less than half of the total income, in some areas actually less than one-quarter. These figures may underestimate agriculture's contribution because as much as a quarter to a third of household income was earned as wages, a large part of which may come from the agricultural sector.

The conclusion may safely be drawn that the 71 per cent of the labour force said to belong to the agricultural sector at the time of the 1980 census is somewhat exaggerated. A figure of less than two-thirds for the mid-1980s, derived from the wet-season average from the Labour Force Surveys, would probably be nearer the truth. This would make the Thai figures somewhat closer to the 1965 figures for Malaysia, another land-surplus country whose income at that time was similar to Thailand's in 1985.

Over the decades, the amount of schooling that Thais receive has been steadily increasing. The results of this investment by the Thai state are shown in Table 2.4. This expansion, particularly of the number of people who have finished primary schooling, has had a considerable impact on productivity growth in Thai agriculture.

Public capital
Expansion of agricultural production in the past has been accompanied by a heavy investment in public infrastructure. The government has invested heavily not only in roads but also in irrigation projects. Between 1950 and 1984, it invested a total of US$3.6 billion (at 1984 prices) on various irrigation schemes across the country, with the bulk going to the Chao Phraya delta, the country's premier rice-growing area. The pace of investment in irrigation has declined recently, partly because of the increasing cost of irrigation, with the easier sites having already been developed, and partly because of the declining

Table 2.3: Total labour force and the share of employment by major sectors, 1977 to 1989

Year	Dry season (January–March)				Wet season (July–September)			
	Total labour force (million)	Agriculture %	Industry %	Services %	Total labour force (million)	Agriculture %	Industry %	Services %
1977	16.101	61.1	15.1	23.8	20.400	73.6	8.6	17.8
1978	16.820	63.0	13.4	23.6	21.807	73.8	8.6	17.6
1979	16.935	57.8	17.1	25.1	21.378	70.9	10.4	18.7
1980	:	:	:	:	22.680	71.0	10.2	18.8
1981	17.543	53.7	17.2	29.1	24.712	72.1	9.5	18.4
1982	18.616	52.6	17.8	29.6	25.369	68.7	10.6	20.7
1983	20.640	55.9	16.7	27.4	25.184	69.1	10.0	20.9
1984	22.321	60.0	14.9	25.1	25.999	69.7	10.6	19.6
1985	22.602	59.2	14.9	25.9	25.046	68.4	10.9	20.6
1986	23.481	57.9	15.8	26.3	26.691	66.7	10.6	22.6
1987	25.189	56.6	15.4	28.0	27.639	64.4	11.7	23.8
1988	25.989	58.4	14.9	26.7	29.464	66.4	11.4	22.2
1989	26.297	57.3	16.6	26.0	:	:	:	:

Source: National Statistical Office, Labour Force Surveys, 1977 to 1989.

Figure 2.3 Relationship between the share of agricultural labour force and GDP per capita, selected Asian countries, 1965 to 1983

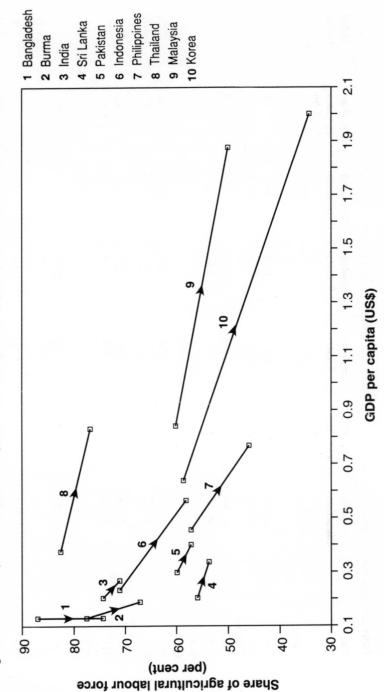

1 Bangladesh
2 Burma
3 India
4 Sri Lanka
5 Pakistan
6 Indonesia
7 Philippines
8 Thailand
9 Malaysia
10 Korea

Table 2.4: Population and educational level, 1960, 1970 and 1980 (per cent of population in each age group)

Age	No education	Completed less than 4 years	Completed 4 years	Completed 5-9 years	Completed 10 years	More than 10 years education	Other studies
1960							
Males							
15+	27.37	13.96	45.99	6.23	2.66	1.92	1.88
45+	60.10	12.59	19.72	3.14	0.68	0.99	2.77
Females							
15+	45.63	11.16	38.45	2.54	1.04	0.84	0.34
45+	90.62	3.43	4.83	0.47	0.11	0.12	0.41
1970							
Males							
15+	17.11	7.78	57.90	6.48	4.12	3.66	2.95
45+	43.38	11.29	31.57	4.21	1.55	2.01	5.99
Females							
15+	30.98	6.99	52.53	3.57	2.00	2.25	1.68
44+	75.58	5.94	13.98	0.93	0.37	0.47	2.73
1980							
Males							
15+	10.00	4.80	58.38	10.00	7.11	8.19	1.52
45+	27.49	8.45	52.00	3.69	3.01	3.02	2.32
Females							
15+	18.35	5.14	58.39	7.06	3.54	6.55	0.96
45+	48.92	8.05	38.37	1.36	0.84	0.99	1.47

Source: National Statistical Office, 1960 Population Census, 1970 and 1980 Population and Housing Census

price of rice. Indeed, since 1983, implementation of large-scale irrigation projects has all but ceased.

Questions have been raised with respect to irrigation investments in Thailand because, in most ex post analyses of the productivity of irrigation investments, their productivity has been found to be low. The utilization of public capital embodied in the irrigation structures remains relatively poor. Not that it is underutilized. On the contrary, the main constraint to dry-season rice production is the amount of water that can be stored during the monsoon in the main storage dams. Rather, the problem is its specificity. Most of the structures were designed to produce rice, but actual cultivation in the Central irrigated areas has largely shifted away from rice. Better utilization of these structures will have to await further investments to upgrade them.

Private capital

Over the years, Thai farmers have made long-term investments in the clearance of new lands, in land development (levelling and so on), in planting perennials, in livestock and in machinery. Few data exist on the total size of these investments and on how they compare with the major public works discussed above. Looking at the factor shares in the cost of production for crops using estimates provided by the government, it is remarkable how small the share of capital is (typically less than 10 per cent). Of course, the share would be larger for the livestock and fisheries subsectors.

New technology

Crop growing in Thailand has undergone relatively little technological change. By and large, there is little application of what is conventionally regarded in the rest of Asia as modern technology. There is little use of modern high-yielding varieties of rice, for example, and the rate of fertilizer application is well below that in most of the rest of Asia. It is only in the use of machinery that Thai farmers are somewhat ahead of farmers elsewhere in Asia. The result is that agricultural yields in Thailand generally lag behind those of other countries.

Despite these observations, to look at technological developments solely at the level of individual crops is to underestimate the technological dynamism displayed by Thai farmers since the 1960s. While they have used age-old techniques to grow a particular crop, Thai farmers have also been adopting new crops with speed, aided by the availability of abundant land resources. And it is because of this same abundance of land that they have been slower to intensify their practices. It must be remembered that acceptance of a new crop is no less an innovation than acceptance of a new technique or a new variety.

The government has expended resources to promote technological change, at least for the crop subsector, but the amounts have not been very significant. In this respect, Thai agriculture has suffered from its success in the world markets. Because Thailand exports most of its agricultural commodities, there is not a sufficiently strong impulse for the government to invest in research. The Thai situation contrasts with India and Indonesia, where the drive to attain self-sufficiency has impelled their governments to invest in research and promote new technology. It is interesting to note that in Thailand import-substituting crops have claimed relatively more research money than export crops such as rice or maize (Table 2.5).

Among the export crops, the research system has not been instrumental in introducing new crops. But once a crop's commercial success has been proven the research budget tends to expand along with its importance in the economy. This behaviour indicates that an important motive of the government in promoting farm productivity is to increase the farmers' income, rather than to protect the competitiveness of the particular crop. In this sense, research has followed rather than led comparative advantage.

The key player in introducing new crops has been the private sector. However, once a crop has been thus introduced, the private sector tends not to play an active role in developing new technologies to grow that crop. Even in poultry production, where the private sector has played a dominant role, the domestic firms have mostly been the conduit for technologies produced by foreign multinationals. Only recently have hybrid-maize seed firms begun to conduct research of their own (Suthad, Sarun and Banlu 1988), and much of that work has capitalized on the success of the Suwan varieties—a success of the public sector research system.

Not to be forgotten as a source of technical progress are the

Thai farmers' trial-and-error methods that have been practised for millennia. These have been especially important in the horticultural sector and, more recently, in the pig industry.

Growth accounting

This section presents a growth accounting exercise for the crop sector. The implicit underlying model is based on the following equation:

$$ln(y/n) = \beta_0 + \beta_1 ln(p) + \beta_2 ln(p_f) + \beta_3 ln(h/n) + \beta_4 ln(k/n) + \beta_5 ln(s) + \beta_6 ln(r)ln(i) + u \tag{1}$$

where y = index of output,
n = agricultural labour force,
p = index of output prices,
p_f = fertilizer prices,
h = cultivated area,
k = index of capital stock,
s = average number of years of schooling,
r = cumulated national research expenditures,
i = cumulated irrigation expenditures, and
u = random term.

The model is run against provincial level data for the period 1961 to 1985. We used panel data consisting of provincial-level observations for all the variables except research expenditures, whose output is regarded as a public good, accessible to all provinces. The details of the estimation are given in Direk and Sakeddao (1990). We give below a brief explanation of its economic assumptions.

Essentially the fitted equation is a supply function, hence the presence of output and fertilizer prices. However, we also assume that in each year, the quantities of land and labour are fixed for each province, as a historical given. This explains the presence of these variables. The estimated equation gives the mean estimate of the sources of growth of output per capita during the period 1961-85. The results are reported in Table 2.6. Because we consider the end of the land surplus in the late 1970s to be an important watershed, we have also reported the growth accounting exercise for the two subperiods before and after that watershed.

Table 2.5: Research expenditure relative to crop value, 1987 and 1988 (per cent of crop value)

Crops	1987	1988
Export crops		
Rice	0.49	0.37
Rubber	0.46	0.54
Maize	0.52	0.20
Tapioca	0.20	0.18
Sugar-cane	0.43	0.23
Mungbean	0.88	0.74
Sorghum	1.01	0.77
Import crops		
Soybean	0.79	0.66
Oil palm	0.72	0.46
Cotton	4.35	2.30
Groundnut	1.20	2.30

Source: Suthad and Khaoborisuth (forthcoming), 'Research budget application of the Department of Agriculture', discussion paper for the Research Priorities in Thai Agriculture Project, Department of Agriculture, Thailand Development Research Institute (TDRI), Australian Centre for International Agricultural Research (ACIAR) and International Service for National Agricultural Research (ISNAR).

The most striking, and surprising, result is the major role played by education in explaining the productivity increase in agriculture. This result appears to be very robust against different specifications of the equation. Considering that much of the increase in schooling took place at the primary level, the result does show that at this level, there is considerable impact on agricultural productivity. A somewhat more obvious result, in view of what we have said earlier, is the role played by increase in per capita land availability. The contrast between the period prior to the late 1970s and the period thereafter should be noted.

We have tried to measure the impact of agricultural research and irrigation, and found these impacts to be relatively small. It should be noted that the result reported in Table 2.6 is not particularly robust, and is obtained against much experimentation with various specifications other than the multiplicative interaction as stated in equation (1) above. The rationalization for this particular specification is that the impact of research is felt only in irrigated areas. We would also conjecture that the main effect of irrigation in Thailand has been the substitution of rice for other crops, but that it has not led to much aggregate increase in productivity.

A specification involving a trend term appears to be insignificant. Nevertheless the shift in the values of the unexplained residual between the first and second period (mostly the effect of u in equation (1) above) should be noted. Although the data do not warrant this, we would still speculate that in the recent past, as land has become more scarce, a more intensive technology has been adopted by Thai farmers.

Institutions

Land property rights

Among Asian countries, Thailand is probably unique in the nature of its land property rights problems. It might have been thought that the abundance of land in Thailand would have made land distribution more egalitarian than in the more overcrowded parts of Asia. To some extent this is true. While tenancy is widespread in some of the older rice-growing parts of the Central Plains region and in the Northern valleys, the incidence of tenancy is quite small in the Northeast region

Table 2.6: Output growth per capita and its sources (per cent per year)

Sources	1961–63 to 1976–78	1976–78 to 1983–85	1961–63 to 1983–85
Output growth per capita	3.13	1.33	2.41
Attributable to:			
Output price	0.19	-0.61	-0.06
Fertilizer price	0.27	0.16	0.24
Land per unit of labour	0.90	-0.50	0.47
Capital per unit of labour	0.59	0.43	0.53
Schooling	1.17	1.12	1.10
Research and irrigation	0.51	0.01	0.39
Unexplained residual	-0.50	0.76	-0.26

Source: See text.

and in the newly settled areas fringing the Central Plains (Table 2.7).

The problem lies in the fact that Thai farmers do not have clear title to the land they till. As many as a million farm households (out of a total of some five million) are technically squatters on land which the government claims is the nation's forest reserve. Farmers on at least 30 per cent of the land outside the reserves have not been able to obtain sufficiently clear title to enable them to use the land as collateral. The statistics cited here (mostly from Thailand Development Research Institute 1986[T]) are necessarily incomplete. There is no firm set of data on which to base more precise statements. The situation is so dynamic that there is difficulty in obtaining current estimates; but there also appears to be a lack of interest in having clear estimates. The agency responsible for issuing such land titles (the Lands Department) is thus unable to give a precise answer to the elementary question of how much land is covered by all the titles it has ever issued.

Two consequences of this record of unclear land titles are especially important. The first concerns the issue of land conservation. Because there are now so many people who are technically squatters on the government's forest land, the government has found it difficult to construct a clear and acceptable set of policies on forestry and conservation. Public opinion appears simultaneously to favour conservation and to oppose eviction of squatters. In 1985, the government formulated a forestry policy which seems to incorporate the worst aspects of both alternatives.

The second consequence concerns agricultural productivity. Empirically well-supported arguments by Feder et al. (1988) show that the lack of land titles does not lead to less security in land tenure. In general, even on forest reserves, the probability of farmers without land titles being evicted from their land is quite low, although not quite zero. Indeed there is an active market in land without titles. Consequently, the impact on agricultural productivity is negligible. However, when the land that farmers hold cannot be placed as collateral for long-term loans (and long-term loans even from informal lenders do require collateral), then farmers are unable to make investments in land or even equipment. This under-investment clearly has an impact on agricultural productivity. Land with title sometimes fetches

Table 2.7: Land holdings, classified by type of tenancy, 1983

	North		Northeast		Central		South	
	(thousands)	Per cent of total	(thousands)	Per cent of total	(thousands)	Per cent of total	(thousands)	Per cent of total
Total land holdings (thousand rai)	27,940	100	53,061	100	27,950	100	14,280	100
Owner-occupied	21,490	76.9	48,732	91.9	20,025	71.7	13,281	93.0
Rented	4,118	14.7	2,099	3.9	7,075	25.3	586	4.1
Others (incl. mortgaged, rented, free, etc.)	2,332	8.4	2,231	4.2	850	3.0	412	2.9
Number of farm households (thousands 1982)	1,236	100	1,946	100	879	100	624	100
Number of renters (1982)	259	20.9	134	6.9	310	35.3	92	14.8

Source: Office of Agricultural Economics, Ministry of Agriculture and Cooperatives. Figures slightly amended for consistency.

as much as double the price of land without title (Feder et al. 1988: 93). The social discounted value of the additional productivity is about 50 per cent of the market value of the land. In areas where credit markets seem to be particularly active, this premium on titling is much lower (Feder et al. 1988: 142–3).

Other factor markets

Labour markets

As with agriculture everywhere, labour demand is highly seasonal. Because much of the supply of labour is from rural households, the supply is also highly seasonal. Much exchange of labour among farm households takes place. In the past, such exchange has been in the form of barter among households within a village. This practice has rapidly declined, apparently for two reasons. First, the rural economy has become more monetized and transactions costs can therefore be reduced by using money instead of inter-household labour debt. Second, the rhythm of agricultural work within a village has become more synchronized, certainly within irrigated villages, but also within some cash-crop growing villages; consequently, farmers have to range beyond their villages in order to procure labour. Such outside labour can only be hired on a cash-wage basis.

The expanded demand for hired labour is partly met by landless households, but the proportion of landless households in Thailand is still relatively small (Table 2.8). Much of the demand for hired labour is met by other farm households, with the Northeasterners being notably in a position of excess supply, and the Central Region farmers (particularly sugar-cane farmers who usually farm very large areas of up to 500 hectares) in a position of excess demand most of the time. Considerable seasonal migration takes place to match these imbalances. The sugar-cane harvest alone requires some 200,000 additional hired hands from the Northeast (Sunee 1978[T]: 201, adjusted for the more recent expanded production). Where considerable numbers of transactions take place, as in this case, sophisticated methods of forward labour contracting (involving a nominally interest-free advance by the employer) have been devised to ensure that adequate labour will be forthcoming at harvest time (Ammar 1990[T]).

Table 2.8: Percentage of landless, near-landless and small farmers

Area	Type of farmers				
	Landless[a]	Near-landless[b]	Small[c]	Other[d]	Total
Selected provinces[e]	10.59	3.25	4.53	81.63	100
	(92,034)	(28,287)	(39,354)	(709,469)	(869,144)
Upper North[f]	13.48	31.37	27.51	27.64	100
	(12,245)	(28,511)	(25,002)	(25,116)	(90,874)
Lower North and some parts of Central Plain[g]	10.11	8.16	9.61	72.12	100
	(74,977)	(60,503)	(71,275)	(534,948)	(741,723)
East and some parts of Central Plain[h]	13.03	7.40	7.86	71.71	100
	(39,802)	(22,593)	(24,006)	(218,973)	(305,374)

Figures in parentheses are the estimated number of farms from the survey.

a Those who do not own any land (excluding home lot) and do not rent any land from other people. They are mainly farm labourers.

b Those who own less than 5 rai of land and have a net cultivated area of not more than 5 rai (including own land and rented land).

c Those who own less than 10 rai and have a net cultivated area of not more than 10 rai.

d Those holding over 10 rai of land.

e The 1979 survey covered three provinces in lower North, one in the Northeast (Khorat), and eight provinces in the Central Plain.

f 1981, covered eight provinces.

g 1982, covered thirteen provinces (three in lower North).

h 1983, covered nine provinces (six in Central Plain).

Source: Agricultural Land Reform Office, data assembled by Anat Arbhabhirama et al. (1988: Table 2.11).

In the Central paddy-growing irrigated areas, on the other hand, where farm sizes are relatively small and where the labour demand in neighbouring areas occurs at the same time, a considerable amount of the farmer's management skill has to be devoted to planning his precise labour requirements, and to acquiring knowledge about neighbouring areas' requirements so as to be able to procure labour when required.

This sketch of the rural labour markets is sufficient to indicate two essential points. First, we can safely jettison the simple surplus labour hypothesis that labour can be removed from the agricultural sector for year-round employment elsewhere without any impact on agricultural production. Second, it is possible that considerable disequilibrium exists in the rural labour markets as there is very little systematic exchange of information between areas that are temporarily in surplus and those that are in deficit (see particularly Chalongphob's chapter in this volume). It is because of these disequilibria that considerable geographical inequalities exist in incomes. The average landless household's income in the Central Region is thus frequently higher than that of an owner-occupier in the Northeast (Ammar and Viroj 1990[T]).

Credit markets

In rural areas, credit has been traditionally provided by informal lenders, for example by better-off farm households within the village or by individuals on fixed incomes (e.g. school teachers) and, outside the village, mostly by traders. The government has long been trying (since 1916 in fact) to replace these informal lenders on account of the 'exorbitant' interest rates they charge. Only with the setting up of the Bank for Agriculture and Agricultural Cooperatives (BAAC) in 1969 has the government acquired an institutional basis to make inroads into the informal sector's role in the rural credit markets. An additional boost was achieved in 1975 when the commercial banks were required to lend a proportion of their portfolio to the agricultural sector. As a consequence of these policies, the share of formal sector loans provided to farm households has gone up from about 10 per cent in the 1960s to almost 50 per cent in the 1980s (Ammar 1990[T]).

Both the informal and formal sectors appear to have been

successful in meeting the short-term credit needs of the better-off and middling farmers. Long-term credit from both these sources is relatively rare and invariably entails putting up land as collateral. There are many market devices which substitute for credit. Large tractors have sometimes been acquired (frequently on hire-purchase) by better-off households, and then leased for custom-ploughing by the other farmers. In the case of the modern livestock sector, large agri-businesses have provided capital to the farmers at the start of their career. Another financial source for rubber growers is the Rubber Replanting Fund, which provides a grant to farmers wishing to replant their trees. The 'repayment' is in the form of a tax levied on all rubber exports. But these examples are mostly ad hoc solutions to the problems caused by the absence of long-term credit. As Thai agriculture becomes more capital intensive, the absence of long-term credit institutions will obviously work against farmers who do not have titled land.

Output markets

Internal trade in agricultural products in Thailand has generally been free from government intervention. As a result, its organization and associated institutions have evolved in response to market pressure and the traders' own needs. The sophistication with which the marketing institutions have evolved varies across different commodities and depends on certain factors connected with the processing technology, the perishability of the products, and the requirements imposed by the final consumers (Ammar 1978). The market organizations for the products of Thai agriculture may be divided into two types: arm's length markets and contract farming systems. This is a broad categorization; some markets have mixed characteristics.

Arm's length markets

Most major commodities are traded on arm's-length basis (i.e. from the farmers through myriads of middlemen, through processors, and so on, down the chain to exporters or final consumers). With the expansion of the market, there would be increasing differentiation of functions, although it is typical for a middleman to deal in many commodities. This occurs because seasonality is even stronger in the trade of agricultural products than in their production. Traders therefore find it worthwhile to handle many commodities.

At the farm level, a farmer usually deals with middlemen in the district towns or directly with a nearby processor. In most arm's length markets, the farmer is generally not tied to any particular middleman but will switch from one to another depending on the prices offered. Exceptions occur in the case of rice (in some poorer areas) and maize, where credit ties will cause farmers to stick with one buyer.

Further along the marketing chain the markets are efficiently organized (see Chirmsak 1977 for a good account of the rice trade). For each commodity, there is typically a central wholesale market where buyers and sellers converge in an informal auction market. Alternatively, where processors or silo facilities are concentrated, prices are posted up and become the market information which is passed along the chain. The information role in the Bangkok wholesale trade (e.g. rice for export) is undertaken by brokers, with whom up-country millers and traders are in constant communication, nowadays by telephone.

Despite allegations to the contrary, research into these types of markets has consistently failed to find evidence of any substantial monopsonistic or monopolistic element (Ammar 1978). A more sophisticated, and probably more valid, charge which could be brought against the present marketing system is that it pays insufficient heed to the quality of the product. For a long time, the cassava trade was subject to adulteration but this disappeared when traders began paying a differential price for the cassava roots according to their starch content. Similarly, more select varieties have always had a marketing channel separate from the less differentiated export rice. However, such non-interventionist moves towards quality improvement take time to develop and may not be appropriate for international trade in high-value horticultural products.

Contract farming
In the last few decades, a new mode of handling certain agricultural products has emerged, particularly in sugar-cane, tobacco and poultry. The specific circumstances that give rise

to such transactions vary. They range from the scheduling needs of the processors (sugar-cane) to the need to control the particular variety to be delivered to the overseas market (tobacco). The success of these arrangements in promoting technical change, for example in the case of poultry, and the fact that many such arrangements appear to reduce the price risk for the farmers, have led many to advocate the expansion of this type of arrangement to other products. Furthermore, where quality is an important consideration, it appears that such types of transactions can convey information regarding consumer preferences better than arm's length markets.

However, there is little understanding of the reasons for the emergence of contract farming in any given branch of agriculture (see Ammar 1978). Without careful planning, introduction of contract farming runs a severe risk of failure. Early pineapple canneries, for example, attempted to copy the contract arrangements prevalent in the sugar industry, only to incur huge losses from contract defaults by the farmers. More recently, questions have been raised regarding the burden of risk borne by farmers, particularly in the case of exotic crops or new technologies introduced by the contracting firms.

Local economic institutions

The role of local (village-level) institutions has received little study from economists. From studies made by non-economists and economic historians, it appears that local economic institutions play a relatively small role in Thai agricultural production. In recent years, their role seems to have diminished even further. A number of reasons can be suggested for this.

First, Thai agricultural systems, except in the upper Northern region, do not depend much on communally constructed and maintained irrigation systems. In the Central Plains region, irrigation systems have been constructed and maintained by the government. Even though the problem of allocation could have given rise to communal organization, a system of de facto rights which gives absolute priority to upstream farmers has developed instead. Even in the North, the communally built and maintained systems are now being replaced by more permanent structures constructed by the government. The traditional systems with their heavy maintenance requirements were the focus of sophisticated communal organizations which levied labour contributions from among the beneficiaries.

Second, local security was traditionally a local matter. With improved transport and communications, the State's presence in the villages became more firmly established and the need for village solidarity against outsiders weakened. The third reason, not entirely independent of the second, is that there is little direct taxation of Thai farmers. The overwhelming majority earn too little to be subject to income tax. Land taxes are very light, which is a further reason for the government's poor record in assigning land property rights. There was thus no need for a village-level collective apparatus to handle taxation, such as existed in pre-colonial Vietnam.

The absence of local economic institutions partly explains the ease with which the forest areas surrounding villages have been cleared for cultivation. Traditionally, until a given piece of land is cleared for cultivation, the land is considered communal property, to which all villagers have access. Once someone clears the land, it is generally recognized as his. While land was plentiful, this traditional practice did not require elaborate organization or formal rules. As land became increasingly scarce during the 1980s, there was thus nothing to prevent massive encroachment on forests by individual villagers or by government officials or a coalition of both. The question of village common land became another strand in the complicated land issue.

However, one local institution is economically important even though it does not directly contribute to agricultural production, namely the village temple. Temple building in Thailand is financed by local contributions and there is a lay committee that oversees its finances. Because the temple is sometimes the only functioning village-level financial organization, villagers themselves and many development agencies have latched on to it to promote and operate communal activities.

Policies

The Thai government has significantly affected the agricultural sector in three different policy areas: through its attempts to manipulate land use; through its expenditure policies, particularly on irrigation and research; and through its pricing policies. It is important to stress that the Thai political system has not produced an articulated set of policies towards the agricultural sector as a whole. Where pronouncements on such policies have been made, as in the development plans, they have not been significant or have not been carried out, except for irrigation. Furthermore, they were not considered in tandem with much more powerful measures applied to agriculture, for example export taxes and restrictions.

Land and land use policies

The government's main failing in the past has been more that of omission than of commission. Essentially, it failed to set up a clear procedure to grant property rights to land that was perfectly well-suited to agriculture, and which was eventually taken over anyway for that purpose. Now that farmers have occupied these lands, the government has decided to shift from the sins of omission to the sins of commission by attempting to resume control over them.

The objective of the land policies announced in 1985 was to reverse the feared environmental damage created by continual deforestation. The intention was to return some of these deforested lands to forest cover. The government defined two categories of forest land: natural forests and economic forests. The natural forests were defined entirely on the basis of environmental considerations (e.g. areas with steep slopes, watershed areas) and were to cover about 15 per cent of the total area of the country. Where these have been denuded, the Royal Forestry Department (RFD) was itself to do the replanting. In contrast, the economic 'forests' were to be planted with tree-crops. From the way the policy was later implemented, it appears that no environmental consideration was involved in the decision to have another 25 per cent of land devoted to economic 'forests'. It was subsequently shown that the calculations of the area to be put under economic 'forests' used estimates of demand for tree-crop products such as rubber, fruit, oil palm and timber, with that demand to be met entirely from domestic sources.

The central motivation behind this set of policies has been

the attempt by the RFD to regain control over the lands occupied by farmers (illegally occupied in the eyes of RFD). The RFD is willing to issue these farmers with non-transferable occupancy certificates (which means that the land cannot be used as collateral), provided they use the land in the manner prescribed by it, namely to plant tree crops. More pointedly, the RFD also has the power to allow private companies to lease, at a nominal rent, the land that it claims (but which may already be occupied by what it calls 'squatters') and use it to grow specified fast-growing trees. In the last few years, the crop of choice is *Eucalyptus calmandulensis*, which is considered highly suitable to produce paper pulp. In recent years, the expansion of agri-businesses entering this field has led to a number of celebrated conflicts with local farmers, and has become a sensitive political issue.

This attempt by the government to expand the area under 'economic forests' has led it to attempt the regulation of land use on economic grounds, something it has never done on such a massive scale. It is unfortunate that this attempt should be based on such dubious economic and environmental grounds; and what is worse is that, in some cases, agri-businesses were given the task of evicting the squatters (farmers who were essentially doing just what the agri-businesses intended to do).

Irrigation
Before 1980, probably the largest impact of government action on agricultural production occurred through its decisions on irrigation investments. The objectives of the Thai government in making these investments are far from clear. As an exporter of rice, the government certainly had little drive to attain self-sufficiency (unlike importing countries such as Indonesia and the Philippines), although it must be acknowledged that changes in the world price of rice do have some impact on the pace of investments (investments fell in 1969–71 and in 1982–85 when rice prices were very low). If a desire to maximize production had been the motivation, the government would have concentrated single-mindedly on areas with the greatest potential. Certainly, the availability of good sites from an engineering point of view would have meant favouring the better-off areas in any case. Thus, the government invested

massively in the Central plains, in a continuing effort that began when the Dutch engineer J. Homan van der Heide proposed the project in 1907. With the completion of the Chao Phraya and the associated Mae Klong and Pitsanuloke projects, the Central system has reached a plateau of development from an engineering point of view.

With this halt in its Central system, the government's attitude to irrigation development became even more ambivalent. Many of the more recent investments have been small scale. In this, the government was and remains guided by equity considerations, notwithstanding the fact that the productivity of these investments appears at best dubious.

Another area of undoubted weakness is the failure to increase the efficiency of the existing systems. Even though the Central system is now used to its capacity in the dry season there is considerable wastage involved. Unpredictable flows have led to inefficient use of water and to the hoarding of water by farmers upstream, thereby reducing supplies downstream where its productivity would be higher. Furthermore, most of the structures were designed with rice production in mind, but much of the irrigated land has since been put to other uses, such as horticulture and aquaculture.

This shift in land use, however, has had little impact on the Royal Irrigation Department's (RID) operations. A rethinking by RID in this matter would have profound implications. In the past, the government has seldom intervened in the farmer's use of his land. A regulatory system with a variegated cropping pattern would be nearly impossible. But if the farmers and RID wish to move away from rice and have the water delivery schedule shifted to take account of this fact, a different arrangement from the current, generally hands-off attitude, is called for. Such a new arrangement could take many forms, but will require stronger management and organizational skills from both RID and the farmers.

Credit
As indicated earlier, the government has intervened in order to make cheap, institutional credit available to farmers. From the farmers' point of view the partial replacement of informal sources by institutional sources brought about by these policies

has been clearly and substantially beneficial. The question is whether this implicit subsidization has been larger than is justifiable.

Three modes of intervention have been used (Ammar and Prayong 1990), each of which implies a subsidization of credit in one form or another:

- commercial banks are required to lend a proportion of their deposits, now set at 14 per cent, to the agricultural sector;
- the Bank of Agriculture and Agricultural Cooperatives (BAAC) has chosen to use an average-cost pricing rather than the marginal-cost pricing rule in its setting of interest rates charged to the farmers; and
- since 1987, the government has introduced a paddy mortgage scheme which gives highly subsidized loans to farmers to store their paddy until later in the marketing season.

These policies together have meant an implicit subsidy to the agricultural sector of about 1 billion baht (US$40 million) in 1987, or less than 1 per cent of value added in the agricultural sector. Of this total, most (about three-quarters) is through the second mode of intervention.

Pricing policies

The most powerful instruments applied to agriculture in the past have been the various border measures applied against agricultural exports and, more recently, against agricultural imports (Ammar and Suthad 1989).

There appears to be a clear trend in government intervention measures. In the past, agriculture tended to be taxed much more heavily, with rice being the most heavily disprotected component. Another traditional export item, also heavily taxed, was rubber. Most of the newer export items were lightly treated. In all cases the taxes were such as to reduce the variability of domestic prices, with the taxes being high when world prices were high, as in 1973–74.

Sugar was an exception. Its domestic price to consumers was maintained at a higher level than the world price in order to subsidize exports. Significantly, sugar was imported until as recently as 1959, and the industry would have continued to be import-competing had free trade prevailed until the late 1960s. The protective policies normal to imports in Thailand thus carried over even after sugar had clearly become an export (i.e. it would still be exported if the government ceased to support it) from about the mid-1970s onward.

The peak years of heavy anti-agriculture bias were the late 1970s and the early 1980s. Thereafter, from about 1982 onwards, disprotection of exportables steadily declined: maize exports were completely liberalized at the end of 1981, all taxes on rice exports were removed in 1986, and taxation of rubber was gradually reduced and then temporarily removed altogether in 1989. At the same time another export commodity, cassava, joined sugar in receiving protective treatment. In this case, the government dissipates the quota rent it receives as a result of the voluntary restraint agreement with the European Community (EC) in favour of higher exports to non-EC markets, thus boosting demand and domestic prices.

This trend away from disprotection of agriculture has several explanations. The dismantling of export taxes in the 1980s is in line with the implicit policy of stabilizing domestic prices. However, when agricultural (particularly rice) prices soared again in 1987–89, the neutral policies remained in place. These events appear to be the strongest confirmation of the alternative hypothesis that the political economy of agricultural pricing policies has indeed begun to shift in favour of agriculture, and that the pro-farmer rhetoric of the post-1973 period is at last beginning to be implemented. Table 2.9 shows the nominal protection coefficients for eight crops, both exports and imports, from 1970 to 1986. The data confirm the decline in the disprotection of the export sector, and also show that the protection rates for imports (except cotton) have been rising.

Among non-tradables, there have long been what appear to be very stringent regulations on the slaughtering of pigs and cattle. A slaughterhouse cannot be privately owned. The transport of live animals and meat across provincial boundaries has to be licensed by local authorities, and at times is banned altogether. An imputed income tax is collected with the slaughtering permit, which is issued for each individual animal. The combined result of these regulations and taxation is that considerable illegal slaughtering takes place, usually under unsanitary conditions. In more recent years, these regulations have begun to be relaxed in a bid to promote exports, particularly of pork.

This account of pricing policies concludes with some estimates of the indirect effects of non-agricultural policies on the relative prices received by the farmers. The method of calculation is given in detail in Ammar and Suthad (1989) and is based on the methodology developed by Krueger, Schiff and Valdes (1988). Briefly, a policy of industrial protection is an implicit tax on exports. The size of this implicit tax could be calculated as the extent of devaluation of the real exchange rate necessary if the industrial protection is removed. Since the 1960s, the degree of implicit export tax has been about 10 per cent. In addition, when the government had a sizeable macroeconomic imbalance (as in the early 1980s) and decided to meet such imbalance not by devaluation but by unsustainable borrowing from abroad, there was an additional implicit taxation on exports as well: in the early 1980s it was of the order of 10–15 per cent. These implicit taxes combined are sizeable and exceeded, for that period, the direct imposts of the government on agricultural exports (compare Table 2.9 with Table 2.10).

Conclusions: future directions

Thai agriculture is now at a crossroads. The two factors that fuelled its past growth—surplus land and a buoyant foreign market—cannot sustain it in the future. While Thailand will still have a comparative advantage in agriculture, the sector's dominance in the economy and in exports will continue to decline. It will have to compete with the manufacturing sector even for that factor of production which it seems to have in abundance, namely labour. The current prognosis is for the labour force in agriculture to decline absolutely sometime in the 1990s.

These developments, as well as the need to cope with the legacy of inadequate land policies, present a set of delicate problems for the government. First, the factor intensity of Thai agriculture will change with the changing trends in the people–land ratio. At the same time, domestic demand will dictate that the more capital-intensive and technology-intensive horticultural sector must expand. Thailand has potential as an exporter of horticultural and livestock products. Whether these exports can be achieved despite rapidly increasing domestic demand and whether government trade policy can be adjusted

Table 2.9: Effect of direct intervention on domestic relative prices of selected agricultural commodities, 1970 to 1986 (proportionate deviation from world relative price)

Year	Rice[a]	Maize	Sugar (grower)	Sugar (miller)	Sugar (consumer)	Rubber	Cassava[a]	Cotton	Soybean	Palm oil
1970	-0.1829	-0.0268	0.2382	0.4085	0.4939	-0.1303	0.0000	1.1780	:	:
1971	-0.2583	-0.0358	0.0216	0.2799	0.4287	-0.1058	0.0000	1.1658	:	:
1972	-0.2682	0.0622	-0.2201	0.0252	0.1451	-0.1101	0.0000	1.0385	:	:
1973	-0.4044	-0.0971	-0.2932	-0.1114	-0.1547	-0.1712	0.0000	1.1054	:	:
1974	-0.4755	-0.0258	-0.6224	-0.4092	-0.5805	-0.1888	0.0000	0.3104	:	:
1975	-0.3176	-0.0650	-0.5578	-0.4082	-0.6353	-0.1661	0.0000	0.4198	:	:
1976	-0.1576	-0.0327	-0.2078	-0.1127	-0.2495	-0.2083	0.0000	0.1774	-0.0753	:
1977	-0.2199	0.0033	-0.0256	-0.0280	-0.1067	-0.2228	0.0000	0.0258	0.1824	-0.0198
1978	-0.3163	-0.0229	0.3491	0.0423	0.1462	-0.2275	0.0000	0.1001	0.1550	-0.0390
1979	-0.2392	-0.0461	0.3921	0.1047	0.2117	-0.2449	0.0000	0.0740	0.1638	-0.0766
1980	-0.2611	-0.0545	-0.0282	0.2105	0.3565	-0.2611	0.0000	0.0870	0.1398	-0.0920
1981	-0.2573	-0.0873	-0.1017	-0.0093	-0.0057	-0.1890	0.0000	0.0301	0.1183	0.0001
1982	-0.1155	0.0000	0.3609	0.0841	0.6005	-0.1312	0.0000	0.0254	0.2886	0.0715
1983	-0.0805	0.0000	0.5158	0.3512	1.3564	-0.1795	0.0000	0.03791	0.2455	0.0934
1984	-0.0611	0.0000	0.5310	0.4857	1.2781	-0.1509	-0.0034	0.2234	0.2606	-0.1395
1985	-0.0442	0.0000	0.9672	0.2380	1.8829	-0.01056	-0.1734	0.4538	0.1553	-0.1186
1986	0.0030	0.0000	0.8085	0.0632	1.6537	-0.1107	-0.2082	0.6423	0.3413	0.3176

[a] For rice and cassava, the deviation is from the world price as it would be if Thailand unilaterally eliminated its intervention.

Source: Ammar and Suthad (1989) for rice, maize, sugar and rubber, and for the period 1970–85; additional calculations made for the remaining commodities and for 1986.

Table 2.10: Combined effect of intervention in the agricultural and non-agricultural sectors and of macroeconomic imbalances on relative prices of agricultural commodities, 1970 to 1986 (proportionate deviation from world relative price)

Year	Rice[a]	Maize	Sugar (producer)	Sugar (miller)	Sugar (exporter)	Rubber	Cassava[a]	Cotton	Soybean	Palm oil
1970	-0.3470	-0.2223	-0.0105	0.1256	0.1938	-0.3050	-0.2012	0.7730	:	:
1971	-0.4006	-0.2208	-0.1744	0.0344	0.1547	-0.2774	-0.1922	0.7225	:	:
1972	-0.3642	-0.0773	-0.3224	0.1094	-0.0052	-0.2269	-0.1317	0.7053	:	:
1973	-0.4619	-0.1842	-0.3613	-0.1971	-0.2363	-0.2512	-0.0966	0.8164	:	:
1974	-0.4994	-0.0702	-0.6396	-0.4362	-0.5806	-0.2258	-0.0453	0.2346	:	:
1975	-0.4266	-0.2143	-0.6284	-0.5027	-0.6936	-0.2993	-0.1617	0.2315	:	:
1976	-0.2835	-0.1773	-0.3262	-0.2454	-0.3617	-0.3267	-0.1518	0.0280	-0.1926	:
1977	-0.3907	-0.2165	-0.2390	-0.2409	-0.3024	-0.3931	-0.2211	-0.1540	-0.0249	-0.1916
1978	-0.4517	-0.2165	0.0818	-0.1642	-0.0809	-0.3806	-0.2000	-0.0776	-0.0315	-0.1942
1979	-0.4148	-0.2663	0.0707	-0.1503	-0.0680	-0.4192	-0.2317	-0.1200	-0.0423	-0.2434
1980	-0.4045	-0.2379	-0.2168	-0.0244	0.0933	-0.4045	-0.1954	-0.1210	-0.0783	-0.2576
1981	-0.4171	-0.2837	-0.2950	-0.2225	-0.2197	-0.3635	-0.2138	-0.1820	-0.1130	-0.2067
1982	-0.2565	-0.1594	0.1440	-0.0887	0.3454	-0.2697	-0.1604	-0.1308	0.0923	-0.0917
1983	-0.3015	-0.2403	0.1516	0.0265	0.7902	-0.3767	-0.2416	-0.0802	-0.0245	-0.1436
1984	-0.2517	-0.2030	0.2202	0.1841	0.8156	-0.3233	-0.2023	-0.0034	0.0269	-0.2990
1985	-0.2203	-0.1843	9.6047	0.0099	1.3517	-0.2704	-0.1492	0.2160	-0.0336	-0.2627
1986	-0.0999	-0.0915	0.6430	-0.0341	1.4109	-0.1920	-0.0446	0.4291	0.2186	0.1971

[a] For rice and cassava, the deviation is from the world price as it would be if Thailand unilaterally eliminated its intervention.

Source: Ammar and Suthad (1989) for rice, maize, sugar and rubber, and for the period 1970–85 with some minor adjustments; additional calculations made for the remaining commodities and for 1986.

to accommodate both domestic and foreign needs, are issues that must be addressed.

Public policy towards agriculture will thus have to address very different issues. No longer can the government be content to let the farmers grow any crop, on whatever land, have middlemen transport it to Bangkok and then collect a toll only when it is exported. Some of the issues confronting Thai agriculture now require a very different organizational framework. The government itself will have to re-examine its legal and regulatory framework and its own role within it.

3

Manufacturing

SOMSAK TAMBUNLERTCHAI

Since the 1960s, the rapid expansion of Thailand's manufacturing sector has been an important contributor to the country's impressive overall growth performance. This chapter describes the structure of the manufacturing sector and the Thai government's policy of industrialization. The various factors contributing to past growth and influencing future growth of the manufacturing sector are also reviewed.

Manufacturing in the Thai economy

Growth and structural change

Thailand has been quite successful in diversifying into non-agricultural sectors. Table 3.1 shows that the GDP share of agriculture (at constant prices) decreased from 27 per cent in 1970 to 17.3 per cent in 1987.[1] By contrast, the manufacturing sector's share in GDP increased from 16 per cent in 1970 to 22.7 per cent in 1987.

Significant diversification has also occurred with exports. The share of agricultural exports declined from 82.7 per cent in 1961 to 62 per cent in 1971 and to 27.9 per cent in 1987, while manufactured exports increased from only 2.4 per cent in 1961 to 10 per cent in 1971 and to 63.1 per cent in 1987 (Table 3.2). Since 1985, the value of manufactured exports has exceeded that of agricultural products, and textile products (including garments) have emerged as the most important foreign exchange earner in the export market. They have even replaced rice which had been the most significant export earner since Thailand first entered into foreign trade in the mid-nineteenth century. Since 1986, the value of garment exports alone has surpassed that of rice.

Table 3.1: Distribution of gross domestic product by economic sector, 1970 to 1988 (at 1972 constant prices, per cent)

Sector	1970	1975	1980	1985	1986	1987	1988
Agriculture	27.0	24.8	20.6	19.9	19.1	17.3	16.9
Mining and quarrying	2.9	2.1	2.6	2.5	2.4	2.3	2.4
Manufacturing	16.0	20.0	21.7	20.7	21.7	22.7	23.0
Construction	5.3	3.7	4.5	4.2	3.9	3.9	4.0
Electricity and water supply	1.0	1.6	2.0	2.5	2.7	2.7	2.8
Transportation and communication	6.5	6.1	6.7	7.2	7.3	7.3	7.4
Wholesale and retail trade	17.4	17.1	16.9	16.3	16.3	16.7	17.0
Banking, insurance and real estate	2.5	2.6	2.8	3.0	2.9	4.0	3.6
Ownership of dwellings	5.6	5.5	4.8	4.4	4.4	4.3	4.1
Public administration and defence	4.4	4.7	5.2	5.4	5.3	5.1	4.8
Services	11.5	11.9	12.2	13.9	14.0	14.2	14.0
Gross domestic product	100	100	100	100	100	100	100

Source: NESDB, *National Income Statistics of Thailand*, New Series, 1970 to 1988.

Table 3.2: Exports by economic sector, 1961 to 1989 (selected years) (per cent)

Sector	1961	1966	1971	1976	1981	1986	1987	1988	1989
Agriculture	82.7	76.9	62.2	51.8	47.7	34.3	27.9	26.4	23.0
Fishing	0.4	1.8	2.0	4.4	4.3	6.4	6.1	5.2	5.5
Forestry	3.3	2.2	1.5	1.7	0.1	0.3	0.3	0.2	0.14
Mining	6.6	11.6	13.7	6.7	7.7	2.7	2.0	1.9	1.6
Manufacturing	2.4	3.8	10.0	26.0	35.8	54.9	63.1	65.4	68.6
Others	4.7	3.9	3.3	9.3	4.3	1.3	0.6	0.9	1.2
Total	100	100	100	100	100	100	100	100	100

Source: Bank of Thailand.

Although Thailand's labour force has continued to shift from agriculture into other economic sectors, the transformation of the economy has been less rapid in employment than in output and exports. In 1985, agricultural labour still comprised nearly 70 per cent of the total labour force, while that of manufacturing was less than 10 per cent (Table 3.3).

There have also been significant changes in the structure of production. By the early 1970s, most of the growth in manufacturing was based on production for the domestic market including a significant amount of import substitution in consumer goods. Various manufacturing industries have since become more export-oriented and some 20 per cent of manufacturing output was being exported by 1980. In 1960, food, beverages and tobacco were important industries accounting for 60 per cent of manufacturing value added, but their shares in total manufacturing value added have declined steadily over time. By contrast, textiles, garments, chemical products and transport equipment have grown in importance (Table 3.4).

In the first half of the 1980s, the growth rate of manufacturing output slowed substantially. During the period 1980–85, the average growth rate was only 4.6 per cent per year, compared with 10.9 and 10 per cent in the 1960s and 1970s, respectively.

Table 3.3: Employment by economic sector, 1971 to 1987 (selected years) (per cent)

Economic sector	1971	1975	1980	1985	1986	1987
Agriculture, forestry, hunting and fishing	77.8	73.0	70.7	68.9	64.0	60.0
Mining and quarrying	0.1	0.2	0.2	0.3	0.2	0.3
Manufacturing	5.6	7.5	7.9	7.9	9.1	11.0
Construction, repair and demolition	1.1	1.1	1.9	2.2	2.7	4.1
Electricity, gas, water and sanitary services	0.1	0.2	0.3	0.3	0.4	0.4
Commerce and banking	6.9	7.6	8.5	9.1	10.7	11.9
Transport, storage and communication	1.3	2.1	2.0	2.0	2.3	2.7
Others	6.9	8.4	8.4	9.3	10.6	11.4

Source: National Statistical Office, *Labour Force Survey*, Round 2 (July–September), various issues.

Table 3.4: Distribution of gross domestic product in manufacturing sector, 1970 to 1988 (selected years) (at 1972 constant prices, per cent)

	1970	1975	1980	1985	1986	1987	1988
Food	16.52	15.72	14.12	16.42	16.35	14.88	14.49
Beverages	11.73	8.89	9.77	10.58	9.64	9.10	8.90
Tobacco and snuff	8.51	7.66	6.56	4.94	4.60	4.27	4.00
Textiles	8.99	13.23	14.48	14.08	14.70	15.09	14.84
Wearing apparel except footwear	9.17	9.71	9.07	10.14	10.42	11.06	10.82
Leather, leather products and footwear	2.49	2.37	1.80	2.34	2.54	3.03	3.17
Wood and wood products	4.07	3.45	2.13	1.50	1.48	1.42	1.41
Furniture and fixtures	1.93	1.22	1.27	1.22	1.18	1.18	1.18
Paper and paper products	1.40	1.00	1.82	1.68	1.65	1.72	1.71
Printing, publishing and allied industries	1.39	1.54	1.60	1.82	1.69	1.47	1.31
Chemicals and chemical products	3.60	3.43	4.18	4.67	4.66	4.53	4.51
Petroleum refining and petroleum products	5.66	7.56	5.18	4.80	4.84	4.46	4.22
Rubber and rubber products	2.62	2.67	2.79	2.48	2.50	2.60	2.80
Non-metallic mineral products	4.03	3.82	3.63	4.07	3.68	3.84	3.89
Basic metals	2.72	1.63	1.82	1.75	1.63	1.44	1.35
Fabricated products	3.09	2.22	1.85	1.83	1.80	1.81	1.83
Machinery	3.11	3.06	3.35	3.68	3.60	3.57	3.62
Electrical machinery and supplies	1.93	1.95	2.93	2.96	3.05	3.20	3.31
Transport equipment	5.54	6.16	7.78	3.90	4.23	4.61	5.20
Other manufacturing industries	1.51	2.71	3.89	5.15	5.79	6.74	7.43
Total	100	100	100	100	100	100	100

Source: NESDB, *National Income Statistics of Thailand*, New Series, 1970 to 1988.

In 1985 in particular, the manufacturing sector experienced a negative growth rate of –0.6 per cent. Industries serving the domestic market were generally experiencing low growth while export industries grew rapidly. Since 1986, Thai economic growth has recovered, especially in manufacturing, and this can be attributed to continued export expansion and increased domestic demand resulting from the economic recovery.

Size and geographical distribution of manufacturing enterprises

Despite government efforts to promote modern, large-scale industries, most manufacturing in Thailand is small scale. Statistics from the Ministry of Industry reveal that, in addition to a multiplicity of home industries, there were a total of 87,221 registered factories at the end of 1987. Almost half of these were rice mills located in provincial towns and rural villages. Large-scale manufacturing enterprises operate under the government investment promotion program administered by the Board of Investment (BOI), with many of them having foreign capital participation.

Industry is heavily concentrated in Bangkok and surrounding provinces, including both larger manufacturing enterprises and many of the small-scale ones. In 1987, about one-fifth of registered factories were located in Bangkok and this proportion would be substantially higher if rice mills were excluded. In 1986, industrial production in the Central region (which includes Bangkok) accounted for 90 per cent of the total value added in the manufacturing sector (Table 3.5). This degree of geographical concentration has not diminished over recent years despite the government's declared objective of industrial decentralization.

The main explanations for the concentration are proximity to the biggest consumer market and the availability of better infrastructural facilities and social services. Bangkok is the country's largest port so transportation costs can be significantly reduced for those port-based industrial enterprises which use large quantities of imported materials. The policy of promoting import-competing industries producing goods for the needs of urban, upper income people, and the heavy reliance on imported materials since 1960, has also contributed to the concentration of industrial activity.

In terms of size distribution, over 90 per cent of registered factories in 1980 were small scale with fewer than 50 employees.

Table 3.5: Regional distribution of manufacturing value-added, 1970 to 1986 (selected years) (per cent)

Region	1970	1975	1980	1986
Bangkok	39.4	38.7	51.7	54.6
Central	37.6	41.4	36.0	35.8
North	7.9	6.7	4.0	3.1
Northeast	8.5	7.3	4.6	4.7
South	6.6	5.0	3.7	1.8
Total	100	100	100	100

Sources: Data for 1970, 1975 and 1980 are from World Bank, *Thailand's Industrial Sector, Background Report Volume I, The Main Report*, August 1982, Table 4.4. Data for 1986 are calculated from the original manufacturing value-added data obtained from the National Economic and Social Development Board (NESDB).

This is shown in Table 3.6, which also confirms the heavy concentration of manufacturing activities in Bangkok and the Central region. The proportion of small enterprises would actually be higher if factories not registered with the Ministry of Industry were also included.

It is difficult to estimate levels of output or employment in small-scale enterprises because of lack of output and

Table 3.6: Manufacturing enterprises by workforce size and location, 1980 (per cent)

Number of employees	Manufacturing enterprises						% of all manufacturing enterprises
	Bangkok	Central	North	Northeast	South	Total	
1-9	48.9	24.1	7.8	11.8	7.5	100	63.3
10-49	45.2	34.7	0.5	12.9	7.8	100	30.2
50-199	29.3	38.3	9.8	16.2	6.5	100	5.3
200 and over	29.6	47.1	10.8	8.0	4.5	100	1.2

Note: The data exclude rice mills, saw mills, ice-making and printing firms.
Source: Division of Factory Control, Ministry of Industry.

employment data classified by size of establishment, discrepancies in the number of enterprises of different sizes among different official sources, and the exclusion of a large number of home industries in the enumeration of industrial enterprises.[2] According to an estimate contained in a study on small and medium-scale industries in Thailand in 1977 (Saeng et al. 1977[T]), small enterprises with less than 50 employees accounted for 34.7 per cent of manufacturing value-added, and 54.8 per cent of employment. This estimate was based on the number of establishments of different sizes registered with the Ministry of Industry and did not include numerous cottage and small-scale firms. It would therefore understate the true contribution of small-scale enterprises.

One of the more interesting findings to emerge from the various surveys of manufacturing establishments is that small and medium-scale enterprises tend to be more labour intensive with a high input of local production materials. On the basis of average capital productivity, they do not appear to be less efficient than larger enterprises. Many small-scale enterprises are also involved in producing export goods, such as gemstones and jewellery, wood handicrafts, plastic goods, footwear, traditional garments, and various food products. Some of these are exported through trading companies, but direct exports by small manufacturers themselves also occur (see, for example, Saeng et al. 1977[T]; Somsak and Chesada 1981).

Foreign trade

Thailand is an open economy and the process of industrialization has been closely related to the development of foreign trade and investment. During the 1960s, industrialization in Thailand was largely characterized by import substitution. The process of import substitution continued in the 1970s, although promotion of industrial exports was increasingly emphasized by the government.

The process of import substitution was reflected in the country's import structure. Although the share of consumer goods in total merchandise imports declined rapidly over the years (Table 3.7), the share of imported consumer durables declined until 1971, indicating the time lag involved in import substitution of consumer durables compared with non-durable consumer goods. For intermediate products and raw materials, the share in total imports increased through the 1960s, then declined until recent years when the share of imports again increased. The same trend also appeared in capital goods imports. The share of 'other imports', which includes mainly motor vehicles, vehicle parts, fuel and lubricants, increased rapidly in the 1970s, but declined more recently, mainly due to the fluctuation in oil prices. With the dramatic increase in oil prices since 1973, the share of fuel and lubricants in total imports increased significantly, reaching 30 per cent in 1980–82. Since 1982, the share of oil imports has declined drastically to between 10 and 13 per cent of total merchandise imports in the late 1980s. This change reflected both the rapid decline in international oil prices and the increasing supply of domestic energy.

The increase in oil prices since 1973 has contributed significantly to the rapid increase in the total value of imports, and also to the change in the structure of imports. The decrease in the import share of capital as well as intermediate products since the early 1970s was partly attributable to increased oil imports. In the late 1980s, as the value of oil imports declined, the share of other goods in total imports naturally increased.

The structure of imports shown in Table 3.7 reveals that the development of domestic industries in Thailand has been highly import-dependent, as the volume of intermediate and capital goods and other imports increased significantly. When merchandise imports are classified by major SITC groups, as in Table 3.8, it can be seen that Thailand's imports have been dominated by machinery, fuel and other industrial products. In recent years, imports in SITC 3 and SITC 5 to 8 accounted for around 85 per cent of the country's total merchandise imports by value, with machinery (SITC 7) being the most significant import item.

Data obtained from a survey of BOI-promoted enterprises in the early 1980s show that about 60 per cent of raw materials and intermediate products for these industries were imported. If machinery and other capital equipment used by these enterprises were taken into consideration, the import content would have been even higher since almost all capital equipment of BOI-promoted enterprises was imported.

Table 3.7: Imports by economic classification, 1961 to 1989 (selected years) (per cent of total imports)

	1961	1966	1971	1976	1981	1986	1987	1988	1989
I. Consumer goods									
A. Non-durable	32.2	17.7	10.8	7.8	6.3	5.3	4.9	4.0	3.9
B. Durable	7.3	8.2	7.1	5.4	4.4	4.7	5.0	3.6	4.6
Sub-total	39.5	25.9	17.9	13.2	10.7	10.0	9.9	7.6	8.5
II. Intermediate products and raw materials									
A. Chiefly for consumer goods	10.9	14.0	18.8	17.5	15.6	24.9	24.8	23.2	23.3
B. Chiefly for capital goods	7.0	7.7	10.4	10.8	9.1	9.4	10.3	11.9	12.1
Sub-total	17.9	21.7	29.2	28.3	24.7	34.3	35.1	35.1	35.4
III. Capital goods									
A. Machinery	13.4	18.0	21.7	18.1	17.0	23.7	23.1	28.3	28.4
B. Others	12.0	13.3	10.7	9.0	9.4	8.2	7.9	11.5	8.2
Sub-total	25.4	31.3	32.4	27.1	26.4	31.9	31.0	39.8	36.6
IV. Other imports									
A. Vehicles and parts	7.9	10.1	8.2	7.2	4.4	3.6	4.5	5.8	6.0
B. Fuel and lubricants	10.1	10.3	10.2	23.4	30.1	13.2	12.9	7.6	9.0
C. Others	0.7	0.6	2.1	0.7	3.7	7.0	6.6	4.3	4.5
Sub-total	18.7	20.9	20.5	31.3	38.2	23.8	24.0	18.0	19.5
Total	100	100	100	100	100	100	100	100	100

Source: Bank of Thailand, Monthly Bulletin, various issues.

Table 3.8: Imports by trade classification, 1960 to 1989 (selected years) (per cent of total imports)

SITC Commodity	1960	1961	1970	1975	1980	1986	1987	1988	1989
0 Food	8.2	5.7	4.1	2.9	3.0	5.4	4.2	4.7	4.5
1 Beverages and tobacco	1.1	1.3	1.1	1.1	0.8	0.8	0.5	0.5	0.53
2 Crude materials	1.5	3.1	5.2	5.9	5.7	6.7	7.4	6.8	6.8
3 Mineral fuels and lubricants	10.7	8.7	8.7	21.3	31.1	13.4	13.2	7.6	9.0
4 Animal and vegetable oil/fats	0.2	0.2	0.1	0.2	0.8	0.1	0.1	0.1	0.1
5 Chemicals	10.2	10.8	13.0	13.6	11.8	16.1	15.2	12.6	11.2
6 Manufactured goods	34.4	31.6	24.0	15.8	14.9	18.1	19.6	21.4	23.0
7 Machinery	25.0	30.7	35.4	34.6	22.8	30.8	32.5	39.6	37.9
8 Miscellaneous manufactured goods	5.5	5.4	5.0	3.2	5.8	6.4	5.0	4.7	4.4
9 Miscellaneous	3.2	2.4	3.3	1.3	3.1	2.2	2.3	2.2	2.6
Total	100	100	100	100	100	100	100	100	100

Source: Bank of Thailand, *Monthly Bulletin*, various issues.

Since 1970, the share of manufactured exports has increased to exceed that of agricultural exports (Table 3.2). Processed foods, textiles, garments, electronic goods (mainly integrated circuits) and jewellery comprise a significant proportion of Thailand's manufactured exports. These five product groups accounted for almost two-thirds of the country's manufactured exports in the late 1980s.

Processed foods comprise various agri-based products, including canned fruits and vegetables, sugar, dairy products and numerous other food items. The exporting of textiles began in the 1960s as an outlet for domestic surplus, but producers realized the necessity of continued export if further expansion of the industry was to be possible and thus efforts were made to maintain and increase the export volume. Export of garments did not start until the early 1970s, and in 1971 the value of garment exports was only 65 million baht. By 1972 it had jumped to 264 million baht and by 1987 exceeded 35 billion baht, accounting for 12 per cent of the country's total export value.

The increase in exports of electronics products was associated with the investment of a small number of multinational firms which had been attracted by the availability of low-cost labour to assemble integrated circuits. These account for 4 to 5 per cent of the country's total exports. The emergence of jewellery as another labour-intensive export item is closely associated with the growth of the tourist industry. The export of jewellery first became significant during the 1960s and has since grown rapidly. At present it accounts for 2.5 per cent of the country's total exports. If gemstones are also included as manufactures, the combined share of precious stones and jewellery in total exports increases to between 5 and 6 per cent. As can be seen in Table 3.9 many products exported in small amounts have registered high growth rates and increased their shares in manufactured exports over time, including footwear, furniture, leather products, rubber products and plastic products.

Most manufactured exports have been directed to industrialized countries, with the European Community, the United States and Japan the three most important markets (Table 3.10). The US market in particular grew rapidly during the 1970s, and these three markets together accounted for nearly 50 per cent of Thailand's manufactured exports in 1980.

The manufacturing sector has become more export-oriented

Table 3.9: Distribution of manufactured exports by industry, 1970 to 1987 (selected years) (per cent of total manufactured exports)

Industry	1970	1974	1978	1981	1984	1985	1986	1987
Processed foods	26.00	38.93	28.26	28.99	22.24	21.26	20.19	16.59
Textiles	20.33	15.82	22.60	14.18	13.13	12.50	11.25	9.39
Garments	0.89	6.32	10.37	12.76	2.69	15.41	16.03	19.31
Footwear	0.03	0.07	0.37	1.15	2.69	2.48	2.49	3.15
Wood products	0.29	3.98	4.24	2.71	1.34	2.04	1.83	2.06
Furniture and fixtures	0.04	0.56	0.80	1.29	2.23	1.38	1.46	1.80
Paper and paper products	0.77	1.21	0.41	0.34	0.32	0.56	0.73	0.73
Leather products	1.48	0.91	2.62	1.43	1.87	1.40	1.37	2.11
Rubber products	0.75	0.45	0.68	1.10	1.13	1.19	1.21	1.35
Plastic products	1.09	0.76	0.82	1.26	1.70	1.32	1.11	1.18
Chemical products	7.49	4.35	0.95	0.73	1.43	1.23	1.26	..
Non-metallic mineral products and glass products	9.92	5.51	1.57	1.07	0.84	1.25	1.21	1.21
Metal products	8.30	4.19	3.24	3.40	3.40	3.64	3.76	2.80
Non-electrical machinery	0.49	0.27	1.02	0.56	0.90	2.63	1.85	2.65
Electric machinery and supplies	0.39	1.82	9.07	12.43	11.71	10.00	10.90	10.09
Transport equipment	0.07	0.24	0.38	0.25	0.33	0.36	0.32	0.36
Scientific equipment	2.02	0.28	0.58	1.12	0.53	1.34	1.09	0.82
Jewellery	17.12	6.77	8.54	9.44	9.86	9.13	10.78	11.08
Miscellaneous n.e.c.	2.54	7.56	3.45	4.83	8.93	10.68	11.19	12.06
Total	100	100	100	100	100	100	100	100

Source: Bank of Thailand.

Table 3.10: Market structure of manufactured exports, 1970 to 1989 (per cent of total exports)

Market	1970	1971	1972	1973	1974	1975	1976	1977	1978	1979
Japan	8.91	7.78	8.90	16.85	20.54	23.87	21.47	14.87	14.46	14.47
United States	23.65	21.46	15.44	13.33	8.80	16.03	12.33	10.99	14.69	13.76
EC	11.51	11.75	8.58	14.50	11.94	8.26	14.60	14.49	19.55	19.34
ASEAN[a]	12.47	12.44	16.38	16.46	12.93	9.71	14.56	15.81	8.34	9.86
Middle East	6.29	6.06	3.74	4.60	13.07	5.87	5.68	6.42	7.80	6.02
Asian NICs[b]	22.37	19.56	21.99	17.74	20.74	16.92	14.30	15.80	16.45	16.02
Others	14.79	20.94	24.96	16.52	11.99	19.34	17.06	21.61	18.70	20.54
Total	100	100	100	100	100	100	100	100	100	100

Market	1980	1981	1982	1983	1984	1985	1986	1987	1988	1989
Japan	8.87	9.18	9.83	10.68	9.10	8.90	9.72	10.56	14.71	18.53
United States	16.99	17.20	17.59	19.43	22.18	23.76	21.84	21.89	31.55	35.29
EC	20.97	16.25	15.75	15.30	16.18	16.22	17.54	18.32	23.15	16.57
ASEAN[a]	10.10	7.63	8.65	7.66	5.19	5.83	5.01	4.14	4.81	1.60
Middle East	9.05	10.01	8.91	9.81	8.61	8.33	7.51	8.81	0.46	0.24
Asian NICs[b]	16.04	16.60	14.46	16.55	15.55	15.43	17.88	17.21	18.01	17.15
Others	17.99	23.04	24.79	20.57	23.20	21.54	20.50	19.07	7.30	10.63
Total	100	100	100	100	100	100	100	100	100	100

a Includes all ASEAN countries except Singapore
b Includes Singapore, Republic of Korea, Taiwan and Hong Kong.
Source: IEDB International Trade System.

as a result of this rapid expansion. The export–output ratio was about 10 per cent in 1972, and increased to 13.8 per cent in 1975, and to 20 per cent in 1980 (Table 3.11). Although more recent estimates are not available, the export–output ratio can be expected to have risen steadily since 1980 because export industries have been growing more rapidly than domestic-market industries. Export-oriented industries with high export-oriented production (i.e. more than 10 per cent of export–output ratio) include rubber products and non-ferrous metals (mainly tin) and also food, textiles, leather products, plastic products, ceramic products and earthenware, fabricated metal, and other manufactured products (with jewellery as the principal export item in this group).

Table 3.11: Export–output ratio by industry, 1975 to 1988 (selected years) (per cent)

Industry	Export–output ratio (%)			
	1975	**1980**	**1985**	**1988**
Refinery and petro. products	1.47	0.18	0.64	1.20
Food products	15.82	21.20	22.55	16.63
Beverages	0.10	0.12	0.19	0.53
Textiles	6.92	10.71	12.24	11.17
Leather products	6.28	39.25	72.98	176.89
Wood products and furniture	12.86	11.64	15.85	34.18
Paper and paper products	1.39	1.05	2.23	3.08
Industry chemicals	3.58	5.39	10.84	11.15
Other chemicals	1.88	2.50	2.07	3.04
Rubber products	1.11	3.75	5.97	7.03
Plastic products	4.39	11.59	16.32	34.99
Pottery, china, earthenware	5.35	14.79	14.83	51.48
Glass products	1.49	3.21	8.53	9.81
Other non-metallic mineral products	14.55	2.40	2.53	6.17
Iron and steel	1.65	4.37	8.62	12.43
Non-ferrous metals	56.24	85.31	36.68	14.74
Fabricated metal products	5.36	9.05	9.11	16.33
Non-electrical machinery	1.65	5.41	25.94	96.62
Electrical machinery	11.08	33.12	43.62	74.26
Transport equipment	0.19	0.75	0.77	1.33

Source: IEDB International Trade System

Despite rapid growth in manufactured exports, Thailand's industrial production is still mainly domestically oriented with over three-quarters of output being sold on the domestic market. Table 3.12 distinguishes between three components of demand for Thailand's manufactured output: purely domestic demand, replacement of imports, and export demand. From 1966 to 1980, domestic demand was the primary source of growth in manufacturing output. From 1966 to 1972, import substitution was an important source of growth; but this had diminished by 1975, indicating that it was domestic production and imports of manufactured goods which had increased to satisfy increasing domestic demand. On the other hand, exports were also increasing in importance as a source of demand for manufactured output, particularly after 1975.

If the manufacturing sector is to maintain a reasonable growth rate, then export expansion must become increasingly important. Apart from export earnings, there is also the benefit of employment absorption because Thailand's manufactured exports are mostly labour intensive. Estimates of direct and indirect labour requirements in producing different categories of manufactured products (based on 1975 input–output data) show that export industries have the highest labour content among industries of different trade orientation (Table 3.13).

As well as being more labour intensive, export industries also tend to have slightly higher backward linkages with lower import content in production compared with other types of industries (Table 3.14). The promotion of manufactured exports is therefore justifiable not only in terms of employment generation, but also in terms of utilization of domestic resources and inducement of investment and production in other industries.

Table 3.12: Growth of manufacturing output, 1966 to 1980 (per cent)

	1966–72	1972–75	1975–78	1978–80
Domestic demand	64.1	91.0	79.5	72.2
Import substitution	29.4	0.5	-7.7	-7.4
Export demand	6.5	8.5	28.2	35.2

Source: World Bank, *Thailand: Managing Public Resources for Structural Adjustment*, 1984, Table 7.4.

Table 3.13: Direct and indirect labour requirements in manufacturing industries by trade orientation, 1983

Labour requirement	Trade orientation of industries			
	Export[a]	Import substitution[b]	Domestic production dominated[c]	Import dominated[d]
Work-years for 1 million baht of final demand				
Direct labour requirement	7.33 (8.21)[e]	3.62	6.33	5.18
Indirect labour requirement	3.54 (4.89)[e]	3.61	5.31	5.19
Total	10.87 (13.10)[e]	7.23	11.64	10.37
Work-years for 1 million baht of value added				
Direct labour requirement	24.33 (21.93)[e]	11.39	16.90	15.54
Indirect labour requirement	11.75 (12.80)[e]	10.57	14.54	15.48
Total	36.08 (34.73)[e]	21.96	31.44	31.02

[a] Export industries (EP): industries with an export value exceeding 10 per cent of total output.

[b] Import-substituting industries (IS): industries with an import to supply (domestic production plus imports) ratio between 20 and 80 per cent.

[c] Domestic-production dominated industries (DPD): industries with a domestic production to supply ratio exceeding 80 per cent.

[d] Import-dominated industries (ID): industries with an import–supply ratio exceeding 80 per cent.

[e] Figures in parentheses are labour requirements for export industries excluding rice milling, tapioca milling, rubber sheet and block rubber, and non-ferrous metals.

Source: Somsak Tambunlertchai, 'Manufactured exports and employment in Thailand' in Pitou van Dijek and Harmen Verbruggen (eds), *Export-Oriented Industrialization and Employment: Policies and Responses, with Special Reference to ASEAN Countries,* Council for Asian Manpower Studies, 1984, Tables 1.1, 1.2, p.114.

Table 3.14: Backward and forward linkages and ratio of imported to total intermediate inputs of manufacturing industry by trade orientation, 1983

Trade orientation[a]	Forward linkages	Backward linkages index	Ratio of imported input to total intermediate input
Export	0.981	1.13	9.37(1980)[b]
Import substitution	1.183	1.063	55.53
Domestic production	0.86	1.13	16.31
Import dominated	0.77	1.04	46.48

[a] Definition of trade orientation same as Table 3.13, notes a-d.
[b] Excluding rice milling, tapioca milling, rubber sheet and block rubber and non-ferrous metals.

Source: Somsak Tambunlertchai, 'Manufactured exports and employment in Thailand' in Pitou van Dijek and Harmen Verbruggen (eds), *Export-Oriented Industrialization and Employment: Policies and Responses, with Special Reference to ASEAN Countries*, Council for Asian Manpower Studies, 1984, Tables 1.1, 1.2, p.114.

Foreign direct investment

Foreign direct investment (FDI) has played an important role in Thailand's industrialization and has increased rapidly since the 1960s. Among the various sectors, FDI has been most significant in manufacturing where it accounted for about one-third of total FDI inflows during the 1980s. Textiles, electronic and electrical goods, chemicals, machinery and transport equipment are among the major industries with substantial FDI (Table 3.15). Much of the FDI in manufacturing has occurred in industries covered by the BOI promotion program which provides various incentives to investors.

The United States and Japan have been the two most important sources of FDI, accounting for over 60 per cent of total FDI inflows between 1970 and 1985 (Table 3.16). Japanese investment in manufacturing industries has largely been concentrated in industries under BOI promotion, and has

Table 3.15: Net private foreign direct investment inflow by industry, 1971 to 1987 (baht millions)

Industry	1971–75	1976–80	1981–85	1986	1987
Financial institutions	2,015.9	–136.3	10.2	510.2	–3,839.3
Trade	1,854.3	2,170.9	5,789.7	1,777.5	842.4
Construction	936.0	1,644.1	5,400.3	1,234.9	1,349.1
Mining and quarrying	1,508.4	990.9	7,207.1	240.2	192.0
Oil exploration	1,396.3	713.4	6,446.9	236.4	251.3
Others	112.1	277.5	760.2	3.8	–59.3
Agriculture	27.2	196.6	215.7	199.8	289.6
Industry	2,640.6	3,319.5	10,813.4	2,107.0	4,709.9
Food	364.2	251.9	607.3	284.2	395.8
Textiles	1,216.5	688.0	889.8	85.0	996.9
Metal and non-metallic	162.5	120.8	1,246.3	–36.0	365.1
Electrical appliances	332.9	1,245.2	3,010.3	617.0	1,136.5
Machinery and transport equipment	52.7	345.5	930.4	14.9	159.9
Chemicals	295.0	487.5	1,406.0	484.0	868.1
Petroleum products	61.3	56.7	2,052.0	8.2	–15.8
Construction materials	53.3	–123.9	84.3	5.4	11.0
Others	102.2	247.8	587.0	674.1	792.4
Services	439.2	1,466.8	3,460.5	810.6	1,167.8
Transportation and travel	187.8	850.5	1,178.6	255.6	220.6
Housing and real estate	91.3	200.5	505.1	39.9	320.0
Hotels and restaurants	93.3	92.1	580.1	100.3	99.6
Others	66.8	323.7	1,196.7	414.8	527.6
Total	9,421.6	9,652.5	32,896.9	1,880.2	4,711.5

Source: Bank of Thailand.

commonly taken the form of joint ventures with local equity participation. By contrast, US investment has been directed to projects outside the scope of BOI promotion, and a significant proportion has been in the energy sector. FDI from newly industrializing countries (NICs) in Asia, particularly Hong Kong, Taiwan and Singapore, has also increased significantly since the mid-1970s. Hong Kong and Singapore are now among the major sources of FDI inflow in Thailand, while Taiwanese companies have invested mainly in BOI-promoted industries, under joint ownership schemes with Thai business people.

The increasing volume of FDI inflow only represents a very small proportion of gross domestic investment in Thailand. The proportion of FDI in private sector investment was also rather insignificant, averaging less than 5 per cent a year between 1970 and 1987. FDI is more important in BOI-promoted industries where approximately 50 per cent of companies with BOI promotional status have some degree of foreign equity participation. At the end of 1988, foreign equity accounted for 38.5 per cent of the total equity capital of all BOI-promoted firms. But the role played by foreign investment enterprises could be more important than the average share of ownership suggests, since Thai investors generally rely heavily on the technological expertise, and sometimes the financial resources, of their foreign partners. As a result, foreign investors often maintain tight control over operations of companies even in cases where they have a minority share. This is particularly true of Japanese companies where the shareholdings of local business people are often dispersed among several individuals, while those of Japanese investors are limited to only one or two companies (Somsak 1977: Ch.3).

Comparison of FDI inflow with gross domestic investment could understate the importance of foreign investors' involvement in the Thai economy, since investment from retained profits and that financed by domestic borrowing is not included. In Thailand, companies with foreign investment are among the largest firms in many industrial groups including textiles, chemicals, electronics products and transport equipment. Among Thailand's 'top one thousand companies' (ranked by sales in 1980), there were 214 foreign manufacturing companies and 64 foreign trading companies. Together, these 278 companies accounted for 51 per cent of total sales of the

Table 3.16: Net private foreign direct investment inflow by country, 1971 to 1987

Country	(million baht)					Percentage distribution				
	1971-75	1976-80	1981-85	1986	1987	1971-75	1976-80	1981-85	1986	1987
Japan	2,485.3	3,063.0	8,974.5	3,049.0	3,268.7	26.38	31.73	27.28	44.32	41.85
United States	3,762.3	2,398.5	10,593.5	1,293.3	791.3	39.93	24.85	32.20	13.80	10.13
United Kingdom	531.8	611.3	1,689.2	245.1	328.9	5.64	6.33	5.13	3.56	4.21
West Germany	71.9	597.0	782.4	160.3	448.1	0.76	6.2	2.38	2.33	5.74
France	251.5	17.5	293.4	91.0	132.9	2.67	0.18	0.89	1.32	1.70
Netherlands	245.3	107.5	2,072.3	-58.0	74.4	2.60	1.11	6.30	-0.84	0.95
Italy	87.1	517.1	243.0	79.2	7.3	0.92	5.36	0.74	1.15	0.09
Canada	48.6	-118.5	225.7	36.2	11.2	0.52	-1.23	0.69	0.51	0.14
Australia	67.0	41.9	386.1	144.0	25.7	0.71	0.43	1.17	2.00	0.33
Hong Kong	932.8	1,327.1	2,837.1	941.6	1,721.9	9.90	13.75	8.62	13.68	22.05
Singapore	496.7	668.3	1,180.1	403.1	220.6	5.27	6.92	3.59	5.86	2.82
Malaysia	100.5	158.8	217.6	7.9	-9.2	1.07	1.65	0.66	0.11	-0.12
Philippines	63.5	-0.6	26.8	59.4	0.4	0.67	0.01	0.08	0.86	0.01
Taiwan	17.2	0.9	257.3	131.9	687.3	0.18	0.01	0.78	1.92	8.80
Others	260.1	262.6	3,117.6	415.0	101.1	2.76	2.72	9.48	4.37	1.29
Total	9,421.6	9,652.4	32,896.6	6,880.2	7,810.6	100	100	100	100	100

Source: Bank of Thailand.

'top one thousand'. Furthermore, companies with foreign involvement appeared to have greater shares in the larger-sized groups among these 'one thousand companies' (Somsak and McGovern 1984).

FDI has contributed to the diversification of Thailand's industrial structure. In many cases, investment by foreign companies was instrumental in promoting production of commodities that would not otherwise have been produced. Contributions made by foreign companies in other areas are less obvious. Empirical studies on the impact of FDI in Thailand have been lacking mainly due to the dearth of necessary data. Scanty evidence obtained from various studies based on BOI-promoted manufacturing industries tends to indicate that the contribution of FDI in terms of income and employment generation has not been significant. Their contribution to foreign exchange earnings and savings by foreign-invested companies also appears to be limited due to the high import content in their production (Somsak 1977; Industrial Management Co. Ltd 1984).

Although FDI in Thailand in the 1960s was concentrated in import-substituting industries, there was some FDI in export industries in the 1970s. Foreign direct investment in export industries has increased significantly in recent years. As can be seen from Table 3.16, net FDI inflow to Thailand increased rapidly between 1981 and 1985, a trend which continued in the late 1980s. Although Thailand's FDI inflow was lower than that of most ASEAN countries in the 1970s, it has picked up rapidly in recent years. Thailand seems to be the preferred site for Japanese investors seeking to relocate their plants because of rising costs following the rapid appreciation of the Japanese yen since 1986. Faced with similar problems (but on a smaller scale), a number of Taiwanese investors have also shifted their investment to ASEAN countries, including Thailand. Statistics from the Bank of Thailand reveal that gross FDI inflow to Thailand increased significantly in the late 1980s, and FDI inflow from Japan accounted for a significant proportion of the total. Statistics from the BOI also show large increases in investment from Japan, the United States, Hong Kong, and Singapore in recent years, and it seems likely that FDI will play a more important role in Thailand's manufacturing sector in the future.

Policies and strategies for industrialization

In the decade following World War II, direct government involvement in the manufacturing sector was extensive. A number of state enterprises were set up to produce a wide range of industrial products including cement, paper, sugar, tobacco and gunny sack . This led to a reluctance on the part of private entrepreneurs to invest in manufacturing activities that would have to compete with these enterprises (World Bank 1959). Because of poor management and widespread corruption within most of these state enterprises, the government initiative was a failure.

In the late 1950s, the government began to invest heavily in public infrastructure to reduce its involvement in manufacturing. Massive public investments in electric power, transportation and communications during the late 1950s and 1960s (made possible by foreign aid and loans) greatly improved the infrastructure for industrial development. The BOI was established and, in 1960, a Promotion of Industrial Investment Act was enacted to facilitate the promotion of private investment. Incentives given to industries under BOI promotion included a period of income tax exemption, tax exemption on capital equipment, and tax exemption or reduction on raw materials and intermediate products.

The First National Economic Development Plan (1961–66) was broad and vague on the role of industry but it demonstrated the government's policy to promote industrialization through private enterprise. In the early 1960s, the aim of investment promotion was largely import substitution. Large-scale production with capital-intensive techniques was given higher priority in the promotion list of the BOI. Consumer goods industries, including assembly-type activities using imported components, were also encouraged.

The Second Five Year Plan (1967–71) continued to stress the importance of industries producing for the domestic market, but also gave attention to industries using domestic raw materials and labour. BOI incentives were revised to reflect the government's intention of reducing the dependence on imports in domestic industrial production.

The strategy of export promotion was set out in the Third Development Plan (1972–76), and concern was expressed about the geographical concentration of industries in and around Bangkok. The investment promotion law was revised to give greater incentives for industrial location in provincial areas. The policies of export promotion and dispersion of industrial plants have continued to be emphasized in all subsequent national development plans.

The Fourth Plan (1977–81) was the first to stress the importance of small-scale industries. The promotion of these had often been mentioned in conjunction with the promotion of rural industries, but few policy measures had been formulated and implemented.

Since the early 1960s, trade policy measures have been used to influence the pace of industrialization, and the most frequently used instrument has been differential tariff rates on imports. Other measures include quantitative restrictions, credit assistance to importers and exporters, and tax rebates on exports. These foreign trade policy measures have played a more important role in Thailand's industrialization process than the official investment promotion program, which has also relied heavily on trade policy measures. This is because promotional privileges have benefited only companies under BOI promotion, while other trade policy measures provide protection to non-promoted firms as well.

Tariff rates in Thailand have been changed frequently since 1960. Tariffs on imported consumer and intermediate goods which could be produced locally are high, while tariffs on other intermediate and capital goods are generally low. It has been pointed out that the tariff structure is biased in favour of import-competing industries and against export-oriented industries (Narongchai 1973). Effective rates of protection (ERPs) are high for consumer goods, both non-durable and durable, while export industries on average receive negative protection (Industrial Management Corporation 1985).

There have been a number of studies of effective rates of protection in the industrial sector in Thailand, but they were undertaken at different times using different data sets and industrial classifications. This hinders the comparison of changes in the protective structure over time. In one study, ERPs in three different years were compared and showed high protection given to domestic import-competing industries. The results are reproduced in Table 3.17. These data show that in 1974 and

1978, when manufactured exports were actively promoted by the government, the tariff protection given to domestic industries was increased. More recent ERP estimates also confirm this bias in the tariff structure in favour of import-competing industries and against export industries. This information is provided in Table 3.18, which also shows the ERP ranking of the 23 industries indicated, with the highest ERP ranked 1, and so forth.

In the Fifth Development Plan (1982–86), several structural problems resulting from past industrialization were identified.

- Heavy reliance on imported capital equipment and intermediate products for manufacturing production which has led to increases in the trade deficit despite rapid growth of import-substituting and export industries.
- Ineffective promotion of manufactured exports which has meant that, although manufactured exports grew rapidly over the decade to 1982, there were still many industries which were not competitive on the world market. Tax and tariff structures were weighted in favour of industries selling on the domestic market reducing incentive for exporting. Export promotion measures were also not effectively implemented.
- Industrial activities were heavily concentrated in Bangkok and its surrounding provinces. Efforts to decentralize industries from the Greater Bangkok metropolis to provincial locations were unsuccessful and the concentration of industries in the Central region continued to increase.
- The employment capacity of the manufacturing sector was still limited due to excessive usage of capital equipment and inadequate promotion of labour-intensive industries in this sector.
- Overall, there was no long-term plan for the development of manufacturing industries.

The Fifth Plan attempted to address these problems with industrial adjustment and regional dispersion of industrial activities. Small, regional and export industries were identified as priority industrial sectors for promotion. There were also plans for developing certain heavy industries along the eastern seaboard, such as chemical plants producing fertilizers and other petrochemical products using natural gas as fuel or raw material.

The plan set a growth target for the manufacturing sector of not less than 7.6 per cent a year with export industries growing

Table 3.17: Average rates of protection 1971, 1974 and 1978 (per cent)

	Nominal rates of protection			Effective rates of protection		
	1971	1974	1978	1971	1974	1978
Processed foods	50.9	5.8	9.0	205.9	-46.6	78.5
Beverages and tobacco	116.5	150.1	69.1	439.2	946.2	4.0
Construction materials	21.8	32.9	12.2	23.4	49.3	91.7
Intermediate products I	11.4	0.3	14.8	15.3	-6.7	16.2
Intermediate products II	36.1	30.0	19.2	50.3	75.4	55.3
Non-durable consumer goods	44.9	39.8	64.6	57.4	134.6	212.4
Consumer durables	45.0	48.2	57.3	93.2	136.2	495.6
Machinery	10.2	28.0	21.4	7.6	23.7	58.3
Transport equipment	58.8	37.9	80.5	146.5	135.0	417.2
All industries	..	30.8	87.3	87.2	18.6	70.2
All industries excluding food, beverages and tobacco	..	..	36.4	44.2	45.9	90.3
Non-import-competing	71.2	34.6	50.8	175.0	39.7	99.6
Import-competing	33.6	24.8	35.7	56.1	44.8	85.9
Export	-7.4	-6.5	13.7	-24.3	-39.9	40.3

Source: World Bank, *Industrial Development Strategy in Thailand*, 1980, Table 7.

Table 3.18: Effective rates of protection by major groups of industries, 1984 (per cent)

Sector	Effective rate of protection (ERP)		
	Balassa	Corden	Ranking by ERP
Agriculture	15.88	13.90	22
Food	97.65	47.27	14
Beverages	213.81	179.77	4
Textiles	307.35	251.67	3
Leather	119.33	78.93	8
Wood and wood products	55.11	41.61	16
Paper and paper products	58.03	44.39	15
Basic industrial chemicals	58.57	40.41	17
Chemical products	94.39	35.49	19
Refineries and petroleum products	1197.65	59.98	10
Rubber and rubber products	21.90	-3,764.39	23
Plastic products	213.36	16.88	20
Ceramic and earthenware	117.16	117.00	5
Glass and glass products	115.39	82.90	7
Other non-metallic products	71.22	83.99	6
Iron and steel	62.93	40.41	18
Non-ferrous metals	-390.02	49.57	12
Fabricated metals	116.65	835.52	1
Machinery	111.29	77.84	9
Electrical ind. machinery and appliances	80.27	52.58	11
Transport equipment	1,376.05	48.93	13
Other manufactured products	21.46	261.54	2
Exporting industries	5.59	4.43	n.a.
Import competing industries	195.58	110.93	n.a.
Non-import competing industries	85.16	66.73	n.a.

Source: Industrial Management Corporation, *Industrial Restructuring Study for the National Economic and Social Development Board*, 1985.

at more than 15 per cent a year, domestic industries at 5.6 per cent, small-scale industries growing at a rate higher than large-scale industries, and regional industries faster than industries located in Bangkok and the Central region. The employment capacity of the manufacturing sector was targeted at 186,400 new jobs or an annual growth rate of 7.6 per cent during the period of the Fifth Plan. The aims of the industrial adjustment plan were the promotion of labour-intensive, resource-intensive and export industries, and the gradual phasing out of inefficient industries through rationalization of the incentive structure. In 1982, an Industrial Adjustment Committee, chaired by the Minister of Industry, was set up for the purpose of planning and implementing the industrial adjustment program. Ten broad industrial groups were identified for restructuring.

With the discovery of natural gas in the Gulf of Thailand in 1981, programs for development of industries using natural gas and its by-products along the eastern seaboard were also incorporated. The development of light industry and export-oriented industries, and the setting up of an export processing zone on the eastern seaboard (the Eastern Seaboard program) were also planned.

In 1986, at the end of the Fifth Plan period, it was evident that few of the plans for industrial adjustment had been implemented and that virtually none of the targets set for the manufacturing sector had been achieved. The adverse international economic environment facing Thailand during the Fifth Plan period was cited as a major reason for these failures. Macroeconomic difficulties included adverse terms of trade, increasing trade and budget deficits, and instability in the domestic financial market. The government was thus largely preoccupied with solving the problems arising from various external shocks, and this led to its neglect of the longer-term objectives of structural adjustment, especially those dealing with the promotion of small-scale and regional industries. Another critical factor was that, although the promotion of small-scale and regional industries was specified in the Fifth Plan, their importance does not seem to have been adequately appreciated by most policy-makers. As a result, little attention was paid to the promotion of these industries.

The development of the Eastern Seaboard (ESB) area, including the establishment of fertilizer and petrochemical plants, was delayed and scaled down due to changing economic circumstances (in particular, the rapid decline in oil prices and lack of government funds). The government, concerned with the adverse impact on its image which might result if the ESB program were to be indefinitely postponed, finally decided to go ahead with parts of it. Construction in the Laem Chabang area began in 1985. This included a deep-sea port, an industrial estate, an export processing zone, a water supply pipeline and a railway line. Similar developments in the Mab Ta Put area, including a deep-sea port, an industrial zone, and heavy industries including fertilizer and petrochemical plants, were also approved.

With the recovery of the Thai economy and the improvement of the financial condition of the government after 1985, the implementation of ESB development programs was accelerated. In mid-1989, the deep-sea ports and industrial estates, and the petrochemical complex (which includes various companies producing intermediate and downstream products of petrochemicals), were under construction. The fertilizer project, on the other hand, was still in doubt. Private sector investors were not enthusiastic about the prospects for this project, mainly because of lower oil prices and the sharp appreciation of the Japanese yen which would substantially increase the construction costs from the original estimates.

In the Sixth Development Plan (1987–91), export, small-scale, and regional industries continued to be emphasized. In addition, agri-based and engineering industries were singled out as the two main industrial groups to be promoted. The industrial structural adjustment program, initiated during the Fifth Plan, was omitted entirely, and various other elements of the Fifth Plan program (such as those concerning technological improvement and rationalization of the incentive structure) were also scarcely mentioned in the Sixth Plan.

Sources of manufacturing growth

In the three decades since 1960, several internal and external factors have favoured the growth of Thailand's manufacturing industries. In 1960, the Thai population was estimated to be 26.4 million. Although per capita income was low, around 2000 baht (approximately US$100) in 1960 prices, the consumption of numerous imported products was considered large enough to warrant local production. In the 1960s, despite population growth at 3 per cent a year, the average growth of GDP per annum in real terms was substantially higher, at 8 per cent. As a result, the domestic market for manufactured products expanded rapidly.

Besides rapid overall economic expansion there were other favourable factors, including abundant natural resources and low labour costs. Policy measures were also conducive to industrial growth. The Thai economy has enjoyed considerable price stability since 1960 compared with other developing countries. The massive public spending on infrastructure during the periods of the First Development Plan (1961–66) and the Second Development Plan (1967–71) greatly improved the facilities for industrial investment. The strong commitment by government since 1960 to promote private investment and reduce direct public involvement in manufacturing had a positive effect in encouraging both domestic and foreign investment in various manufacturing industries. The stable but somewhat overvalued Thai currency, together with various incentives offered to manufacturers (including tariff protection and tax exemption in capital goods and intermediate products), also served effectively to induce investment in various import-substituting activities in the 1960s and early 1970s.

Thailand was late in promoting its manufactured exports compared with other open economies at similar levels of development. By the time the country was attempting to increase its manufactured exports in the 1970s, protectionist practices prevailed in world trade. But, as a marginal supplier of manufactured products in the world market, Thailand seemed little affected by the worldwide recession and the increased trade barriers of the 1970s. The rapid growth of textile and garment exports from Thailand could initially have benefited from the quota restrictions set by industrial countries on the textile exports of Hong Kong, Taiwan, and the Republic of Korea, which were the major exporting countries of textile products in Asia. Since textile exports from these countries were restricted by quota agreements, some excess demand could have spilled over to Thailand.

As already noted, the other major manufactured exports from Thailand are processed foods, precious stones and jewellery, and electronics components. These are either labour-intensive or resource-based products which were not greatly affected by trade restrictions. Given the country's resource endowments, it is surprising that it was only in the 1970s that Thailand began to exploit its comparative advantage by exporting these manufactures. During the 1960s, when manufactured exports from the Asian NICs were expanding dramatically, Thailand was still in the process of import substitution. The rapid increase in domestic demand for industrial products together with the incentives provided for domestic sales were not conducive to the development of manufactured exports. Selling manufactured products abroad requires competitiveness in price and quality, and development of industrial exports in many countries including Thailand came after this stage of import substitution. Thailand's abundant natural resources also delayed the industrialization and exportation of manufactured products to a certain extent. The country relied on primary exports for foreign exchange earnings, so there was no urgent need for development of industrial exports. The country faced a trade deficit in the 1960s, but the balance of payments showed a surplus due to various capital inflows and service incomes. It was the balance of payments deficit from 1969 to 1971, after many years of surplus, that caused government officials to turn their attention to promotion of manufactured exports.

Only modest incentives have been offered to exporters of manufactured products in Thailand (Somsak 1984). But the government's emphasis on export promotion since the early 1970s served to bring the potential of the export market to the attention of manufacturers. The success of export promotion undoubtedly owes much to the efforts made by individual exporters in finding their marketing channels and improving the quality of their products.

Another important factor in the shift to exports was the saturation of domestic demand for some manufactured products, including textiles (Somsak and Yamazawa 1983). Foreign investment in certain industries has also been helpful for export expansion. Production of canned pineapple and electronics components (integrated circuits) are examples of multinational enterprises which made use of Thailand's abundant labour and natural resources.

The movement in international exchange rates in the 1970s was also an important factor contributing to export growth in Thailand. The pegging of the Thai baht to the US dollar, together with the realignment of major currencies since 1971, enabled the baht to depreciate substantially against non-dollar currencies and improved the competitiveness of Thailand's exports throughout the decade.

Conditions affecting Thailand's industrialization have changed significantly in the 1980s. Along with other petroleum importers, Thailand was adversely affected by the second oil crisis in 1979–80 and the subsequent worldwide recession, and the country became more dependent on external trade at a time when the external terms of trade moved against it. In the first half of the 1980s, growth in the Thai economy slowed down. With 4.1 per cent GDP growth in 1982, Thailand again experienced a growth recession during 1985 and 1986, with real GDP growth rates estimated at 3.5 and 4.5 per cent, respectively. In 1985, the manufacturing sector experienced negative growth for the first time in two decades. The large budget deficit and rapid public debt accumulation constrained the government's ability to finance economic expansion. The resulting austerity measures of expenditure cutbacks had a further depressing effect on the domestic economy.

The Thai government devalued the baht against the US dollar in 1981 and 1984, reflecting increasing trade deficits and rapid appreciation of the US dollar (to which the baht had been tied) relative to other currencies. The 1984 devaluation was accompanied by a change in the exchange rate system, with the baht tied to a basket of currencies instead of to the US dollar alone.

In the latter half of the 1980s, general economic conditions in Thailand improved substantially. Several factors, including the decline in oil prices, reduction in international interest rates and recovery in export commodity prices, assisted in this upturn. Foreign investment inflow, both in terms of direct investment and investment in the Securities Exchange of Thailand, increased significantly in 1987 and 1988. Manufactured exports continued to expand rapidly. International currency realignment since 1986, together with more flexible management of the Thai exchange rate, were helpful in maintaining the international competitiveness of Thai products.

Conclusions: future directions

There are good prospects for further growth of the manufacturing sector in the 1990s. Most investment projects which applied for Board of Investment (BOI) promotion in the late 1980s will come into operation. Many of these are export-oriented. Various projects located on the eastern seaboard will also start operating. The manufacturing sector will continue to grow in importance within the Thai economy and the structure of the manufacturing sector will become more diversified. Although traditional industries such as food and textiles will remain important, they will be joined by others, including chemicals, plastic and metal products.

Despite the favourable medium-term growth prospects, the long-term prospects for the Thai economy, including its manufacturing sector, are not so reassuring. There is no certainty that the country will be able to maintain the high growth rates it enjoyed in the late 1980s. Thailand's manufactured products are still directed mainly at the domestic market and the expansion of this market could help stimulate manufacturing growth. Most Thai citizens still live in rural areas and any increases in their incomes should theoretically expand the market for manufactured products. However, as a result of limits on the expansion of arable land and the slim prospects for further improvement in agricultural prices, the growth of the agricultural sector is likely to slow down. Firm action on rural development and rural industrialization have been seriously lacking and unless development policies and strategies can be changed, prospects for expanding the domestic market through rural industrialization appear remote.

Further growth in the manufacturing sector will thus rely heavily on export expansion. But Thailand will have to face increasing trade protection from major importing countries as well as competition from other developing countries keen to promote their manufactured exports. Thailand's main advantages are low-cost unskilled labour and an abundant supply of agricultural raw materials. But this competitive strength will gradually be eroded when countries like China, Indonesia, Vietnam and Burma begin to launch their manufactured products onto the world market.

Despite better than expected economic growth and rapid inflow of foreign investment, various constraints to the Thai economy have been identified, including a lack of qualified manpower, support services and infrastructure facilities for industry. Massive investment will be needed to build up infrastructure facilities to accommodate further industrial

growth. This will be constrained by the country's deteriorating
financial position—in the late 1980s, the deficits in the trade
and current account were already large and increasing. It will
also take time to increase the supply of qualified workers. This
in turn will constrain Thailand's ability to move up the ladder
of comparative advantage when faced with increasing
competition in labour-intensive products from countries with
lower labour costs. Thus, the outlook for further industrialization
in Thailand is by no means rosy despite prevailing optimism
based on the economic boom of the late 1980s.

Notes to Chapter 3

[1] The national income statistics of Thailand have recently been
revised. The revised series extends back to 1970. Calculations
presented in this chapter of GDP shares and growth rates for 1970
and thereafter are made according to the revised series. GDP shares
before 1970 are calculated from the old GDP series.

[2] Manufacturing enterprises which are required to register with the
Ministry of Industry are those with seven or more workers or those
using machinery of two-horsepower or more. Statistics of small
enterprises not required for registration are unavailable.

4

Services

PASUK PHONGPAICHIT and SAMART CHIASAKUL

Since the early 1970s, Thailand's service sector has accounted for over half of total GDP, dwarfing the contributions of agriculture and industry. The service sector has also been a major factor in labour absorption; in the late 1980s it accounted for about 27 per cent of the total employed labour force. It has also been a major contributor to foreign exchange earnings. Yet, despite this major role, the service sector rarely attracts the same attention as agriculture or manufacturing. Indeed, it tends to be treated as a mere residual.

The role played by the service sector since the early 1970s has, to a considerable extent, been the result of deliberate policy-making, resulting in important structural effects on the economy as a whole. Thai planners and government agencies set out to boost the service sector, with consequences for labour policy, employment planning, environmental control and income distribution. This chapter examines the context in which the growth of the service sector became a major aspect of Thai policy-making, and reviews some of the major consequences of these policies.

The role of the service sector in developed and developing economies[1]

In developed economies, employment in the secondary sector tended to expand in advance of any employment growth in the tertiary sector. Industries grew first, absorbing labour from the primary sector. Growth in the service sector usually occurred later as a consequence of industrial maturity. Colin Clark (1957) explained this pattern in terms of two variables: changes in labour productivity, and consumption of goods and services. As labour productivity and incomes rise, demand for services expands and contributes to rapid growth of the service sector. Clark's hypothesis was supported by the studies of Kuznets (1966, 1971) and Fuchs (1969).

The Clark–Kuznets approach attributes a passive role to the service sector in the development process. Services expand as a result of growth in productivity and income in other sectors, especially manufacturing. The development process is portrayed as passing through three main stages: a pre-industrial stage based on agriculture; a stage dominated by industrialization; and then a post-industrial stage based on growth of services with high technology. This analysis suggests that there is no need for special policy measures to deal with the service sector. It is also customary for writers adopting this perspective to view services as a low productivity sector with low economic value compared with manufacturing.

The pattern of structural change in the present day developing countries has been substantially different from that seen previously in the now-developed countries (Table 4.1). The growth of employment in services has to some extent been related to the growth of secondary industry (in accordance with the pattern of the developed countries) but it has also tended to expand of its own accord in advance of growth in manufacturing. Thus, the relative size of the service sector of developing countries can be much larger than the secondary sector even in the early stages of economic development when per capita income is still relatively low.

This 'premature' growth of the service sector in developing countries has been attributed to their inability to industrialize fast enough to absorb excess labour. It has also been found that the high capital intensity of present day industrialization (even in circumstances of abundant labour supply) limits the rate of labour absorption by industry.[2] The slow pace of industrialization causes rural–urban migration in developing countries to exceed the rate of labour absorption. Sabolo found that in developing countries 'when the rate of the rural–urban drift rises, the incremental increases in the size of the population shifts from the agricultural sector towards the tertiary sector' (Sabolo 1975: 27).

Table 4.1: Percentage share of employment in primary, secondary and tertiary sectors (selected countries)

	Primary sector	Secondary sector	Tertiary sector
Germany			
1885	39.8	39.0	21.2
1907	36.8	41.0	22.2
1925	30.5	40.8	28.7
1933	28.9	40.5	30.6
1939	26.0	42.2	31.8
1946	29.2	38.5	32.3
1950	23.2	42.9	33.9
1961	13.9	47.8	38.3
1970	8.9	49.2	41.9
United Kingdom			
1901	9.1	51.2	39.7
1911	8.8	51.5	39.7
1921	7.1	47.6	45.3
1931	6.0	46.1	47.9
1951	5.1	49.1	45.8
1961	3.6	47.4	49.0
1966	3.1	46.6	50.3
United States			
1900	37.6	30.1	32.3
1901	31.6	31.6	36.8
1920	27.4	34.4	38.2
1930	22.0	31.1	46.9
1940	17.6	32.5	49.9
1950	11.9	34.5	53.6
1960	6.5	35.1	58.4
1964	6.6	34.1	59.3
1970	4.3	33.6	62.1
Egypt			
1907	69.1	10.8	20.1
1917	69.2	8.4	22.4
1927	60.3	9.5	30.2
1937	70.7	10.0	19.3
1947	63.7	12.2	24.1
1960	58.0	12.2	29.8
1985–88	38.2	13.4	48.4

Table 4.1: *continued*

	Primary sector	Secondary sector	Tertiary sector
Thailand			
1960	82.3	4.2	13.5
1970	79.3	5.9	14.8
1981	72.0	9.6	18.4
1987	64.4	12.7	22.9
India			
1921	72.5	11.4	16.1
1931	67.2	10.5	22.3
1951	73.6	8.1	18.3
1961	72.9	11.4	15.7
1985–88	62.6	10.8	22.6

Sources: Thailand: data are from Population Census, 1960, 1970 and *Report of the Labour Force Survey* Round 2, 1981 and Round 3, 1987. For other countries, see Yves Sobopo, *The Service Industries, a WEP Study*, ILO, Geneva, 1975, pp.7, 9, 16, Word Bank, World Development Report, 1987, and UNDP, Human Development Report, 1991.

The service sector in Thailand

In the early post-war years, Thailand followed the pattern of service growth propelled by surplus labour. In the 1960s, although the manufacturing sector started to grow, the service sector grew significantly faster in terms of contribution to GDP (Tables 4.2 and 4.3) and contribution to employment (Table 4.4). Between 1961 and 1970, manufacturing's share of GDP grew from 12.6 to 16.0 per cent, while that of services as a whole grew from 46.5 to 54.1 per cent (Table 4.1). From 1960 to 1970, manufacturing's share of total employment grew from 3.4 to 4.1 per cent, while the share of the tertiary sector expanded from 14.1 to 16.2 per cent, with the major increase occurring in services (Table 4.3).

From the early 1970s onwards, there was a significant change in government attitude to the service sector. Rather than passively watching the gradual growth of services' contribution

Table 4.2: Percentage distribution of GDP, 1961 to 1990 (selected years)

	1961	1965	1970	1975	1980	1981	1982	1983	1984	1985	1986	1987	1988	1989	1990
Agriculture	39.8	34.9	27.0	24.8	20.6	20.4	20.2	19.7	19.4	19.9	19.1	17.4	16.9	16.1	14.4
Mining	1.1	2.1	2.9	2.1	2.6	2.4	2.4	2.3	2.5	2.5	2.4	2.3	2.5	2.6	2.9
Manufacturing	12.6	14.2	16.0	19.9	21.7	21.7	21.4	21.6	21.5	20.7	21.8	22.6	23.3	23.9	24.7
Services	46.5	48.8	54.1	53.2	55.0	55.5	55.9	56.4	56.5	56.9	56.7	57.7	57.3	57.4	58.0
Construction	4.6	5.6	5.3	3.7	4.5	4.5	4.3	4.4	4.6	4.2	3.9	4.0	4.3	4.7	5.2
Electricity and water supply	0.4	0.8	1.0	1.6	2.0	2.1	2.3	2.3	2.4	2.5	2.7	2.7	2.7	2.9	3.0
Transport	7.5	7.1	6.5	6.1	6.7	6.5	6.8	6.9	7.1	7.1	7.3	7.2	7.1	7.1	7.1
Trade	15.2	16.5	17.4	17.1	16.9	17.3	16.4	16.2	16.3	16.3	16.4	16.9	17.1	17.6	17.6
Banking, insurance and real estate	1.9	2.6	2.4	2.6	2.8	2.6	2.8	3.0	3.0	3.0	2.9	3.5	3.8	4.4	5.3
Ownership of dwellings	2.8	2.5	5.6	5.4	4.8	4.7	4.7	4.5	4.4	4.4	4.4	4.2	3.9	3.7	3.6
Public administration	4.6	4.3	4.4	4.7	5.1	5.3	5.4	5.7	5.2	5.4	5.4	5.1	4.7	4.1	3.8
Other services	9.6	9.5	11.5	11.9	12.3	12.5	13.3	13.4	13.5	13.9	13.9	14.1	13.6	12.9	12.3
Total	100	100	100	100	100	100	100	100	100	100	100	100	100	100	100

Sources: 1961 and 1965: Bank of Thailand, *Monthly Review*, various years.
1970–85: National Statistical Office, *National Income of Thailand New Series 1970–1987*, Bangkok.
1986–88: National Statistical Office, *National Income of Thailand*, 1989, Bangkok.
1989–90: *Bank of Thailand Quarterly Bulletin*, 31(4), December 1991, Table 67.
1990: estimate.

Table 4.3: Gross domestic product, Thailand, 1961 to 1990 (selected years) (billions of baht, constant 1972 prices)

	1961	1965	1970	1975	1980	1981	1982	1983	1984	1985	1986	1987	1988	1989	1990
Agriculture	29.5	36.1	42.1	50.7	61.8	65.1	67.1	70.1	74.0	78.5	78.8	78.6	86.6	92.4	90.7
Mining	1.0	1.7	4.5	4.3	7.9	7.6	8.1	8.0	9.5	9.9	9.8	10.5	12.8	15.1	18.1
Manufacturing	9.1	14.0	24.9	40.7	65.0	69.1	70.8	76.8	82.0	81.5	90.3	102.3	119.5	137.3	156.0
Services	33.7	47.0	4.3	108.7	164.8	176.6	185.4	200.6	215.1	224.2	234.6	261.2	293.6	329.4	366.7
Construction	3.5	5.7	8.2	7.6	13.5	14.3	14.2	15.8	17.5	16.6	16.2	18.3	22.2	26.9	33.0
Electricity and water supply	0.3	0.5	1.6	3.3	5.9	6.6	7.5	8.3	9.0	9.9	11.0	12.3	14.0	16.5	19.2
Transport	4.7	6.3	10.1	12.4	20.0	20.6	22.7	24.5	27.1	28.2	30.2	32.7	36.2	40.7	45.1
Trade	12.0	16.2	27.1	34.9	50.7	55.1	54.5	57.6	62.1	64.2	67.6	76.4	87.9	101.1	111.4
Banking, insurance and real estate	1.5	2.6	3.8	5.3	8.3	8.4	9.2	10.5	11.5	11.8	12.0	15.8	19.6	25.2	33.7
Ownership of dwellings	2.2	2.4	8.7	11.2	14.3	14.9	15.5	16.1	16.6	17.4	18.0	19.0	20.2	21.4	22.7
Public administration	3.4	4.3	6.9	9.7	15.4	16.8	17.8	20.1	19.9	21.4	22.2	22.9	24.0	23.7	24.1
Other services	7.1	9.6	17.9	24.3	36.7	39.9	44.0	47.7	51.4	54.8	57.5	63.8	69.5	74.1	77.6
Total	73.3	98.9	155.8	204.4	299.5	318.4	331.4	355.5	380.6	394.1	413.5	452.6	512.5	574.2	631.6

Sources: As for Table 4.2.

to the economy, the government began actively to promote the sector's growth. In the first two national development plans (1961-66 and 1967-71), the service sector received little attention. However, in the Third Plan (1972-76) the government began to stress tourism as one of the major sources of potential foreign exchange earnings, as other sources (especially US grant aid, loans and other foreign inflows) were declining. The Fourth and Fifth Plans (1977-81 and 1982-86) put even more emphasis on tourism, and in the Sixth Plan (1987-91) this sector was promoted vigorously as a major source of foreign exchange and a provider of employment.

The Sixth Plan emphasized the promotion of direct labour exports. It also stressed diversification of these exports into new countries because the demand from the Middle East was declining. This plan also advocated measures to promote Thai construction firms overseas and the development of various service industries to save foreign exchange arising out of the payments to overseas firms for business services such as marketing, management, public relations, quality control, packaging, freight and insurance, and information services relating to marketing.

By the early 1980s, the service sector had become a major subject for study by government bodies and by academic institutions responsive to government thinking. These studies demonstrated the importance of the service sector to the Thai economy and suggested a wide range of measures to promote faster service sector growth. Two such studies were carried out in response to the National Economic and Social Development Board's suggestion that economists pay more attention to the role of services in promoting employment because experience had shown that the manufacturing sector would not be the major absorber of new entrants to the labour force. A study by Suwat (1983) focused on ways to increase the rate of labour absorption in the service sector through such techniques as marketing campaigns for service producers.

Other studies focused on the market structure of the service industry (Udom 1983), on the contributions of traded services to Thailand's balance of payments and on the policy issues involved in promoting traded services. A study by Thwatchai et al. (1989) analysed the interlinkages, relationships, supply conditions, barriers, and regulation of the Thai service sector

Table 4.4: Employment by industry, 1960 to 1987 (selected years)

	Share of total workforce						Growth rate[a]				
	1960	1970	1975	1979	1984	1987	1960-79	1970-75	1975-79	1979-84	1984-87
Agriculture	82.3	79.3	72.7	70.5	69.7	64.4	11.5	0.1	3.1	3.8	-0.6
Mining	0.2	0.5	0.4	0.4	0.5	0.2	11.5	-1.0	2.6	5.2	-28.6
Manufacturing	3.4	4.1	7.4	8.1	7.6	8.8	3.8	14.7	6.2	2.9	7.0
Tertiary	14.1	16.1	19.5	21.0	22.1	26.6	3.2	5.6	6.0	5.3	8.4
Construction	0.5	1.1	1.1	1.9	2.1	2.3	10.1	2.6	18.7	5.4	6.1
Utilities	0.1	0.2	0.2	0.3	0.5	0.4	5.2	10.3	7.1	19.4	-5.6
Transport	1.2	1.6	2.0	1.9	2.0	2.3	4.9	7.3	2.8	4.0	7.1
Commerce	5.7	5.3	7.5	8.1	8.5	10.8	1.2	9.4	6.2	4.9	10.5
Services	4.7	7.1	8.3	8.5	9.1	10.7	6.1	5.2	4.5	5.4	7.7
Others	1.9	0.8	:	:	0.2	0.1	:	:	:	:	75.4
Total	100	100	100	100	100	100	1.9	1.8	3.9	4.1	2.1

a Annual compound growth rate.
Source: National Statistical Office, *Labour Force Survey*, July–August 1975, 1979, 1984; NSO *Labour Force Survey*, August 1987; NSO *Population Census* 1960 and 1970.

in the domestic and international context. Using the 1975 and 1980 input–output tables, the study showed that service industries have the highest linkage effects to the rest of the economy and that the forward linkage effects are more important than the backward effects. The study also showed that most traded services in Thailand were subject to government regulations which prohibit aliens from certain service activities or allow them only a minority participation. Exchange controls, differential tax treatments, subsidies through promotional licensing, and discriminatory purchasing procedures were also important in controlling trade in services. Thammanoon and Somchai (1989) analysed the balance of payments contribution of selected service industries, namely tourism, transport, banking, insurance and overseas labour services, and emphasized the potential importance of liberalized trade policies in transport, banking and telecommunications in order to promote faster growth.

Why the attention to services?

The government's changing attitude towards the service sector largely reflected balance of payments considerations. In the 1950s and 1960s, Thailand's economic growth was propelled by the rapid expansion of extensive agriculture, induced by favourable world demand for commodities, and supported by government expenditures on transport into previously inaccessible agricultural areas. The foreign exchange earnings from primary exports expanded rapidly and underwrote the growing demand for consumer and capital goods for urban expansion. But demand for imports grew faster than export earnings and, from 1952 onwards, Thailand's balance of trade was in deficit in most years. However, during the 1960s the deficit was more than offset by the inflow of foreign exchange from US grant aid and loans, and other capital inflows.

By the late 1960s the economy was facing a crisis, partly as a result of fluctuating earnings from primary exports, but also as a result of two other developments. The first was the change in the US policy in Indo-China, beginning in the second half of the 1960s, and resulting eventually in US withdrawal from Indo-China in 1975. After this, US grant aid and loans to Thailand declined steeply. The second factor was the declining rate of growth of the agricultural sector, which became critical after 1976 as commodity prices slumped worldwide. Earnings from traditional agricultural exports, especially rice, fell in real terms between 1978 and 1979 and again between 1981 and 1982. For the period 1977–82, agricultural value-added in constant prices grew at an average annual rate of 4.1 per cent. This was much lower than the high growth rate of 5.5 per cent a year in the 1960s.

The decline in export earnings widened the trade deficit. The deficit rose from 3–4 per cent of GDP in the 1960s to 9 per cent in 1970, declined to about 6 per cent in 1973–76, and then rose again to over 8 per cent from 1978 to 1980. To combat the widening trade deficit, Thailand never took the option of reducing the demand for imports. The philosophy of an open economy was first to increase foreign exchange earnings by whatever means, and only to consider curbing imports when all else failed. Because agriculture, the traditional foreign exchange earner, faced a long-term resource constraint, policy-makers saw the prospect of earning foreign exchange by sending migrants to work overseas and by promoting tourism. From the early 1980s, these two strategies became major components of Thai economic policy.

The second oil crisis in the early 1980s affected Thailand less severely than some other countries, but it caused agricultural growth to slow further, as well as raising problems for other sectors. The trade deficit continued to widen, and the debt service ratio, which traditionally had been insignificant, began to rise alarmingly. The slump in commodity prices continued and, in addition, there was a slowing down in the world demand for manufactured goods. Thailand's GDP growth rate fell to an average of 5.3 per cent a year over the period 1981–86. The recorded unemployment rate rose from its usual level of 1–2 per cent to 3–4 per cent in 1986–87, and invisible unemployment and underemployment increased even more sharply. Rising unemployment on top of the increased debt burden and widening trade deficit threatened to create political as well as economic instability.

To overcome the crisis of the mid-1980s, policy-makers again turned to the service sector to act as a major source of foreign exchange earning and employment creation. Whereas in the

1970s, promotion of services had seemed to be a timely expedient, by the mid-1980s it had become a major policy platform (International Labour Office, ARTEP 1984).

Promotion of the service sector was effective for two main reasons. First, the development of tourism and labour migration required relatively small investment on the part of the government. Thailand had plenty of scenic sites, natural resources and exotic local culture to attract tourists. It also had plenty of cheap, but trainable and entrepreneurial labour suitable for engaging in service activities, or for working overseas. Second, Thailand's shift of policies coincided with the increased demand for workers in the Middle East, Brunei and Singapore (and later in Japan and Taiwan) and also with the growth of travel to Asian destinations in the 1970s and 1980s.

Promoting labour migration

Private employment agencies were set up to recruit and handle overseas migrant labour from the early 1970s, and by the mid-1980s 329 agencies were registered (Thailand, Dept of Labour 1986[T]). From 1978, the Department of Labour provided employment services to migrant workers alongside private employment agencies. In the 1980s, the government took a more active role by incorporating measures to promote overseas migration into the Fifth Plan (1982–86). The Department of Labour was asked to publicize labour market information about jobs overseas, and to collaborate with other ministries to facilitate overseas migration. The issuing of passports was made easier, and workers could apply for an exemption of the transit tax at the airport upon leaving Bangkok. As the number of Thais working overseas increased, the government also set up an Office of the Labour Attaché to provide assistance in Saudi Arabia, Iraq, Kuwait and Singapore. In late 1985, the government passed the Recruitment and Job Seeker Protection Act in a positive move to protect job seekers overseas.

For decades there had been some privately organized overseas migration by Thai workers, but the appearance of private and state-sponsored overseas employment agencies completely transformed the scale of migration. The number of Thais working overseas increased rapidly following the increased demand from the Middle East after the mid-1970s. The recorded number of Thais working overseas on a yearly basis as shown in Figure 4.1 included only those who informed the Labour Control Office at Bangkok's Don Muang Airport, and are therefore an underestimate. Since 1986 the yearly figures reported are higher than previous years. They are closer to the actual number of migrants because the Act passed at the end of 1985 made more stringent requirements on employment agencies to report to the Labour Control Office.

More than 100,000 Thais travelled overseas to work each year throughout the 1980s. Most of these were unskilled or semi-skilled workers, and more than 80 per cent went to the Middle East. In 1989, over 260,000 Thais were working overseas, mostly in the Middle East and Asia (Table 4.5). This number is equivalent to about 10 per cent of the employed workers in the manufacturing sector of Thailand.

Figure 4.1 Numbers of Thai overseas migrant workers, 1973 to 1989

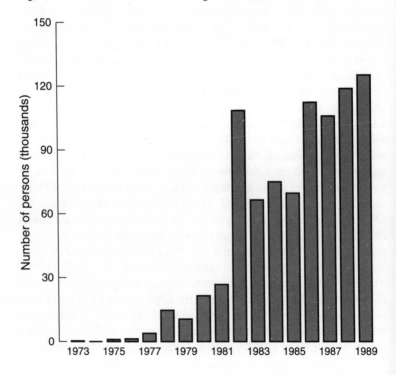

Table 4.5: Thai workers outside Europe and USA by country of work, 1989
(thousands)

Saudia Arabia	140.0
Iraq	5.0
Qatar	3.8
Bahrain	3.0
United Arab Emirates	2.0
Kuwait	6.5
Other Middle East	2.3
Libya	25.0
Other Africa	0.5
Malaysia	10.0
Singapore	30.0
Brunei	11.0
Hong Kong	9.5
Other Asia	18.1
Total	264.6

Source: Data sheet from the Department of Labour.

Promoting tourism

In its initial attempts to promote tourism as a foreign exchange
earner, the government concentrated on increasing the number
of foreign tourist arrivals. Later, in the Sixth Plan, more attention
was paid to increasing the length of stay and to promoting
domestic tourism in order to enhance employment in provincial
areas. Nevertheless, maximization of the number of tourists
remained the essential policy.

The Tourist Authority of Thailand (TAT), a government agency
with the status of a public enterprise, is responsible for tourist
policies in Thailand. But TAT has limited human and financial
resources and by the nature of its work TAT must cooperate
with many other agencies. Thus, it promotes tourism in
cooperation with other public enterprises such as the Airport
Authority of Thailand, and with many other departments in
different ministries, especially the Ministry of Interior. The
Ministry of Interior controls various district-level and provincial-
level offices which are important for tourist promotion measures
in different localities. In the Sixth Plan, tourism was promoted

not only as a foreign exchange earner but also as a panacea for the slump in commodity prices and as a provider of employment in areas outside Bangkok. Following this guideline, tourist promotion plans were drafted in a number of provinces with the cooperation of the Ministry of Interior. Both TAT and ministry officials searched for scenic sights all over Thailand to be promoted as tourist spots for both local and foreign tourists. They revived all kinds of local festivals as well as inventing new ones to provide added attractions for tourists.

The Ministry of Interior also controls the police. As part of the tourist promotion, a tourist police force was set up to provide more security for foreign tourists. The Ministry of Interior is also responsible for the prevention of prostitution. But, as is well known, prostitution has become a tourist attraction. The blatant existence of a large-scale sex trade would have been impossible without the tacit blessing of the Ministry of Interior.

The number of foreign tourists visiting Thailand increased rapidly in the 1980s. In 1978 there were 1.5 million foreign tourists. In 1983, the number increased to 2 million. Five years later, following the government-sponsored 'Visit Thailand Year' in 1987, this number had doubled to over 4 million. About half of the tourist arrivals came from East Asia and the Pacific. Another quarter came from Europe, and the remainder came from the United States, other Asian countries and the Middle East. The government plans to increase this number to 6 million by 1991 (Thailand, NESDB 1990^T).

Impact of service development on the economy

Between 1970 and 1987, the contribution of 'services' (i.e. the tertiary sector plus public utilities, defence and public administration, ownership of dwellings, construction and other services) to GDP rose from 54.1 per cent to 57.9 per cent (Tables 4.2 and 4.3). Most of this rise came from the sub-sector of 'other services' which includes: education, health, recreation and entertainment, hotels, restaurants, personal services, domestic services, business services, non-profit institutions and repair works. This rise in terms of the value-added contribution to

GDP was relatively modest, but in terms of contribution to employment and foreign exchange earnings, services played a significant role.

The service sector's share of the total labour force grew from 16 per cent in 1970 to 27 per cent in 1987. Again, the major part of this rise came under the 'other services' which saw a rise from 7.1 per cent to 10.7 per cent. And the rate of growth was significantly faster in the 1980s than the 1970s. Over these two decades, the service sector absorbed labour at more than double the rate of the manufacturing sector; and the 'other services' sub-sector, as defined above, alone absorbed as much labour as the total manufacturing sector.

Available evidence indicates further that the service sector is an important employer of rural migrant workers who face economic problems in their locality.[3] The sex industry in Bangkok (Pasuk 1982) and in Hadyai in the south for instance is dominated by young girls from rural areas. Child labour in small industries in Bangkok is also dominated by country girls. A study of the pattern of rural–urban migration in Thailand showed that young members of small and medium farming households in the northeast and other parts of rural Thailand migrate temporarily during the off-farm season to work in urban areas as taxi-drivers, housemaids, bar girls, massage girls, waitresses and construction workers (Fuller et al. 1983). The flow of migration increases in the years of severe drought or other natural disasters.

For many villages in the northeast and the north, temporary migration by young men and women in the off-farm season is now a regular event as a means of earning extra income for the family. A major contributing factor is the contraction of average farm sizes because of increasing population and because virgin land is no longer available at low cost. Small rice farmers in the northeast (even with 20 rai of rice land—3.2 hectares or 7.9 acres) can no longer afford to rely on traditional paddy crops to sustain their families. Temporary migration to work for cash in urban areas is the most viable way out of this situation. Indeed, in the case of external migrant workers to the Middle East and other Asian countries, migrants from the northeast also dominated the flow. The expansion of the service sector has provided a safety valve for absorbing underemployed and unemployed labour from rural areas.

The income earned from tourism and the remittances of migrant workers working overseas are the two most important contributions of services to foreign exchange earnings. As shown in Table 4.6, the net income from tourism was negative before 1970, but increased rapidly thereafter. In some years such as 1986 and 1987, when the deficit fell because of lower oil prices, tourism income more than covered the total trade deficits.[4] The contribution of workers' remittances has been much less than that of tourism, but has increased in importance from virtually zero in the early 1960s to over 17 per cent of the trade deficit in most years since 1980–81. It should be noted that the data on remittances as recorded by the Bank of Thailand are an underestimate because they include only those payments made via commercial banks. As shown in Table 4.6, the increases in net income from tourism and remittances of overseas workers have become very important as a means of bridging the trade deficit.

Consequences of service promotion

As a short-term device to obtain quick inflow of foreign exchange the promotion of tourism and migrant labour was very effective. Furthermore, the rapid expansion of the service sector provided employment for the growing labour force and helped reduce unemployment and underemployment. It also widened the base of the economy, reducing the country's heavy reliance on agricultural products. Finally, it facilitated a transition between rural culture and fully fledged urbanism. Service occupations, including overseas migrant labour, offered many people of rural background an opportunity to sample urban culture and values without being totally subsumed by them.

But service-oriented development also entailed less favourable consequences for the economy and society. Perhaps most important in this respect was the impact on education policy. The success of service-oriented development delayed the need to transform the education system. As long as the employment and foreign exchange problems could be solved by diverting more poorly educated and low-skilled workers into service occupations, there was little need to overhaul the education system and create the new skills needed for industrial

Table 4.6: Receipts from tourism and overseas workers' remittances relative to the trade deficit,[a] 1960 to 1989

					(billions of baht)				
	1960	1965	1970	1975	1980-81	1982-83	1984-85	1986-87	1988-89[b]
Trade deficit	0.9	2.6	12.2	20.1	61.9	62.7	65.2	29.1	121.5
Receipts from tourism	0	0	0.9	1.7	14.1	17.4	22.1	34.8	69.2
	(0)	(0)	(7.4)	(8.5)	(22.8)	(27.8)	(33.9)	(119.5)	(56.9)
Workers' remittances	0	0	0	0.1	8.4	15.8	20.4	20.8	21.1
	(0)	(0)	(0)	(0.5)	(13.6)	(25.2)	(31.3)	(71.5)	(17.4)

[a] Figures in brackets are percentages of trade deficit.
[b] 1989 figures are estimates.
Source: Data sheets from the Bank of Thailand.

growth. As a result, Thailand continued with an unduly 'bottom-heavy' education pyramid. In the mid-1980s, over 90 per cent of all people in the relevant age group went through four to six years of elementary education, but less than half progressed to secondary education. And of those who completed secondary education, less than 10 per cent went on to higher education. Once manufacturing industry started to grow rapidly in the late 1980s, the lack of suitably educated personnel quickly became a major constraint. The reliance on services and external migration to absorb labour may also have delayed efforts to improve technology and human capabilities in rural areas.

There were also some directly negative effects of tourism—particularly the expansion of the sex industry, the related spread of AIDS and other diseases, damage to the environment, and localised socio-economic problems in the major tourist locations. The reluctance of the government to take any serious measures to restrict the expansion of the sex industry appeared to confirm that it tacitly condoned the industry as a means of promoting tourism and thus increasing foreign exchange earnings.[5] As Thailand emerged as one of the most critical areas of AIDS expansion in the late 1980s, this convenient neglect appeared positively malign.[6]

Similarly, the cavalier promotion of tourism caused extraordinarily rapid degradation of the environment in the key tourist locations. In less than five years, Pattaya was transformed from a relatively sleepy resort town into an environmental disaster area. Several areas of outstanding natural beauty such as Phi Phi, Samui, Krabi and Tarutao were quickly ravaged by uncontrolled development. By the late 1980s, local pressures were emerging to counter and control such haphazard development, but the government still had no planning mechanism to provide suitable infrastructure and environmental control in the areas singled out for major tourist development.

Wanee (1983) compared the redistributive impact of 'new services', namely tourism and its associated industries (hotels, transport, gift making, restaurants), with that of 'old services' or informal sector activities such as vending, petty trading, domestic service and other personal services. In particular, this study questioned whether the development of 'new services' would help reduce the imbalance between Greater Bangkok (Bangkok metropolis and the surrounding five provinces) and the rest of the country. The study found that the 'old services' probably redistribute a greater proportion of income towards rural areas outside Greater Bangkok than do the 'new services' because a portion of the informal sector workers are migrants who remit income back to their homes in the villages. Tourism probably creates more imbalances between urban and rural areas because tourist activities tend to be concentrated in urban areas. Human resource development and regional planning in areas outside Greater Bangkok may help to draw modern services into rural areas and thus promote more balanced development.

Conclusions: future directions

In the late 1980s, the manufacturing sector began to expand rapidly. By 1989, manufactured exports accounted for more than half of all commodity exports. However, this did not mean that there would be no further impetus to promote the service sector. First, manufactured export growth did not solve the problem of the trade deficit. Indeed, because Thailand's industrial growth relied so heavily on imported technology, the growth in manufacturing actually caused a net negative effect on the balance of trade. The National Economic and Social Development Board projected that the trade deficit would be in the order of 7 per cent of GNP during the Seventh Plan period (1992–97) (Thailand NESDB 1990[T]).

Second, the late 1980s saw the beginnings of a serious restructuring of Thailand's agriculture which promised to displace more labour from the rural sector. Medium and large farms, in the best position to apply new technology to improve their efficiency or to diversify into higher value products, began to squeeze out small farms and to push more of the marginal rural population onto the labour market. While some may be absorbed as wage labour on medium and larger farms, others will be forced into self-employment and the usual fringe occupations of the informal sector. Given the trends towards capital-intensive and skill-intensive industries, manufacturing development is unlikely to increase the demand for industrial labour at a commensurate rate. Services will continue to offer the only viable alternative employment opportunity for some time to come.

Notes to Chapter 4

[1] Definitions of the service industry vary. The ILO and the OECD
equate the service sector with the tertiary sector.
Their classification is:
- primary sector: agriculture, hunting, forestry and fishing
- secondary sector: mining and quarrying, manufacturing,
  electricity, gas, water and construction
- tertiary sector: commerce, financing, insurance, real estate and
  business services, transport, storage and communication,
  community, social and personal services, and activities not
  elsewhere defined.

In this chapter, a broad definition is used covering the tertiary
sector plus electricity, gas and water construction. Thus, our service
sector includes all activities except agriculture, mining and
manufacturing.

[2] Somsak (1984) for instance found that during the 1970s new
industries operated by foreign or joint venture firms which received
promotional privileges from the Board of Investment tended to have
a higher capital intensity ratio compared with non-promoted firms.
The high capital intensity can explain the low labour absorption rate
of modern industries.

[3] Data based on the population census of 1970 show that of the total
out-migration of 940,000 people in 1970 from rural areas, 25 per cent
were in services, 60 per cent in agriculture, and 15 per cent in
manufacturing and industries not elsewhere classified (United
Nations, *Migration, Urbanisation and Development of Thailand*, New
York, 1982). More recent data for 1981 show that about 10–18 per
cent of employed workers in commerce, transport, community,
recreation and personal services were migrants (calculated from
the National Statistical Office, *Report of the Labour Force Survey*,
July–August 1981). In 1985, of all migrants in the Bangkok
metropolis (Bangkok, Nonthaburi, Pathumthan Samut Prakan,
Nakhon Pathom and Samut Sakhon) who were employed, 55 per
cent obtained jobs in service activities, 19 per cent in manufacturing,
and the remaining 26 per cent in agriculture and mining (National
Statistical Office, *Survey of Migration into the Bangkok Metropolis, 1985*,
Bangkok). This same survey showed that 35 per cent of all the
migrants who moved to Bangkok did so to look for work during
the slack agricultural seasons.

[4] It was estimated that in developing countries, the tourist industry
itself consumed about 40 per cent of the income from tourism as
imports (De Kadt 1979). The estimate of the import content of the

tourist industry for Thailand was 34.24 per cent (Inthapanya and Jumlong 1985T).

5 The reluctance of past and present administrations to take any action to curb the sex industry stems from a number of reasons, including the deeply-entrenched apathetic attitude towards prostitution and the fear that tourism, the country's top money earner, would be 'hurt'. (Article in *Bangkok Post*, 11 August, 1990.)

6 Dr Praphan Panupark of Chulalongkorn Hospital, a doctor involved in treating AIDS sufferers in Bangkok, attributed the government's slowness in waking up to the AIDS menace to its concern with tourism and the impact on the industry of adverse publicity (*Bangkok Post*, 11 August, 1990).

5

Monetary Policy

BHANUPONG NIDHIPRABHA

In the two decades since 1970, Thailand's average annual growth rate of Gross Domestic Product (GDP) was 6.8 per cent. Growth was positive in every year, even in per capita terms. The stability of the price level was another remarkable achievement. The annual average rate of inflation over these two decades was 7 per cent. The rate never exceeded 25 per cent and there were only four years in which it exceeded 10 per cent. The two oil price shocks of 1973–74 and 1979–80 did not lead to runaway inflation, and price stability was restored relatively quickly after each shock. The highest current account deficit was 7.6 per cent of GDP in 1979. Thailand's unemployment statistics are unreliable (as with most developing countries) but the negative deviation of actual income from the trend income level, which presumably moves in the same direction as true unemployment, reached 3 per cent at its worst in 1985. It cannot be denied that the story of Thailand's economic performance has been largely one of success. But to what extent was this success the result of macroeconomic policy?

Thai monetary policy is controlled by the government's central bank, the Bank of Thailand. Its most important objective is economic stabilization. This chapter analyses the Bank of Thailand's stabilization program by reviewing the impact of the bank's policies. The main focus is the degree to which these policies resulted in the achievement of the bank's objectives. The characteristics of Thai monetary policy between 1970 and 1989 are outlined together with Thailand's monetary volatility and controllability of the monetary base. A review of interest rate policy is followed by discussion of the effectiveness of monetary policy in achieving economic stabilization over the same 1970–89 period. The analysis suggests that the Thai authorities have largely succeeded in their attempts to stabilize the economy through discretionary monetary interventions.

Discretionary monetary policy

Thai authorities employ various monetary measures to counter cyclical movements of income. Interest rate policy instruments, such as the Bank of Thailand's lending interest rate to commercial banks and interest rate ceilings (which the bank also sets), have been employed more frequently than other monetary instruments such as the legal reserve ratio and open market operations. Several monetary aggregates have been used as intermediate targets for policy response, but according to Chaiyawat (1984) the monetary base is regarded by the monetary authorities as an operational target since it can be more readily controlled and monitored than most other monetary targets. This analysis will focus on the movement of the monetary base as an indicator of the direction of monetary policy.

If a stable relationship exists between monetary aggregates and the authorities' ultimate goal variables, monetary authorities can attain those goals in principle by manipulating monetary aggregates. However, the objectives of maintaining high growth, price stability and external equilibrium may not be compatible. The success of the direct targeting approach also depends heavily on the stability and predictability of the demand for and velocity of circulation of money.

The four basic goal variables of the monetary authorities are: output growth, inflation, the current account deficit, and unemployment. The performance of the Thai economy in relation to these ultimate targets is summarized for the period since 1971 in Table 5.1. The change in the growth rate of the monetary base is also included in the table to indicate the direction of monetary policies pursued. It should be noted that the first column in Table 5.1 shows the actual change in the growth rate of the monetary base. This observed change may differ from any intended change. The two magnitudes can be equal only if monetary authorities succeed in attaining their intermediate targets precisely. Therefore, the characterization of the direction of monetary policy should always consider the policy measures undertaken (such as the change in the bank rate) in addition to the observed change in the level of monetary aggregates.

The period 1970 to 1989 can be categorized according to the type of monetary policy pursued by inspecting the movement of the bank rate and the change in the growth rate of the monetary base. The results are summarized in Table 5.2, with each period identified as either expansionary (+) or contractionary (−). The average income growth rate over the period when the policy was applied is also given. Table 5.2 thus provides a historical description of the changing nature of Thailand's monetary policy through the 1970s and 1980s. Monetary policy has been counter-cyclical. In general,

Table 5.1: Thailand's monetary base and key economic variables, 1971 to 1989 (per cent)

	Change in monetary base growth rate	GDP growth rate	Current account	Inflation	Deviation from GDP trend
1971	11.90	4.96	2.37	0.50	0.43
1972	10.55	4.07	0.62	4.77	−2.16
1973	−0.60	9.86	0.45	15.54	0.62
1974	−6.16	4.35	0.64	24.32	−1.71
1975	6.85	4.85	4.08	5.36	−3.54
1976	8.72	9.38	2.59	3.73	−1.24
1977	3.17	9.90	5.55	7.60	1.60
1978	6.76	10.44	4.80	7.90	5.03
1979	7.30	5.31	7.62	9.91	3.54
1980	1.40	4.78	6.44	19.67	1.56
1981	−1.83	6.33	7.37	12.70	1.09
1982	8.00	4.06	2.82	5.23	−1.53
1983	6.75	7.25	7.28	3.75	1.14
1984	5.74	7.13	5.08	0.85	−0.87
1985	7.77	3.51	4.13	2.43	−3.95
1986	8.15	4.92	−0.59	1.85	−5.67
1987	15.87	9.47	0.74	2.48	−3.34
1988	8.14	13.22	2.78	3.85	2.44
1989	10.40	12.21	3.67	5.37	7.60

Sources: Calculated from *Monthly Bulletin*, Bank of Thailand; *National Income of Thailand*, National Economic and Social Development Board, various issues.

expansionary measures were associated with periods of slow economic growth, and contractionary measures with strong economic growth. The exception is the 1975–77 period, when the policy applied was expansionary even though the income growth rate remained as high as 8 per cent.

During 1971–72, growth fell to 4.5 per cent, well below the average growth path, and the monetary policy applied was expansionary. However, because of the export commodity boom and the first oil price shock in 1973, inflation rose to 20 per cent over the period 1973–74. The Bank of Thailand felt compelled to adopt a contractionary policy. When the world recession led to a fall in exports in 1975, the Bank of Thailand reverted to an expansionary monetary policy to prevent economic recession. A contractionary policy was reintroduced during the 1978–81 period, when a strong economic recovery was threatened by the balance of trade deficit and the second oil price shock.

It should be noted that shortly after the first oil shock (1973–74) the monetary measures applied were essentially expansionary, while after the second oil shock (1979–80) they were contractionary. After this second shock, the objectives of the monetary authorities seemed to shift away from emphasizing high economic growth to maintaining external equilibrium when it became obvious that the deficit in the balance of payments was unsustainable. The average size of the current account deficit between 1978 and 1981 was 6.9 per cent of GDP.

As a result of the strong deflationary measures introduced between 1978 and 1981, the economic growth rate fell to 5.7 per cent during 1982–83, as compared with 6.7 per cent over the preceding four years. Consequently, the monetary policy response was expansionary during 1982 and 1983. The impact of this monetary expansion was felt in 1984, when the growth rate rose to 7.1 per cent. The strong recovery implied a rising demand for imports, and the subsequent deterioration in the balance of trade resulted in monetary tightening. Economic growth slowed to 5.9 per cent during 1985–87 and the monetary authorities then tried to encourage further growth through a monetary relaxation.

Table 5.2 suggests that monetary policy might have considerable lag effects on income since monetary measures take a longer time to affect nominal GDP than to affect monetary aggregates. The growth rate observed in each period described

Table 5.2: Direction of monetary policy and average key economic indicators, 1971 to 1989 (per cent)

Year	Direction[a]	Real GDP growth rate	Inflation	Deviation of actual income from trend income	Current account deficit/GDP	Monetary base growth rate	Government budget deficit/GDP
1971–72	+	4.52	2.63	-0.86	2.16	14.37	4.65
1973–74	–	7.11	19.93	-0.55	2.09	15.60	0.63
1975–77	+	8.04	5.56	-1.06	4.36	11.20	2.98
1978–81	–	6.72	12.55	2.80	6.95	13.55	2.79
1982–83	+	5.66	4.49	-1.34	5.66	11.21	3.80
1984	+	7.13	0.85	-0.87	5.51	5.58	3.49
1985–87	+	5.97	2.25	-4.31	1.91	13.63	2.60
1988–89	0	12.71	4.61	5.02	3.60	15.89	-2.93

[a] (+) indicates expansion, (–) indicates contraction, (0) indicates no change.
Directions of monetary policy are evaluated from the direction of change in the bank rate and the growth rate of monetary base.
Source: (As for Table 1).

in the table was actually the outcome of the policy measures undertaken in the previous period. Therefore, the seemingly counter-cyclical policy could prove to be a destabilizing overreaction if applied too late or too strenuously.

The relationship between real income level and the monetary base is captured in Figure 5.1, which shows the percentage difference between the actual growth rate and the trend growth rate of real income and the monetary base, lagged one period. The correlation coefficient between the two variables is 0.52. The fact that the rate of change in output moves more closely with the previous rather than the current period rate of change in base money growth indicates some degree of lag in the effect of monetary policy. Figure 5.1 reveals that the fluctuation in the growth rate of real income in the 1970s was higher than the fluctuation in the first half of the 1980s. The standard deviations of the real growth rate over the 1971-79 and 1980-85 periods were 2.6 and 1.5, respectively. The existence of large external shocks in the first period explains this greater fluctuation. The commodity boom in 1973 produced a surge in real income, while subsequent oil shocks brought about a sharp decline in growth rates in 1974 and 1979. A strong economic recovery occurred between 1975 and 1978. The second half of the 1980s was more volatile than either of these periods, however, and the standard deviation of real income growth was 3.1 for the whole of the 1980s.

Although there was less deviation from the trend during the 1978-85 period, the growth rate was also below the trend path. The contractionary monetary measures employed from 1979 to 1981 were responsible for the slower economic growth. Table 5.2 shows the period average percentage deviation of actual income level from the potential income path, which was obtained by fitting the real income level against a time trend. The actual income path remained above the potential (trend) level between 1979 and 1981. However, the lag effects of monetary restraint were felt later, from 1982 to 1985, when income fell below its potential level. This implies a decreasing rate of employment of domestic resources. The reduced domestic demand, in turn, produced a period of price stability.

From 1985 to 1990 income growth accelerated, putting pressure on the price level which also rose at an increasing rate. As long as the current account deficit was sustainable

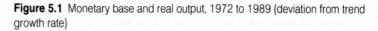

Figure 5.1 Monetary base and real output, 1972 to 1989 (deviation from trend growth rate)

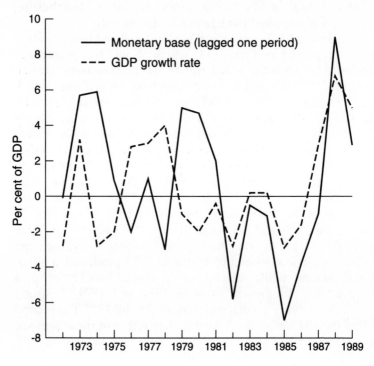

through capital inflows, and inflation was tolerable, no major adjustments in monetary policy were made to combat domestic demand pressure. Growth was especially rapid in 1988 and 1989, with no disruption from domestic policy. The high growth rate generated high government tax revenues, reducing the average size of the public deficit as a percentage of GDP to 3.6 per cent, as opposed to 7 per cent from 1978 to 1984. The automatic fiscal stabilizer resulting from this—the tendency for higher growth to reduce the fiscal deficit—helped lessen the demand pressure on the price level during the boom period.

Volatility of money supply and controllability of the monetary base

As described above, the discretionary monetary measures applied to restore internal and external equilibrium led to fluctuations in the growth rate of monetary aggregates, which in turn affected the variation in income. As illustrated in Figure 5.1, the movement of the monetary base is correlated with the movement of output. In this section the sources of the variations in the monetary base are analysed and the relationships between money supply, bank credit, and the monetary base are explored.

The volatility of monetary growth was most pronounced in the period 1979 to 1985. As Table 5.3 indicates, the coefficients of variation for the growth rates in M1 and the monetary base were largest in this period. The largest variations were also observed for the money multiplier, credit multiplier, and velocity of money. Table 5.3 also indicates that growth rates of the monetary base and money supply were lower from 1979 to 1985 than in the previous six years, 1973 to 1978. Although the growth rates of monetary aggregates were lower after the second oil price shock, they were also more volatile. From Table 5.3, the money multiplier seemed to be the least volatile, while the credit multiplier was growing steadily and showed the largest variation. The variation in the velocity of money was larger than that of the money multiplier. Thus, domestic credit or nominal GDP may not be as appropriate an intermediate target as the money supply.

From 1986 to 1989, the monetary base and M1 increased at a faster rate than in the previous period, as a result of the expansionary measures implemented between 1985 and 1987. Of the monetary variables shown in Table 5.3, the fluctuations from 1986 to 1989 also became less volatile, as can be seen from the small coefficients of variation. The return to a more stable relationship can be explained in terms of the waning effects of the external shocks from rising foreign interest rates. There was no necessity for the monetary authorities to adjust the bank rate as they had in the period between 1979 and 1985. Given a stable relationship between money supply and the monetary base, greater control over the latter will improve the controllability of monetary aggregates. Under the fixed exchange

Table 5.3: Monetary volatility, 1973 to 1989

	Year	Average growth rate (%)	Coefficient of variation[a]
Money Supply (M1)	1973–78	14.07	0.39
	1979–85	6.82	0.86
	1986–89	19.49	0.29
Monetary base	1973–78	13.62	0.23
	1979–85	10.53	0.35
	1986–89	16.05	0.22
		Average value	Coefficient of variation
Money multiplier	1973–78	1.24	0.02
	1979–85	1.15	0.08
	1986–89	1.11	0.02
Credit multiplier	1973–76	2.91	0.17
	1979–85	4.85	0.18
	1986–89	6.32	0.09
Velocity of money	1973–78	8.38	0.06
	1979–85	10.34	0.09
	1986–89	10.12	0.04

[a] Coefficient of variation is the ratio of standard deviation to the mean value.
Source: Calculated from Bank of Thailand, *Monthly Bulletin*.

rate regime prior to 1978, and with the subsequent continued intervention of the Bank of Thailand in maintaining exchange rate stability, the net foreign assets component of the monetary base becomes an uncontrollable item. It is affected by the condition of the balance of payments. The two controllable items in the monetary base component are the claims on government and the claims on financial institutions by the Bank of Thailand. The latter two components are subject to the discretion of the Bank of Thailand.

The relative importance of each item, expressed relative to the uses of the monetary base, is given in Table 5.4. The relative share of net foreign assets (NFA) declined between 1979 and 1985. However, the NFA share increased between 1986 and 1989 as a result of the favourable balance of payments. On the other hand, the share of the net claims on government (NCG) by the Bank of Thailand increased above the share of NFA between 1979 and 1985, but during the subsequent years of the late 1980s were again below the share of NFA. The share of claims on financial institutions (CFI) also increased, reflecting the increasing importance of the export credit promotion scheme of the Bank of Thailand as well as the credit which had been extended to some shaky financial institutions for liquidity purposes.

The average growth rates of each source component of the monetary base are given in Table 5.5 for the years 1973 to 1989. It is clear that the volatility of the monetary base in the 1979–85 period was largely the result of changes in net foreign assets, which are uncontrollable items. The Bank of Thailand's claims on financial institutions and governments, the controllable items, also showed the greatest variation during this period.

During the period 1986 to 1989, a very high growth rate of net foreign assets and a negative growth rate of net claims on government resulted from the balance of payments surplus and the redemption of public debt, respectively. Figure 5.2 suggests a negative relationship between the rates of change in the net foreign assets and the change in the Bank of Thailand's net claims on government. The correlation coefficient between the two variables is –0.74, indicating that the Bank of Thailand had attempted to offset the change in the monetary base which stemmed from the movement in the balance of payments.

The Bank of Thailand lending rate

The Bank of Thailand controls short-term market rates of interest by adjusting the bank rate and intervening in the repurchase market. The bank rate was adjusted more frequently in the period 1980–82, when foreign interest rates were especially volatile. Table 5.6 provides a summary of the adjustments in the bank rate made between 1979 and 1989 by indicating the number of times that the adjustment was made per year, the direction of the adjustment, and the net change in the rate over the year.

The net percentage change in the bank rate provides useful information for classifying the course of discretionary monetary policy. Information from Table 5.6 is therefore the basis for the

Table 5.4: Components of the monetary base, 1970 to 1988 (average ratio relative to uses of base)

| | Sources of base | | | | Uses of base | |
	Net foreign assets	Net claims on government	Net claims on financial institutions	Net other liabilities	Currency held by private sector	Deposits held by private sector
1970–78	1.12	0.43	0.16	-0.71	0.82[a]	0.18[a]
1979–85	0.72	1.07	0.40	-1.18	0.87	0.13
1986–89	1.13	0.44	0.47	-1.04	0.83	0.17

a 1976–78.

Source: Calculated from Bank of Thailand, Monthly Bulletin.

Table 5.5: Growth and variation of the components of the monetary base, 1971 to 1989 (per cent)

	Net foreign assets	Net claims on government	Net claims on financial institutions	Net other liabilities
1971–78				
Average growth rate	13.71	35.57	39.40	22.02
Coefficient of variation	1.20	1.39	0.94	0.61
1979–85				
Average growth rate	2.77	19.58	23.43	13.65
Coefficient of variation	7.05	0.67	1.21	1.08
1986–89				
Average growth rate	51.48	-61.53	12.88	8.95
Coefficient of variation	0.14	-1.06	1.59	0.47

Source: Calculated from Bank of Thailand, *Monthly Bulletin.*

Figure 5.2 Net foreign assets and net claims on government, 1971 to 1989

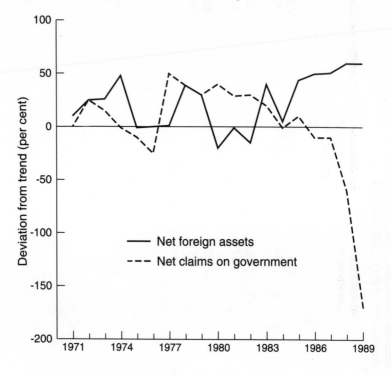

Table 5.6: Adjustment of the Bank of Thailand lending rate, 1979 to 1989

	Number of adjustments	Direction		Net rate of change (%)
		+	-	
1979	2	2	0	2.5
1980	6	3	3	0.0
1981	5	3	2	1.0
1982	4	1	3	-2.0
1983	2	1	1	0.5
1984	1	0	1	-1.0
1985	1	0	1	-1.5
1986	3	0	3	-3.0
1987	0	0	0	0.0
1988	0	0	0	0.0
1989	0	0	0	0.0

Source: Calculated from Bank of Thailand, *Monthly Bulletin*.

construction of Table 5.2. The same method of classification has been applied from 1970 onwards. Although the net change in the bank rate in 1983 was 0.5 per cent, that particular year was classified as one of restrictive monetary policy, since the bank rate was lowered by one percentage point between January and November. The increase of 1.5 per cent was only made in December, resulting in a positive net change over the year of only half a percentage point. The year 1984 was classified as contractionary because a ceiling was imposed on credit growth at 18 per cent. There was no change in the bank rate in 1987, 1988 or 1989. Since the bank rate was kept at a low level, 1987 was considered to be expansionary. Table 5.1 indicates that the change in the growth rate of the monetary base in that year was 15.9 per cent. The following year, 1988, can be considered restrictive, or at least less expansionary, due to the slowdown in the growth rate of the monetary base. The net claims on government of the Bank of Thailand were reduced by 61.5 per cent, as a result of the government budget surplus in 1988.

From time to time the bank rate has been adjusted either to induce capital inflow or to prevent capital outflow. The monetary authorities aim to keep the domestic rate of interest in line with foreign interest rates, but periodically use a differential between these two rates to influence capital movements. As Table 5.7 suggests, a positive difference between the bank rate (RB) and the Eurodollar interest rate (RF) induces more capital inflow, since it is cheaper to borrow from abroad than from the central bank. This produces a decline in the ratio of commercial banks' borrowings from the central bank relative to foreign banks (CB/FB). The last column in Table 5.7 shows the percentage change in the CB/FB ratio. Given the size of the central banks' lending, a negative sign in this column would indicate capital inflow, while a positive sign would indicate capital outflow.

In 1975, the Bank of Thailand provided considerable credit for commercial banks for liquidity purposes. Commercial banks tried to reduce their outstanding foreign loans due to excess liquidity. Except for the above two years, a negative correlation is observed between the interest rate differential (RB–RF)—the Thai bank rate minus the Eurodollar rate—and the rate of change of the commercial banks' borrowing ratio. Table 5.7 suggests that adjustments in the banks' lending rate can be employed to affect the balance of payments position. The correlation coefficient between the variables RB/RF and FB/CB is 0.2. The positive relationship between the two ratios can be seen in Figure 5.3. Weak correlation was due to other factors such as exemption of the 10 per cent withholding tax on foreign borrowings to encourage capital inflows during periods of tightened credit. Tax exemptions were made available sporadically from 1970 to 1983. The proportion of capital inflows that stemmed from commercial banks' borrowings was 31 and 37 per cent in 1979 and 1983, respectively. In 1988 and 1989, the Ministry of Finance attempted to secure increased inflow of long-term capital funds by providing an interest tax exemption for foreign borrowings with a maturity of three years or longer.

Figure 5.3 Foreign borrowing and the bank rate, 1970 to 1988

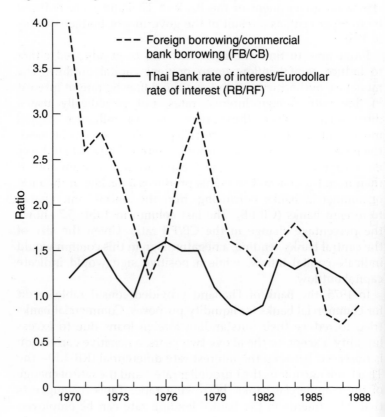

Year	Bank rate[a] (%) (1)	Eurodollar rate[b] (%) (2)	(1)-(2) (3)	Ratio of commercial bank borrowings[c] to foreign borrowing[d] (4)	Rate of change of (4) (%) (5)
1970	9.00	8.52	0.48	0.25	n.a.
1971	9.00	6.58	2.42	0.39	56
1972	8.00	5.46	2.54	0.36	-8
1973	10.00	9.24	0.76	0.42	17
1974	11.00	11.01	-0.01	0.53	26
1975	10.00	6.99	3.01	0.91	72
1976	9.00	5.58	3.42	0.60	-34
1977	9.00	6.05	2.95	0.40	-33
1978	12.50	8.78	3.72	0.33	-17
1979	12.50	12.01	0.49	0.47	42
1980	13.50	14.06	-0.56	0.65	38
1981	14.50	16.82	-2.32	0.67	3
1982	12.50	13.16	-0.66	0.81	21
1983	13.00	9.60	3.40	0.61	-25
1984	12.00	10.78	1.22	0.52	-15
1985	11.00	8.34	2.66	0.66	27
1986	8.00	6.77	1.23	1.29	95
1987	8.00	7.11	0.89	1.44	12
1988	8.00	7.91	0.09	1.09	-24
1989	8.00	9.10	-1.10	0.59	-46

[a] Bank rate or loan rate.
[b] Eurodollar rate in London.
[c] Commercial bank borrowings from Bank of Thailand.
[d] Borrowings from banks abroad.
Source: Calculated from Bank of Thailand, *Monthly Bulletin*, and the International Financial Statistics (IFS).

The capital flows through commercial banks' portfolio adjustments indicate that the use of the bank rate for achieving internal equilibrium may be partly offset by capital movement. On the other hand, employing the bank rate for achieving external equilibrium will interfere with internal equilibrium. Additional instruments are therefore required to meet both goals.

Maximum interest rates

Apart from intervening in the short-term money market, the Bank of Thailand sets maximum interest rates on both lending and borrowing. The two interest rates were kept constant at 14 and 7 per cent, respectively, from 1966 to 1973. In 1974 they were each raised by one percentage point. Nevertheless, as Table 5.8 shows, the real deposit rate was negative.

In 1980, during the second oil shock, the interest rate ceilings were each raised by three percentage points. However, the real deposit rate was still negative. As can be seen in Figure 5.4, the ratio of quasi-money to GDP actually declined from its rising trend after the real interest rate became negative. The introduction of an interest tax on time deposits in 1977 delayed its return to the pre-shock path. The ratio resumed its increasing trend after interest rates were restructured in 1980 and 1981 to re-establish positive real interest rates. The escalating real net deposit interest rate between 1982 and 1984 resulted in a sharp increase in the rates of time and saving deposits to GDP after 1982.

Demand conditions permitting, a surge in the growth rate of quasi-money is likely to be followed by a sharp increase in credit growth. Figure 5.5 shows the growth rates of bank credit and total deposits. The slowdown in the growth rate of deposits between 1977 and 1979 led to a sharp decline in credit expansion between 1978 and 1980. A sharp rise in credit growth can be seen between 1981 and 1983. On the other hand, the increase in the volume of bank credit resulted from the enormous financial savings accumulated in the past in response to unusually high returns on financial savings through commercial banks. The Bank of Thailand did not adjust the maximum interest rates, the argument being that, since the actual interest rates

	Loan rate	Time deposit rate	Interest tax rate	Net deposit rate	Inflation rate[a]	Real net deposit rate
1970	14.00	7.00	0.00	7.00	-0.09	7.09
1971	14.00	7.00	0.00	7.00	0.44	6.56
1972	14.00	7.00	0.00	7.00	4.91	2.09
1973	14.00	7.00	0.00	7.00	15.47	-8.47
1974	15.00	8.00	0.00	8.00	24.30	-16.30
1975	15.00	8.00	0.00	8.00	5.30	2.70
1976	15.00	8.00	0.00	8.00	4.20	3.80
1977	15.00	8.00	10.00	7.20	7.60	-0.40
1978	15.00	8.00	10.00	7.20	7.90	-0.70
1979	15.00	9.00	10.00	8.10	9.90	-1.80
1980	18.00	12.00	10.00	10.80	19.70	-8.90
1981	19.00	13.00	10.00	11.70	12.70	-1.00
1982	19.00	13.00 (12.5)[b]	12.50	10.94	5.20	5.74
1983	17.50	13.00 (12.5)	12.50	10.94	3.80	7.14
1984	19.00	13.00 (12.5)	12.50	10.94	0.90	10.04
1985	19.00	13.00 (11.0)	12.50	9.63	2.40	7.23
1986	15.00	9.50 (7.25)	15.00	6.16	1.90	4.26
1987	15.00	9.50 (7.25)	15.00	6.16	2.50	3.66
1988	15.00	9.50 (8.63)	15.00	7.34	3.85	3.49
1989	15.00	9.50 (9.88)	15.00	8.40	6.31	2.09

a The real net deposit rate is the difference between the nominal time deposit rate and current inflation rate.
b The figures in parentheses are the actual rate of interest paid by commercial banks. Before 1982, the banks' deposit rates were equal to the maximum rates.
Source: Bank of Thailand, Monthly Bulletin.

Figure 5.4 Quasi money and M1, 1970 to 1988 (per cent of GDP)

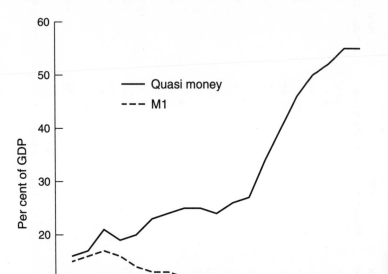

were below the ceiling rates, market forces would naturally lead to a decline in the market interest rates. Chaiyawat (1984) contends that this rapid credit expansion contributed to a deterioration in the balance of payments. In 1984 the monetary authorities applied a credit restraint policy by requiring commercial banks to restrict the growth rate of credit in the first half of 1984 to 9 per cent, and for the whole year to 18 per cent of the level of credit outstanding in 1983.

The US credit restraint program introduced by the Federal Reserve Board in 1980 lasted for only four months, but according to Goldfeld and Chandler (1986), it had a substantial con-tractionary impact on the US economy. The 18 per cent credit restraint imposed by the Thai monetary authorities in 1984 lasted for eight months and it too had a considerable impact. In mid-1984, the Thai Farmers Bank encountered an 86 per cent rate

Figure 5.5 Bank credit and total deposits (growth rate), 1972 to 1989

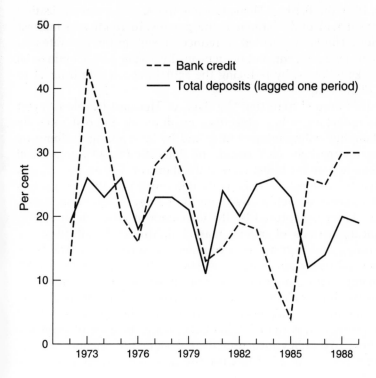

of dishonoured cheques by value compared with only 3 per cent for the corresponding period in 1983 (*Far Eastern Economic Review*, 6 September 1984). The monetary authorities hesitated in reducing the interest rate ceiling, despite the widely held view that downward rigidity of interest rates results from the oligopolistic structure of the Thai banking industry. As a result, commercial banks were not willing to reduce deposit rates even though the real rate of interest rose to 11.6 per cent in 1984. With the credit restraint program being implemented, commercial banks found themselves unable to dispose of excess liquidity.

By 1985, the time deposit rate actually paid by commercial banks had fallen from 12.5 to 11 per cent. It was another three years before the deposit rate finally came down. The implementation lag of interest rate policy thus retarded economic growth; the level of real investment fell in 1985. Finally, in 1986, the Bank of Thailand came to the important realization that it had underestimated the downward rigidity in interest rates. The bank decided to reduce maximum interest rates on loans by 4 per cent, and on deposits by 3.5 per cent. Commercial banks followed by reducing the actual deposit rate from 11 to 7.25 per cent.

It is argued here that the Bank of Thailand is able to exert its monetary policy objectives on domestic interest rates by changing ceiling interest rates and by intervening in domestic money markets. As a result, the domestic rate of interest will deviate from the foreign rate in the short run. Figure 5.6 suggests that the domestic rate is partly determined by the foreign rate of interest as well as by domestic money market conditions. The latter is captured by the loan–deposit ratio which is high during periods of money market tightness. By affecting the lending and borrowing of commercial banks the central bank can indirectly affect the domestic lending rate. In June 1989, an important change in interest rate policy was made. The ceiling on the interest rate of long-term fixed deposits of more than 12 months was abolished. Furthermore, the interest on fixed deposits of less than 200,000 baht was to be exempt from tax. These two policy measures were designed to encourage long-term savings in a bid to close the expected widening resource gap.

Effectiveness of monetary policy

Monetary policy would be totally ineffective in an economy with a fixed exchange rate regime and an open capital market. The central bank would be unable to alter the quantity of money in domestic circulation. An expansion (or contraction) of monetary policy would lead to a reduction (or increase) in the domestic interest rate, thereby inducing capital outflows (inflows). In the long run, the quantity of money supply and therefore the level of the interest rate would remain unchanged with no effect on aggregate demand.

It is argued that there are many reasons to believe that in Thailand, at least in the short term, the level of aggregate demand can be affected by monetary policy. The effectiveness of

Figure 5.6 Domestic and foreign interest rates (end of period), 1970 to 1989

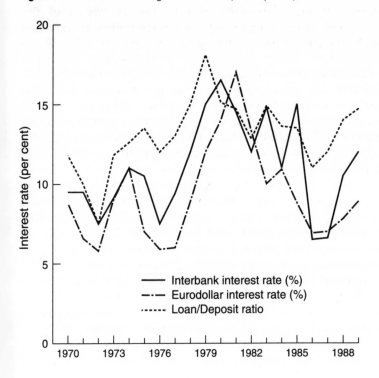

monetary policy depends on several conditions. First, it depends on the success of the sterilization process of the central bank—the systematic policy of adjustments designed to offset the effect that changes in the balance of payments would otherwise have on the domestic money supply. As Figure 5.2 indicates, the strong negative relationship between the rate of change in the level of net foreign assets and net claims on the government (a component in the sources of the monetary base) suggests that the central bank was trying to stabilize the economy by adjusting the controllable components of the monetary base in a counter-cyclical manner. Monetary policy will be effective in the short run at least—a period during which the effects of external disturbances can be expected to subside. A second condition for the effectiveness of monetary policy is the controllability of the international movement of capital.

Although it might be possible to move capital by over-invoicing imports or under-invoicing exports, the exemption of the 10 per cent withholding tax rate on foreign borrowing interests will have some impact on the degree of capital mobility in the short term.

There are various monetary instruments other than the bank rate that can be employed to affect the monetary base. The legal reserve ratio of commercial banks was altered in 1969 and again in 1974 for contractionary purposes. The ratio has remained at 7 per cent since 1974. The last adjustment was made in 1979 by changing the defined combination of legal assets to include cash on hand and government bonds, each at the maximum of 2.5 per cent of total deposits. Open market operations were employed by the Bank of Thailand in 1988 to reduce the excess liquidity of the commercial banking system in 1988. In addition, the minimum capital-risk asset ratio was reduced in 1983 from 8.5 to 8 per cent to stimulate the economy, although it had a negative impact on the stability of financial institutions. The commercial banks' branching conditions, which require banks to hold government bonds at 16 per cent of total deposits, further provides the central bank with some degree of manoeuvrability in terms of the excess reserves of commercial banks.

Even if the central bank cannot affect the quantity of money in the long run, monetary policy can still be effective as long as it has some impact on credit availability. The domestic rate of interest cannot remain the same after the introduction of an expansionary or contractionary monetary policy since the level of investment demand or credit-sensitive aggregate demand will be altered. The credit availability effect of monetary policy has long been noted by Tobin (1978). Empirical evidence on this issue in developed and less-developed countries is provided by Mishkin (1976) and Leff and Sato (1980), respectively.

The effectiveness of monetary policy also depends on the ability of the central bank to predict future macroeconomic values. The longer the lag effects of monetary policy, the more precise must be the forecasts. Unfortunately, it is more difficult to predict future events for many quarters ahead. As shown in Table 5.9, the errors in the Bank of Thailand's four quarters ahead forecasts of the real GDP growth rate and inflation were significant. The extent to which the Bank of Thailand employed these forecasts in its stabilization policy is unknown. Given that the model employed by the Bank of Thailand was a correct representation of the Thai economy, the forecast errors would stem partly from the effect of the responses to policies already introduced as well as from the errors in the assumed values of exogenous variables. Meltzer (1987) also warns that it is dangerous for monetary authorities to react to forecasting values because they are usually inaccurate.

Aside from the accuracy of the forecast values, the demand for money must be stable if hitting the intermediate monetary target implies achieving the ultimate targets. Figure 5.7 shows the movements in the velocity of circulation of money, both M1 and M2. The velocity of M2 was more stable than that of M1. The latter exhibited an increasing trend from 1972 to 1985. There is no inherent tendency for velocity to decline with increasing income while the structure of the economy is being transformed from a predominantly agricultural to an industrial one. The scope for Thailand to employ active monetary policies to transfer resources for investment purposes with non-inflationary expansion is therefore limited. In this respect the situation in Thailand may be quite different from that in some other developing countries (Driscoll and Lahiri 1983).

Figure 5.8 compares the financing pattern of the government budget deficit over the periods 1971-80 and 1981-86. It shows that the deficit in the latter period was less inflationary than in the first period of deficit financing, since it was financed through borrowing from the commercial banks and the government savings bank, rather than relying heavily on

Table 5.9: Actual values and 'four quarters ahead forecast' by the Bank of Thailand, 1985 to 1988 (per cent)

	GDP growth forecast	Actual rate	Inflation forecast	Actual rate
1985	6.1	3.2	6.7	2.4
1986	4.0	3.6	3.5	1.9
1987	5.0	5.6	2.5	2.5
1988	5.8	10.9	3.8	4.0

Source: Bank of Thailand.

Figure 5.7 The velocity of money, 1970 to 1988

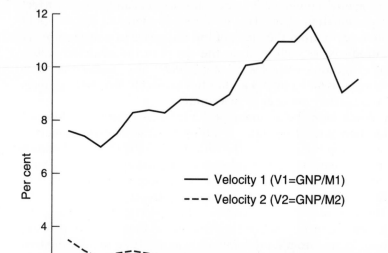

borrowing from the central bank. The changing deficit financing pattern suggests non-excessive monetary growth in the period when velocity was rising. The period of price stability is therefore partly due to the proper coordination of monetary and fiscal policies.

Conclusions: monetary stabilization

Until 1986, the most frequently used monetary instrument was the Bank of Thailand's lending rate. The Thai monetary authorities have engaged in fine-tuning of the economy by adjusting this bank rate. It has been used to spur growth, contain inflation, avoid recession, and induce capital inflows or prevent capital outflows.

Figure 5.8 Government deficits (net domestic borrowings), 1970 to 1989

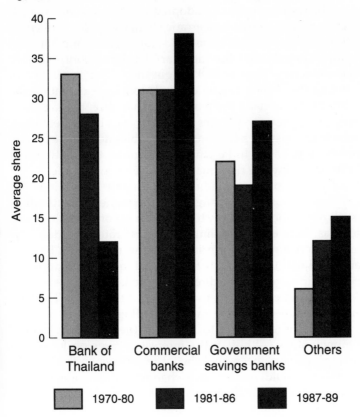

When the emphasis on each goal variable changes, a switching pattern of monetary policy between expansion and contraction (or less expansion) is observed. Each policy episode lasts about two or three years. The Thai monetary authorities can perhaps be said to have a strong adherence to what Modigliani (1977) called the fundamental practical message of Keynes' General Theory—the economy needs to be stabilized, can be stabilized, and should be stabilized by appropriate monetary and fiscal policies. According to Friedman (1968), an appropriate monetary policy should avoid drastic and erratic changes of direction. Discretionary policy can also be destabilizing if monetary policies have considerable and variable lag effects. The 18 per cent credit restraint program adopted in 1984 was an example of overreaction, a drastic and erratic change of policy direction.

Although there exists a close and stable relationship between the money supply and the monetary base, the controllability of the monetary base is still in question. The feasibility of controlling the money supply depends to a large extent on the stability of the demand for money. Furthermore, the lag effect of monetary policy complicates the timing of its implementation. Economic forecasts of key economic variables need to be precise if monetary policy is to be employed counter-cyclically in the right direction, by the right magnitude, at the right time.

If balance of payments adjustment cannot be attained via free movement of the exchange rate, the monetary authorities must allow the money supply to expand or to contract. However, as long as there exists a ceiling on interest rates, the domestic interest rate cannot perform its balancing role. If the Bank of Thailand adjusts the bank rate for external equilibrium purposes the domestic sector will be directly affected.

To promote flexibility in the system, the Bank of Thailand should abandon the ceiling rate on lending, thereby allowing the domestic interest rate to adjust to the changing level of the money stock. Although the interest ceilings on long-term time deposits have been abolished, the ceilings on some types of deposits should remain as a channel for the operation of monetary policy. By adjusting the ceilings on deposit rates so as to achieve realistic deposit interest rates, the monetary authorities can have a powerful direct effect on aggregate demand through credit availability and an indirect effect on the lending interest rate.

The bank rate should be free from involvement in external equilibrium adjustments. Provided that an appropriate sterilization is made, monetary authorities can concentrate the use of the bank rate on domestic demand management so as to avoid erratic changes and to reduce discretionary adjustment errors. From 1986 to 1989, there were no changes in the bank rate. Other policy instruments, such as exemption of the withholding tax rate on foreign borrowing, have been used more frequently for inducing capital inflows. This is a step in the right direction.

6

Fiscal Policy

CHAIPAT SAHASAKUL

Fiscal policy refers to the determination of government revenues and expenditures. As with all developing countries, Thailand's fiscal policies have had an important influence on its pattern of development. To familiarize the reader with fiscal policy in Thailand, this chapter provides, first, a general overview of Thai fiscal policy, second (and most importantly), a description of the interaction between the state of the economy and fiscal policy, and third, a review of selected features of the tax system and government expenditures. The Appendix Table gives relevant background data on fiscal policy variables. Most of the discussion relates to the calendar years 1970–88.[1]

Government budget definitions

The government budget is basically a match between sources and uses of funds. Government funds come from tax revenue (T_t), other revenue (N_t) and borrowing (B_t-B_{t-1}), where other revenue includes rent interest and dividend income, and contributions from state enterprises. The sources have to match uses (i.e. government expenditures) which involve government purchases (G_t), transfer payments (P_t) and interest payments on public debt (RB_{t-1}).

Algebraically, one can write the government budget constraint as follows:

Tax revenue   =   Government purchases
+ Other revenue   + Transfer payments
+ Borrowing   + Interest payments on public debt
or

$$T_t + N_t + (B_t - B_{t-1}) = G_t + P_t + RB_{t-1}, \tag{1}$$

where the subscript t indicates the period, B_t is public debt at the end of period t, and R is the interest rate on public debt.

The left-hand side of equation (1) shows the sources of government funds and the right-hand side, the uses of these funds or government expenditures. When the government spends more than its revenue, that is $G_t + P_t + RB_{t-1} > T_t + N_t$, it may borrow from an international or local credit market. This borrowing net of any repayment is a change in public debt or $B_t - B_{t-1}$ and is commonly known as a budget deficit. Alternatively, when the government spends less than its revenue, it is said to have a budget surplus.

This formal definition will enable the fiscal policy variables cited below to be more fully understood.

An overview of fiscal policy: 1970 to 1988

Government revenue grew at an annual rate of 13.9 per cent for the period 1970–88 and expenditures grew at an annual rate of 12.8 per cent for the same period. Since revenue grew faster than expenditures, the budget deficit shrank at an average annual rate of 3.1 per cent.

As a proportion of gross national product (GNP), government revenue averaged 15.9 per cent for 1970–88 with a clear upward trend from 14.1 per cent in 1970 to 17.4 per cent in 1988. Likewise, the ratio of government expenditures to GNP also rose from 17.8 per cent in 1970 to 19.2 per cent in 1987, then declining to 16.4 per cent in 1988, with an average of 18.6 per cent over the whole period. However, the size of budget deficits relative to GNP averaged 3.1 per cent for 1970–88 with no clear trend. Interestingly, in 1974 the government budget was in surplus, at 0.8 per cent of GNP, and again in 1988 at 2.6 per cent of GNP. As Table 6.1 clearly shows, the government obtains most of its revenue from taxes. The ratio of tax revenue to government revenue averaged 90 per cent for 1980–88 with no clear trend.

So far, the cited figures have referred to general government (central and local). However, in comparing the size of revenue and expenditures of central government with general government during the 1970–88 period, approximately 90 per cent and 92 per cent, respectively, of general government revenue and expenditures came from the central government.

Finally, the size of public debt (excluding the government's guarantee obligation) held by the private sector and foreigners gained momentum in recent years (1982–88).[2] When expressed relative to GNP, public debt rose from 7.7 per cent in 1970 to 14.8 per cent in 1982 and to 24.6 per cent in 1987. It dropped slightly to 21.6 per cent in 1988, mainly reflecting rapid economic growth over the year.

Fiscal policy and the economy

This section reviews the interaction between fiscal policy and the aggregate economy since 1970. The presentation in Table 6.2 is grouped into five sub-periods, each covering three consecutive years. The discussion below sketches the government revenue, expenditures and deficits as related to key macroeconomic indicators. Note that the term 'government' as used here includes both central and local governments but excludes public enterprises.

1970–78: strong growth

The Thai economy was relatively strong from 1970 to 1978, despite experiencing adverse effects from the first oil shock in 1973 and 1974. As a result, the government budget was relatively manageable and acceptable.

The growth rate of real gross national product (GNP) for 1970–72 averaged 4.2 per cent per year, somewhat below the annual average of 6.4 per cent for the period 1970–88. The growth rate rose to an average of 6.5 per cent per year for 1973–75, despite the first oil shock in 1973–74 because world market prices of farm products, including Thailand's major exports at the time, also rose sharply. The average growth rate for 1973–75 of principal exports of farm products (rice, rubber, maize, tapioca products and sugar) ranged from 38 per cent to 89 per cent per year.[3] The Thai economy adjusted quickly to the oil shock and surpassed its previous growth rate of real GNP with a record of 9.6 per cent per year from 1976 to 1978.

Since the economy was relatively strong, government revenue also grew at a higher rate than government expenditures during this period. This resulted in a relatively low government deficit.

Table 6.1: Nominal gross national product (GNP) and ratios of key fiscal policy variables, 1970 to 1988 (GNP in billions of baht and ratios in per cent)

Year	Nominal GNP	Ratio to GNP		Deficit (-)	Ratio of tax revenue to total revenue	Ratio of central government to total government		Ratio of public debt to GNP
		Central govt revenue	Central govt expenditure			revenue	expenditures	
	(1)	(2)	(3)	(4)	(5)	(6)	(7)	(8)
1970	147.6	14.1	17.8	-3.7	88.7	90.6	92.6	7.7
1971	153.3	14.0	18.8	-4.8	88.9	92.5	94.4	9.2
1972	169.5	13.9	18.2	-4.3	89.6	91.6	93.6	12.0
1973	221.2	13.3	15.7	-2.4	91.1	92.6	93.7	10.0
1974	279.1	15.0	14.3	0.8	90.5	91.4	91.0	8.3
1975	303.3	14.4	16.7	-2.2	89.6	89.2	90.6	8.4
1976	345.6	13.9	18.5	-4.7	90.7	90.9	93.2	9.2
1977	402.3	14.8	17.9	-3.1	92.3	90.6	92.3	8.8
1978	484.6	14.9	17.5	-2.6	92.0	90.2	91.7	9.4
1979	552.6	15.8	18.2	-2.4	92.3	90.0	91.3	10.2
1980	653.1	16.7	20.7	-3.9	90.7	87.4	89.8	10.9
1981	748.2	16.8	19.7	-2.9	89.0	89.0	90.6	12.0
1982	807.1	16.4	21.5	-5.1	89.8	87.4	90.4	14.8
1983	903.4	17.9	20.4	-2.5	88.6	88.9	90.3	15.1
1984	962.0	17.4	20.8	-3.4	91.0	88.7	90.5	19.1
1985	996.8	17.9	21.8	-3.9	88.2	90.1	91.9	22.4
1986	1072.2	18.0	21.1	-3.2	87.8	88.2	90.0	24.9

1987	1211.4	18.5	19.2	-0.7	88.6	90.4	90.8	24.6
1988	1482.2	17.4	16.4	2.0	93.6	94.9	99.2	21.6
Average for 1970–88		15.9	18.6	-3.1	90.2	90.3	92.0	13.2

Sources: Data on nominal GNP for 1970–85 in column (1) are from National Economic and Social Development Board (no date). Those for 1986–88 are obtained directly from National Economic and Social Development Board.

Data on total revenue, expenditures, deficits and tax revenue used in calculating in columns (2)–(5) are from lines 1, 2, 3, 4, 7 and 17 of the Appendix Table, where tax revenue is the sum of direct taxes on households and corporations and indirect taxes.

Data on revenue and expenditures of the central government used in calculation of columns (6), (7) and (8) are from Bank of Thailand (various issues). For example, data for 1983–88 are from the issue of January 1989, Table 25, pp.36–7, lines 1 and 2.

Data on public debt refer to that held by private sector and foreigners and are from line 20 + line 21 of the Appendix Table.

Table 6.2: Selected macroeconomic variables and fiscal policy variables, 1970 to 1988 (per cent, unless specified otherwise)

	1970-88 (average)	1970-72 (average)	1973-75 (average) First oil shock	1976-78 (average) Recovery	1979-81 (average) Second oil shock	1982-84 (average) Structural adjustments	1985-87 (average)	1987 Rapid growth	1988 Rapid growth
Macroeconomic variables									
1 Growth rate of nominal GNP	13.4	7.2	21.8	16.9	15.6	8.8	8.1	13.0[a]	18.9[a]
2 Growth rate of real GNP	6.4	4.2	6.5	9.6	5.3	6.3	5.2	8.6[a]	11.1[a]
3 Inflation rate (GNP deflator)	6.7	2.9	14.3	6.7	9.7	2.4	2.7	4.1[a]	7.0[a]
4 Current account/ GNP	-3.6	-2.1	-1.7	-4.2	-7.1	-5.0	-1.6	-1.4	-1.6
5 Inter-bank lending rate[b]	11.0	8.8	10.4	9.7	15.2	12.6	9.3	6.5	10.6
6 Exchange rate: baht/US$	22.02	20.91	20.45	20.38	20.86	23.14	26.36	25.74	25.3[c]

Fiscal policy variables

7 Growth rate of revenue	13.9	6.2	20.5	16.6	18.4	9.4	9.7	15.0	24.3[d]
8 Growth rate of expenditures	12.8	8.0	16.5	17.3	18.2	10.3	5.0	2.6	4.1[d]
9 Growth rate of deficits	-3.1	14.2	-39.2	19.5	16.5	14.3	-38.2	-117.6	-321.3
10 Average interest rate on treasury bills sold at tender	7.7	6.4	6.1	6.5	10.0	10.5	6.6	3.7	5.8

[a] Directly obtained from National Economic and Social Development Board.
[b] As at December.
[c] Average of January–November.
[d] Of central government.
Source: National Economic and Social Development Board, and *Bank of Thailand* ((various issues).

Interestingly, the government raised rice premiums and export duties (essentially an export tax on rice) when the world price of farm products soared in 1973–74 in order to stabilize the domestic price of rice. As a result, the growth rate of government revenue jumped from 6.2 per cent in 1970–72 to 20.5 per cent in 1973–75 while the deficit declined at an average rate of 39.2 per cent for the same period.

The first oil shock of 1973–74 raised inflation and interest rates. The inflation rate rose to an average of 14.3 per cent per year for 1973–75 from an average of 2.9 per cent per year for 1970–72. The corresponding figures for the inter-bank lending rate, a measure of the short-term market interest rate, were 10.4 per cent and 8.8 per cent, respectively. However, this did not affect average interest rates on treasury bills (sold at tender) which averaged 6.1 per cent for 1973–75 and 6.4 per cent for 1970–72.

1979–81: weak growth

Unlike the first oil shock, world prices of farm products during the second oil shock in 1979–80 were unfavourable, resulting in an average growth rate of real GNP for 1979–81 of 5.3 per cent. The three major adverse effects of the second oil shock were: a high current account deficit of 7.1 per cent of GNP for 1979–81; a high inflation rate of 9.7 per cent per year for 1979–81, compared with 6.7 per cent per year for 1970–88; and a high inter-bank lending rate of 15.2 per cent for 1979–81 compared with an average of 11 per cent per year for 1970–88.

Government revenue in nominal terms also grew at a relatively high rate over this period but this was mainly because of high inflation. The high inflation also gave the government no alternative but to raise employee compensation and increase other spending. Government deficits continued to grow at an average annual rate above 15 per cent for the 1976–81 period and the average interest rate on treasury bills also rose as the inter-bank lending rate rose, from 6.5 per cent for 1976–78 to 10 per cent for 1979–81.

1982–84: worldwide recession and domestic structural adjustments

Worldwide recessions and high interest rates since 1981, caused by the second oil shock, slowed the growth rates of Thailand's real GNP, exports and imports, but raised the real interest rate (nominal interest rate minus inflation rate), particularly in 1982. The government also launched structural adjustment programs aimed at improving the efficiency of the domestic economy. The programs were supported by various international organizations, such as a two-year standby arrangement with the International Monetary Fund (IMF) and the first and second structural adjustment loans (SAL I and SAL II) from the World Bank (Chaipat et al. 1989). The Bank of Thailand also devalued the baht in November 1984 by 14.8 per cent against the US dollar as the latter had been appreciating against the major currencies since 1983.

Some of the structural adjustment programs, such as tax-rate cutting and tax structure improvements, tended to reduce tax revenue in the short term, although their ultimate aim was an improvement in the efficiency of the economy, leading to an expansion in the tax base and thus increased tax revenue in the long term. The reduction in tax revenue worsened over this period because, during the worldwide recessions, the tax base also shrank. As a result, growth of government revenue for 1982–84 slowed to an average annual rate of 9.4 per cent compared with 13.9 per cent per year for the entire 1970–88 period. On the expenditure side, the annual growth rate for 1982–84 was also slow (at 10.3 per cent) compared with the average annual growth rate of 12.8 per cent for 1970–88 (Table 6.2).

There were at least two reasons for this drop in expenditure growth. First, the government limited the growth of its personnel to 2 per cent per year when the comparable average growth rate for 1981–84 was 7.6 per cent (Vuthiphong 1987b: 53–4). Second, the government also imposed ceilings on annual public borrowing from abroad. In 1983, the ceiling had been reduced from US$2.4 billion to US$2.06 billion under SAL II and it was eventually reduced to US$1 billion.[4] This 'public' borrowing included borrowing not only by central government and local governments, but also by state enterprises. This ceiling reduction effectively constrained the growth of government expenditures.

Although growth rates of government revenue and expenditures for 1982–84 were slow compared with the entire 1970–88 period, expenditures still exceeded revenue. As a result, government deficits for 1982–84 continued growing at an average annual rate of 14.3 per cent. Finally, the average interest rate

on treasury bills sold at tender was also in line with the high
interest rate in the international credit market. The rate on
treasury bills for 1982–84 averaged 10.5 per cent, somewhat
higher than the average of 7.7 per cent for 1970–87.

1985–88: economic recovery

The baht devaluation against the US dollar in November 1984,
coupled with other domestic structural adjustments for 1982–84,
apparently restored Thailand's competitiveness in the world
market and provided a solid foundation for an impressive
recovery since the middle of 1986. The world economic recovery
since 1985 has also boosted Thai exports and growth of the
Thai economy. As a result, growth rates of real GNP increased
from 3 per cent in 1985 to 8.6 per cent in 1987 and finally reached
11.1 per cent in 1988, the highest since 1970.

Economic recovery since mid-1986, and a continuous boom
in 1988–89, have totally changed the fiscal picture. The growth
rate of revenue jumped to 15 per cent in 1987 and to
approximately 25 per cent in 1988. However, fiscal restraint since
the structural adjustment period has kept growth rates of
government expenditures to 2.6 per cent in 1987 and
approximately 4 per cent in 1988. Government deficits have
rapidly declined and the government budget returned a surplus
in 1988.[5]

A summary of features of the tax system

This section discusses important features of the tax system
in Thailand, some drawn from Chaipat (1987). Because
approximately 90 per cent of tax revenue comes from the central
government, the discussion in this section is limited to the
central government tax system. It begins with the revenue share
of seven taxes: personal income, corporation income, business,
excise, import, export and other taxes, followed by a brief
description of each.

Revenue share

Table 6.3 presents the revenue share of seven types of tax for
the period 1970–88. The majority of tax revenue in Thailand

comes from indirect taxes. Business, excise and import taxes account for almost 75 per cent of total tax revenue; personal and corporation income taxes account for approximately 20 per cent; and export and other taxes for 3.4 and 2.1 per cent, respectively. However, the revenue share over time reveals an upward trend in personal income tax, corporation income tax and excise tax and a downward trend in import and export taxes. No clear trend is apparent for business and other taxes. This implies that the government is attempting to collect more revenue from direct taxes (personal and corporation income taxes) and sale taxes on selected items (excise tax). The government has also placed greater emphasis on improving Thailand's competitiveness in the world market by reducing export taxes and duties and by trying to reduce protection on domestic industries by lowering import duties and taxes. The reduction of export and import duties and taxes has been part of the structural adjustment programs since 1982.

Structure of selected taxes

The emphasis here is on personal income tax since its structure is more complicated and its importance is increasing as the economy develops.

Personal income tax

Personal income tax is collected from an individual, an ordinary partnership or an estate. The structure is quite complicated. The tax rate schedule, effective for income starting on 1 January 1989, contains rates ranging from 5 to 55 per cent over six income brackets (Table 6.4). It exempts many types of income and allows numerous deductions and credits. As a result, the structure of personal income tax has a narrow base and a highly progressive rate schedule. The assessable income for tax purposes includes earned income, interest, dividends, rent, self-employed income and income from business. For certain types of assessable income, taxpayers are allowed standard deductions which are a percentage of the corresponding assessable income. Some deductions have a cap or a maximum limit. For example, in 1989, earned income is allowed a 30 per cent standard deduction with a maximum limit of 50,000 baht. As a consequence, standard deductions (being a percentage of assessable income) effectively lower marginal tax rates applying to that income. Furthermore,

Table 6.3: Revenue share of various central government taxes, 1970 to 1988 (per cent)

	Total tax revenue (billions of baht) (1)	Personal income (2)	Corporation income (3)	Business (4)	Excise (5)	Import (6)	Export (7)	Other (8)
1970	15.645	8.3	5.8	23.6	19.5	34.5	5.4	2.9
1971	15.929	9.1	6.2	25.1	21.3	33.2	2.6	2.6
1972	17.447	8.9	5.8	24.9	22.3	32.2	2.3	3.6
1973	22.463	7.8	6.7	25.0	21.8	30.7	4.6	3.3
1974	32.872	6.4	8.5	22.8	20.5	25.5	15.2	1.3
1975	32.197	8.5	11.3	24.9	23.0	26.5	4.5	1.4
1976	36.184	8.4	10.3	25.8	24.1	26.3	3.8	1.4
1977	45.130	8.4	10.4	25.5	22.9	27.6	3.7	1.5
1978	55.005	9.7	11.7	24.8	21.9	26.7	3.5	1.6
1979	66.941	9.4	11.7	22.7	24.3	25.8	4.5	1.6
1980	80.611	9.0	11.9	22.8	26.4	24.1	4.2	1.5
1981	94.803	9.5	14.2	22.7	26.1	23.1	3.0	1.4
1982	99.053	12.1	12.9	22.7	28.5	20.4	1.8	1.6
1983	118.133	12.4	11.2	21.8	27.0	23.7	2.2	1.8
1984	130.311	13.2	11.2	23.2	26.3	22.8	1.4	2.0
1985	136.672	14.5	11.3	21.6	27.5	22.5	0.8	4.0
1986	143.638	13.4	10.8	19.6	32.3	21.7	0.6	1.7
1987	173.588	11.1	10.2	20.0	32.9	23.0	0.7	2.1
1988	230.511	10.6	11.9	22.5	26.5	25.4	0.4	2.7
Average for 1970–1987		10.0	10.2	23.3	25.0	26.1	3.4	2.1

Notes: Data on various types of taxes of the central government are from *Bank of Thailand* (various issues). For example, data for 1982–88 are from the issue of January 1989, Table 23, pp.34–5. Total tax revenue comprises personal income, corporation income, business, excise, import, export and other taxes but excludes items of fiscal monopolies, royalties, licences and fees that Bank of Thailand treats as

the amount of standard deductions varies from one type of assessable income to another. Effective marginal tax rate schedules are as numerous as the number of assessable income types.

The revenue code also allows taxpayers to deduct personal exemptions and itemized deductions. The allowable amounts of personal exemptions vary, depending on whether taxpayers are individuals, partnerships or estates. In 1989, the personal exemption was 15,000 baht, with another 15,000 baht for a spouse and an additional exemption of 7,000 baht for each child. The main feature of the exemption is that it is a per head allowance and the size of the allowance does not vary with the income of the taxpayer.

The allowance of itemized deductions is a way of using tax policy to encourage some specific activities relative to others. The five items allowed for deductions are charitable contributions, life insurance premiums, interest payments on loans for residential purposes, employee's contribution to a provident fund, and educational allowances for dependent children. Nevertheless, all itemized deductions are capped.

Taxable income is derived after subtracting deductions and exemptions from reported income. To obtain 'taxes before credit', the tax rate schedule is applied to taxable income. Tax credit for dividends paid by domestic companies is therefore deducted from 'taxes before credit' to arrive at 'taxes after credit'. This tax credit on dividends is a novel feature of the structure since it tends to reduce any adverse effect resulting from double taxation of both personal and corporate incomes.

The low tax rate is another interesting feature of the personal income-tax structure since it partially discourages tax evasion by excessively exploiting various deductions. The minimum tax rate is 0.5 per cent of the assessable income aside from earned income, without allowing for all deductions, exemptions and credits. Income brackets in the statutory tax rate schedule are stated in nominal terms; inflation tends to push taxpayers into higher tax brackets regardless of the fact that their real incomes may stay constant over time. Inflation also tends to reduce the real value of exemptions and certain deductions because they are stated in nominal terms and are not adjusted as quickly as the changes in inflation occur.

Table 6.4: Statutory vs effective marginal tax rates for selected types of assessable income, 1989 (per cent)

Net income class (thousands of baht) (1)	Statutory rates (2)	Effective marginal tax rates for		
		Earned income (3)	Interest income (4)	Dividends paid by domestic companies (5)
0–50	5	3.5	5	−23.5
50–166.67	10	7.0	10	−17.0
166.67–200	10	10.0	10	
200–500	20	20.0	10	−4.0
500–1000	30	30.0	15	9.0
1000–2000	40	40.0	15	22.0
Over 2000	55	55.0	15	41.5

Notes: Statutory rates in column (2) are from the Royal Decree No.15, B.E. 2532. Effective marginal tax rates for earned income in column (3) are 70 per cent of the statutory rates for the net income class of 0–166,666 baht since a standard deduction rate for earned income is 30 per cent. When the net income is greater than 166,666 baht, the standard deduction hits the ceiling of 50,000 baht and the effective rates are the same as the statutory rates.

Though no deductions are allowed for interest income, taxpayers may elect to pay a 15 per cent tax rate on certain kinds of interest income such as interest on government bonds and on time deposits with commercial banks in Thailand. This option is not taken by taxpayers whose net income is below 200,000 baht because the corresponding statutory tax rates would be below 15 per cent. However, for taxpayers whose net income is over 200,000 baht, this option reduces the effective marginal tax rates for interest income from 20–55 per cent to the rate of 15 per cent.

Dividend income paid by domestic companies, though not allowed standard deductions, is the only type of income that receives tax credit. In 1989, the tax credit was at 30 per cent, the same rate of corporation income tax if the corporation has been listed on the Securities Exchange in Thailand. This tax credit is first treated as part of the assessable income for the purpose of calculating taxes before credit. Then, the same amount of tax credit is deducted from taxes before credit to arrive at the taxes after credit. As a result, the effective marginal tax rate is negative for the net income class below 500,000 baht.

Corporate income tax

Corporate income tax is subject to the criticism that it is double taxation—that is, a tax is levied first on corporation profits and then again on dividends received by individuals. This criticism does not apply fully to corporation income tax in Thailand since individuals receive a tax credit of 30 per cent on dividends earned. Further, realized capital gains earned from trading stocks in the Securities Exchange of Thailand (SET) are free from personal income tax. Another feature of Thai corporation income tax is that it does not provide investment tax credit nor accelerated depreciation allowance, as provided by US tax laws, which generally widen effective tax rates across firms and industries though the statutory tax rate is uniform.

Corporate income tax is collected from legally incorporated companies or partnerships on their net profits or income or other proxies such as sales. The income-tax base for large corporations is generally net profits whose tax rate is currently at 30 per cent when listed on the SET and at 35 per cent when not listed. Gross receipts or sales are usually used as a proxy for the income-tax base of small companies whose accounting practices are inadequate. From an economic viewpoint, a tax on gross receipts or sales of small companies is basically a sales tax rather than an income tax and the rate on gross receipts or sales is 5 per cent. There are other types of proxies for corporation income but the income taxes generated from these are insignificant (Chaipat 1987: 34–9).

The corporation income tax structure has been complicated by the investment privileges provided by the Board of Investment (BOI). These privileges granted by the Investment Promotion Act include a period of income-tax holidays and an exemption from import taxes on machinery and equipment. They reduce government revenue and redistribute scarce resources between promoted and non-promoted firms. Another problem with the structure of corporation income tax relates to the depreciation allowance. Depreciation is based on historical costs and is understated during periods of inflation and, therefore, the net profit is overstated, resulting in some tax on the capital itself.

Business tax

Business tax in Thailand is a general sales tax and is mostly collected from importers and producers of goods and services on their gross receipts, because of low administration costs. The rates vary, depending on the type of business, type of taxpayer, and stage of production. There are fourteen categories of businesses subject to the tax and rates range from 1 to 50 per cent. Since the tax is collected from importers and manufacturers, the effective tax rate tends to escalate as goods move to the retail level.[6] To overcome the escalation effect, the Ministry of Finance has proposed replacing most of the business tax with a value-added tax (VAT). The disadvantage of VAT is that, to obtain a rebate for taxes on purchases from other firms, each firm requires a good book-keeping and invoice system, which tends to increase their compliance costs.

Excise tax

Excise tax, like business tax, is another form of consumption tax which is levied on the sale of a particular commodity or group of commodities. In Thailand this tax is collected from domestic producers and importers of the following nine commodities: petroleum and petroleum products, tobacco, spirits, non-alcoholic beverages, cement, matches, mechanical lighters, snuff, and playing cards. These commodity taxes are levied at specific rates (for example, baht per litre of gasoline or per gram of tobacco) and at ad valorem rates (for example, 38 per cent of retail price). The applicable rate depends on whichever tax rate generates the higher tax revenue. Only three of the above commodities contribute a substantial share to the total excise tax—petroleum and petroleum products, tobacco and spirits (Chaipat 1987: 57–74).

Import duties

For the purpose of product identification, the Customs Department of Thailand sets out the classification of imports based on the Harmonized Commodity Description and Coding System, effective from 1 January 1988. Tax rates used for imports are, for some commodities, ad valorem and, for others, specific. Several commodities use both ad valorem and specific tax rates. The tax rate for any given year differs from one type of commodity to another and the rate for any given commodity may also differ over time. The Customs Department occasionally issues Customs Tariff Decrees to modify the schedule of import tariff rates.

Some imported commodities are subject to relatively high tariff rates in order to protect domestic industries, for example tobacco (1988 tariff rate of 50 per cent) and passenger cars (1988 tariff rate of 200 per cent). Other imported commodities are subject to relatively low tariff rates such as raw materials or essential production inputs, for example cotton (1988 tariff rate of 5 per cent).

Export taxes
Very few items are at present subject to export tariffs. In 1990 there were seven of them: rice and glutinous rice in various forms (rate temporarily set at zero); metal scraps of every kind; rawhides of bovine animals; rubber in various forms; certain kinds of wood and sawn wood; raw-silk and silk yarn; and pulverized or baked fish unfit for human consumption. The policy of not taxing most exports increases the international competitiveness of Thai exports in the world market. Among the taxed items, rubber duties now generate most of the total export duties.

Selected features of government expenditures

This section describes changes in the composition of government expenditures over the period 1970–88. It looks mainly at changes in the shares of the composition as shown in Tables 6.5 and 6.6.

One way to break down government expenditure is to look at the national income accounts where some items have a direct effect on aggregate output and some do not. The former category can broadly be called purchases of goods and services. The latter category comprises subsidies, transfer payments and interest payments on public debt. As shown in Table 6.5, government purchases (column 1) accounted for an average of 87.8 per cent of government expenditure from 1970–88; interest payments (column 3), 9.5 per cent; and subsidies and transfer payments (column 2), 2.7 per cent. Interestingly, the shares of both subsidies/transfer payments and interest payments have increased steadily over time. An increase in the share of

Table 6.5: Expenditure share of the general government, 1970 to 1987 (per cent)

	Purchases of goods and services (1)	Subsidies and transfers (2)	Interest on public debt (3)	Consumption (4)	Investment (5)	Compensation of employees (6)
1970	93.8	0.7	5.5	63.2	30.6	35.9
1971	92.9	0.9	6.2	61.4	31.5	35.9
1972	91.6	0.4	8.0	60.3	31.3	37.5
1973	90.2	0.8	9.0	62.4	27.8	38.9
1974	89.9	1.5	8.6	65.6	24.4	44.3
1975	90.9	2.2	6.8	61.9	29.1	41.2
1976	91.5	2.5	6.0	59.3	32.2	36.0
1977	90.1	3.1	6.7	59.6	30.5	35.6
1978	90.5	2.5	7.1	64.2	26.2	37.9
1979	89.8	2.4	7.8	66.4	23.4	38.6
1980	87.1	4.8	8.1	60.3	26.8	37.7
1981	86.7	3.4	10.0	65.9	20.7	37.4
1982	85.2	4.1	10.7	63.4	21.8	39.2
1983	82.6	5.7	11.7	64.3	18.3	41.7
1984	84.6	2.2	13.1	65.0	25.3	39.7
1985	82.4	3.7	14.0	65.8	16.5	39.6
1986	81.5	2.6	15.9	63.7	17.8	39.9
1987	79.6	4.3	16.1	66.2	13.4	41.2
Average for 1970–1987	87.8	2.7	9.5	63.3	24.9	38.8

Notes: Data on components of government expenditures used to calculate percentage shares are from the Appendix Table. Theoretically, columns (1)+(2)+(3) = 100 per cent, columns (4)+(5) = column (1), and column (6) is part of column (4). However, this may not be exactly

subsidies/transfer payments is partly because the government has put more emphasis on public welfare, while an increase in the share of interest payments is because of rapid expansion of the public debt in the 1980s and because interest rates on the public debt were relatively high in the early 1980s.

Looking at the composition of government purchases, government consumption (column 4 of Table 6.5) averaged 63.3 per cent of government expenditures over the 1970 to 1987 period with no clear trend. In fact, the percentage share of government consumption was relatively stable over this period because approximately 60 per cent of government consumption came from the stable item of compensation of employees (column 6 of Table 6.5).

By contrast, the share of public investment in GDP declined in the 1980s. This is partly because the government put a ceiling on public borrowing when revenue was depressed by the slow economy during the early 1980s and government expenditures were constrained. Since the government could not easily cut down its consumption, public investment was cut or deferred.

When classified by major functions for 1980–88, defence accounted for the largest share of total government consumption (approximately one-third). When expressed relative to GNP, defence expenditures accounted for only an average of 3.8 per cent (column 9 of Table 6.6). Of the non-defence consumption (columns 3–8 of Table 6.6), general administration accounted for approximately a quarter of total government consumption, with a downward trend over the 1970–87 period. Another quarter went to education and research with an upward trend. The other four items—justice and police, health and special welfare services, transport and communication facilities, and other services—together accounted for an average of approximately 20 per cent. Consistent with the increase in subsidies and transfer payments over time discussed above, the share of health and special welfare services rose but the share of transport and communication facilities declined significantly.

Conclusions: fiscal discipline

This chapter has provided both an overview of fiscal policy in Thailand since 1970 and a detailed examination of some of

Table 6.6: Composition of government consumption classified by major functions, 1970 to 1987 (per cent)

Year	Defence	Non-defence	Share of government consumption						Ratio of defence to GNP
			General administration	Justice and police	Education and research	Health and special welfare services	Transport and communication facilities	Other services	
	(1)	(2)	(3)	(4)	(5)	(6)	(7)	(8)	(9)
1970	30.3	69.7	29.9	8.3	18.8	4.6	7.2	0.9	3.4
1971	30.6	69.4	28.2	8.5	19.8	5.0	7.0	0.9	3.5
1972	29.8	70.2	27.8	8.6	22.0	5.0	5.9	1.0	3.3
1973	31.3	68.7	26.1	8.9	22.2	5.0	5.7	1.0	3.1
1974	29.2	70.8	24.8	9.6	25.2	5.1	4.8	1.2	2.7
1975	26.5	73.5	24.2	9.0	25.5	5.5	8.0	1.3	2.7
1976	29.0	71.0	22.5	8.2	23.9	6.7	8.4	1.3	3.2
1977	33.4	66.6	23.0	8.2	22.9	6.7	4.4	1.3	3.6
1978	34.3	65.7	21.3	8.6	24.4	6.3	3.9	1.2	3.9
1979	36.1	63.9	21.4	7.9	23.7	6.3	3.4	1.2	4.4
1980	32.2	67.8	23.7	7.7	25.5	6.1	3.4	1.4	4.0
1981	34.3	65.7	24.3	7.4	23.4	6.1	3.3	1.2	4.4
1982	31.8	68.2	22.0	8.0	26.8	6.8	3.2	1.4	4.3
1983	31.6	68.4	21.5	8.4	27.2	7.4	2.8	1.2	4.1
1984	32.1	67.9	20.6	8.3	27.8	7.4	2.5	1.4	4.3
1985	33.6	66.4	19.8	8.7	27.1	7.6	2.1	1.1	4.8

	(1)	(2)	(3)	(4)	(5)	(6)	(7)	(8)
1980	31.5	68.5	19.8	8.1	29.0	7.7	2.3	1.7	4.2
1987	31.7	68.3	19.5	7.4	29.3	7.8	2.2	2.1	4.1
Average for 1970–1987	31.6	68.4	23.4	8.3	24.7	6.3	4.5	1.3	3.8

Notes: Data on government consumption, its classification by major functions and GNP used to calculate share and ratio are from National Economic and Social Development Board (no date), Table 2, pp.18–19 and Table 42, pp.86–87.
Theoretically, columns (1)+(2) = 100 per cent and columns (3)+(4)+(5)+(6)+(7)+(8) = column (2). However, this may not be the case due to rounding.

its components. The size of general government expenditures and revenue (central and local governments but excluding state enterprises) has been small when compared with the size of the economy proxied by gross national product (GNP). The ratio of government revenue or expenditures to GNP was below 20 per cent during the study period. The average size of public debt relative to GNP was also comfortable at approximately 13 per cent from 1970 to 1988. However, as the economy has developed, the size of fiscal policy variables has also been increasing. For example, the ratio of public debt to GNP was slightly over 20 per cent in 1988. Nevertheless, it is still low by international standards.

The main reason for the relatively small size of fiscal policy variables is the fiscal discipline of Thai governments since the early 1970s. They have tended to keep their expenditures in line with revenue generated, resulting in only minimum or moderate borrowing at home and abroad. Therefore, it is not surprising that Thailand has never been considered by the international community to be a heavily indebted country. With a relatively small amount of public debt, there has been no need for the Thai government to finance its debt by printing money and therefore monetary policy can be used for other objectives.

In the absence of this link between public debt and money printing, hyperinflation has been unknown in the recent economic history of Thailand, and the exchange rate between the baht and the US dollar has been relatively stable for more than three decades.

...ment, 1970 to 1976 (millions of baht)

	Line	1970	1971	1972	1973	1974	1975	1976
Revenue	1	20,757	21,506	23,506	29,359	41,949	42,824	47,936
Direct taxes on households[a]	2	1,146	1,597	1,712	1,950	2,301	2,986	3,413
Direct taxes on corporations	3	903	981	1,006	1,503	2,789	3,629	3,733
Indirect taxes	4	16,097	16,541	18,341	23,305	32,864	32,657	36,315
Income from property and entrepreneurship[b]	5	1,091	1,259	1,359	1,639	2,853	2,743	2,803
Transfers from households, corporations and foreigners	6	1,250	1,128	1,088	962	1,142	1,809	1,672
Expenditures	7	26,238	28,787	30,789	34,667	39,780	40,554	64,091
Purchases of goods and services[c]	8	24,607	26,742	28,204	31,259	35,774	45,977	58,666
Consumption	9	16,578	17,676	18,572	21,635	26,085	31,290	38,009
Compensation of employees	10	9,422	10,347	11,543	13,480	17,612	20,848	23,103
Other consumption[c]	11	7,156	7,329	7,029	8,155	8,473	10,442	14,906
Investment[d]	12	8,029	9,066	9,632	9,624	9,689	14,687	20,657
Subsidies and transfer payments	13	189	255	133	273	580	1,122	1,609
Subsidies	14	⋮	⋮	⋮	⋮	383	815	1,081
Transfer payments to households and foreigners	15	189	255	133	273	197	307	528
Interest on public debt	16	1,442	1,790	2,460	3,135	3,426	3,455	3,816
Surplus (+) or deficit (-)	17	-5,481	-7,281	-7,291	-5,308	2,169	-6,730	-16,155
Public debt (excluding government's guarantee obligation)[e]	18	27,316	32,990	42,427	47,340	45,861	48,031	60,696
Held by government agencies[f]	19	15,889	18,919	42,427	47,340	45,861	48,031	60,696
Held by private, domestic investors[g]	20	7,755	10,094	15,977	17,352	18,153	20,606	24,692
Held by foreigners[h] (or government external debt)	21	3,671	3,978	4,369	4,879	4,986	4,819	7,121

Appendix Table: *continued*

	Line	1977	1978	1979	1980	1981	1982
Revenue	1	59,526	72,261	87,377	109,302	125,774	161,485
Direct taxes on households[a]	2	4,217	5,723	6,736	7,831	9,647	12,821
Direct taxes on corporations	3	4,696	6,459	7,857	9,625	13,467	12,881
Indirect taxes	4	46,051	4,296	66,052	81,662	88,768	93,465
Income from property and entrepreneurship[b]	5	2,801	3,310	3,565	5,315	8,075	7,884
Transfers from households, corporations and foreigners	6	1,761	2,473	3,167	4,869	5,817	5,689
Expenditures	7	71,984	84,976	100,531	134,960	147,134	173,860
Purchases of goods and services[c]	8	64,881	76,866	90,289	117,592	127,506	148,094
Consumption	9	42,923	54,583	66,798	81,431	96,981	110,162
Compensation of employees	10	25,617	32,241	38,783	50,826	55,033	68,069
Other consumption[c]	11	17,306	22,342	28,015	30,605	41,948	42,093
Investment[d]	12	21,958	22,283	23,491	36,161	30,525	37,932
Subsidies and transfer payments	13	2,267	2,099	2,449	6,439	4,938	7,125
Subsidies	14	1,271	1,339	1,556	5,439	3,997	6,091
Transfer payments to households and foreigners	15	996	760	893	1,000	941	1,034
Interest on public debt	16	4,836	6,011	7,793	10,929	14,690	18,641
Surplus (+) or deficit (-)	17	-12,458	-12,715	-13,154	-25,658	-21,360	-41,120
Public debt (excluding government's guarantee obligation)[e]	18	72,596	92,078	113,381	140,035	168,838	209,503
Held by government agencies[f]	19	37,211	46,556	56,997	68,675	79,396	90,312
Held by private, domestic investors[g]	20	27,160	30,625	33,170	41,105	48,059	700,059
... for government		41,383			30,255	41,383	49,132

Line		1983	1984	1985	1986	1987	1988
	Revenue						
1	Direct taxes on households[a]	167,033	178,119	178,119	192,567	223,815	289,061
2	Direct taxes on corporations	15,621	18,168	20,887	20,345	20,949	26,602
3	Indirect taxes	13,325	14,753	15,526	15,705	18,003	27,908
4	Income from property and entrepreneurship[b]	114,162	119,089	12,071	133,149	159,573	208,399
5	Transfers from households, corporations and foreigners	13,224	8,491	13,273	15,737	17,325	17,045
6		5,153	6,532	7,732	7,729	8,766	9,107
	Expenditures						
7	Purchases of goods and services[c]	184,309	200,216	217,085	226,717	232,676	243,500
8	Consumption	152,230	169,443	178,793	184,779	184,728	196,343
9	Compensation of employees	118,572	130,095	142,917	144,594	147,410	156,703
10	Other consumption[c]	76,787	79,386	85,965	90,419	94,579	101,383
11	Investment[d]	41,785	50,709	56,952	54,175	52,831	53,320
12	Subsidies and transfer payments	33,658	39,348	35,876	40,185	37,310	39,640
13	Subsidies	10,560	4,470	8,001	7,371	11,281	7,123
14	Transfer payments to households and foreigners	9,656	3,381	6,784	6,100	9,892	5,419
15	Interest on public debt	904	1,089	1,217	1,271	1,389	1,704
16	Surplus (+) or deficit (−)	21,519	26,303	30,291	35,933	36,667	40,034
17	Public debt (excluding government's guarantee obligation)[e]	−22,824	−33,183	−38,960	−35,516	−8,861	45,561
18	Held by government agencies[f]	242,532	292,923	351,136	413,596	451,228	437,942
19	Held by private, domestic investors[g]	106,483	109,481	127,665	147,038	152,670	126,704
20	Held by foreigners[h] (or government external debt)	79,332	109,663	121,558	154,197	169,541	178,174
21		56,717	73,779	101,883	112,361	129,107	133,064

Appendix Table: *continued*

Notes: Line 1 = lines 2+3+4+5+6; Line 7 = line 1–line 17; Line 13 = line 14 + line 15; Line 8 = line 7–13–16; and Line 12 = line 8–line 9.

a Including private non-profit institution.

b Profit of government enterprises, rent, interest, dividend and other unclassified items.

c Purchases from enterprises and foreigners less purchases by households and enterprises.

d Estimated as residuals; lines 7, 8 and 12 may include other unclassified items plus errors and omissions.

e Data on public debt are taken at the end of December.

f Government bonds and treasury bills held by Bank of Thailand, Government Savings Bank and Exchange Equalization Fund plus IBRD loans participation certificates held by Bank of Thailand plus promissory notes held by Government Savings Bank.

g Commercial banks, financial institutions and other domestic sectors.

h Baht equivalent.

Sources: Data on lines 2, 3, 4, 5, 6, 9, 10, 11, 14, 15 and 16 are from National Economic and Social Development Board (no date), Table 57, pp. 110–11, Account 5, pp. 10–11 and Table 42, pp. 86–7. Data on line 17 and lines 18–21 are from *Bank of Thailand* (various issues); for example, those for 1983–88 are from the issue of January 1989, Table 25, pp. 35–7, line 3, Tables 26 and 27, pp. 38–9.

Notes to Chapter 6

1 Note that Thailand's fiscal year starts in October and ends in September of the following calendar year.

2 Public debts held by government agencies, such as the Bank of Thailand and the Government Savings Bank, are not taken to be real liabilities of the government since profit earnings of these agencies are transferred back to the government.

3 See Chaipat et al. (1989: Table 1.3, p. 13).

4 In 1989, the ceiling was raised to US$1.2 billion.

5 The government cut personal income tax rates and raised the public payroll in 1989 to pass on some of the surplus to the public and government employees.

6 For discussions on the pyramid effect of business tax see Chaipat (1987: 48–54) and Thailand Development Research Institute (1987T). For more discussions on VAT, see for example, Ando et al. (1985: 174–6) and Thailand Development Research Institute (1987T).

7

Commercial Banking

NARIS CHAIYASOOT

The Thai financial system is unusual in the crucial role played by its commercial banks. As with most countries of similar economic development, Thailand's financial system includes a wide range of institutions (Table 7.1), but unlike most, its commercial banks have maintained their dominant role since the end of World War II. As Goldsmith (1969) observed, commercial banks' shares in assets normally decline as a country's financial system develops, and more specialized financial institutions begin operating. In Thailand, however, in terms of total assets, total savings mobilized and total credit extended, the shares of commercial banks have remained high (Figure 7.1). In 1987, for example, they stood at 69 per cent, 73 per cent and 76 per cent, respectively. This chapter provides an overview of the development of commercial banking in Thailand, its structure, its sources of funds and its performance.

The development of commercial banking

Foreign banks dominated the early history of commercial banking in Thailand. In 1888, a branch of the British-owned Hong Kong and Shanghai Banking Corporation was established in Bangkok. The Chartered Bank (British) and the Banque de L'Indochine (French) followed, respectively. These foreign banks were primarily engaged in financing European trade. The first indigenous bank, the Siam Commercial Bank, was founded by Prince Chaiyanantamongkol in 1906 (Pannee 1986[T]). Others mostly Chinese local banks, were established later, mainly to support Chinese rice milling and exporting businesses and to transmit remittances to mainland China. The Thai commercial banks generally lacked trained personnel and played a minor role compared with European banks.

European bankers had only scant knowledge of native languages and local business conditions, and thus employed local people, mostly prominent Chinese businessmen, as their compradores. The European banks prospered under this system. Their main function was to attract business and act as guarantors for all loans advanced by the banks. They received commissions on the volume of loans made.

This buoyant period for European banks ended with World War II. In 1942, Thailand sided with Japan and declared war against the Allies. All foreign banks, except the sole Japanese bank, were forced to suspend operations, and this provided an opportunity for five Thai banks to replace them. These Thai banks flourished during the war because there was a shift in

Figure 7.1 Share of commercial banks' assets in total assets of all financial institutions, 1971 to 1987

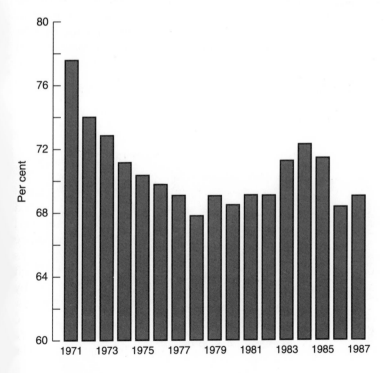

Table 7.1: Thai financial institutions, 1987

	Year operations began	No. of institutions	No. of branches	Deposits equivalent[a]	Borrowing[a]
1. Commercial banks	1888	30	1,986[b]	752,568	73,124
2. Finance companies	1969	94	36	96,933	23,029
3. Life insurance companies	1929	12	732	20,413	24
4. Agricultural cooperatives	1916	(1157)[c]	...	(602)	(4,474)
5. Savings cooperatives	1946	(732)	...	(2,878)	(513)
6. Pawnshops	1866	336	n.a.,	n.a.	3,184
7. Credit finance companies	1969	21	...	1,989	1,051
8. Government Savings Bank	1946	1	470[d]	19,641	...
9. Bank of Agriculture and Agricultural Cooperatives (BAAC)	1966	1	70	19,641	9,757
10. Industrial Finance Corporation of Thailand (IFCT)	1959	1	6	...	7,412
11. Government Housing Bank	1953	1	2	7,838	4,160
12. Small Industrial Finance Office[d]	1964	...	...	...	...
Total		2,284	3,302	1,002,082	148,053

	Household savings[a]	Capital account[a]	Credit extended[a]	Investment[a]	Total assets[a]
1. Commercial banks	588,728	57,469	672,906	127,780	920,095
2. Finance companies	60,272	10,885	116,182	22,887	159,955
3. Life insurance companies	20,413	459	7,652	9,818	24,951
4. Agricultural cooperatives	(2,506)	(3,790)	(8,097)	(192)	(11,248)
5. Savings cooperatives	(19,858)	(20,360)	(21,563)	(496)	24,348
6. Pawnshops	n.a	(1,400)	(4,800)	n.a	(5,400)
7. Credit finance companies	1,989	596	2,441	255	3,834
8. Government Savings Bank	96,897	5,555	3,634	86,834	111,533
9. Bank of Agriculture and Agricultural Cooperatives (BAAC)	4,524	2,067	25,104	..	33,515
10. Industrial Finance Corporation of Thailand (IFCT)	..	-3,010	8,679	264	22,552
11. Government Housing Bank	7,833	2,183	12,671	20	15,441
12. Small Industrial Finance Office[e]	..	57	42	..	57
Total	803,025	107,835	883,776	248,550	1,333,013

a Units in millions of baht, current prices.
b Not including head offices of 16 Thai banks and 14 foreign banks in Thailand.
c Figures in parentheses are estimates.
d Including four amphur (district) agencies.
e At end of September 1987.
Source: Bank of Thailand.

foreign trade from Europe to Japan and neighbouring occupied countries (Manas 1982). In addition, the Bank of Thailand imposed the requirement that all export proceeds be sold to it with an authorized commercial bank's guarantee that exporters had conformed to the Thai law. Thai commercial banks gained handsome commissions on the export proceeds, and the Thai banking business expanded.

After the war, additional banks were established or re-established by native entrepreneurs and foreigners. In 1955, the Thai cabinet passed a resolution calling for restraint on the approval of new banks (Emery 1970) and it became difficult for local entrepreneurs to acquire licences. Foreign banks were not allowed to open new banks if their countries were already represented by banking businesses in Thailand. Exceptions were only made where reciprocal banking agreements promised to be mutually beneficial. This protection provided an opportunity for commercial banks incorporated in Thailand to grow without serious competition, and to become involved in activities beyond remittances and financing of foreign trade. Their operations soon surpassed those of foreign banks in terms of the value of deposits, capital and credit extended. As shown in Tables 7.2 and 7.3, there were 16 banks incorporated in Thailand in 1986 and 14 banks incorporated abroad. By the middle of 1988, the share of assets, deposits and credit extended by Thai commercial banks was 96, 98 and 95 per cent, respectively, of the overall banking sector in Thailand (Table 7.4). Some economists have argued that there is a tendency to underestimate the importance of foreign banks by considering only the size of assets (Skully 1984); but the foreign banks in Thailand are only engaged in certain areas of wholesale banking. Moreover, much of this business is conducted offshore and is not reflected in local asset holding. This chapter concentrates on the operations and structure of banks incorporated in Thailand.

The structure of the banking sector

Several studies have examined the degree of concentration in the Thai banking industry (Supoj 1976; Nampech 1979[T]; Direk and Pairoj 1982[T]; Amnuey 1984[T]; Yokporn 1986[T]). From the more recent data in Table 7.5 it can be seen that the Bangkok Bank

Table 7.2: Commercial banks incorporated in Thailand, 1986

Bank	Year of opening
1. Siam Commercial Bank	1906
2. Nakornthon Bank[a]	1933
3. First City Bank of Bangkok[b]	1934
4. Bank of Asia	1939
5. Siam City Bank	1941
6. Bangkok Bank of Commerce	1944
7. Bangkok Bank	1944
8. Bank of Ayudhya	1945
9. Thai Farmers Bank	1945
10. Laem Thong Bank	1948
11. Union Bank of Bangkok	1949
12. Thai Danu Bank	1949
13. Bangkok Metropolitan Bank	1950
14. Thai Military Bank	1957
15. Siam Bank[c]	1965
16. Krung Thai Bank[d]	1966

[a] Formerly called the Wang Lee Bank (until April 1985).
[b] Originally called the Tan Peng Chun Bank, but later renamed the Thai Development Bank (1977).
[c] Formerly called the Asia Trust Bank (until 6 December 1985) when the government took it over.
[d] Established in March 1966 as a result of a merger between the Bank of Agriculture (founded in 1950) and the Provincial Bank (founded in 1943).
Source: Bank of Thailand.

dominates approximately one-third of the Thai banking sector. The Thai Farmers Bank and the Krung Thai Bank also have large shares. The assets of the first four major banks taken together account for more than three-fifths of the banking industry. The same result is obtained by examining the shares of deposits and credit extended. This indicates that a degree of concentration prevails, even though, in terms of the four main banks, this concentration has not increased significantly over the past decade.

Supoj (1976) claims that two factors are involved in the concentration of banking in Thailand. He argues that the larger banks are able to keep expanding because they can site new offices in productive areas and channel the funds back to head

Table 7.3: Commercial banks incorporated abroad with branches in Thailand, 1986

Bank	Nationality	Year of opening
1. Hong Kong and Shanghai Bank	British	1888
2. Standard Chartered Bank[a]	British	1894
3. Indosuez Bank	French	1897
4. Four Seas Communication Bank	Singapore	1906
5. Bank of Canton	Chinese	1919
6. City Bank[b]	American	1923
7. Bank of China	Taiwanese	1947
8. Bharat Overseas Bank	Indian	1947
9. Bank of American NT & SA	American	1949
10. Mitsui Bank	Japanese	1952
11. Bank of Tokyo	Japanese	1962
12. Chase Manhattan Bank	American	1964
13. United Malayan Banking Corp.	Malaysian	1964
14. European Asian Bank	German	1978

[a] Formerly called the Chartered Bank.
[b] The City Bank replaced the Mercantile Bank.
Source: Bank of Thailand.

Table 7.4: Number of branches, assets, deposits and credit extended, commercial banks in Thailand, 1989

Bank	Number of branches[b]	Total assets[c]	Total deposits[c]	Credit extended[c]
		(millions of baht)		
Commercial banks	2,098	1,252,693	942,780	907,479
Thai banks	2,082	(96)[a]	(98)	(95)
Foreign banks	16	(4)	(2)	(5)

[a] Figures in parentheses are percentage share of total.
[b] At the end of May 1989.
[c] At the end of December 1988.
Source: Bank of Thailand.

Table 7.5: Shares of assets, deposits and credit extended, commercial banks incorporated in Thailand, 1979 to 1988 (per cent)

	Assets					
	1979	1981	1983	1985	1987	1988
Bangkok Bank	36.8	36.8	33.5	33.5	30.4	29.6
Thai Farmers Bank	13.7	12.7	13.4	13.4	13.3	13.2
Krung Thai Bank	13.0	13.4	11.9	11	14.9	14.9
Siam Commercial Bank	5.7	6.8	8.2	8.2	8.9	8.7
Bank of Ayudhya	4.6	4.5	4.7	4.7	5.5	5.9
Thai Military Bank	2.9	3.6	4.8	4.8	5.6	5.9
Bangkok Metropolitan Bank	4.6	4.4	4.3	4.3	3.9	3.8
Bangkok Bank of Commerce	4.4	4.2	3.8	3.8	3.4	3.2
Siam City Bank	3.0	2.9	3.6	3.6	3.6	3.9
First City Bank of Bangkok	3.6	3.2	3.5	3.5	3.8	4.0
Siam Bank	2.0	1.7	2.2	2.2	:	:
Bank of Asia	2.0	2.2	2.0	2.0	2.5	2.7
Union Bank	1.6	1.5	1.6	1.6	1.6	1.6
Thai Danu Bank	1.0	1.0	1.0	1.0	1.1	1.2
Nakornthon Bank	0.5	0.6	0.7	0.7	0.8	0.9
Laem Thong Bank	0.6	0.6	0.5	0.5	0.5	0.4

Table 7.5: *continued*

	Deposits				
	1981	1983	1985	1987	1988
Bangkok Bank	35.3	35.6	32.4	28.7	29.2
Thai Farmers Bank	14.0	13.0	14.3	14.4	13.8
Krung Thai Bank	13.9	14.1	13.1	15.4	15.8
Siam Commercial Bank	5.7	7.0	8.7	9.7	9.1
Bank of Ayudhya	5.0	4.8	5.1	5.4	5.7
Thai Military Bank	3.2	3.6	4.6	5.9	6.1
Bangkok Metropolitan Bank	4.1	4.0	3.7	3.6	3.5
Bangkok Bank of Commerce	5.1	4.9	4.3	3.8	3.5
Siam City Bank	3.4	3.3	3.8	3.5	3.5
First City Bank of Bangkok	2.9	2.6	2.8	3.2	3.2
Siam Bank	1.7	1.3	1.4	:	:
Bank of Asia	2.1	2.2	2.2	2.3	2.3
Union Bank	1.6	1.6	1.7	1.7	1.6
Thai Danu Bank	0.9	0.9	1.0	1.2	1.2
Nakornthon Bank	0.3	0.5	0.7	0.8	0.9
Laem Thong Bank	0.6	0.5	0.4	0.4	0.4

Credit extended

	1981	1983	1985	1987	1988
Bangkok Bank	40.1	39.2	35.4	33.3	31.6
Thai Farmers Bank	14.1	13.2	13.5	13.2	13.0
Krung Thai Bank	11.2	11.8	10.9	13.0	12.9
Siam Commercial Bank	5.7	7.0	8.4	8.3	8.5
Bank of Ayudhya	4.4	4.6	4.8	5.9	6.4
Thai Military Bank	2.8	3.5	4.8	5.4	5.7
Bangkok Metropolitan Bank	4.5	4.5	4.2	3.9	3.8
Bangkok Bank of Commerce	3.9	3.7	3.7	3.4	3.2
Siam City Bank	2.8	2.8	3.4	3.4	3.9
First City Bank of Bangkok	3.3	2.8	3.5	3.7	3.9
Siam Bank	1.8	1.3	1.8	··	··
Bank of Asia	1.3	2.0	1.9	2.4	2.8
Union Bank	1.5	1.5	1.6	1.6	1.6
Thai Danu Bank	1.0	1.0	1.1	1.1	1.3
Nakornthon Bank	0.5	0.6	0.6	0.7	0.9
Laem Thong Bank	0.7	0.6	0.5	0.5	0.5

Source: Computed from data released by the Bank of Thailand.

office. These funds can then be re-used for establishing new bank offices and so a pattern of circular growth develops.

The second factor is the growing demand for banking services, measured in terms of advances offered by banks. This argument contrasts with conventional economic theory which would predict a negative relationship between growth of demand and concentration. As demand grows, prices increase and attract new entrants. These new entrants, in conjunction with the already established firms, serve to reduce the level of concentration. But Supoj (1976) argues that in Thailand, where regulations are enforced against the entry of new commercial banks, a different dynamic arises. He claims that the major banks enjoy increasing market shares because they are already endowed with the advantages of size and efficiency. His argument needs empirical support, however, because a 1984 study revealed that the smallest Thai bank, Laem Thong, was far more efficient than the fourth largest, the Siam Commercial Bank (Amnuey 1984: 39^T).

Besides a concentration in market shares, there is also concentration in terms of ownership. Many of the local commercial banks that were incorporated during the pre- and post-war years were owned by Chinese groups holding Thai citizenship. Initially, each bank was owned by many families, usually belonging to the same dialect group (Suehiro 1985). In the 1960s and early 1970s, there was a shift towards industrial family-controlled banks. The Sophonpanich family became the largest shareholder in the Bangkok Bank in the 1960s. The same was true for the Lamsam family and the Ratanarak family, who control the Thai Farmers Bank and the Bank of Ayudhya, respectively. The Tejapaibul family became the major shareholders in the Bangkok Metropolitan Bank and the Bank of Asia in the 1970s.

It is notable that the shares in deposits of the four major family-owned banks increased over time from 32 per cent in 1962 to 59 per cent in 1972, and remained at 56 per cent in 1988. This means a concentration of deposits as well as capital in the banks owned by these four major families. The Thai government has equity in the Thai banking business and is the major shareholder of the Krung Thai Bank and Siam Bank. It also holds minor shares in the Bangkok Bank, Siam Commercial Bank, Bank of Ayudhya, First Bangkok City Bank and the Union

Bank of Bangkok. The political implications of this degree of government involvement are explored in Krirkkiat (1987[T]). The Crown Property Bureau also has a large share in the Siam Commercial Bank.

Concern about concentration in the banking industry led the Thai monetary authorities to seek ways to reduce it. In the early 1970s, policies were adopted to encourage the entry of more finance companies and place more competitive pressure on the commercial banks. The policy failed because many of the finance companies had Thai banks as major shareholders. Nine of Thailand's ten largest finance companies are affiliated to the four major banking groups and the Siam Commercial Bank group (henceforth called the 'five major banking groups'). As well as having large shareholdings in many finance companies, these five major banking groups have also invested in other financial firms, for example credit financiers, life and non-life insurance companies, and investment companies. In 1980, the volume of assets belonging to these five major banking groups was estimated at 265 billion baht, representing 62 per cent of the total assets of all financial firms in the country. This indicates a significant degree of financial concentration in Thailand. There is also the possibility of a biased loan portfolio as these five major banking groups engage in other non-banking activities. In 1979, these five major banking groups were already investing in 225 non-financial firms.

Other measures to reduce concentration included capital divestiture requirements. In 1979, amendments were made to the Commercial Banking Act of 1962 which made it illegal for a major shareholder to hold more than 5 per cent of the shares of a particular bank. These requirements were not retrospective and applied only to new holdings. The amendments also forced each commercial bank to have at least 250 individual shareholders, each holding no more than 0.5 per cent of bank shares and at least 50 per cent of total shares. This amendment had to be effected within five years and when the deadline was reached in 1984, most banks had complied with the regulation. There are now more shareholders but little has changed in terms of the patterns of control within each bank except for the Siam Bank, which was taken over by the Bank of Thailand). Small shareholders have been unable to unite and fight in order to take control of the banks. More importantly, former major shareholders were able to use other people, or their related companies, to buy new shares (Suehiro 1985) thereby enabling them to maintain control.

Sources of funds

In 1988, almost 75 per cent of commercial bank funds came from their deposits. Other significant sources were commercial borrowing and the capital account which constituted 10 and 6 per cent, respectively.

Deposits

The commercial banks maintain three types of deposits: demand deposits, savings deposits and time deposits. As shown in Table 7.6, the interest rate paid on demand deposits in 1988 was zero because of unremunerative book-keeping costs involved in maintaining these balances. The practice of using post-dated cheques drawn against these demand deposits is very popular in Thailand as a means of conducting business. For savings deposits, the interest rate paid was 6.25–7.25 per cent a year in 1988. Savings deposits can be withdrawn at any time. In December 1988, rates paid on time deposits varied according to maturity from zero (under three months) to 8.75–9.5 per cent (two years or more). Time deposits can be withdrawn before the end of the term and the interest rate adjusted accordingly, except for long-term deposits (2 years and over) which have a penalty rate.

In the early 1980s, the Bank of Thailand began to restructure interest rates by lifting the maximum rates on deposits and lending. The Bank of Thailand has encouraged the banking sector to drop those rates on their own initiative, in a move towards a more flexible interest rate policy. Most have been reluctant to do so, mainly through fear of losing their market share, and the Bank of Thailand has occasionally been called to initiate such a move.

In the middle of June 1989, there was an abrupt change in the regulations covering deposit rates. The monetary authority—the Bank of Thailand—abolished the ceiling on interest rates paid on deposits of more than one year maturity

Such deposits are now allowed to move freely and banks can pay a more competitive interest rate. According to the authority, the reasons for the change were, first, to diminish the influence of the informal money market, secondly, to give more flexibility to commercial banks in managing their funds, and finally to reduce excess profit earned by commercial banks. The Bank of Thailand considered the spread of 5.5 per cent (the rate that the commercial banks were then receiving) to be too high.

It is too early to assess the effects of this deregulation of deposit rates, but the following consequences are expected:
- savings mobilized in the formal money market sector will increase;
- there will be more competition in terms of deposit rates offered by commercial banks, while the extent of non-interest competition (especially in 'under the table' interest rate payments) will be reduced;
- as ceilings on loan rates have not been lifted, less efficient banks may face a difficult time due to higher costs, and the smaller banks may be affected because their main source of income is from lending; and
- finance companies may be more deeply affected than commercial banks (the latter now being able to pay a more competitive rate of interest).

As shown in Table 7.7, time deposits are the most important form of deposits, accounting for 69 per cent of all deposits in 1988 (savings and demand deposits accounted for 32 and 5.6 per cent, respectively). This is a significant change from the situation in the early 1960s when demand deposits were predominant. Several factors have been responsible for such a dramatic growth in time and savings deposits over the years. In the late 1940s and early 1950s, commercial banks had no interest in soliciting time deposits since they had no access to high-yielding investments (due to the government's policy of maintaining low interest rates on government securities). After 1954, however, time deposits began to increase rapidly due to an increase in public debt rates (Trescott 1971). Together with other measures (such as the exemption of interest paid on time deposits from income tax, maintaining a relatively low interest rate tax, and reducing the interest rate paid on demand deposits) this contributed to a more attractive environment for savings and time deposits.

Table 7.6: Deposit rates of commercial banks in Thailand[a] (per cent)

Year	Demand deposits	Saving deposits	Time deposits			Foreign currency deposits
			3 to less than 6 months	6 to less than 12 months	12 months to less than 2 years	
1945	4.50	—	5.00	5.50	5.50	—
1962	0–0.50	4.50	6.00	8.00	8.00	—
1963	0–0.50	4.50	5.00	6.00	7.00	—
1964	0–0.50	4.50	5.00	6.00	7.00	—
1965	0–0.50	4.50	5.00	6.00	7.00	—
1966	0.10	3.50	5.00	6.00	7.00	—
1967	0.10	3.50	5.00	6.00	7.00	—
1968	0.10	3.50	5.00	6.00	7.00	12.00
1969	0.10	3.50	5.00	6.00	7.00	12.00
1970	0.10	3.50	5.00	6.00	7.00	12.00
1971	0.10	3.50	5.00	6.00	7.00	12.00
1972	0.10	3.50	5.00	6.00	8.00	12.00
1973	0.10	3.50	5.00	6.00	8.00	12.00
1974	0.10	4.50	6.00	7.00	8.00	12.00
1975	0.10	4.50	6.00	7.00	8.00	12.00
1976	0.10	4.50	6.00	7.00	8.00	12.00
1977	0.10	4.50	6.00	7.00	8.00	12.00
1978	0.10	4.50	6.00	7.00	8.00	12.00
1979	—	5.50	9.00	7.00	8.00	Floating

Year					
1980	—	8.00	10.00	10.00	12.00–14.00
1981	—	8.00	10.00	11.00	13.00
1982	—	9.00	10.00	11.00	12.50
		(9.00)	(10.00)	(11.00)	(13.00)
1983	—	8.50	10.00	11.00	12.50
		(9.00)	(10.00)	(11.00)	(13.00)
1984	—	9.00	11.00	12.00	12.50
		(9.00)	(13.00)	(13.00)	(13.00)
1985	—	8.50	10.50	10.50	11.00
		(9.00)	(11.00)	(11.00)	(11.00)
1986	—	5.50	6.75	7.00	7.25
		(7.25)	(9.50)	(9.50)	(9.50)
1987	—	5.50	6.75	7.00	7.25
		(7.25)	(9.50)	(.50)	(9.50)
1988	—	6.25–7.25	6.75–9.50	7.00–9.50	7.75–9.50
		(7.25)	(9.50)	(9.50)	(9.50)

[a] As offered by the four largest commercial banks.
[b] Figures in parentheses are the ceiling rates.

Table 7.7: Deposits of commercial banks in Thailand classified by type, 1976 to 1988 (millions of baht)

	1976	1977	1978	1979	1980	1981	1982
Total deposits	99,464	121,811	146,285	164,285	205,473	244,157	310,006
	(100)a	(100)	(100)	(100)	(100)	(100)	(100)
Demand deposits	15,118	16,392	21,082	22,156	25,133	25,014	24,071
	(15.2)	(13.5)	(14.4)	(13.5)	(12.2)	(10.3)	(7.8)
Saving deposits	8,879	10,672	14,241	17,202	27,115	36,751	60,131
	(8.9)	(88)	(9.7)	(10.5)	(13.2)	(15)	(19.4)
Time deposits	74,955	94,089	110,748	124,009	152,321	181,115	224,380
	(75.3)	(77.2)	(75.4)	(75.5)	(74.1)	(74.2)	(72.4)
Foreign currency deposits	383	389	457	570	568	844	1,052
	(0.40)	(0.3)	(0.3)	(0.3)	(0.3)	(0.3)	(0.3)
Marginal deposits	173	267	293	346	336	432	298
	(0.2)	(0.2)	(0.2)	(0.2)	(0.2)	(0.2)	(0.1)

	1983	1984	1985	1986	1987	1988
Total deposits	392,266	479,630	534,504	599,822	720,654	855,708
	(100)	(100)	(100)	(100)	(100)	(100)
Demand deposits	23,269	29,090	25,328	30,475	44,466	48,075
	(5.9)	(6)	(4.7)	(5.1)	(6.17)	(5.62)
Savings deposits	93,576	101,692	111,372	157,705	226,526	273,499
	(23.9)	(21.2)	(20.8)	(26.3)	(31.4)	(31.9)
Time deposits	274,163	347,592	396,471	409,663	446,320	531,276
	(69.9)	(72.5)	(74.2)	(69.3)	(61.9)	(62.1)
Foreign currency deposits	848	891	1,052	1,689	2,938	2,435
	(0.2)	(0.2)	(0.2)	(0.3)	(0.4)	(0.3)
Marginal deposits	408	355	279	287	403	423
	(0.1)	(0.1)	(0.1)	(0.05)	(0.1)	(0.1)

a Figures in parentheses are percentage share of total.
Source: Bank of Thailand.

Table 7.8: Share of commercial bank deposits in the Bangkok metropolis and other provinces[a], 1976 to 1988 (per cent)

	1976	1977	1978	1979	1980	1981	1982	1983	1984	1985	1986	1987	1988
Time deposits													
Bangkok metropolis	45.3	47.3	46.9	46.5	45.0	43.8	42.2	41.3	44.2	45.1	42	39.4	39.5
Other provinces	28.4	28.6	27.9	27.6	28.3	29.4	29.3	29.2	27.8	28.4	25.8	22.4	22.3
Savings deposits													
Bangkok metropolis	4.1	3.8	4.1	4.5	6.4	8.1	11.2	14.3	13.9	13.5	17.1	21.1	21.2
Other provinces	4.7	4.7	5.4	5.9	6.7	6.9	7.9	9.2	7.4	7.5	90.2	10.1	10.6
Demand deposits													
Bangkok metropolis	14.0	12.5	12.5	12.4	10.5	9.1	7.2	5.4	5.3	4.3	4.8	5.7	5.2
Other provinces	3.5	3.1	3.2	3.1	3.1	2.7	2.2	1.6	1.4	1.2	1.1	1.1	1.0

[a] Including inter-bank deposits.
Source: Bank of Thailand.

As people become wealthier, they tend to deposit more in savings and particularly time deposit accounts. This is shown in Table 7.8 where Bangkok residents show a preference for time deposits and poorer provincial residents a preference for savings deposits. Because time deposits can be withdrawn at any time with minimal penalty, most people prefer to place their savings in time deposits to get higher returns. It is also standard practice for banks to lend to persons already holding time deposit accounts. A further significant impact on the growth of savings and time deposits comes from the growth of bank branches. This helps cut costs to customers by increasing accessibility to bank services (Virabongsa 1975; Nalinee 1984). Favourable balance of payments and level of government deficits are also important in that they increase both the spending/saving power of the public and expand the monetary base of the banking system.

Borrowing

The second most important source of funds for commercial banks in Thailand is borrowing (over 100 billion baht in 1985, see Table 7.9). Commercial banks can borrow from the Bank of Thailand, from domestic financial institutions, and from banks abroad. Borrowing from banks abroad has constituted more than half of total borrowing by commercial banks during the last three decades. Borrowing from the Bank of Thailand is next in importance. The most common method of borrowing from the Bank of Thailand is by placing government bonds or other government-guaranteed bonds as collateral. In 1985, this method accounted for 90 per cent of the amount borrowed from the Bank of Thailand. Another practice is the use of the rediscount facilities of the Bank of Thailand in which the bank will rediscount commercial papers which have already been discounted by commercial banks for exporting, industrial undertakings and agricultural undertakings. When borrowing from domestic financial institutions, commercial banks generally turn to other commercial banks through the interbank call-loan market. This interbank market borrowing is small compared with the aggregate level of borrowing by commercial banks.

A number of studies have attempted to explain the reasons behind this pattern of borrowing. Most focus on the motives

Table 7.9: Borrowing by commercial banks, 1971 to 1988 (millions of baht)

	1971	1972	1973	1974	1975	1976	1977	1978	1979
All banks									
1. From Bank of Thailand	1,996[b]	1,263	2,811	3,984	7,297	5,530	5,952	8,140	16,733
	(25.9)	(25.7)	(28)	(32.6)	(46.2)	(35.9)	(28.3)	(24.5)	(31.5)
2. From other financial institutions in Thailand	62.7	160	260	642	425	660	349	204	927
	(1.3)	(3.2)	(2.5)	(5.2)	(2.6)	(4.2)	(1.6)	(0.6)	(1.5)
3. From banks abroad	3,283	3,486	6,898	7,574	8,051	9,204	14,703	24,804	35,421
	(70.7)	(70.9)	(68.7)	(62)	(51.0)	(59.7)	(70)	(74.8)	(66.8)
4. Total	4,642	4,910	10,040	12,201	15,773	15,395	21,005	33,150	52,982
	(100)	(100)	(100)	(100)	(100)	(100)	(100)	(100)	(100)
Banks incorporated in Thailand									
5. From Bank of Thailand	1,214	1,116	2,692	3,575	6,832	4,945	5,324	7,390	15,775
	(30)	(28.2)	(33.1)	(38)	(52.7)	(41.2)	(31.6)	(26.2)	(33.7)
6. From other financial institutions in Thailand	3.7	42	49	198	88	448	211	88	147
	(0.1)	(1.1)	(0.6)	(2.1)	(0.6)	(3.7)	(1.2)	(0.3)	(0.3)
7. From banks abroad	2,818	2,792	5,369	5,630	6,045	6,598	11,283	20,659	30,801
	(69.8)	(70.66)	(66.2)	(59.8)	(46.6)	(55)	(1)	(73.4)	(65.9)
8. Total	4,036	3,952	8,110	9,404	12,965	11,992	16,818	28,137	46,724
	(100)	(100)	(100)	(100)	(100)	(100)	(100)	(100)	(100)

Banks incorporated abroad

9. From Bank of Thailand	81	146	189	409	46,437	584	627	750	957
	(13.4)	(15.3)	(9.8)	(14.6)	(16.5)	(17.1)	(15)	(14.9)	(15.3)
10. From other financial institutions	59	118	211	444	337	211	138	115	680
	(9.7)	(12.3)	(10.4)	(15.8)	(12)	(6.2)	(3.3)	(2.3)	(10.8)
11. From banks abroad	465	693	1,529	1,943	2,006	2,605	3,420	4,145	4,620
	(76.6)	(72.3)	(79.2)	(69.4)	(71.4)	(76.5)	(81.7)	(82.7)	(73.8)
12. Total	606	958	1,930	2,797	2,808	3,402	4,186	5,012	6,258
	(100)	(100)	(100)	(100)	(100)	(100)	(100)	(100)	(100)

Table 7.9: *continued*

	1980	1981	1982	1983	1984	1985	1986	1987	1988[a]
All banks									
1. From Bank of Thailand	16,710	20,156	20,919	23,366	24,275	26,103	33,631	42,030	57,573
	(38.4)	(38.4)	(42.4)	(36.1)	(33.2)	(36.9)	(53.5)	(57.4)	(48.9)
2. From other financial institutions in Thailand	1,074	1,586	2,679	2,664	2,148	4,764	3,167	1,824	7,303
	(2.4)	(3)	(5.4)	(4.1)	(2.9)	(6.7)	(5)	(2.5)	(6.2)
3. From banks abroad	25,645	30,064	25,738	38,539	46,660	39,660	25,987	29,268	52,834
	(59)	(58)	(52.1)	(59.6)	(63.8)	(56.2)	(41.3)	(40)	(44.8)
4. Total	43,430	51,817	49,333	64,569	73,084	70,600	62,786	73,124	117,711
	(100)	(100)	(100)	(100)	(100)	(100)	(100)	(100)	(100)
Banks incorporated in Thailand									
5. From Bank of Thailand	15,613	18,776	19,731	22,096	22,726	24,340	31,544	39,977	53,567
	(41.3)	(43.1)	(44.7)	(37.5)	(35.6)	(39.4)	(55.9)	(59.1)	(52.2)
6. From other financial institutions in Thailand	264	176	638	623	927	1,404	2,030	340	2,074
	(0.7)	(0.4)	(1.4)	(1)	(1.4)	(2.2)	(3.6)	(0.5)	(2)
7. From banks abroad	21,842	24,591	23,722	36,141	40,031	35,971	22,848	27,326	46,799
	(57.9)	(56.4)	(53.8)	(61.4)	(62.8)	(58.2)	(40.4)	(40.4)	(45.6)
8. Total	37,720	43,543	44,092	58,861	63,685	61,717	56,423	67,643	102,441
	(100)	(100)	(100)	(100)	(100)	(100)	(100)	(100)	(100)

Banks incorporated abroad

9. From Bank of Thailand	1,097	1,380	1,187	1,270	1,549	1,762	2,087	2,054	4,006
	(19.2)	(16.8)	(22.6)	(22.2)	(16.4)	(19.8)	(32.7)	(37.4)	(26.2)
10. From other financial institutions	810	1,420	2,040	2,041	1,220	3,359	1,138	1,485	5,230
	(14.1)	(17.1)	(38.9)	(35.7)	(12.9)	(37.8)	(17.8)	(27)	(34.2)
11. From banks abroad	3,802	5,473	2,012	2,397	6,628	3,761	3,139	1,943	6,035
	(66.6)	(66.1)	(38.4)	(41.9)	(70.5)	(42.3)	(19.3)	(35.4)	(39.5)
12. Total	5,709	8,274	5,240	5,708	9,398	8,883	6,364	5,481	15,270
	(100)	(100)	(100)	(100)	(100)	(100)	(100)	(100)	(100)

[a] Preliminary.
[b] Figures in parentheses are percentage share of total.
Source: Bank of Thailand.

of need and profit. In terms of need, banks are seen to borrow when reserves fall below the level that is required by law or their own requirements (Goldfeld 1966). Such situations might arise when customers make unexpected loan demands or withdraw the balance of their accounts. Under the profit motive, banks will borrow if they see the opportunity of enhancing their profit margins, but this is constrained by banks' reluctance to borrow. The results of these investigations seem to support the theory that commercial banks in Thailand borrow primarily to satisfy their needs (Somkid 1972; Direk and Supaporn 1983[T]). These results imply that it may be more effective to use 'quantitative' rather than 'interest rate' measures as a means of controlling the amount of credit extended by commercial banks in Thailand.

Borrowing from banks abroad has also been investigated in a number of studies (Nimit 1976[T]; Ruengwit 1981[T]). A factor relevant to foreign borrowing by both Thai commercial banks and branches of foreign commercial banks is the withholding of tax exemptions. While withholding tax exemption leads the local banks to borrow more from abroad, branches of foreign banks respond quite differently. Being required by their head offices to buy forward cover, these banks found that when interest rates soared it was cheaper to borrow from commercial banks incorporated in Thailand than to borrow from abroad, due to the government withholding tax exemptions. Another factor is the interest rate charged on commercial banks by the Bank of Thailand, particularly when commercial banks borrow by pledging government bonds or government-guaranteed bonds. The studies found that although the interest rate charged by the Bank of Thailand has a negative effect on the amount borrowed, it has no bearing on foreign bank branches. This means that loans from the Bank of Thailand become a substitute for foreign borrowing by banks incorporated in Thailand but not for foreign banks. One possible explanation is that branches of foreign banks do not hold large numbers of government bonds and their collateral is quickly depleted.

It has been suggested that changes in the Thai economy may also lead to different patterns of foreign borrowing behaviour by commercial banks (Nimit 1976[T]; Ruengwit 1981[T]). In the 1960s short-term borrowing for import purposes was the predominant form of borrowing by banks incorporated in Thailand. In the

1970s, however, up-graded credit worthiness for Thai commercial banks meant they could borrow over longer periods and for different purposes. For banks incorporated abroad, imports still remained an important factor, since their borrowers were mostly foreign firms engaged primarily in importing businesses.

Capital account or shareholders' equity

In 1988, shareholders' equity was 6 per cent of total commercial bank liabilities, a figure which had not changed significantly over the previous ten years. This has raised concerns about the capital adequacy of commercial banks in Thailand. In the opinion of many economists, low capital means risky operations, but others question the importance of shareholders' capital in this respect. Because the Bank of Thailand has the capacity to help an ailing bank during a financial crisis, some believe that concerns about capital adequacy are unfounded. Some worry about the competitiveness of Thai commercial banks in the world economy because capital regulations in Thailand are harder to meet than those of many other countries. As of 1986, each commercial bank in Thailand was required to maintain a capital account equal to 8 per cent of its risk assets.

A further feature of the capital account is that, on average, the larger the bank, the lower its capital account relative to its total liabilities (Yokporn 1986[T]). This suggests that either there might be some economies of scale in the operation of commercial banks or that larger banks are more aggressive in their operations than smaller ones. Further discussion on economies of scale and bank operations within the banking industry is found later in this chapter.

Uses of funds

The main uses of funds are: advances, investments, and cash and balances.

Advances

Total advances outstanding at the end of 1988 were over 68 billion baht, amounting to 76 per cent of total assets.

Advances are composed of overdrafts, loans and discounted bills. Overdrafts, although the most popular form of credit extended by commercial banks, constituted approximately 49 per cent of total advances during 1975–84 (Bandid and Madee 1987[T]). Overdrafts are generally arranged for one year. They are often extended over several years, but can be made payable as soon as the one year has elapsed, unlike a fixed period in a term loan. Bank loans are not as popular as overdrafts and represented 23 per cent of total advances in that same period. The rest are discounted bills, including trust receipts.

Many restrictions are imposed on bank advances. For instance, amendments to the Commercial Banking Act in 1962 and 1979 set a limit to the amount of credit extendable to one customer (at present no more than 25 per cent of the bank's capital fund). They also empowered the monetary authority to limit the extension of credit to certain categories of business (non-priority sectors) and to regulate the ratio of capital funds to risk assets. The authority has also imposed a maximum lending rate for commercial banks. Customers often have to pay higher interest rates on advances than those specified by law. Although illegal, this has become an accepted fact of life in the market place.

One interesting question concerns the degree to which the commercial banks will extend their credit in the form of bank advances (see for example, Trescott 1971; Prasan 1973). It has been suggested that commercial banks have desired reserves and when these are exceeded banks tend to expand their credit in the form of advances to dissipate the excess, i.e. a reserve adjustment process. Not all observers agree with this, and it has been argued that banks expand credit for reasons other than to dissipate excess reserves (see Rozenthal 1970), but it is widely held that commercial banks try to accommodate the volume of loans demanded. The extent of these loans depends on a number of factors such as value of imports, flow of private investment expenditures, level of economic activity and seasonal variations (Sataporn 1987[T]; Chaiyong 1984[T]).

Commercial banks in Thailand have long been criticized for advancing funds for the benefit of export, import and domestic trade, while directing little into the agricultural sector. Table 7.10 shows that agriculture's credit share was only 6.6 per cent in 1988, despite government efforts to direct funds to that sector. Financing agriculture is riskier than financing most other activities owing to its unpredictable and seasonal character. The manufacturing share was 25.8 per cent, but many complain that this is insufficient and only large business customers appear to get such loans. In maximizing profits, banks prefer larger customers because of the economies of scale involved. The inclination towards financing trade rather than production is inevitable given banks' historical development and need for asset security. Nevertheless, loans for foreign and domestic trade are important elements in financing the sales of agricultural products.

A number of measures have been taken to channel more funds to priority sectors. For example, the Bank of Thailand now provides a rediscount facility for promissory notes arising from export and from industrial undertakings, agriculture and animal husbandry. This enables exporters, industrialists and farmers to borrow at below market interest rates. Under the provisions of law, each bank also has to direct a certain percentage of its deposits to the agricultural sector. In 1986, banks were required to lend the equivalent of 13 per cent of their deposits to agriculture, 2 per cent of which must go to agri-based industries, and the rest to farmers or into deposits with the Bank for Agriculture and Agricultural Cooperatives (BAAC), a government-owned financial institution. In early 1987, the Bank of Thailand increased the aggregate requirement to 20 per cent of total deposits, but also redefined the recipients from the agricultural sector as coming from the 'rural' sector.

These measures were not without problems. For example, if used without limit, the rediscount facility tends to increase economic instability (an expansion of rediscount implies an expansion of the cash base and money supply). Because of the interest rates through the rediscount facility, Thailand was accused by the United States of trading unfairly with regard to rice, and the United States imposed countervailing duties on Thai rice exports. The policy of compulsory lending to agriculture also caused problems. Wealthier farmers benefited most because commercial banks sought to avoid loan losses and therefore extended loans only to those with enough collateral (Nipon 1987[T]). Depositing loans with the BAAC also caused problems because it could not find sufficient numbers of creditworthy customers. In 1986, the BAAC faced a liquidity glut because most commercial banks chose to deposit funds with them.

Table 7.10: Bills, loans and overdrafts from commercial banks classsified by purpose[a], 1976 to 1988 (millions of baht)

Institution	1976	1977	1978	1979	1980	1981	1982
1. Agriculture	4,121	6,340	8,656	10,774	11,090	16,042	22,139
	(4.3)[b]	(5.2)	(5.4)	(5.4)	(5.6)	(6.2)	(7.2)
2. Mining	1,115	688	1,078	1,250	1,293	1,806	1,895
	(1.2)	(0.5)	(0.7)	(0.6)	(0.7)	(0.7)	(0.6)
3. Manufacturing	17,586	23,846	29,579	34,331	35,489	58,329	64,893
	(18.2)	(19.4)	(18.4)	(17.3)	(18)	(22)	(21.2)
4. Construction	4,372	6,003	8,418	1,014	10,894	13,033	16,073
	(4.5)	(4.9)	(5.2)	(5.1)	(5.5)	(5.1)	(5.2)
5. Real estate business	3,633	3,841	4,394	6,003	6,170	6,972	8,471
	(0.3)	(3.1)	(2.7)	(3)	(3.1)	(2.7)	(2.8)
6. Imports	13,367	15,585	18,318	26,426	26,265	25,110	23,987
	(13.9)	(12.7)	(11.4)	(13.3)	(13.4)	(9.7)	(7.8)
7. Exports	12,529	13,119	17,853	25,556	23,544	26,077	28,991
	(13)	(10.7)	(11.1)	(12.9)	(12)	(10.1)	(9.5)
8. Wholesale and retail trade	20,812	28,129	38,497	44,384	44,059	58,816	76,530
	(21.6)	(22.9)	(23.9)	(22.4)	(22.4)	(22.8)	(24.9)
9. Public utilities	1,306	2,631	3,959	4,503	5,977	5,963	5,648
	(1.3)	(2.1)	(2.5)	(2.3)	(3)	(2.3)	(1.8)
10. Banking and other financial business	5,846	7,017	9,590	12,474	9,666	12,748	16,849
	(6.1)	(5.7)	(6)	(6.3)	(4.9)	(4.9)	(5.5)
11. Services	4,067	5,425	6,311	6,944	6,747	12,032	16,008
	(4.2)	(4.4)	(3.9)	(3.5)	(3.4)	(4.7)	(5.2)

12. Personal	7,597	10,155	14,191	15,407	15,483	21,184	25,298
	(7.9)	(8.3)	(8.8)	(7.8)	(7.9)	(8.2)	(8.3)
13. Others	18	45	25	159	178	—	—
	(–)	(0.1)	(–)	(0.1)	(0.1)		
Total	96,377	122,810	160,878	198,363	196,861	258,117	306,787
	(100)	(100)	(100)	(100)	(100)	(100)	(100)

Table 7.10: continued

Institution	1983	1984	1985	1986	1987	1988
1. Agriculture	30,450	37,409	39,355	39,694	46,137	57,184
	(7.4)	(7.8)	(7.4)	(7.2)	(6.7)	(6.6)
2. Mining	2,439	2,844	3,361	3,169	3,478	4,623
	(0.7)	(0.6)	(0.6)	(0.6)	(0.5)	(0.5)
3. Manufacturing	88,713	106,048	122,576	12,945	162,238	223,868
	(21.5)	(22)	(23.1)	(22.8)	(23.4)	(25.8)
4. Construction	21,773	26,143	29,427	30,555	31,801	37,381
	(5.3)	(5.4)	(5.5)	(5.6)	(4.6)	(4.3)
5. Real estate business	12,218	16,781	19,446	20,764	31,006	54,054
	(3)	(3.5)	(3.7)	(3.8)	(4.5)	(6.2)
6. Imports	34,566	36,048	34,188	32,388	39,240	45,947
	(8.4)	(7.6)	(6.5)	(5.9)	(5.7)	(5.3)
7. Exports	32,022	39,733	45,019	50,144	60,809	72,168
	(7.8)	(8.2)	(8.5)	(9.1)	(8.8)	(8.3)
8. Wholesale and retail trade	101,271	133,012	122,256	127,619	140,221	164,213
	(24.6)	(23.34)	(23)	(23.2)	(20.3)	(19)
9. Public utilities	6,552	7,476	9,548	9,511	12,628	13,683
	(1.6)	(1.6)	(1.8)	(1.7)	(1.8)	(1.6)
10. Banking and other financial business	25,713	30,302	33,067	33,406	63,038	54,842
	(6.2)	(6.3)	(6.2)	(6.1)	(9.1)	(6.3)
11. Services	19,703	24,251	26,926	28,548	36,023	49,238
	(4.8)	(5)	(5.1)	(5.2)	(5.2)	(5.7)

12. Personal	36,537	41,800	45,555	48,281	65,162	89,662
	(8.8)	(8.7)	(8.6)	(8.8)	(9.4)	(10.4)
13. Others	—	—	—	—	—	—
Total	411,962	481,851	530,729	549,024	691,781	866,863
	(100)	(100)	(100)	(100)	(100)	(100)

a Including interbank transactions.
b Figures in parentheses are percentage share of total.
Source: Bank of Thailand.

Investment in securities

Investment in securities by commercial banks amounted to 140 billion baht in 1988 or almost 12 per cent of total assets. Nearly all assets classified in investment categories are Thai government securities. There are several reasons why government securities are attractive to commercial banks. First, part of the legal reserve requirement can be met by holding government securities and, because these securities generally yield interest, they are preferable to non-interest bearing deposits in the Bank of Thailand. Second, in attaining approval for a new branch, a bank must hold at least 16 per cent of total deposits in the form of government bonds or government-guaranteed bonds. This measure is intended to ensure that at least that portion of the commercial banks' investments remains risk-free. Third, government securities can be used as collateral in securing funds from the Bank of Thailand. The opening of the repurchase market at the Bank of Thailand in 1979 has increased the attractiveness of government securities where they are the main instruments. Fourth, as mentioned earlier, government securities are not considered risky assets, so they are not under the constraints set by the Bank of Thailand to maintain a capital–risk asset ratio of 1:8. Finally, the growth in holding government securities in recent years stems from the increase in time deposits.

Commercial banks can also invest in domestic and foreign securities, but measures are imposed to safeguard bank operations as well as to prevent any concentration of ownership within the banking system. For example, a commercial bank is limited to holding just 10 per cent of another company's shares in the total outstanding shares of that company. Each bank can purchase other companies' shares and debentures up to a maximum of 20 per cent of the bank's shareholders' funds. Commercial banks are also prohibited from holding shares of another commercial bank except for debt repayment reasons. Such shares must be disposed of by sale within six months.

'Cash and balances'

Cash held by commercial banks is used for legal reserve requirement purposes and for daily operations. Cash on hand may also include foreign currency purchased in the course of banking operations. Balances at the Bank of Thailand are held to meet the reserve requirement, and for cheque-clearing purposes. Balances with banks abroad are the most important item in the 'cash and balances' category. Because commercial banks can convert unobligated government bonds into cash with little risk, they are counted as liquid assets apart from cash and balances. Cash and balances accounted for 6 per cent of total assets in 1986.

A study of commercial banks' motives in holding liquid assets revealed many similarities with those relating to advances (Nipon 1984[T]). One factor which might explain the demand for liquid assets by commercial banks is the withdrawal risk which positively affects the holding of liquid assets of banks incorporated in Thailand. Smaller banks are more responsive than larger ones to increases in the withdrawal risk. This may imply that larger banks have economies of scale in the holding of liquid assets. Banks incorporated abroad are not sensitive to withdrawal risk because their funds are not mobilized domestically and can be transferred from their headquarters on demand. Liquid assets are also affected negatively by borrowing. This appears to contradict the conventional idea that when costs of borrowing rise, commercial banks need to hold more liquid assets. A possible explanation for the negative relationship lies in banks trying to accommodate the demand for loans when costs of borrowing are high. Changes in legal reserve requirement ratios are also observed to have asymmetric effects on liquid asset holding. Not all commercial banks raise their holdings of liquid assets when the reserve requirement ratio increases, or reduce their holdings when the ratio falls. This might be because it is harder for banks to increase cash reserves when a raise is announced, since that implies a reduction in existing loans or an increase in external borrowing. Similarly, in the case of a reserve requirement reduction, a bank can increase advances to relatively new projects at an earlier stage and thus reduce its liquid asset holdings. Seasonal factors are also important in banks' demand for liquid assets, especially for relatively smaller banks and those incorporated abroad. This is because their activities are not as diversified as those of larger banks (see also Nipon 1984[T]).

Performance of commercial banks

The brief assessment of the overall performance of commercial banks provided in this section will focus on two criteria: profitability and stability.

Profitability

The most common method of measuring profitability of commercial banking in Thailand involves calculating the return on capital. This return is the ratio of net profit from any period to capital in that period. We shall concentrate on profit rates of banks incorporated in Thailand only; branches of foreign banks can remit their profits periodically through the year, so making profit calculations very difficult. Table 7.11 shows that net profit rates of banks incorporated in Thailand ranged from 9.1 to 13.5 per cent between 1979 and 1985, somewhat lower than the 16 per cent computed in the late 1960s and early 1970s. This implies that Thai commercial banks in the 1980s no longer have an edge in terms of profit rates over other industries but it is difficult to confirm this point without knowing the rate of return on invested capital in Thailand. Using the opportunity cost approach, bank profit rates are comparable to rates of return on government bonds of 11 to 12.8 per cent during the same period. The decline in profitability of commercial banks in the 1980s might also stem from recessions in the economy, which affected every sector in the early years of the decade.

An interesting feature of Table 7.11 is the contrast between profit rates of the four large banks and the rest. The much higher rates of the larger banks have prompted some economists to investigate the factors underlying different profit rates. Their results seem to suggest that economies of scale in banking are the key factors (Supoj 1976; Yokporn 1986[T]). They found that larger banks do not exert their market power over prices which may perhaps be explained in terms of risk avoidance behaviour (Sirichai 1982; Galbraith 1967; Caves 1970). This accords with Hicks' idea that 'the best of all monopoly profits is the quiet life' (Hicks 1935). In other words, firms with monopoly power may choose to forgo some of their potential profit by choosing safer portfolios than those in a more competitive market.

Table 7.11: Rate of return to capital of commercial banks

Authors	Period of study	Net profit/capital (per cent)	Rate computed for
Yokporn (1986[T])	1979–83	12.31	Average of all commercial banks incorporated in Thailand
Bandid and Madee (1987[T])	1980	12.5	Average of all commercial banks incorporated in Thailand
	1981	13.3	Average of all commercial banks incorporated in Thailand
	1982	12.3	Average of all commercial banks incorporated in Thailand
	1983	13.5	Average of all commercial banks incorporated in Thailand
	1984	12.4[a]	Average of all commercial banks incorporated in Thailand
	1985	9.1[b]	Average of all commercial banks incorporated in Thailand
Bhanupong and Atchana (1987[T])	1982–85	12.48	Four largest banks[c]
		7.07[d]	Five medium-sized banks
		6.20	Seven smallest banks

[a] Does not include Siam Bank, which was running at a loss in that year.
[b] Does not include Siam Bank and Laem Thong Bank, which were running at losses in that year.
[c] Sizes of banks are classified according to sizes of capital funds.
[d] Does not include Siam Bank.

Sources: Yokporn (1986[T]: 36); Bandid and Madee (1987[T]: 2, 60); Bhanupong and Atchana (1987[T]: 3, 14).

There is a degree of dispute among economists as to the excessiveness of bank profits. A rudimentary measurement of profit—the spread between ceiling interest rates paid on time deposits and ceiling interest rates charged for accommodation—gives a figure of about six percentage points in the period 1981–85.

Those who believe this does not imply excessive profits argue that there are constraints on the management of commercial banks' assets. For example, banks are obliged to maintain a certain volume of liquid assets and to extend a proportion of their loans to the agricultural sector as well as to areas where their branches are located (Tarisa 1987T). Many banking services are given free of charge (e.g. maintaining current accounts, use of cheques, opening deposit and credit accounts, and the initial use of automatic teller machines). Commercial banks in Thailand also face competition from abroad and need to lower their loan rates to win customers who have access to foreign funds (Sataporn 1987T). It is also argued that the profit-spread figure has to incorporate the high real costs of bad debts.

However, those who argue that such a spread is too large, point to other countries. Rozenthal, for example, states that profit-spread in the United States is less than half that in Thailand (Rozenthal 1970: 151). Some argue that in practice many loans are made at higher than the current ceiling rate. Not all deposits are made for one year and demand deposits do not pay interest. Yet banks can earn substantial income from foreign exchange, commissions and fees.

Stability

Since the early 1970s, there have been four financial crises in commercial bank operations which have prompted major intervention by the Bank of Thailand (Table 7.12). Attempts have been made to explain this apparent instability and three major factors have been identified.

First, unfavourable economic conditions (especially in the 1980s) played a major role (Bandid and Madee 1987T). Economic recession, particularly in the agricultural sector, cut back about a quarter of the profits normally accruing to commercial banks largely because of excess liquidity and the banks' inability to adjust their spread. Second, the instability may relate to the

Table 7.12: Crises in commercial banks' operations, 1970 to 1987

		Problems	Action taken by the Bank of Thailand
1970	Thai Development Bank	Liquidity and fraudulence	• Asked other banks to help with the liquidity problem • Withdrawal of old shareholders • Sent in some government officials to help with the management
1984	Asia Trust Bank	Fraudulent management started bank runs	• Ordered capital reduction • Government took over the ownership
1986	First City Bank of Bangkok	Huge losses	• Ordered capital reduction • Changed top level management
1987	Siam City Bank	Huge losses	• Ordered capital reduction • Changed top level management

Source: Compiled from Naris et al. (1987ᵀ:1.120, 1.127).

banks' own management. At the heart of many problems has been dishonest management and the misappropriation of funds. Another form of mismanagement is the capital inadequacy of some Thai commercial banks. Despite substantial growth in banking activities, banks rarely mobilize their own funds but rely instead on deposits and borrowed money. This increases their overall vulnerability.

The third factor contributing to instability is the ambivalent attitude of the authorities (Naris et al. 1987T). Although government authorities will prevent a bank from going bankrupt, they lack the authority to take necessary actions against problem banks. The establishment of a Fund for the Development and Rehabilitation of Financial Institutions and Development of the Financial System (to which each bank must contribute) aims to provide the ailing banks with soft loans to see them through their difficulties. The fund operates on the basis that inefficient banks should not be allowed to fail. Although the authority requires commercial banks to submit detailed information on their operations to the Bank of Thailand, most of this information is withheld from the public for fear they might be alarmed and react irrationally.

Conclusions: banking regulation

It is possible to characterize the regulatory attitude of the Bank of Thailand as 'father knows best' in deciding which commercial banks may have problems. This attitude leads to the question of whether the Bank of Thailand is more prudent than the public who own their deposit funds. Suspicion also arises over bank supervision. The monetary authority in Thailand occasionally attempts to solve the problems of ailing commercial banks by appointing their own personnel as top executives to those banks. Such a practice clearly calls into question the subsequent impartiality of those executives and the degree to which their performance is critically reviewed.

8

Public Enterprises

KRAIYUDHT DHIRATAYAKINANT

Public enterprises play an important role in the Thai economy. In 1988 their revenues represented 21 per cent of GDP and their capital expenditure was equivalent to 8 per cent of GDP. While employment in public enterprises is small, only one-seventh as large as the central government, their recurrent expenditure is now larger than that of the central government and constitutes 19 per cent of GDP. The operation of Thailand's public enterprises is politically sensitive, particularly in relation to their pricing policies.

This chapter reviews the nature of Thailand's public enterprises. It begins by outlining their official definition and the methods by which they can be established. This is followed by discussion of their economic significance, the complicated system of government control, the mechanisms of price setting, their impact on Thailand's foreign debt, and an assessment of the overall performance of the public enterprise sector. It concludes with discussion of the politics of privatization and possible future directions.

The scope of the public enterprise sector in Thailand

Definition

Official definitions of public enterprise in Thailand can be found in two principal Acts. According to the National Economic and Social Development Board Act (1959), a public enterprise refers to an activity in which the government holds total capital of more than 50 per cent of the equity. A more specific yet broader definition is found in the Budget Act (1959). Here, public enterprises are defined as:

(i)   government organizations or business units owned entirely by the government;

(ii) a company or registered partnership of which more than 50 per cent of the capital is contributed by a government unit;

(iii) a company or registered partnership of which more than 50 per cent of the capital is contributed by a government unit, a public enterprise, or a combination of both;

(iv) a company or registered partnership of which more than 50 per cent of the capital is contributed by a government unit and/or public enterprise under (i) and/or (ii) and/or (iii); and

(v)   a company or registered partnership of which more than 50 per cent of the capital is contributed by a government unit and/or public enterprise under (i) and/or (ii) and/or (iii) and/or (iv).

On the basis of these two official definitions, Thailand's public enterprises are listed in Appendix 1 to this chapter.

The generally accepted criteria for identifying public enterprises are ownership, control, autonomy and the degree of marketing of the output (Jones 1975: 24). The key criterion in the official definitions presented above is the nature of ownership. Another criterion is the legally defined autonomy of the enterprise in question. It does not matter whether the good/service produced by the enterprise is marketed. Thus, certain public organizations which provide their services free of charge and which would generally be treated as departmental units are included in the list of public enterprises. The list presented in Appendix 1 is not sufficiently comprehensive, however, to convey the extent of government involvement in commercial enterprise. For instance, over one hundred radio stations owned by military and civilian agencies throughout Thailand have been excluded despite the fact that they sell their air time for a fee to private operators who in turn secure their revenue from radio commercials. Similarly, certain printing presses owned by government departments are not treated as public enterprises simply because they have not been established under any of the public enterprise Acts. In addition there are enterprises owned by the government but which hav less than 50 per cent ownership; by official definition they are not public enterprises.

Methods of establishing public enterprises

Legally, there are a number of ways by which a public enterprise can be established. The first is establishment by a specific Act of Parliament. This type of public enterprise is wholly owned by the government. The second method is established by a Royal Decree under the Public Enterprise Establishment Act (1953). Again, this type of public enterprise is totally owned by the government. The third method is establishment by the Commercial Code and the Commercial Bank Act. Public enterprises established by this method have legal status as limited companies. They may either be wholly owned or partly owned (but by over 50 per cent) by the government. The fourth method is establishment by a Cabinet resolution. Enterprises so established are wholly owned by the government but do not enjoy the same legal status as those established by the preceding methods. Any legal commitment of these public enterprises has to be made by the ministries under which they are supervised.

The different methods of establishment serve to distinguish the basic nature of public enterprises. If their activities relate to provision of public utilities and economic and social infrastructure, then establishment is carried out by an Act of Parliament. Public enterprises servicing so-called public goods or goods with externalities (either in the fields of manufacturing, commerce, services or agriculture) are set up by a Royal Decree. Public enterprises established by a specific Act enjoy far greater privileges than those established by Royal Decree. One important privilege is tax exemption. For example, the Port Authority of Thailand is exempted from import duties, income tax and land tax. Furthermore, there is no limitation on the kind of activities that can be undertaken by public enterprises established by parliamentary Act (Paisan 1976: 80–1ᵀ).

Public enterprises established by the Commercial Code or similar codes produce private goods and carry out their business in a similar manner to private enterprises. They are subject to the same privileges and duties as stipulated by those codes. Except for the case of the Tobacco Monopoly of Thailand, all public enterprises set up by Cabinet resolution are small-scale operations compared with those established by specific Act or Royal Decree.

The economic significance of the public enterprise sector

An overview

Recurrent expenditure of the public enterprise sector has increased noticeably over the past twenty years (from 9.5 per cent of GDP in the fiscal year for 1970 to 20.4 per cent in 1985) with the proportion falling slightly in 1988 (Table 8.1). The public enterprise sector has now become more important than the central government in terms of the economic impacts generated by recurrent expenditure. In 1970 it contributed over 78 per cent of the central government's recurrent expenditure; by 1982, this proportion had risen to some 115 per cent. The two sectors were about the same size in 1985 but the public enterprise sector has edged ahead since.

Viewed from the perspective of capital expenditure, the role of the public enterprise sector has increased even more rapidly. Public enterprise capital expenditures are separate from those of the central government, but their relative magnitudes have changed radically. Public enterprise capital expenditures were equivalent to only 33 per cent of the central government's capital expenditure in fiscal year 1970 and 80 per cent in 1981. This proportion jumped sharply to 167 per cent in 1985 and to 265 per cent in 1988. Although the proportions between years may fluctuate, they suggest that capital investment of the public enterprise sector has expanded much faster than that of the central government. The figures also reflect the ever-increasing need for infrastructural expansion to keep pace with the growth of the Thai economy. The greater part of this capital investment was incurred by utilities.

The revenue generating capacity of the public enterprise sector has also increased. From slightly less than the revenue of the central government in fiscal year 1980-81, the public enterprise sector has since generated more revenue than the central government. However, relative to the central government, this revenue raising capacity of the public enterprise sector declined in 1987 and 1988, a reflection of the increased level of tax collection by the central government during this period of rapid economic growth. Expressed in relation to GDP the public enterprise sector increased its revenue generating capacity from a proportion of 11.2 per cent in 1970, to 17.7 per cent in 1982, and to 22.1 per cent in 1985. The slightly smaller proportions in 1986–88 reflected the greater rates of increase in GDP.

In terms of employment, the public enterprise sector played a smaller role. The employment level of the public enterprise sector did not increase noticeably but fluctuated throughout the 1980s.

The financial profile of the public enterprise sector

Data on the financial profiles of 61 individual public enterprises, representing almost the entire public enterprise sector in Thailand, have been consolidated in Table 8.2 in the form of a balance sheet for fiscal year 1986 (columns 1 and 2). In terms of profit, the table indicates that the overall performance of these enterprises generated positive income, making profits of 16 billion baht. The total losses incurred by the 16 public enterprises which reported net losses were only 14 per cent of the total profits generated by the public enterprise sector in that year. This amount would be still smaller if the excluded public enterprises, all of which made profits, were included. Indeed, 85 per cent of the losses were incurred by two major public enterprises, namely, the Bangkok Mass Transit Organization (BMTO) and State Railways of Thailand (SRT). Table 8.2 also shows, in columns (3) and (4), the financial profiles of the 18 largest public enterprises (listed in Appendix 1). These 18 account for 84 per cent of the total revenue of all public enterprises, for 80 per cent of their net profit, and for 94 per cent of their remittances of profit to the central government.

Table 8.3 shows the net profit situation of the public enterprises by economic sector for two selected years, 1982 and 1988. The overall picture is encouraging, with a trend of increasing net profits. In 1982 the utility group was the only one which suffered losses (some 476 million baht). However, utilities as a group improved their net profit in 1988, despite

Table 8.1: Indicators of the role of public enterprises in the Thai economy, 1981 to 1988

	1981	1982	1983	1984	1985	1986	1987	1988
Recurrent expenditure (fiscal year)								
Public enterprise[a] (million baht)	94,956	138,801	166,859	184,600	207,012	221,904	234,797	261,856
Rate of increase (%)	36.49	46.18	20.24	10.63	12.14	7.19	5.81	11.52
Government[b] (million baht)	103,004	12,029	170,551	186,417	211,043	213,900	224,274	239,831
Public enterprise/government(%)	92.2	115.4	97.8	99.0	98.09	103.74	104.69	109.18
Public enterprise/GDP (%)	12.1	16.2	18.0	18.6	20.4	20.2	19.2	18.9
Capital expenditure (calendar year)								
Public enterprise[c] (million baht)	28,013	27,099	31,494	34,380	58,289	83,069	71,813	106,879
Government[c] (million baht)	34,915	36,946	36,267	37,191	34,845	34,267	36,008	40,311
Public enterprise/government (%)	80.23	73.34	86.83	92.44	167.28	242.42	199.44	265.14
Public enterprise/GDP (%)	9.0	8.4	3.4	3.4	5.98	7.55	5.87	7.74

	1981	1982	1983	1984	1985	1986	1987	1988
Revenue (fiscal year)								
Public enterprise[a] (million baht)	105,093	151,858	182,521	206,419	224,540	241,916	259,471	286,727
Government[b] (million baht)	110,476	113,835	136,604	147,847	162,210	165,628	197,502	245,577
Public enterprise/government (%)	95.1	133.4	133.6	139.6	138.43	146.06	131.37	116.76
Public enterprise/GDP (%)	13.4	17.7	19.7	20.8	22.1	22.0	21.2	20.8
Employees (fiscal year)								
Public enterprise[a] (thousands of persons)	223	243	240	249	262	254	258	266
Government[d] (thousands of persons)	889	933	1,612	1,356	1,531	1,483	1,569	1,727
Public enterprise/government	26.2	26.0	14.89	18.36	17.11	17.13	16.44	15.40

Sources: a Budget Bureau, Annual Fiscal Report.
b Bank of Thailand, Monthly Economic Report.
c Bank of Thailand, Economic Account of Thailand.
d Civil Service Commission

Table 8.2: The balance sheet of Thai public enterprises, 1986

	Total public enterprises[a]		The 18 largest public enterprises[b]		(3)/(1) %
	million baht (1)	% of total revenue (2)	million baht (3)	% of total revenue (4)	
Total revenue from operation	216,252	99.0	180,855	99.9	84
Subsidy/compensation	2,712	1.0	146	0.1	5
Total	218,964	100.0	181,001	100.0	83
Less operating cost	187,927	86.0	153,040	84.6	81
Profit (loss) from operation	31,037	14.0	27,961	15.5	90
Add other incomes	5,327	2.0	3,542	2.0	66
Less other cost	19,506	9.0	18,125	10.0	93
Profit (loss) before income taxes	16,858	8.0	13,378	7.4	79
Less corporate income taxes	1,016	1.0	689	0.4	68
Net profit	15,841	7.0	12,689	7.0	80
Size of profits[c]	18,458		14,915		81
Size of losses[c]	2,616		2,226		85
Remittance to the government from net profit	7,127	45.0[d]	6,673	56.7[d]	94
Total remittance to the government (excluding Bank of Thailand)	6,643		6,133		92

ᵃ includes data on 61 of the 64 public enterprises listed in Appendix A. The three excluded are: Bank of Thailand, Bang Chak Petroleum Co. and PTT Exploration and Production Co.
ᵇ These 18 largest public enterprises are listed in Appendix A.
ᶜ The number of public enterprises making a profit was 45, of which 16 were from the group of the 18 largest public enterprises. The number of public enterprises making a loss was 16, of which only 2 were from the group of the 18 largest public enterprises.
ᵈ Percentage of net profit.
Source: Public Enterprise Division, Dept. of the Comptroller-General.

Table 8.3: Performance of public enterprises by sector, 1982 and 1988 (millions of baht)

Sector	1982			1988		
	Revenue	Expenditure	Net profit	Revenue	Expenditure	Net profit
Mining	19,621	18,420	1,201	38,164	35,454	2,710
Agriculture	5,299	4,874	355	6,389	6,454	-64
Communications and transport	32,278	30,507	1,771	66,690	57,923	8,767
Commerce and service	6,612	6,476	135	90,033	82,219	7,814
Utilities	2,826	3,302	-476	5,482	4,982	499
Energy	80,926	75,048	5,878	78,531	73,464	5,066
Social	143	123	19	1,434	1,356	78
Total	147,639	138,753	8,885	286,727	261,856	24,871

Source: Public Enterprise Division, Dept of the Comptroller-General.

the continued losses suffered by the BMTO. This situation reflects the ever greater profits enjoyed by electricity enterprises within the utilities sector (see also Table 8.4). In 1988, it was public enterprises within the agricultural sector which suffered net losses.

Table 8.4 shows the relative standing of the 20 most profitable public enterprises, ranked by profit.

Some public enterprises require heavy capital investment. This is particularly so in the case of utilities and other infrastructural concerns. Table 8.5 shows that these public enterprises have grown in importance relative to others. Their total assets and debts, as a percentage of the entire sector, had each risen to about 90 per cent in 1988.

Table 8.6 shows the capital budget of Thai public enterprises in 1986, and reveals the importance of a small number of public enterprises in relation to the entire sector. Although the 18 public enterprises included in Table 8.6 (identified in Appendix 1) do not include all 13 public enterprises listed in Table 8.5, the two tables do indicate that the story of the Thai public enterprise sector is largely the story of only about 20 major public enterprises out of the total of 64.

Government control of public enterprises

Being state owned, public enterprises are nominally under direct government control. Although this control is not considered truly effective, public enterprises must be under the direct supervision of a ministry or the equivalent (the Office of the Prime Minister). The supervising ministry oversees all aspects of public enterprise operation, such as their annual budgets, investment projects, corporate plans and appointment of board members, the chief executive and deputies. However, the supervising ministry must refer these matters to the Cabinet for final approval. This degree of supervision generates unnecessary red tape and delay, although the majority of decisions are made on a routine basis. The supervising ministry and the Cabinet are usually concerned only with principal decisions that significantly affect the economy and the interest of certain economic groups. Even these decisions are usually

	Ranking by profit			Total profit		
	1979–82	1983–85	1986–88	1979–82	1983–85	1986–88
Electricity Generating Authority of Thailand	2	1	1	6,669	11,951	14,226
Bank of Thailand	1	2	7	7,978	7,319	4,044
Petroleum Authority of Thailand	7	3	6	1,678	6,780	5,272
Telephone Organization of Thailand	5	4	2	4,105	4,939	7,922
State Lottery Bureau	4	5	3	4,498	4,631	7,304
Thailand Tobacco Monopoly	3	6	5	5,861	2,397	5,863
Communications Authority of Thailand	6	7	4	1,979	1,886	6,221
Airports Authority of Thailand	10	8	9	1,227	1,685	2,764
Port Authority of Thailand	13	9	10	734	952	1,562
Krung Thai Bank Ltd	11	10	12	914	942	774
Provincial Electricity Authority	8	11	11	1,412	820	1,323
Forest Industry Organization	9	12	14	1,408	683	563
Government Savings Bank	12	13	8	824	580	3,894
Bank for Agriculture and Agricultural Cooperatives (BAAC)	15	14	15	405	544	561
Government Pharmaceutical Organization	19	15	13	343	487	712
Government Housing Bank	16	16	17	398	368	162
Thai Plywood Co. Ltd	18	17	16	365	153	219
Marketing Organization for Farmers	17	18	20	392	145	–492
Marketing Organization	14	19	18	667	102	34
Offshore Mining Organization	20	20	19	296	96	28
Others				1,381	1,280	6,601
Total				43,534	45,596	69,557

Sources: Budget Bureau, *Annual Fiscal Report*, various issues; and Cheseda Loohawenchit, 'State enterprises and their impact on the government budget', n.d. (for period 1979–82).

Table 8.5: Assets and debts of thirteen key public enterprises, 1986 and 1988 (millions of baht)

Ranking in 1986	1986		1988	
	Assets	**Debts**	**Assets**	**Debts**
1. Krung Thai Bank Ltd	105,600	101,200	176,900	169,850
2. Electricity Generating Authority	97,644	73,779	108,390	77,250
3. Government Savings Bank	94,147	88,458	127,323	119,328
4. Petroleum Authority	38,165	27,598	37,814	25,650
5. Telephone Organization	32,696	26,915	45,126	37,453
6. Provincial Electricity Authority	30,668	26,868	36,441	31,154
7. Thai Airways International	30,035	30,701	60,094	48,835
8. BAAC	29,359	26,701	37,681	34,807
9. State Railways of Thailand	18,511	11,470	20,644	13,975
10. Metropolitan Electricity	15,776	11,913	17,975	13,228
11. Metropolitan Water Works Authority	15,135	12,050	19,307	14,742
12. Government Housing Bank	13,768	12,436	17,704	16,268
13. National Housing Authority	7,301	6,158	7,619	6,312
(i) Total	528,809	456,253	712,843	608,856
(ii) Total assets and debts of whole public enterprise sector	729,757	618,141	790,843	652,725
(i) As percentage of (ii)	72	73	90	93

Source: Budget Bureau, *Annual Fiscal Reports.*

Table 8.6: The capital budget of Thai public enterprises, 1986 (millions of baht)

	64 public enterprises[a] (1)	18 largest public enterprises (2)	(2) as % of (I)
Capital expenditure Project capital	29,309[b]	28,781	98.2
Non-project capital	7,226[b]	6,804	94.2
Total	36,535[b]	35,585	97.4
Financing Own income	13,402	12,862	95.9
Annual government budget	922	822	89.2
Loans Domestic borrowing	4,635	4,374	94.4
External borrowing	17,353	17,302	99.7
Total loans	21,988	21,677	98.6
Others	233	223	100.0
Total financing	36,545	35,585	97.4

[a] Excluding Bank of Thailand, Bang Chak Petroleum Co. and PTT Exploration and Production Co.
[b] Not including capital spending of financial institutions and Dhipaya Insurance Co.
Source: Public Enterprise Division, Dept of the Comptroller-General.

confined to issues relating to the large public enterprises (invariably those in the utility and infrastructure sectors).

Certain aspects of public enterprise operation must be submitted not only to the supervising ministry, but also to other relevant core agencies and two committees (Figure 8.1). As detailed below, all development projects within public enterprises require prior review by the National Economic and Social Development Board (NESDB). A public enterprise capital budget or annual investment plan must be screened by the Capital Budget Committee. The National Debt Policy Committee must review all investment development projects that require loan financing, be it internal or external and any proposed changes to a public enterprise are analysed by the National State Enterprise Committee. The recommendations of these relevant authorities obviously influence the final decision to be made by the Cabinet. The Budget Bureau reviews and approves all subsidy requests made by public enterprises, and also requires all such enterprises to submit their annual operation reports for examination. The Comptroller General's Office supervises the legality of expenditure disbursement by setting up standard methods and procedures of accounting. It also determines the size of remittances made by public enterprises to the treasury. Similarly, the Auditor General's Office audits the enterprises' financial statements but no single agency is charged with the auditing or monitoring of the overall performance of the public enterprise sector.

The same structure of control applies to all public enterprises regardless of the size or the nature of their operations. Economically important public enterprises are subject to the same supervision as less important ones, and those which are efficient and well-run are just as closely scrutinized as those which are not. However, despite this meticulous yet fragmented supervision, any overall picture of the performance of the public enterprise sector remains beyond the grasp of the relevant supervising authorities. The World Bank has noted that 'the present structure of control over-regulates certain aspects of operations (salary structures or some routine purchases, for example) yet fails to provide the government with adequate control of performance' (World Bank 1986: 217).

Price setting within the public enterprise sector

Prices set by public enterprises are controlled by the government; the greater the likely impact of the price on the economy, the closer is the control of its formulation. As a rule, primary responsibilities for setting prices rest with the boards of individual public enterprises. For small, economically unimportant public enterprises, prices are freely fixed by their boards but within the range determined by the supervising ministry. However, for important public enterprises (i.e. those in the utility and the infrastructure sectors) any change in price must gain ministerial approval. Moreover, a few of these publi

Figure 8.1 Structure of public enterprise supervision

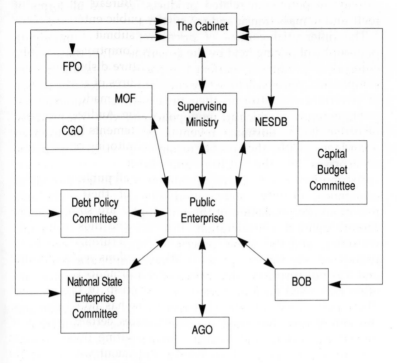

AGO	Auditor General's Office
BOB	Bureau of the Budget
CGO	Comptroller General's Office
FPO	Fiscal Policy Office
MOF	Ministry of Finance

enterprises must also submit their prices to Cabinet for final approval. These requirements in effect make price setting a political decision. For this reason, price increases in these public enterprises are very difficult to effect; they fail either at the level of the supervising ministry or in the Cabinet.

More specifically, the Metropolitan Water Works Authority and the Telephone Organization of Thailand are required by law to submit their proposals for price changes directly to Cabinet for approval. Similarly, changes in electricity tariffs must first be reviewed by the Electricity Tariff Rate Committee and approved by the Cabinet. This approach to rate fixing also extends to petroleum related products (gas and all forms of fuel), and to mass transit and rail systems.

The differential control of prices reflects the underlying philosophy of pricing held by the government. For those public enterprises producing marketed services and facing market competition, prices will be set by competitive forces. The degree of government control on their price setting is minimal. For public enterprises which are monopolies and where the principal objective is to maximize revenue, prices will be fixed in accordance with the profit maximizing rule. For public enterprises in the utility and infrastructure sectors, redistribution objectives may predominate. During periods of economic volatility, stabilization objectives also become important. Reconciliation of these multiple objectives requires careful political consideration, just as much as economic reasoning, and the whole process of price setting can be a protracted one. Raising prices is always unpopular politically and it is not surprising that prices of certain basic services are often kept fixed for long periods and at artificially low levels. These prices may not reflect the rising costs of production and the enterprises concerned may find themselves undergoing forced expansion and deficit financing. For two public enterprises, Bangkok Mass Transit Organization and State Railways of Thailand, such a pricing policy has resulted in heavy losses.

Public enterprise investment and the foreign debt

At present, because of concerns over foreign debts and the public sector deficit, investment by public enterprises is officially subject to government control. Thus all development projects must be approved by the board of directors and the supervising minister. In submitting the development project to Cabinet for final approval, public enterprises must first present to NESDB a detailed study of the project's technical, economic and financial feasibility and its potential sources of financing. NESDB reviews the proposed development project in terms of its consistency with the priorities of the five-year plan and the availability of suitable financing. The Cabinet's ruling usually follows the recommendations forwarded by NESDB.

In addition to gaining approval for development projects, all public enterprises are required to submit their annual operating and capital budgets to NESDB for review. The review focuses on the assumptions behind the formulation of the capital budget, the feasibility of the investment program and its compatibility with overall development priorities of the public sector. Implementation of the investment program is also monitored by NESDB which checks the disbursement of loan funds against planned expenditures and carries out ex-post evaluation of the programs which are to have follow-up projects.

Whether the development project or investment program is recommended to Cabinet for final decision depends on the criteria applied by NESDB. Such criteria include the degree to which the planned investment is compatible with the capability (absorptive capacity) of the public enterprise concerned, the desired financing composition and whether the rate of return to investment is considered adequate. However, financing composition and rate of return criteria are differentially and selectively applied.

For public enterprises which are set up as promotional services (for example, tourism and sports) neither the requirement of an adequate rate of return nor the financing composition are applicable. Similarly, for public enterprises producing commercially competitive products, application of the above criteria is not warranted. Being small relative to those enterprises in the utility and infrastructure sectors, their individual impact on the development process is not easily analysed.

However, for public enterprises in the utility and infrastructure sectors, the decision criteria can be more systematically applied. The criterion of 'development consistency' must always be satisfied, so too absorptive capacity. Although a 'fair' rate of return is required of an investment program, the most crucial dimension is the program's potential effects on the foreign debt (i.e. its sources of finance, especially foreign loans). Such a concern is understandable. Public enterprises are the largest generators of foreign debt and account for about two-thirds of the foreign debt outstanding since 1980 (Table 8.7). However, this proportion may now be declining with the trend towards using the domestic capital market for needed resources and the popular appeal of privatization. Annual debt servicing by public enterprises constitutes more than half of the total debt servicing burden placed on the public sector (Table 8.8). This obviously places a limit on expansion of the government sector because it constrains the ability of the economy to generate foreign exchange and to meet its overall domestic and external debt servicing.

Thus, because of the country's foreign debt position and the important role of the public enterprise sector in generating this debt, the introduction of stringent procedures for debt control is inevitable. Public enterprises must submit a borrowing plan for both guaranteed and non-guaranteed foreign and domestic debts to the National Debt Policy Committee, which makes its recommendation to the Cabinet for final approval. The Fiscal Policy Office of the Finance Ministry negotiates and signs all public enterprise loans.

Government subsidies and public enterprise remittances

The initial capital funds for setting up a public enterprise must, by definition, come wholly or partly from the central government. Even when public enterprises have been in existence for many years the need for central government financial assistance still exists for certain public enterprises (Table 8.9).

Public enterprises which receive the largest financial subsidy from the central government belong to the utility and infrastructure groups. The State Railways of Thailand received by far the greatest amount of financial assistance for the period 1981–1988, followed by the Provincial Water Works Authority. By the very nature of their services, these enterprises require substantial investment in physical plant and basic equipment, yet for economic and/or political reasons they are unable to fix their prices to cover costs. Other public enterprises established under special policies, also receive subsidies from the central government. The majority of these public enterprises do not market their services.

Table 8.7: Outstanding foreign debt of the public enterprise sector, 1980 to 1988 (US$ millions)

	Government foreign debt	Per cent of total foreign debt	Public enterprise foreign debt[a]	Per cent of total foreign debt	Total foreign debt	Per cent of GDP
1980	1,463	36.6	2,537	63.4	4,000	12.3
1981	1,797	35.4	3,261	64.6	5,078	14.8
1982	2,131	35.4	3,890	64.6	6,021	16.4
1983	2,461	35.8	4,404	64.2	6,865	17.0
1984	2,445	35.6	4,423	64.4	6,867	16.2
1985	2,724	36.9	4,664	63.1	7,388	19.7
1986	3,500	36.9	5,977	63.1	9,477	22.8
1987	4,126	37.2	6,967	62.8	11,093	23.5
1988	5,207	42.9	6,943	57.1	12,150	22.2

[a] Including both government guaranteed and non-guaranteed loans.

Sources: Watananuling 1985, Table 1 for 1980 to 1983; and Bank of Thailand for 1984 to 1988.

Table 8.8: Foreign debt servicing of the public sector, 1980 to 1988 (US$ millions)

	1980	1981	1982	1983	1984	1985	1986	1987	1988
Foreign debt servicing of the public sector	442.4	643.0	813.5	903.2	920.5	1341.3	910.5	782.0	994.7
Government debt servicing	200.7	280.7	305.9	368.8	338.0	645.9	245.5	91.8	221.7
Public enterprise guaranteed debt servicing	234.4	329.1	496.2	533.7	582.5	695.4	665.0	690.2	773.0
(Per cent of total)	(53.0)	(51.2)	(61.0)	(59.0)	(63.3)	(51.8)	(73.1)	(88.3)	(77.7)
Public enterprise non-guaranteed debt servicing[a]	7.3	33.2	11.4	0.7	—	—	—	—	—
(Per cent of total)	(1.6)	(5.1)	(1.4)	(0.2)	—	—	—	—	—

[a] Public enterprise foreign debt was publicly guaranteed from 1984 onwards.
Source: Bank of Thailand.

Public enterprise	1981	1982	1983	1984	1985	1986	1987	1988
Utility and infrastructure sector								
1. Electricity Generating Authority	676.9	463.5	—	—	—	—	71.6	64.4
2. Metropolitan Water Works Authority	384.7	289.5	38.4	—	—	—	89.2	266.0
3. Provincial Water Works Authority	760.6	637.2	588.5	—	—	—	127.9	323.6
4. Provincial Electricity Authority	212.0	75.0	75.0	—	—	—	12.6	326.6
5. Ports Authority	60.0	80.0	105.0	—	—	—	—	—
6. Expressways and Rapid Transit Authority	242.3	238.8	—	—	—	—	42.9	67.3
7. Industrial Estate Authority	—	—	—	—	—	191.0	119.3	55.5
8. National Housing Authority	317.0	252.1	149.8	—	—	—	242.4	199.0
9. Bangkok Mass Transit Organization	—	—	439.5	2113.0	2113.0	—	—	—
10. State Railways of Thailand	511.1	683.1	766.9	192.2	13.7	77.7	904.0	1009.9
11. Communications Authority	—	—	—	—	—	—	—	8.0
Special policies								
12. Fish Marketing Organization	5.0	—	—	—	—	—	0.5	—
13. Rubber Estate Organization	—	—	—	—	—	—	0.6	0.7
14. Public Warehouse Organization	—	—	—	—	—	—	—	280.0
15. Tourism Authority	109.9	124.5	140.5	199.3	216.6	233.1	384.4	503.7
16. Sports Promotion Organization	51.0	65.6	86.7	80.8	97.1	118.2	143.4	155.6
17. Zoological Organization	5.5	6.1	2.9	—	—	—	7.7	8.1
18. Science and Technology Research Institute	—	56.8	78.7	84.5	82.8	92.4	112.7	118.9
19. Science and Technology Teaching Promotion Institute	—	—	21.5	23.1	22.5	29.9	39.3	40.4
Total	2,469.7	2,972.2	2,493.4	2,692.9	2,545.7	742.3	2,278.5	3,427.7

Source: Budget Bureau, Budget documents.

In the past, subsidies were looked upon as important sources of investment financing and were granted leniently. However, due to recent financial problems, the government has discouraged this source of revenue for project financing. In addition to public enterprises providing non-marketed services, only those operating in accordance with, or at a loss as a result of, special government policy can receive a government subsidy. The amount of annual subsidy requested must be submitted to the Budget Bureau for review and then to Cabinet for final approval.

The reverse of government subsidy is of course remittances from public enterprises to the government. An annual remittance to the government is required of every public enterprise at a minimum rate of 30 per cent of its profits. Such remittances are viewed as dividends for state equity investment in public enterprises. Nevertheless, it has been noted that a large part of public enterprise dividend payments are not really returns to the owner on the initial investment but a tax payment (often partial) to the state (World Bank 1986: 219). This view reflects the fact that most public enterprises are exempted from corporate income tax and some do not pay business taxes. Thus, any profits include taxes that might otherwise have accrued to the government.

Although public enterprises often complain about the high rate of remittance required, the majority do not remit the specified amount. The actual remittance is a result of annual negotiation and depends on the relative urgency of the government's need for revenue and the need for internal financing of the public enterprise. Thus, in 1986, the total remittance of the entire sector was only 45 per cent of net profits (Table 8.2).

The performance of public enterprises

As noted earlier, the public enterprise sector as a whole generates a healthy surplus and the majority of Thai public enterprises are profit-makers, not money-losers. Thus, at this level, the overall performance of the public enterprise sector can be considered to have been good. However, at the level of individual enterprises, the story is less rosy.

It must be stressed that there is as yet no review system by which the performance of individual public enterprises can be evaluated. Indeed, evaluation of performance is probably the weakest aspect of the Thai public enterprise system. As already stated, in spite of numerous authorities overseeing individual aspects of public enterprise functions, there is no single agency which is charged with the responsibility of overall evaluation of public enterprise performance. Even the profit-loss indicator can say little about the efficiency of individual public enterprises since profit may be more the result of monopolistic position than the result of efficiency, and loss more the result of uneconomic interference by the state than the result of inefficiency. Nevertheless, it is widely believed by observers of Thai public enterprises that their operations are inefficient. The reasons can be drawn from certain aspects of the state-public enterprise relationship, particularly the appointment of executive management staff.

An appointment by the supervising ministry of a chief executive officer to a public enterprise is often determined not by the competence and relevant experience of the appointee, but by his affiliation with powerful politicians or a certain political party. The appointment is usually regarded as a reward for loyalty and/or an extension of close control. Most appointees are former bureaucrats, and this is reflected in their management style. This situation is reinforced by appointment of board members who mostly represent their respective supervising agencies. They can rarely provide the level of management ability needed for efficient business performance. In addition to these managerial shortcomings, the enterprises also often lack relevant operational guidelines except for certain isolated regulations such as those related to the compensation structure.

In relation to labour costs, public enterprises must follow a pay scale formulated by the Finance Ministry. Pay structures are similar for all public enterprises although the upper limits vary according to size and profitability. Increases in wages for the lowest paid employees automatically result in higher pay for all other employees, including top management. Not surprisingly then, demands for high wages and fringe benefits by labour unions have not been resisted by top management, and labour costs have accordingly risen relatively faster in the public enterprise sector. Moreover, the bonus system does not differentiate between sources of profit; inefficient but monopolistic public enterprises generate bonuses for their employees while efficient but highly competitive public enterprises do not. The bonus system thus rewards the inefficient and penalizes the efficient. It is in this uniformity of measures, applied to all public enterprises regardless of size and nature of services, that the real problem lies. In fact it is probably the main reason behind the failure of government supervision of the public enterprise system.

In 1988 the government ordered all public enterprises to draw up five-year corporate plans in an effort to improve performance. Most public enterprises have produced these plans, with varying quality and structures. However, little use has been made of such plans; the many supervising agencies have yet to understand the significance of the corporate plan in controlling public enterprises and have not reviewed the plans submitted to them.

A five-year corporate plan can be viewed as a statement of actions to be undertaken in order to achieve certain goals and objectives regarded as desirable by the executives of that public enterprise. The content of a corporate plan can thus also be used for evaluating the performance of individual public enterprises. In order to establish the appropriate link between the government and an individual public enterprise, the objectives to be pursued must be set in consultation with the government. They must be negotiated in detail and in terms of the specific targets identified in the corporate plan. Moreover, the plan's assumptions (such as size of subsidy, remittance and price changes) should be explicitly stated (after agreement with the government). These measures and conditions can then be used for year-end evaluation and total evaluation of the plan.

Privatization: a possible solution for better performance

Experience before the 1980s

If the spirit of the first five national development plans, spanning the years from 1961 to 1986, is taken as a manifestation c

'privatization' policies, Thailand had already embarked on the road to privatization well ahead of many other countries. The development plans essentially stated that the government would try to restrain its expansion of the public sector and refrain from intervention in the free enterprise economy. The move towards privatization is evident from the number of public enterprises operating in 1958 (74) compared with the number in 1978 (62) (Kraiyudht 1987). A number of small companies involved in trading and manufacturing services were liquidated, some were reorganized and several lost their status as public enterprises by changes in definition. It should also be noted that 12 new public enterprises were created between 1978 and 1981 (Appendix 2).

Thailand's experience in the 1980s

With the popularization in Thailand of the term 'privatization' in the years of the Fifth National Development Plan (1982–86), and with its formal induction into the Sixth National Development Plan (1987–93), a number of public enterprises have been privatized or have ceased operating. For some, their operating rights and factories have been franchised/leased to private interests, others have sold shares to private organizations or entered into joint ventures with private enterprises, while others have contracted out certain services.

Although the majority of public enterprises in Thailand have not been offered for sale, there seems to be interest among them, especially at management level, in franchising part of their operations. The State Railways of Thailand has franchised its on-train catering and its affiliated hotel service in a resort area. It has also leased its vacant land for building construction. The Bangkok Mass Transit Organization has also franchised a few of its routes operated by air-conditioned and regular buses. Likewise, the Port Authority of Thailand has franchised its crane operation service.

The main form of contracting-out, which is promoted as a means of privatization, concerns that of the final output or service provided by a public enterprise. An example is the Telephone Organization of Thailand which has recently contracted out its telephone installation service. Contracting out of intermediate services or output has been practised for quite some time (even before the word 'privatization' became popular) although admittedly on a small scale. The Electricity Generating Authority of Thailand and the Bangkok Mass Transit Organization, for example, have contracted out certain areas of their maintenance services.

No liberalization of rules and regulations imposed by the government on public enterprises has been attempted. Thai public enterprises, large and small, whether utilities, industrial or commercial concerns, still remain more or less subject to the same control mechanisms and sets of regulations. However, the tight control over price fixing has been relaxed somewhat with the government allowing an increase in the prices charged by public utilities (electricity and piped water). Of course, the government still retains its approval authority so that all price initiatives by these enterprises must be sanctioned by the government (see Kraiyudht 1989).

The future of privatization

The pursuit of privatization is a political decision. Thus, the adoption of a privatization policy which details the strategy and procedures for privatization rests solely with the government. At the end of the 1980s the position of the Thai government was unclear. Indeed, the term privatization as applied to the public enterprise sector was less popular than before and seldom mentioned in official circles. This was particularly so in the case of 'divestiture', or privatization in its extreme form.

However, the concept of privatization has proved popular when linked to new activities of existing public enterprises or to the initiation of a new activity where no particular agency is legally in charge. The present 'sky train' project, for example, is to be run as a private enterprise, as is the construction and operation of a new international airport for Thailand (either via joint venture, franchising, or turn-key). The operation of a new deep-sea port, yet to be completed, is also a possible area for privatization. Likewise, the speedy introduction of ultra modern telecommunications systems (for example, the car phone, modular telephone and telepaging) is frequently suggested in the context of privatization.

Conclusions: an uncertain future

On the basis of the preceding discussion there can be no doubt that the public enterprises together represent a major sector in the economy, similar in terms of economic size to the central government. Previous governments have established public enterprises for varying purposes. These have included revenue generation—for example, the Thailand Tobacco Monopoly and the State Lottery Bureau. The government also set up public enterprises to provide certain services necessary for the well-being of the people, and to provide the basic infrastructure necessary for economic development.

Several public enterprises, such as the Bangkok Mass Transit Organization, the Provincial Water Works Authority and the Krung Thai Bank, were intended to solve immediate problems faced by the government. A few were the result of a transfer of ownership from the private to the public sector (a reverse of 'privatization') or of a lack of private interest (for example, Thai Maritime Navigation Co. Ltd and Bangkok Dock Co. Ltd). The demands of national security also prompted the establishment of certain public enterprises. The final group of public enterprises was set up to promote activities which could have been carried out via departmental organizations (for example, the Sports Promotion Organization and the Science and Technology Teaching Promotion Institute). It has also been suggested that underlying these explicit objectives there always existed an implicit goal of creating channels by which high ranking and influential military and civilian bureaucrats might be given positions to increase their income (Riggs 1965; Silcock 1967).

The economic and social acceptability of these explicit objectives for setting up public enterprises must be examined in the context of each specific case and the circumstances in which each came into being. Although the establishment of a public enterprise may have been the best means for achieving chosen objectives under specific circumstances, it does not follow that it will remain the best solution under a new economic setting. The government seems to be unaware of this since it keeps re-stating the same set of objectives under which each public enterprise was established years ago as if the Thai economy had remained unchanged over the corresponding period.

Whether or not public enterprises presently operating have a rightful place in the Thai economy of the 1990s, and whether or not their respective objectives are well articulated, the fact remains that the public enterprise sector plays a very significant role in the economy and its operation has enormous impact on its performance. Resource utilization of these public enterprises has both positive and negative effects on the availability of savings to the public as well as to the private sector and on the well-being of the people. As such it is imperative that the central government should have full knowledge of the effectiveness of resource utilization of the public enterprise sector and should take control of the direction of this utilization to assure the generation of economic benefits expected by the Thai community.

Appendix I

Public enterprises in Thailand, 1989

A. Established to generate revenue

1. Thailand Tobacco Monopoly[a]
2. State Lottery Bureau[a]

B. Established to provide services in utilities and infrastructure

Utilities
1. Electricity Generating Authority of Thailand[a]
2. Metropolitan Electricity Authority[a]
3. Provincial Electricity Authority[a]
4. Metropolitan Water Works Authority[a]
5. Provincial Water Works Authority[a]

Infrastructure
1. Expressway and Rapid Transit Authority of Thailand[a]
2. Airports Authority of Thailand[a]
3. Port Authority of Thailand[a]
4. State Railways of Thailand[a]
5. Bangkok Mass Transit Organization[a]
6. Telephone Organization of Thailand[a]

7. Mass Communications Organization of Thailand[a]
8. Communications Authority of Thailand[a]
9. Aeronautical Radio of Thailand Ltd
10. National Housing Authority[a]
11. Industrial Estate Authority of Thailand[a]

C. Established to service special state policies

Finance
1. Bank of Thailand
2. Krung Thai Bank
3. Government Savings Bank
4. Government Housing Bank
5. Bank for Agriculture and Agricultural Cooperatives
6. State Pawn Shops, Department of Social Welfare

Natural and Mineral Resource
1. Petroleum Authority of Thailand
2. PTT Exploration and Production Co. Ltd
3. Bang Chak Petroleum Co. Ltd
4. Offshore Mining Organization
5. Forest Industry Organization

Agriculture and Commerce
1. Dairy Farming Promotion Organization of Thailand
2. Rubber Estate Organization
3. Marketing Organization for Farmers
4. Fish Marketing Organization
5. Government Cold Storage Organization
6. Marketing Organization
7. Public Warehouse Organization
8. Prachin Buri Provincial Co. Ltd
9. Lampoon Provincial Co. Ltd
10. Surin Provincial Co. Ltd
11. Thai Plywood Co. Ltd
12. Police Printing Press
13. Playing Cards Factory, Excise Department
14. Liquor Distillery Organization, Excise Department
15. Government Pharmaceutical Organization
16. Express Transportation Organization
17. Thai Maritime Navigation Co. Ltd
18. Thai Airways International Ltd[a]

19. The Transport Co. Ltd
20. Bangkok Dock Co. Ltd

Promotion
1. Tourism Authority of Thailand
2. Sports Promotion Organization of Thailand
3. Zoological Park Organization of Thailand
4. Institute for the Promotion of Science and Technology Teaching
5. Science and Technology Research Institute of Thailand
6. Office of the Rubber Replanting Aid Fund

D. Established for reasons of national security

1. Preserved Food Organization
2. Glass Organization
3. Textile Organization
4. Battery Organization
5. Tanning Organization

E. Others

1. Dhipaya Insurance Co. Ltd
2. Syndicate of Thai Hotels and Travel Co. Ltd
3. Northeast Jute Mill Co. Ltd
4. Sugar Factory, Department of Industrial Works
A total of 64 public enterprises

[a] These constitute the 17 most important public enterprises in Thailand which are analysed in Table 8.2. The 18th public enterprise indicated in Table 8.2 is Thai Airways Co. Ltd, which is presently an integral part of Thai Airways International Ltd.

Appendix 2

Public enterprises formed since 1978

1. Dairy Farming Promotion Organization of Thailand (1971
2. Industrial Estate Authority of Thailand (1972)
3. Expressway and Rapid Transit Authority of Thailand (1972
4. National Housing Authority (1973)
5. Marketing Organization for Farmers (1974)

6. Offshore Mining Organization (1975)
7. Bangkok Mass Transit Organization (1976)
8. The Communications Authority of Thailand (1976)
9. The Mass Communications Organization of Thailand (1977)
10. Provincial Water Works Authority (1979)
11. Airport Authority of Thailand (1979)
12. The Petroleum Authority of Thailand (1980)

9

Energy Policy

PRAIPOL KOOMSUP

As a small, oil-importing developing country, Thailand cannot escape the effects of fluctuating oil prices. Energy is important to all sectors of its economy and oil imports are a major portion of the country's imports. Energy has become an important issue in economic planning and management. This chapter describes and analyses two policy measures which play a prominent role in the energy sector—namely oil pricing and the legal arrangements governing petroleum exploration and development. To set these in perspective, I begin with an overview of Thailand's energy demand pattern and its energy supply profile.

Energy demand pattern

The rapid growth of the Thai economy during the past two decades has been associated with industrialization, farm mechanization, urbanization and expanding transport activities. As a result, the consumption of modern energy, particularly oil products, has grown rapidly, averaging some 12 per cent per year since 1970. The two oil crises of 1973-74 and 1979-80 significantly dampened economic growth and energy demand. Energy consumption grew at less than 2 per cent per year in the post-shock years of 1974 and 1980. High oil prices also encouraged energy conservation and the substitution of indigenous energy for imported oil. Nevertheless, oil is still the most important energy source in Thailand, accounting for close to half of total energy requirements and over two-thirds of modern fuels.

In 1988, almost 70 per cent of total energy consumption was in the form of commercial or non-traditional energy, nearly

80 per cent of which was petroleum products (Table 9.1). The demand for commercial energy grew at 16 per cent per year during the 1960s, but its growth was reduced to 9 per cent per year in the 1970s and to an even lower rate in the 1980s. Traditional or non-commercial energy accounted for 30 per cent of total energy consumption in 1988 and consisted mainly of charcoal and fuel-wood. The data on the sectoral use of energy for 1979 to 1988 (Table 9.2) indicate that transport and households each accounted for over 30 per cent of total energy demand over most of this decade, followed by industry which consumed 27 per cent.

The most important oil product is diesel oil, most of which is used in transport, particularly in commercial vehicles. Gasoline is also used, mainly in road transport. Virtually all the secondary energy consumption of fuel oil is in industry, notably cement.[1] About one-third of liquefied petroleum gas (LPG) is used in transport, leaving about one-third to be used in cooking, and the rest in services and industry. The three biggest users of electricity are industry (44 per cent), services (25 per cent) and households (25 per cent). The use of traditional fuels is sectorally concentrated. While charcoal and fuel-wood are predominantly used in rural households, bagasse[2] is used in sugar mills, and most paddy husk is burnt in rice mills.

Following the first oil crisis, significant changes occurred in the pattern of energy use. The changes were caused not only by the structural change and growth of the economy but also by the government's energy pricing policy and production increases in indigenous energy, mainly natural gas and lignite. These changes can be summarized as follows:

- The large price differentials among transport fuels encouraged motorists to switch from gasoline to LPG and diesel oil, and from premium gasoline to regular gasoline. There was also the practice of mixing kerosene with diesel oil. These inter–fuel substitution activities, though privately profitable, were said to cause economic losses to the economy and imbalances between the country's refining and consumption patterns. In electricity generation, the development of local natural gas and lignite enabled the Electricity Generating Authority of Thailand (EGAT) to reduce its use of fuel oil (its main energy source before 1984).

In industry, the efficiency of fuel use was improved for most of the sector. The cement industry, in particular, switched

Table 9.1: Total energy consumption by type of energy, 1979 to 1988 ('000 metric tonnes crude oil equivalent)

	1979	1980	1981	1982	1983	1984	1985	1986	1987	1988
Modern energy sources										
Coal	43	59	42	101	108	144	213	141	196	240
Lignite	53	55	70	155	151	157	233	323	478	568
Petroleum products	8,157	7,913	7,892	7,834	8,639	9,342	9,463	10,071	11,263	12,747
Natural gas	—	—	—	—	32	194	178	87	40	60
Hydroelectricity	1,060	1,121	1,179	1,281	1,441	1,583	1,707	1,878	2,121	2,408
Sub-total	9,313	9,148	9,183	9,371	10,371	11,420	11,794	12,500	14,098	16,023
	(59.3)[a]	(60.6)	(59.1)	(57.8)	(60.9)	(62.5)	(62.5)	(63.9)	(67)	(69.9)
Renewable energy sources										
Fuel-wood	2,657	2,578	2,613	2,676	2,740	2,837	2,875	2,885	2,835	2,825
Charcoal	2,193	2,289	2,253	2,227	2,183	2,161	2,138	2,103	2,103	2,066
Paddy husk	522	431	534	560	564	742	830	838	788	729
Bagasse	1,021	653	968	1,387	1,164	1,112	1,219	1,230	1,224	1,284
Sub-total	6,393	5,951	6,368	6,850	6,651	6,852	7,062	7,056	6,950	6,904
	(40.7)	(39.4)	(40.9)	(42.2)	(39.1)	(37.5)	(37.5)	(36.1)	(33)	(30.1)
Total energy consumption	15,706	15,099	15,551	16,221	17,022	18,272	18,856	19,556	21,048	22,927
	(100)	(100)	(100)	(100)	(100)	(100)	(100)	(100)	(100)	(100)

[a] Figures in parentheses are percentages.
Source: Thailand Energy Situation 1988, National Energy Administration.

Table 9.2: Total energy consumption by economic sector, 1979 to 1988 ('000 metric tonnes crude oil equivalent)

	1979	1980	1981	1982	1983	1984	1985	1986	1987	1988
Agriculture	1,041	1,130	1,004	1,117	1,043	1,029	841	881	835	834
	(6.6)[a]	(7.5)	(6.5)	(6.9)	(6.1)	(5.6)	(4.5)	(4.5)	(4)	(3.6)
Mining	85	85	71	74	102	86	74	53	49	49
	(0.5)	(0.6)	(0.5)	(0.5)	(0.6)	(0.5)	(0.4)	(0.3)	(0.2)	(0.2)
Manufacturing	4,515	3,995	4,293	4,728	4,547	4,930	5,219	5,250	5,598	6,062
	(28.7)	(26.5)	(27.6)	(29.1)	(26.7)	(27)	(27.7)	(26.8)	(26.6)	(26.5)
Construction	98	128	125	111	78	100	125	123	111	98
	(0.6)	(0.8)	(0.8)	(0.7)	(0.5)	(0.5)	(0.7)	(0.6)	(0.5)	(0.4)
Residential and commercial	5,375	5,395	5,402	5,502	5,622	5,760	6,029	6,203	6,393	6,650
	(34.2)	(35.7)	(34.7)	(33.9)	(33)	(31.5)	(32)	(31.7)	(30.4)	(29)
Transportation	4,206	4,008	4,268	4,328	5,084	5,953	6,360	6,820	7,875	8,914
	(26.8)	(26.5)	(27.4)	(26.7)	(29.9)	(32.6)	(33.7)	(34.9)	(37.4)	(38.9)
Others	386	358	388	361	546	414	208	226	187	320
	(2.6)	(2.4)	(2.5)	(2.2)	(3.2)	(2.3)	(1)	(1.2)	(0.9)	(1.4)
Total	15,706	15,099	15,551	16,221	17,022	18,272	18,856	19,556	21,048	22,927
	(100)	(100)	(100)	(100)	(100)	(100)	(100)	(100)	(100)	(100)

[a] Figures in parentheses are percentages.
Source: Thailand Energy Situation 1988, National Energy Administration.

heavily from fuel oil to natural gas. Some cement plants have been converted to use lignite and imported coal.

- In households, the main shifts have been from traditional fuels to modern fuels. In urban areas, charcoal as a cooking fuel has been gradually replaced by LPG. Rural households are in the process of moving from fuel–wood to charcoal in cooking, and from kerosene to electricity in lighting.
- In the past decade, the demand for electricity grew at close to 10 per cent per year as a result of a high income elasticity of demand and rural electrification. Rates in 1990 are between 5 and 7 per cent.

Most of these changes are likely to continue in the future, subject to various constraints and factors within and outside the energy sector. Four major conditions determine Thailand's energy demand prospects: world oil prices, the national macroeconomic situation, the potential supply of domestic natural gas, and opportunities for increased energy efficiency.

Not only is oil the nation's most important energy source, but it is also a major import item (Table 9.3). Therefore, changes in the world oil price have very significant effects on Thailand's energy situation. The perspective of the international oil market has changed since the second oil price shock of 1979–80. The growth of world oil consumption has moderated; the development of indigenous resources in several oil importing countries has been accelerated; and non-OPEC oil supplies have expanded. Oil prices fell in the mid- to late 1980s. Their future movements are unpredictable. Much depends on the political will and discipline of OPEC.

Thailand's macroeconomic environment is also relevant. Its economy is closely linked with the world economy. Financial instability and economic recession in the world in the early 1980s adversely affected Thailand's economic performance. However, GDP growth substantially rose in the latter half of the 1980s, and in 1990 was expected to remain high in the first five years of the 1990s. Inflation was expected to remain moderate at about 5 per cent per year, and the current account deficit was expected to remain stable. A constant shift in the production structure was expected in the 15 years to 2005 when manufacturing would be the most significant sector of the economy. Population growth was expected to decline from the 1.8 per cent per year experienced in the 1979–85 period t

1.2 per cent over the years to 2001. Urbanization was expected to continue, with the urban population growing from 8 million in 1982 to 13.5 million in 2001.

Another factor influencing the demand for specific fuels is the availability of alternative supplies of energy. In the Thai context, the most promising local energy resources which can replace imported oil are natural gas and lignite. Demand for energy may be reduced by improvements in energy efficiency and by energy conservation. Efforts to improve energy efficiency are aimed mainly at the two sectors dominating the demand for modern energy—industry and transport. To some extent they also involve other sectors—services and households. In industry, possible energy-saving measures range from low-cost housekeeping measures to medium-cost retrofitting investments, and higher-cost investments in new equipment and processes. It is possible that industrial energy saving during the next 15 years could result in a 14 per cent decline in energy output ratios by 2001.

In transport, opportunities for energy savings are to be found in improving overall fuel efficiency of road vehicles, reducing Bangkok's traffic congestion, and shifting to more efficient transport modes in Bangkok. There could be scope for saving as much as 55 per cent of energy demand in Bangkok transport by the year 2001. In services, commercial and government sectors, energy saving can mainly be achieved by more efficient modes of air-conditioning and lighting. In households, the potential for improved efficiency is in the use of charcoal in cooking stoves, and in the manufacture of charcoal itself. To realize these saving potentials, appropriate government policies are needed. Besides energy pricing, which is the central policy instrument, there are non-price interventions which include information, education, training, financial and fiscal incentives, as well as regulations and standards.

Energy supply

Although Thailand's potential energy resources are diversified, the development and use of modern energy supplies (natural gas, oil, lignite and hydro-power) are below potential. The resource bases of gas, oil and lignite are still relatively unknown and most of the exploitation of these fuels has occurred in the last five years, partly as a result of policy initiatives to promote the development of domestic energy resources so as to reduce oil imports.

Traditional fuels such as fuel–wood, charcoal, bagasse and paddy husk were the main domestically derived energy sources, providing about 35 per cent of total energy demand in 1985. Modern fuels, which supplied the remaining 65 per cent, were dominated by oil products and most of the oil used in Thailand was imported.

The recent record of increased domestic production of modern fuels is impressive. Both oil and gas production have increased from minimal quantities in 1980 to some 38,000 barrels per day of oil plus condensate, and to about 580 million cubic feet per day of gas in 1988. The generation of electricity from the use of lignite has increased from 210 megawatts (MW) in 1980 to over 900 MW in 1988. Each of these increases in domestic production has contributed to reducing the country's dependence on imported oil. Nevertheless, the contribution of domestically produced modern energy supplies was only about 30 per cent of total energy requirements.

In summary, the supply situation in the late 1980s was as follows: some 35 per cent of supplies were domestic traditional fuels, about 25 per cent were domestic modern fuels, and the remaining 40 per cent were imported modern fuels (mainly oil and oil products). Consequently, a basic issue in supply policy is to find ways of increasing the domestic production of natural gas, oil, lignite and hydro-power.

Oil and gas production

Oil production in Thailand began in the 1950s when the Defence Energy Department established a small refinery close to the Fang oil field in Chiang Mai. Production has ranged from 400 to 1,000 barrels per day, although it is said that considerably more could be produced through the application of enhanced recovery techniques and additional exploration and development drilling in that area.

As well as the Fang basin there are other basins in Thailand in which oil or gas have been found. None of these basins has been fully explored, as is illustrated by the fact that only 12 exploration wells were drilled in all concession areas in Thailand (onshore and offshore) between 1975 and 1990. No estimates of the overall hydrocarbon potential of the country have been published by the government but exploration results so far suggest that the geology is complex. The known and potential reservoirs are fragmented so that economically recoverable reserves are likely to be only a small fraction of reserves in place. The experience of the Erawan Gasfield in the Gulf of Thailand, where recovery factors were reduced from an expected 82 per cent to about 35 per cent, is often cited as an illustration of this point. A more comprehensive understanding of the geology and ultimate production potential of the various basins will only come about through additional exploration drilling (and subsequent production) and a systematic compilation and review of geological and related data by a responsible agency of the government.

The World Bank has estimated the 'ultimate potential' oil reserves at some 1.15 billion barrels and gas reserves at some 19.3 trillion cubic feet (TCF). These are indeed only estimates, but they would indicate that the scope for oil discoveries is considerable. The estimated 'proven and possible' reserves of oil are only some 180 million barrels suggesting that only about 16 per cent of oil reserves have been discovered. For natural gas, however, the 'proven and possible' reserves have been estimated at some 12.9 TCF implying that 67 per cent of the 'ultimate' reserves have already been discovered. The likely reality is that the 'ultimate' gas reserves are considerably larger and the 'proven and possible' reserves may not be as much as 12.9 TCF. In any event, given the present lack of knowledge about the hydrocarbon basins in Thailand, these statistics at least point to the potential for additional reserves of oil and gas. They suggest that intensified petroleum exploration in Thailand can be profitable to the private sector, and worthwhile to the country.

Lignite production

Another indigenous energy resource is lignite. Although abundant, it has not been extensively utilized. Before the sharp increases in oil prices in 1974, oil was less costly and more convenient to use. The use of lignite was thus underdeveloped.

Most of the mined lignite is used at Mae-Moh electricity generating plant in the north, but it is also used at Changwad Lampang, at the North Bangkok plant, Changwad Nonthaburi and at the Krabi plant. It is also used in a fertilizer plant, and in the cement and other industries.

Since the 1970s, the role of lignite in supplying energy has gradually increased. There have been various initiatives to accelerate and develop it as a substitute for fuel oil. This can be seen in the increase of electricity generation by lignite; in 1972 the capacity was only 72 MW, but this had increased to 585 MW in 1984. The use of lignite in electricity generation increased (by a factor of about 15) from 326,000 tonnes in 1972 to over 5 million tonnes in 1988. In the industrial sector, utilization of lignite increased from 7,271 tonnes in 1972 to over 1 million tonnes in 1988. It is expected that lignite utilization will rise with increasing electricity generation capacity as well as increasing industrial demand.

Most of the lignite found in Thailand is of low quality. It is found in the Northern and Southern regions. The calorific value ranges from 2,000 to 6,000 Kcal/kg. Anthracite has also been discovered during oil exploration at Fang, but in limited quantities.

According to the reports of the Department of Mineral Resources (DMR), National Energy Administration (NEA), and EGAT, there are more than 75 lignite deposits in Thailand. In the Northern and Southern regions, there are 11 explored deposits with total (geological) reserves in place of about 1,730 million tonnes, and proven reserves of over 900 million tonnes. Moreover, there are 15 more deposits under exploration or still being planned. Taking all the 26 deposits together, it is expected that there are geological reserves of about 2,600 million tonnes of lignite. It is believed that proven reserves would increase if there was additional exploration in various unexplored deposits. Indeed the estimates of reserves in place would most likely also be raised.

Hydroelectric power generation

Since hydro-power is a renewable energy source which car be developed and used as electricity, it can reduce reliance or foreign petroleum and help to stabilize the country's energy supply in the long run. Hydroelectricity in Thailand is more appropriate for the generation of electricity for peak demand than as the base load. Operating costs of generation are also low. Moreover, the development of hydroelectricity through creation of dams can provide other benefits such as irrigation, fisheries and tourism.

Domestic hydroelectric potentials can be divided into three types:
- large and medium scale (more than 6 MW);
- hydro-power plant (reversible pump type);
- and small scale (less than 6 MW).

The total domestic hydroelectric potential is estimated at 10,051 MW, with an annual average electricity generation capacity of about 17,000 million kilowatt/hour. There are 98 large and medium-scale potential hydro sites in various regions, providing 3,520 MW in Northern regions, 477 MW in the Northeastern region, 6,013 MW in the Central region, 740 MW in the Southern region. There are also 250 small-scale potential hydro sites in various regions, with total production capacity of 291 MW.

The potential for hydroelectric production along Thailand's borders is from large-scale project sites with total capacity of about 17,866 MW. The annual average rate of production could be about 107,800 million kilowatt/hour. The power would be obtained from two major rivers:
- The Maekong River, with dam construction between Thailand and Laos, and seven projects having total production capacity of 9,623 MW. Among these, the Kheun Pha-Mong project is the largest, with the capacity of 4,800 MW.
- The Salawin River, involving a joint project between Thailand and Myanmar (formerly Burma) with four projects having total production of 8,243 MW. The Salawin project is the largest project among the four, with a production capacity of 5,850 MW.

The total hydroelectric potential both from the domestic and the international sources is 27,917 MW.

Utilization of hydro-power in electricity generation in Thailand started in 1964 at Bhumibol Dam, in Tak Province. The project was equipped with two generators, giving a total capacity of 140 MW. At the end of each national plan, the capacity was increased. At the end of 1989, the total installed capacity of all hydroelectric projects was about 2,250 MW or 30 per cent of the country's total electricity generation capacity.

Taking into account the appropriateness and the possibility of future development in hydro-power, the water resources which can be further developed and utilized in the generation of electricity are rather limited. The remaining domestic water resources are only suitable for medium or small-scale electricity projects. Moreover, there are problems of environmental impact, especially regarding deforestation and population resettlement. A good example is the Nam Chone Dam project, with potential installed capacity of 400 MW, but which was shelved by the government in 1987 after strong protests by environmentalists. This problem will limit the development of potential domestic water sources potentially usable for hydroelectric generation. The possibility of international hydro projects going ahead also seems remote, depending upon the political situation on the country's borders.

Energy policies

The oil crises in the 1970s and early 1980s affected the Thai economy adversely by creating large trade and balance of payments deficits, high inflation rates, growing foreign debts, and energy shortages. The share of oil in total imports, which was relatively stable at about 10 per cent before the first oil crisis, shot up rapidly after 1973. Thailand's oil import value in 1981 accounted for over 40 per cent of its total export earnings and about 30 per cent of its total import bill (Table 9.3). Although these percentages have declined in recent years, the prospect of another oil crisis is still a real threat.

Several policy measures have been used to cope with the energy-related problems. This chapter deals only with those policies specifically targeted at the energy sector. They are classified into two groups: energy demand management policy and energy supply policy.

Energy demand management policy

The most significant policy measure in energy demand management is energy pricing. Since the first energy crisis

Table 9.3: Imports by economic classification, 1965 to 1989 (selected years) (millions of baht)

	1965	1973	1974	1979	1980	1983	1984	1985	1986	1987	1988	1989
Consumer goods	4,113	6,311	7,995	15,933	19,286	22,308	22,692	23,966	24,466	33,844	39,793	55,220
	(26.7)a	(15)	(12.5)	(10.9)	(10.2)	(9.4)	(9.3)	(9.5)	(10.1)	(10.1)	(7.8)	(8.4)
Intermediate products and raw materials	3,210	13,621	18,370	43,500	45,312	66,474	69,613	75,772	84,333	119,792	181,485	234,385
	(20.8)	(32.3)	(28.7)	(29.8)	(24)	(28.1)	(28.4)	(30.2)	(34.9)	(35.8)	(35.4)	(35.7)
Capital goods	4,775	12,826	19,808	39,902	46,075	69,814	73,607	75,404	78,316	105,916	201,147	239,807
	(30.9)	(30.4)	(30.9)	(27.3)	(24.4)	(29.5)	(30)	(30)	(32.4)	(31.7)	(39.2)	(36.5)
Othersb	3,335	9,426	17,871	46,826	78,013	78,013	79,243	76,028	54,243	74,657	90,689	127,015
	(21.6)	(22.3)	(27.9)	(32)	(41.3)	(33)	(32.3)	(30.3)	(22.5)	(22.3)	(17.7)	(19.3)
Fuels and lubricants	1,353	4,661	12,571	32,647	58,733	57,065	57,353	56,718	32,354	44,177	38,829	58,414
	(8.8)	(11)	(19.6)	(22.3)	(31.1)	(24.1)	(23.4)	(22.6)	(13.4)	(13.2)	(7.6)	(8.9)
Others	1,982	4,765	5,300	14,179	19,280	20,948	21,890	19,318	21,889	30,480	51,860	68,601
	(12.8)	(11.3)	(8.3)	(9.7)	(10.2)	(8.9)	(8.9)	(7.7)	(9.1)	(9.1)	(10.1)	(10.5)
Total imports	15,433	42,184	64,044	146,161	188,686	236,609	245,155	251,170	241,358	334,209	513,114	656,427

a Figures in parentheses are percentage shares of total.
b Other imports include vehicles and parts, gold bullion, and miscellaneous items.
Source: Bank of Thailand, *Statistical Bulletin*, various issues.

energy prices have been one of the main variables in economic planning and management. In Thailand, the government has some control over the prices of most commercial energy products including oil products, natural gas, electricity and lignite. Although the prices of non-commercial energy products (mainly fuel-wood, charcoal, paddy husk and bagasse) are not directly regulated by the government, it is reasonable to believe that they are influenced by the prices of commercial energy. The main emphasis of this section is on the pricing of oil products, both at the ex-refinery and retail levels.

The Sixth Economic and Social Development Plan describes energy pricing policy in terms of an energy demand management strategy with the key element that energy prices paid by users (or retail prices) reflect the real cost to the economy. The objectives of this policy are to:

• reduce energy consumption growth;
• reduce oil imports, and lower the energy dependence on imported oil; and
• avoid wasteful inter-fuel substitution.

All these objectives imply that energy pricing should lead to better energy efficiency by energy conservation and by the substitution of oil by other energy sources, particularly indigenous sources. Since oil is a major import item, such energy pricing should also relieve the balance of payments problem.

On the supply side, oil pricing at the ex-refinery import levels should ensure adequate oil supplies, domestically refined or imported, at competitive prices. While local refineries should be maintained for supply security reasons, ex-refinery pricing must also force them to be efficient and competitive. An appropriate pricing system should also encourage competition in the wholesale and retail distribution of oil products.

Oil products have long been an important source of government revenue. The main problem is how to tax different oil products in such a way as to generate a 'reasonable' amount of government revenue, while at the same time not inducing inefficient uses of energy, ensuring adequate and efficient oil supplies and distribution, and not causing excessive inflation and price instability.

Since oil prices have significant effects on energy demand and supply, it is very important for the government to implement an oil pricing policy which allows domestic oil prices to reflect the real cost of imported oil. There is an understandable reluctance by the government to impose hardship on low- and middle-income sections of the population by raising oil prices. In Thailand, the pricing of oil products has become such a sensitive political issue, because of its significant impact on the cost of living, that one government was brought down in 1980 after it sharply raised the retail prices of oil products and electricity. In setting oil prices, the government must trade off among conflicting policy objectives. This includes a trade-off between an equitable distribution of the burden of higher petroleum prices (and the implications of costs of living for the various income groups) and the saving of foreign exchange which would have been spent on imported oil.

The government imposes a price control on all oil products because it regards them as being vital to the livelihood of the population. It is debatable whether this price control is desirable, for political and economic reasons, some of which are noted above. But the government finds it necessary to influence domestic oil prices.

For locally refined products in Thailand, the government controls prices at two levels, namely retail and ex-refinery. Excise, municipal and business taxes are collected at different rates for different types of product.[3] In addition, there is a component called the 'oil fund' which is equivalent to a variable tax or subsidy allowing the government to change the ex-refinery price without changing other components and the retail price. The remaining component of the retail price is a marketing margin which includes marketing costs and profits of oil traders. The breakdown of retail price components for a locally refined product is as follows:

Retail price = ex-refinery price + excise tax + municipal and business taxes, + oil fund + marketing margin.

There is no import tax on crude oil imports. For imported refined products, the government collects an import tax as well as business and municipal taxes. The rates of these taxes are based on the 'import price' set by the government on the basis of the c.i.f. price. The retail price components of an imported refined product are as follows:

Retail price = import price + import tax + municipal and business taxes + oil fund + marketing margin.

It is clear that the government has been trying to control not only the retail prices of oil products, but also those components of the prices. Therefore, it is interesting to examine some of these components individually.

Ex-refinery price

Prior to the first oil crisis in 1973–74 the government set the ex-refinery price for the biggest local refinery (the Thai Oil Refining Company, or TORC) by using the following formula:

Ex-refinery price = f.o.b. ex-refinery price in Singapore + Singapore–Bangkok transport cost + insurance cost + losses (0.5 per cent of c.i.f. Bangkok price).

After the world oil price began to rise very sharply at the end of 1973, transport and insurance costs, including losses, were taken out of the formula. Since then the ex-refinery price in Thailand has been tied to the Singapore f.o.b. ex-refinery price (or posting price), though the prices still differ slightly for some products. Because Singapore is the biggest refining centre in the region and is likely to have the economies of scale which ensure efficiency, such a price-setting formula should force local refineries to be as efficient as those in Singapore. One interesting issue is whether this method of ex-refinery price determination is appropriate. Different conditions in the two countries may require differences in their ex-refinery prices. These include, for example the price of imported crude oil, oil demand patterns, refinery yield patterns, and domestic cost components in refineries.

It has been observed that an incentive provided to Thailand's local refineries for producing fuel oil is relatively greater than for diesel oil; and this contributed to shortages in diesel oil in the past and will lead to fuel oil surpluses in the future when lignite and natural gas will substitute for much of the fuel oil used in electricity generation. Price differentials among different products as well as among different refineries need to be considered by taking into account various cost and demand differences.

Taxes and the oil fund

Before the first oil crisis, taxes were the biggest component added to the ex-refinery prices of all oil products. All taxes a percentages of ex-refinery prices ranged from over 100 per cent for gasoline and LPG to 30 per cent for diesel oil. After December 1973, these percentages began to decline as the government tried to reduce the oil tax burden in order to soften the impact of import prices on domestic prices. Retail prices remained stable from December 1975 to March 1977, and the relative tax shares reached the lowest level for gasoline and diesel oil during that period. These shares picked up gradually until early 1980 when political pressure, which caused a change in the government, pushed them down again. In May 1984, fuel oil and LPG were subject to only minimal taxes, while the tax shares on gasoline, diesel oil, and kerosene were slightly lower than those in early 1973.

Oil is one of the very few commodities bringing substantial tax revenue to the government. The excise tax revenue from oil products is in fact the largest among the various types of excise tax. As a percentage of total tax revenue, the revenue from oil excise tax seemed to be directly related to oil price increases after 1974. It went down from 7.2 per cent in 1974 to 6.6 per cent and 6.3 per cent in 1975 and 1976, respectively, when domestic oil prices remained constant; then it climbed up to 8.4 per cent and 12.9 per cent in 1979 and 1980, respectively, when international oil prices rose again. The percentage went down again to about 10 per cent in 1981–83 when the tax rates on oil products were reduced to prevent the retail prices from increasing at high rates (Table 9.4).

The revenue from the import tax on oil products follows a similar pattern, reaching the lowest level of about 1 per cent of total tax revenue in 1975 and 1976. The revenue from both taxes as a percentage of total tax revenue reached its peak at 16 per cent in 1980. This seems to imply that high domestic oil prices in 1980 were caused not only by OPEC's action but also by the government's action, intentional or not, of shifting its tax base towards oil products. However, the tax share fell in the 1980s to 12 per cent, which, though lower than in 1980, was still higher than in the 1970s.

Because the taxes on oil products are indirect taxes, most of the oil tax burden falls on the final users. Like other indirect taxes, the oil taxes tend to be regressive, generating a proportionally larger burden for the poor than the rich, but since the government taxes the types of oil product used mainly

Table 9.4: Oil tax revenue as proportion of total tax revenue, 1970 to 1987 (per cent)

	Oil excise tax revenue	Oil import tax revenue	Revenue from oil excise and import taxes
1970	6.2	3.2	9.4
1971	8.1	1.8	9.9
1972	7.4	1.5	8.9
1973	7.0	1.4	8.4
1974	7.2	1.5	8.7
1975	6.5	1.1	7.6
1976	6.3	1.3	7.6
1977	6.7	1.3	8.0
1978	6.3	1.9	8.2
1979	8.4	2.4	10.8
1980	12.9	3.4	16.3
1981	10.5	2.3	12.8
1982	10.9	1.1	12.0
1983	9.5	0.8	10.3
1984	9.1	1.5	10.6
1985	9.2	0.5	9.7
1986	11.0	0.5	11.5
1987	13.1	0.4	13.5

Source: *Annual Report*, Department of Excise Tax, Ministry of Finance, various issues; *Statistical Bulletin*, Bank of Thailand, various issues.

by the rich (e.g. gasoline) at higher rates than those used mostly by the poor (e.g. kerosene and fuel oil), the degree of tax regressivity should be reduced or even reversed.

Apart from the oil taxes mentioned above, the 'oil fund' is essentially another type of government levy. This fund was set up in 1974 when the government collected the oil company's windfall profit arising from higher retail prices of the 'old cost' oil stock. In 1975, the government began to collect the oil fund from oil users by adding it as another component of the retail price. The component is a positive levy every time the government raises the controlled retail prices, and it is reduced when ex-refinery prices are raised, as a result of higher oil import prices, in order to keep the retail price constant. For kerosene, fuel oil and LPG, the retail prices and taxes have been set a such low levels that the oil fund often becomes negative, i.e. subsidies are given by drawing from the oil fund, until there is another round of retail price adjustments. It is only for gasoline that the oil fund remains largely positive.

From 1975 to 1977 and from 1979 to 1981, payments were drawn from the oil fund to subsidize the prices of fuel oil and diesel oil used by EGAT to keep down the price of electricity. These subsidies, the rates of which were quite high,[4] were one of the main causes of a large deficit in the oil fund. It was estimated that the oil fund deficit amounted to 3,600 million baht at the end of 1980. To the extent that electricity is used mainly by people in big cities, particularly Bangkok, these large subsidies benefit city dwellers at the expense of the rural sector, thus worsening the distribution of the oil tax burden.

When the taxes and the oil fund are combined, it is worth noting that oil subsidies by the government became widespread during and after the second oil crisis. From the middle of 1980 to March 1983, all oil products except gasoline were subsidized for most of the time through compensation paid out of the oil fund (i.e. negative oil fund), which more than offset taxes. It was not until April 1983 that the government began to remove subsidies for kerosene, diesel oil and fuel oil as the import prices of oil started to decline.

In practice, the importance of the various goals of the oil pricing policy vary according to the urgency of the energy problem, the political strength of the government, the government's fiscal position, and the external balances of the economy in monetary and trade areas. During the past oil crises, oil pricing by the government was oriented towards short-run objectives such as inflation, short-run economic growth and industrial competitiveness.

Following the second oil crisis, more consideration was given to the position of the oil fund which had accumulated an increasing deficit since the first crisis. Attempts were made to use the tax and oil fund revenue from gasoline to subsidize other oil products, thus leading to price disparities which encouraged undesirable inter-fuel substitution. These price differences were reduced in 1983 when the OPEC oil price started to decline. Even then, reductions in retail prices were delayed so that the government might turn the oil fund deficit into a surplus. It was during July 1979 and March 1980 that oil prices

were substantially adjusted to reflect fully the higher import
costs and to promote energy conservation. As already observed,
this was done at a high political cost. The baht devaluation
in November 1984 increased the baht cost of imported oil and
led to some oil subsidies. In June 1985, fuel oil and cylindered
LPG were subsidized[5] and the oil fund deficit was about
180 million baht per month. As a result of differential taxes
and oil fund levies, the retail/import price ratio varied
significantly among different oil products. The price ratios and
the retail prices in June 1985 are shown in Table 9.5.

While the retail price of gasoline was about double its import
price, the corresponding difference for diesel and LPG was about
30 per cent and was negligible for kerosene and fuel oil. Because
of this, the inter-fuel price differentials at the c.i.f. level were
further widened at the retail level, as shown in Table 9.6. The
cases of high price differentials were gasoline on the one hand,
and diesel oil, LPG and kerosene on the other. Though the c.i.f.
prices of gasoline were 10 to 30 per cent above those of the
other three products, the differences in their retail prices were
increased to 60 to 100 per cent.

This distorted retail price structure has led to a number of
undesirable consequences:

• Inefficient use of transport fuels. From a purely economic
  standpoint, diesel oil is the most cost-efficient fuel for heavy
  forms of transport (buses and heavy trucks), and gasoline
  is the most cost-efficient fuel for light transport (private cars,
  taxis, pick-ups and small trucks). The relatively low retail
  prices of LPG and diesel have encouraged their use in transport

Table 9.5: Retail and import price ratios of petroleum products, 1985

	Retail price/ import price	Retail price (baht/litre)
Premium gasoline	1.91	11.70
Regular gasoline	2.13	10.80
Kerosene	1.08	6.12
High-speed diesel	1.29	6.76
Fuel oil 1500	0.91	4.05
LPG (cars)	1.27	5.90

Table 9.6: Petroleum product price differentials at import and retail levels, 1985[a]

	Import price	Retail price
Premium gasoline/high-speed diesel	1.18	1.75
Premium gasoline/LPG (cars)	1.32	1.98
Premium gasoline/regular gasoline	1.09	1.08
Premium gasoline/kerosene	1.00	1.91
Regular gasoline/high-speed diesel	1.08	1.61
Regular gasoline/LPG (cars)	1.21	1.83
Regular gasoline/kerosene	0.99	1.76
High-speed diesel/LPG (cars)	1.12	1.14
High-speed diesel/kerosene	0.91	1.09

[a] As of 25 June 1985.

as a substitute for gasoline, notably the use of LPG in taxis and private cars, and the use of diesel in pick-ups, small trucks and private cars. The relatively cheap kerosene has also been added to diesel without significantly affecting engine performance or lifetime. These inter-fuel substitution practices create substantial economic losses, which may exceed 1,000 million baht per year, mostly in the form of foreign exchange spent on imported oil.

- Product imbalance. The distorted prices have caused imports of diesel oil to rise rapidly. There is a likelihood that gasoline will be in surplus and will have to be exported at a discount. Under the existing domestic oil price structure, it is expected that diesel oil imports will continue to grow, while gasoline will be exported during the next five years. These product imbalances not only cause real economic losses, but also imply a lower degree of supply security. The increasing reliance on imported diesel oil appears excessive because too much of a single product in the resulting supply mix will be exposed to world price changes and possible supply disruption. Although this problem could be alleviated by the expansion and/or modification of local refineries, this is a very costly option which could be avoided by improvements in the pricing policy.

Fiscal deficit. The government has been subsidizing some oil products by running a deficit in the oil fund. In June 1985, the deficit amounted to 180 million baht per month. Although this had been reduced from a level of 400 million baht per month in November 1984 because of lower import prices, the remaining fund was at a low level. The oil fund deficit only aggravated the already tight government budget situation; and there is no strong economic reason why some oil consumers should be subsidized.

However, despite these economic costs, the oil price structure had some merits, most of which concern distributive and sectoral impacts. These merits are as follows:

- The fishing industry and the transportation sector rely heavily on diesel oil as the fuel used in their production activities. A high price of diesel oil would tend to hurt these two sectors; and a high transport cost could lower the farm-gate prices of most agricultural commodities.
- Kerosene is widely consumed for lighting purposes by rural households without access to electricity. Therefore, a low price of kerosene is regarded as a policy instrument for reducing the hardship of the rural poor.
- Fuel oil is mainly used in industrial production, and its high price could increase industrial production costs and reduce the industry's international competitiveness.
- The oil fund enables the government to keep the prices of most oil products relatively low and more stable than import prices, thus creating lower inflation rates and a higher degree of price stability, at least in the short run.
- Gasoline is directly consumed by the rich, rather than the poor. Given the present inefficient income tax system, relatively high gasoline taxes can also act as a supplement to the income tax.

The problems arising from the oil pricing policy can be summarized as follows:
(i)   retail price relativities and levels:
    - the diesel oil price is too low relative to gasoline and LPG
    - the price of LPG is too low relative to gasoline; in other words, gasoline is too expensive compared with diesel and LPG;
    - the price of kerosene is too low relative to diesel oil;
    - the price differential between premium and regular gasoline is too large; and

- all oil products except gasoline and diesel oil are effectively subsidized, and their retail prices (excluding marketing margins) are below their import and ex-refinery prices.
(ii) adjustments in prices, taxes and oil fund:
  - retail price adjustments have not been frequent and large enough to reflect long-run changes in world prices and exchange rates;
  - the oil fund, which is designed to be a buffer insulating retail prices from short-run fluctuations in world prices and exchange rates, has been used as the only device by which long-run adjustments in retail prices are possible; and
  - taxes have not been allowed to change in order to accommodate long-run price adjustments; and the tax ceilings for some products are too low for such adjustments.

In 1988, when the world oil prices fell dramatically, the government adjusted retail prices and taxes in such a way that inter-fuel price differentials were reduced somewhat. For instance, in 1989–90 the retail price differences between gasoline and the other three products (high-speed diesel, kerosene and LPG) were cut to 30–50 per cent.

As for price adjustments, even though the government has agreed with the Sixth Plan objective of the floating of petroleum product retail prices, the prices have still been controlled and rarely adjusted. This price rigidity has been reflected by fluctuations in the flow and the size of the oil fund. There were constant inflows and build-ups of the oil fund in 1986 when the world oil prices went down sharply. But in 1989, when world petroleum prices picked up, the outflows consistently reduced the size of the oil fund, which eventually fell into deficit in the first two months of 1990.

Besides oil pricing, the government has tried to manage energy demand by adopting other measures, most of which are either short-run or ineffective without appropriate energy pricing. Those measures temporarily used during the oil crises include various kinds of quantitative restrictions on the use of oil products and electricity, such as limiting the operating time of petrol stations, television stations, and entertainment establishments. Energy conservation by the public has also been promoted by periodic publicity campaigns and some fiscal incentives and disincentives.

Energy supply policy

As mentioned above, the main thrust of Thailand's energy supply policy is to encourage the domestic production of local energy resources (natural gas, oil, lignite and hydro-power) in order to lessen the degree of reliance on imported energy. Because natural gas, and to a lesser extent, crude oil, have the most promising supply potential, this section emphasizes the policy measures concerning local petroleum exploration and development.

The legal framework for petroleum exploration and development in Thailand is provided in the 1971 Petroleum Act, amended in 1973, which gives a concessionaire the right to explore, produce, store, transport and sell petroleum, but not the right to refine it. The petroleum exploration period under a concession may not exceed eight years and is subject to one renewal of no more than four years. The concession holder is entitled at any time to relinquish the whole or any part of his exploration area. Compulsory relinquishment at the end of the fifth year of the exploration period applies to an area of 50 per cent of each exploration block; at the end of the eighth year an aggregate area of another 25 per cent of the remaining area must be relinquished. The production period may not exceed 30 years, following the termination date of the exploration period. The production period may be extended once for a period not exceeding ten years. The law prohibits the government from nationalizing the concessionaire's properties and his rights to conduct petroleum operations, and from restricting the export of petroleum, except in a national emergency.

So far, even though the government has played no active role in petroleum exploration and production, it has been instrumental in making possible petroleum production by the oil companies that find commercial deposits of oil and natural gas. The government, through the state oil company (the Petroleum Authority of Thailand, or PTT), is the sole buyer of local oil and gas. It has also invested significant funds in the construction of gas pipelines, control stations and other facilities all of which have facilitated the transportation of natural gas from the Gulf of Thailand. And without the use of gas by the government-owned power plants, natural gas production would not be possible because other large private consumers of natural gas do not yet exist in Thailand. Some feasibility studies on gas utilization and the future construction by the government of infrastructure facilities will further encourage more exploration and production of natural gas. This instrumental role played by the government in the case of crude oil produced by Shell is perhaps less important because local processing activities and a domestic market already exist for oil.

While the royalty on petroleum is specified in the Petroleum Act, taxation on profits comes under another law, the Petroleum Income Tax Act of 1971. According to these Acts, royalty is collected in cash or in kind at 12.5 per cent of petroleum sales, and profits from production are taxed at 50 per cent. For exploration in a water depth exceeding 60 metres, which requires sophisticated technology and large investment involving higher risks, the royalty is 8.75 per cent of the petroleum produced, and the income tax remains unchanged. In addition to these taxes, the government usually demands and receives a so-called 'signature bonus' which is a lump sum payment made when a concession is granted.

With more hydrocarbon deposits found in Thailand, in 1982 the government added a 'production-sharing' feature to the existing 'royalty and tax' system. The so-called 'additional petroleum benefit' (APB) condition requires a concessionaire in onshore areas to pay, on top of the royalty and profit tax, a bonus to the government at a rate ranging from 27.5 per cent to 43.5 per cent of sale value when oil production exceeds 10,000 barrels per day (bpd). Moreover, deductible expenses in each year must not exceed 20 per cent of the value of petroleum sold in the same year. Under the new system, the government's share would increase from 46.25 per cent of oil sales when production is below 10,000 bpd to 68 per cent in the case of production exceeding 30,000 bpd.

Because the government, through PTT, is so far the sole buyer of natural gas and oil produced in the country, an additional government benefit can be gained if the wellhead prices of the resources are low. The government's attempt to maximize this benefit has led to lengthy price negotiations between the PTT and the oil and gas producing oil companies. The wellhead price of natural gas from the Erawan Gasfield in the Gulf of Thailand was agreed upon on a cost plus basis, taking into account also the market price of fuel oil, the product substituted by natural

gas. There is an agreement on the price of crude oil from the
Sirikit Oilfield in Northern Thailand linking the domestic crude
price with the prices of imported crudes. In any case, the law
requires that the price obtained by a concessionaire cannot
exceed the import and export prices for crude oil and natural
gas respectively.

Although the present petroleum supply policy has enabled
the country to discover and produce some natural gas and crude
oil, it is believed that more improvements can be made in light
of new information and the world oil market situation. The
geology of Thailand is now known to be complex and
fragmented, implying that future discoveries will probably be
relatively small and high cost. The world oil price has been
rather erratic and, in recent years, has been weaker than earlier
predicted, tending to slow down exploration. These factors
suggest that the government should provide more and better
incentives for further exploration and production of petroleum.

The fiscal terms for concessions in onshore areas appear to
be quite onerous and inefficient. The combination of royalties,
the annual bonus, the tax-deductible expense limit, and the
petroleum income taxes leads to government taking some 40
to 50 per cent of gross production revenues for a modest
discovery, and higher rates for fields with production levels
over 20,000 barrels per day. These royalty and tax arrangements
could be perverse in their application because less profitable
oil fields could be taxed at higher rates on actual net profits
than more profitable ones. This result is inconsistent with the
basic requirement of a fiscal regime, which is that the net
government taking should be geared progressively with actual
field profitability. The principle is simply that a low profit field
should pay a low tax rate and that, as profitability increases,
the effective tax rate should increase. The fiscal regime relates
the government's net tax take to levels of production value
(gross revenues), presumably in an attempt to approximate this
principle, but field production value (especially given petroleum
engineering and the geology in Thailand) may not be a good
indicator of the net profitability of a field. Therefore, the fiscal
regime would tend to preclude production of higher cost fields
and/or inhibit exploration.

Another policy issue is the pricing of natural gas and crude
oil at the wellhead. At present, natural gas prices in Thailand

are established through the provisions of four contracts. This has been a good way to get the production of gas onstream and the related pipelines and production facilities in place. However, there are outstanding problems. First, exploration companies need to have good estimates of the value of gas discoveries. This means that prices for new gas, wherever it is found, should be easily estimated at least for a few years in the future. This requires that a solid, ongoing government pricing policy applicable to all new gas should be used instead of price negotiations with long delays. Second, exploration companies also need to know that any gas from new discoveries can obtain access to the pipeline transmission system and thereby find a market. In this respect, it seems desirable to clarify the role of PTT in natural gas transmission. It has been suggested that the transmission system should be equally available to all suppliers and gas consumers who are prepared to pay for transmission. A transmission tariff should therefore be set, based on capital and operation costs, so that the pipeline system assets earn a reasonable rate of return. As a result, the link between the wholesale gas price and the net back price to the producer should be the true transmission cost.

Domestic crude oil pricing appears to present less problems than gas pricing because the present practice in the contract between Shell and PTT sets the price of oil on a net back basis related to the prices of some imported crudes less a discount. Even in this arrangement, however, there has been some debate about the small 'effective discount' which puts the price of the domestic crude below that of international crude oils.

There are a number of lesser but nevertheless important aspects of the regulations that should be improved.

- Obligation to produce. Companies can obtain 40-year production licences (30 years plus 10) giving them substantial rights but no obligations to produce. Once the pricing basis and market access is clarified, it would be reasonable to include firm production obligations in any production licence.
- Exploration/production periods. Overall exploration (12 years) and production (40 years) periods are long by international standards, and could usefully be reduced.
- Relinquishments. In some cases exploration is aimed at optimizing relinquishment obligations rather than at bringing discoveries onstream quickly. A number of countries have

built flexibility into their regulations so that government can defer the relinquishment obligations in the event of a discovery, in order that the discovery can be delineated promptly.
- Confidentiality. Thailand's provisions for data acquired by oil companies to remain confidential as long as the licence is in effect and for several years thereafter, are more restrictive than most countries. Further, the confidentiality provisions are rigidly interpreted by the DMR as their sole responsibility; a ministerial request is necessary for other government bodies to obtain access. Thus, valid uses of such data for national five-year plans, gas network and railroad planning, and PTT and EGAT counterpart investments are substantially inhibited. The promotion of Thailand's hydrocarbon potential in the international industry is also neglected under the guise of confidentiality. In other countries confidentiality periods are for only a few years and this would serve in Thailand to encourage more companies to get involved with exploration.

In August 1989, the government succeeded in making substantial amendments to the Petroleum Act and the Petroleum Income Tax Act. The changes are intended to correct some of the weaknesses mentioned above. Significant amendments to the legal arrangements were as follows:
- The maximum period for exploration was reduced to six years, with an extension of not more than three years. The limits on concession areas were lowered, and the compulsory relinquishment of half of the area would occur one year earlier. These measures were designed to speed up exploration.
- The maximum period for production was cut to 20 years, with a possible extension of not more than 10 years.
- Instead of being a fixed rate of 12.5 per cent, the royalty rate was made variable with the rate of production, ranging from 5 per cent when production is under 5,000 barrels per day to a maximum of 15 per cent when production is over 50,000 barrels per day.
- A new concept of 'annual income per metre of well-depth' was introduced, taking into account the exploration costs represented by the depth of drilling and the field geology. In addition to the royalty and income tax, a 'special bonus' was to be progressively collected if such an annual income

showed high profitability. However, a flexible 'special deduction' from the annual income was allowed in cases where additional incentives were needed to attract investment in marginal fields. Consequently, the government share became more positively related to field productivity and profitability than before.

• The confidentiality period for company-acquired data was shortened to only one year after being reported to DMR.

Conclusions: declining import dependence

Because Thailand is an oil-importing developing country, the instability of international oil prices continues to present difficult economic problems. High and unpredictable oil prices and potential oil supply shortages have forced its policy-makers to try to achieve a balance between reducing short-run inflationary impacts and encouraging the local supply of energy, as well as promoting energy conservation. Under various social and political constraints, energy pricing policy has led to some demand distortions in the energy market. On the supply side, the legal framework and high oil prices have stimulated the exploration and production of natural gas, crude oil and lignite. As a result, oil import dependence has declined substantially from over 80 per cent in the 1970s to 40 per cent in the late 1980s. After sharp falls in oil prices in 1986, some steps were taken to adjust the energy policies in terms of both their demand and supply aspects. Price gaps between different oil products were narrowed, fiscal subsidies on some oil products were reduced or eliminated, and the fiscal regime for petroleum exploration and development was revised, taking into account low oil prices and high production costs. While more steps could be taken to improve the energy policies, these changes have been in the right direction.

Notes to Chapter 9

The secondary energy consumption of fuel oil excludes the use in power generation.

Bagasse is a fibrous residue which remains after extracting juice from sugar-cane.

3 A business tax has been exempted for locally refined products since
   February 1979.

4 In 1979, for instance, the price paid by EGAT for fuel oil was
   1.58 baht/litre while the market price was 2.86 baht/litre. The
   subsidy amounted to 1.28 baht/litre or nearly 50 per cent of the
   market price.

5 Both taxes and oil fund are combined in determining whether a
   product is subsidized.

10

Education Policy

SIRILAKSANA KHOMAN

As in most developing countries, education expansion in Thailand has been phenomenal since the 1970s. School enrolments have increased at all levels and literacy has improved radically. This chapter reviews the consequences of this expansion of Thailand's education system. The discussion focuses on the overall performance of the education sector in Thailand, giving particular attention to the interrelated problems of access and equity, education quality, relevance of curricula, educational efficiency, and the problem of education sector financing.

The growth studies of Schultz, Denison, and Griliches, which prompted a spurt in budgetary outlays for education elsewhere in the early 1960s, were also influential in Thailand. Education figured prominently in each of the first six national development plans and its importance was reflected in the central government's budgetary allocations. Education expenditures now account for about 20 per cent of the central government's budget, with approximately 50 per cent going to primary, 15 per cent to secondary and 12 per cent to higher education. Technical education accounts for 10 per cent while grants to private schools range between 2 and 3 per cent.

While government intervention still dominates the education sector, it has gradually been matched and reinforced by private involvement, as individuals become increasingly aware of education's contribution to earning capacity and social mobility. At the inception of economic planning in the early 1960s, education was considered a panacea for increasing the income, skill and productivity of the workforce. But there have been problems. Thailand's education system has undergone considerable change since the early 1960s, when policy-makers, scholars and advisers wrestled with conflicting ideologies and the basic issues of equity, efficiency, and relevance. These issues have now become more pressing in the face of growing fiscal austerity on the one hand and mounting demand for expansion, especially at higher levels, on the other. The economic merits of Thailand's educational expansion are somewhat uncertain in view of the apparent mismatch between supply and demand, evidenced by the simultaneous increase in the number of educated unemployed since 1975 and shortages of highly-trained personnel in medicine, science, engineering and technology.

Access and equity

Along with other ASEAN countries Thailand has made significant progress over the past two decades in providing access to primary education. Considering the high rate of population growth during this period, this has been an impressive feat. A rough indication of this achievement is the gross enrolment ratio, defined as the ratio of the number of pupils of all ages enrolled in primary school to the total population in the official primary school age group. It is evident from the high gross enrolment ratios presented in Table 10.1— some exceeding 100 per cent—that universal enrolment of the official school-aged population has virtually been attained in the ASEAN region. Growth of primary school enrolment has now stabilized with the decline in birth rates during the last decade. For Thailand, primary enrolment is now increasing at about 3 per cent per year.

The ratios presented in Table 10.1 provide some insight into overall participation in education and the small disparity of access to education between females and males. Nevertheless, they conceal other important considerations such as the large disparity in participation rates between rural and urban populations, and between different socio-economic groups.

The Survey of Children and Youth in Thailand (Thailand, National Statistical Office (NSO) 1977) revealed that of the total number of children and youths not attending school, 91 per cent lived in rural areas; and more recent data (NSO 1983) show

Table 10.1: Comparison of gross enrolment ratios at the primary level in ASEAN countries[a], 1970, 1975 and 1986 (per cent)

	1970			1975			1986		
	MF	**M**	**F[b]**	**MF**	**M**	**F**	**MF**	**M**	**F**
Indonesia	80	70	73	86	94	78	118	121	116
Malaysia	87	91	84	91	92	89	101	101	101[c]
Philippines	108	··	··	107	··	··	106	107	106
Singapore	105	109	101	110	113	107	115	118	113[d]
Thailand	83	86	79	83	87	80	99	··	··

a Statistics for Brunei are not available.
b Refers to 1987.
c Refers to 1984.
b MF denotes all students; M denotes males, and F denotes females.
Source: UNESCO, *Statistical Yearbook 1988*, Table 3.2

that the proportion is virtually unchanged. Provision of education is unequal with respect to geographic distribution and population served. Except for primary schools run by provincial authorities, which are evenly located in rural and urban areas, a disproportionate number of schools are situated in towns and cities, particularly in Bangkok. Recent education statistics (Ministry of Education (MOE) 1986) show that of the 2,923 private secondary schools, almost half (1,046) are located in Bangkok, and of the 894 municipal schools 427 were in Bangkok, with enrolment almost identical to the total enrolment for the rest of the country. All public kindergarten schools are located in urban areas, as well as the great majority of private kindergartens and schools.

School location has important implications for the cost of education for rural families. These costs are prohibitive for some rural Thai families. Attending secondary school in town adds costs, and the additional time involved means forgone productive capacity for those whose after-school labour contribution to family production might be substantial if schools were located closer to home. In addition, because quality of schools can differ markedly, children in rural schools are further penalized unless families can pay for them to attend better quality urban schools from primary level onwards.

Economic development raises wages and increases the opportunity cost of additional schooling for those who would otherwise be employed. For those who would not be employed, the opportunity cost of schooling depends on the marginal product of their time in home production. Evidence indicates that a disproportionate burden of education cost is borne by the poor. In 1983, the estimated total time and money cost to a village household of sending a child to a public lower secondary school in town was 2,882 baht per year, almost four times the cost of the same child's primary education. Public schools normally select students by a competitive entrance examination and the cost of sending a child who failed this examination to private school was approximately 4,400 baht per year (NSO 1983) which would be more than half of their total annual income. The cost of upper secondary schooling was almost 6,000 baht per year, still in 1983 prices, and more than 10,000 baht for the upper secondary vocational streams. Because of the sequential nature of the curriculum, if it is perceived that only completion of the higher level would make the lower level worthwhile, and if the total financial burden of completing the curriculum up to the highest level is prohibitive, there is little incentive to go on to lower secondary school.

The Survey of Children and Youth (Thailand, NSO 1977) also found that students in urban areas tended to leave school at a higher level of education than rural students. About 60 per cent of youths aged 15–19 were still in school in urban areas, whereas the corresponding figure for rural youths in that age group was a mere 20 per cent. The next Survey (1983) found a similar pattern, with about 60 per cent of the youths aged 15–19 still in school in urban areas, and only 18 per cent of this age group still in school in rural areas.

Both surveys suggest that financial difficulties were a major cause of non-continuation into secondary school, a problem that further exacerbates the existing inequality of opportunity and income. Even when remaining in school, children from poor families do not perform as well as others. The main causes of drop-out and repetition of grades were found to be poverty, malnutrition, illness and absenteeism, and parental preference In order to progress up the education ladder, several screening examinations have to be passed. A National Education Council survey (Thailand, NEC 1977) studying performance in these examinations showed that children from lower socio-economic backgrounds invariably registered lower scholastic achievement than their more advantaged classmates. A survey relating nutritional status to school grades (Sirilaksana 1986) also showed that malnutrition has a negative impact on examination scores, independent of family income and other socio-economic variables.

Thailand's record is therefore far from impressive when secondary enrolment is considered. Even though enrolments at the lower secondary level doubled during the period 1960 to 1970, and tripled at the upper secondary level (with secondary enrolment as a whole continuing to grow at an annual rate of 12 per cent throughout the 1970s), the gross enrolment ratios (which in any case overstate the number remaining in school) were still low. Table 10.2 shows that Thailand's secondary school enrolments are drastically lower than the impressive numbers in primary enrolment, and fall far behind most other ASEAN countries. Statistics on continuation rates by cohort also support this conclusion.

While the percentage of students continuing to the next grade is high—between 86 and 97 per cent in the primary grades (Primary 1 to Primary 6 from 1982–86)—the percentage of those continuing on to secondary school after completion of the final primary grade drops dramatically to around 45 to 55 per cent of total primary school students. Of the total number of primary school students, about 30 per cent actually continue on to secondary school. Analysis of the 1981 Socio-Economic Survey data (Chalongphob et al. 1988) also found that children in own-account households are less likely than those in other types of households to continue beyond the compulsory level, reflecting the higher opportunity cost of time of school attendance and the low perceived relevance of formal schooling to informal sector work. Chalongphob (1987) showed that returns from education above the primary level are low or almost nil for employees in the informal sector.

A study of farm productivity in Thailand by Jamison and Lau (1982) also indicates that in traditional agriculture there is no clear evidence of any returns from education above the primary level. A recent study of farm households by Suganya and Somchai (1988) again shows that the education of the household head had no perceptible effect in improving farm

Table 10.2: Comparison of gross enrolment ratios at the secondary level in ASEAN countries, 1970, 1975 and 1986 (per cent)

	1970			1975			1986		
	MF	**M**	**Fa**	**MF**	**M**	**F**	**MF**	**M**	**F**
Indonesia	16	21	11	20	25	15	41	··	··
Malaysia	34	40	28	42	46	38	59	59	59b
Philippines	46	··	··	54	··	··	68	66	69
Singapore	46	47	45	52	71	52	71	70	73c
Thailand	17	20	15	26	28	23	29	··	··

a MF denotes all students; M denotes males, and F denotes females.
b These figures are for 1987.
c These figures are for 1984.
Source: UNESCO, *Statistical Yearbook 1988*, Table 3.2.

income per worker. Only in the formal labour market, particularly in the public sector and the larger private firms, are there clear returns from education. For example, in Bangkok the annual differential between the private formal and informal sector for males can be as high as 1,883 baht for secondary education and 6,253 baht for university graduates. The corresponding differentials for females are 1,960 baht for secondary and 5,596 baht for university education (Chalongphob 1988b).

The returns from education depend on the student's eventual occupation. Therefore, if the prospect of gaining employment in the formal sector is low, many poor rural families would opt for no schooling beyond the primary level because of the high cost and low perceived returns. Members of farm households and labourer households have lower expected returns from education and consequently drop out at a younger age.

This situation compounds the problem of inequity since low education begets low incomes, which are then transmitted across generations. This intergenerational perpetuation of inequality is likely to accelerate in future as production technology becomes increasingly more complex and employment shifts increasingly out of agriculture and into industry. The demand for educated workers will increase and their wages will rise relative to those with less education. Low

secondary enrolment is therefore the single most important
problem of Thailand's education system today. On the demand
side, the problem lies partly in the perceived irrelevance of the
curriculum for productive activity. It also lies partly in the
demonstrated low returns that education generates in the
informal sector, where the majority of the less-educated labour
can expect to find employment. For pupils with the expectation
of informal sector employment, continuation onto secondary
school is seen by their families to be uneconomic.

At the tertiary level, Thailand's enrolment has jumped from
about 55,000 in 1970 to well over one million in 1990. The single
most important cause of this increase is the government's policy
of accommodating the huge increase in demand for university
places by creating two 'open' universities, admission to which
is unrestricted, and hence unlimited. These two universities,
Ramkamhaeng University and Sukhothai University, founded
in 1971 and 1978 respectively, accounted for 56 per cent of tertiary
enrolments in 1978 and 88 per cent in 1989. Private universities
and colleges have also been encouraged, but these still account
for less than 10 per cent of total enrolments.

The gross tertiary enrolment ratios in Table 10.3 reflect this
large increase, with Thailand's ratio jumping from 1.7 per cent
in 1970 to 25 per cent in 1982 and declining somewhat to
20 per cent in 1985. Latest estimates for this ratio are around

Table 10.3: Comparison of gross enrolment ratios at the tertiary level in ASEAN
countries, 1970, 1975 and 1985 (per cent)

	1970			1975			1985		
	MF	M	Fa	MF	M	F	MF	M	F
Indonesia	2.6	4.0	1.3	2.4	··	··	6.5	8.9	4.2b
Malaysia	1.6	2.3	0.9	2.8	4.0	1.6	6.0	6.7	5.3
Philippines	19.8	17.4	22.2	18.4	··	··	38.0	35.5	40.3
Singapore	6.7	9.3	4.1	9.0	10.7	7.3	11.8	13.3	10.2c
Thailand	1.7	1.9	1.4	3.4	4.0	2.7	19.6d	··	··

MF denotes all students; M denotes males, and F denotes females.
These figures are for 1984.
These figures are for 1983.
It is interesting to note that this ratio has fallen from 25.0 in 1982.
Source: UNESCO, *Statistical Yearbook 1988*, Table 3.2.

20 per cent. The large increases in tertiary enrolment in Thailand are clearly evident when compared with other ASEAN countries. Table 10.4 shows tertiary enrolment in Thailand increasing at an annual rate of 28 per cent over the 1970–83 period, about four times that of Indonesia, the Philippines, and Singapore.

The policy of passively accommodating demand for tertiary study by providing quick and ready admission into fields of study that are relatively low cost, such as social sciences and the humanities, should be critically reviewed. It leads to an imbalance between demand and supply, and to fiscal strain. The system of heavy subsidy is costly to the education system and raises a range of efficiency and equity issues.

The inequity induced by this system is apparent when we consider the beneficiaries. From Table 10.5, students from professional and commercial backgrounds are substantially over-represented in the student population. A value of one for the Selectivity Index (alternatively called the Ratio of Advantage) would roughly indicate equality of access, i.e. that the proportion of the student population from a particular background corresponds to the proportion of that occupational category in the total population. Even though the index ignores factors such as different family sizes and age structures, the magnitudes indicate clearly that differential access is a major consideration. An index value above one indicates over-representation, and below one, under-representation. With indices of 0.16 and 0.12 respectively, it is clear that students from farming and working-class backgrounds are under-represented in the student population.

Table 10.4: Average annual growth rates of student enrolments, ASEAN countries (per cent per year)

	Period	Primary level	Secondary level	Tertiary level
Indonesia	1970–82	5.4	8.5	7.9
Malaysia	1970–83	1.8	5.2	12.1
Philippines	1970–81	1.8	5.0	6.1
Singapore	1970–83	-1.7	2.0	7.
Thailand	1970–83	2.0	9.2	27.

Source: Calculated from UNESCO, *Statistical Yearbook*, 1985 and 1988.

Table 10.5: Distribution of university students by father's occupation, with selectivity index, 1983

Occupation	Population distribution (%)	Students' distribution (%)	Selectivity index
Professional	3.05	27.35	8.97
Commerce	8.99	45.36	5.05
Farming	68.52	11.15	0.16
Production worker	10.41	1.29	0.12
Others	9.03	14.85	1.64

Sources: National Statistical Office (1984); National Education Council (1985).

Table 10.6 compares the average family incomes of university students and other population groups. It shows that the average family income of university students exceeds that of the general population by 5 to 7 times, and is up to 10 to 20 times higher than farming and working-class families. Looking at affordability of university education, it can be seen from Table 10.7 that, on average, tuition fees amount to only 2.5 per cent of the annual family income of university students. A special-purpose survey of first-year Thammasat University students in 1986 (Sirilaksana 1987) revealed that tuition fees amounted to only 1.2 per cent of average family income per year.

Analysis of candidates sitting for the university entrance examination each year reveals a similar imbalance. In 1983, more than 35 per cent had parents whose residence was in Bangkok, far in excess of Bangkok's share in the total population and 73 per cent had parents who were proprietors or government officials. Of the total number of successful candidates, 46 per cent were Bangkok residents and 74 per cent children of proprietors or government officials (Thailand, Ministry of University Affairs 1987).

Clearly, low-income families are not the main beneficiaries of the present situation of low fees and heavy government subsidy of higher education in Thailand, but an increase in fees would further limit the chances of the poor. Given the sequential nature of formal education, and the evidence on the pattern of enrolment and participation among different population groups at the lower levels of education, it would appear that

Table 10.6: Students' average family income per month in relation to other population groups, 1983 (baht per month, 1983 prices)

Population	Average monthly family income (baht)
Students in public universities	11,197
Students in private universities	15,477
Total population	2,380
Farmers	578
Manual/production workers	1,362

Sources: National Education Council (1985); National Statistical Office (1983).

Table 10.7: Tuition fees as a percentage of annual family income, 1986 (baht per annum, 1986 prices)

Institution	Average annual family income (baht)	Tuition fees	Tuition fees/ family income (%)
All universities	137,364	3,328	2.5
Lowest tuition[a] (Thammasat)	155,505	2,455	1.6
Highest tuition[a] (King Mongkut)	97,774	6,103	6.2

[a] The level of tuition fees mainly reflects the nature of the courses offered (for example, humanities as opposed to the sciences).
Source: National Education Council (1985).

the most disadvantaged groups are excluded from the education system even before they have a chance to qualify for admission to higher education.

One area in which accessibility has progressed steadily in Thailand is adult and informal education. These programs have grown from traditional intensive-learning schools to a range of services which are both diverse in nature and comprehensive in area coverage. In 1980, there were a total of 3,784 schools offering courses to almost half a million adult students. Many programs are established outside Bangkok, such as the 829 functional literacy schools, and the mobile vocational-training units. Informal learning groups sponsored by the Ministry o

Education have grown rapidly and are now numbered in the thousands. Training in vocational skills at correctional institutions is also widely organized, and some 14 schools have been set up. While there has been no systematic assessment of the success of these programs or their relative contribution, they appear to have contributed to the declining adult illiteracy rate that UNESCO reports for Thailand (Table 10.8) even though these reported rates are suspiciously low.

Quality and relevance

Quality measures

The task of defining 'quality' is perhaps intractable. It can be viewed from many different perspectives, each imperfect because of education's multi-dimensional nature. Analysts use measures such as examination scores, cognitive tests, length of time needed for students to attain a target level, standardized tests of reading ability, language, mathematics and sciences,

Table 10.8: Estimates of adult illiteracy[a], ASEAN countries (per cent)

			% illiterate	
	Year	Total	Male	Female
Brunei	1981	22.2	14.8	31.0
Indonesia	1980	32.7	22.5	42.3
Urban		16.5	8.8	24.0
Rural		37.6	26.8	47.7
Malaysia[b]	1980	28.4	20.0	36.0
Urban		19.0	12.0	26.0
Rural		32.0	24.0	41.0
Philippines	1980	16.7	16.1	17.2
Urban		6.9	6.0	7.7
Rural		23.1	22.4	23.9
Singapore	1980	17.1	8.4	26.0
Thailand	1980	12.0	7.7	16.0

Adult population is defined as the population aged 15 and above.
Adult population aged 10 and above.
ource: UNESCO, Statistical Yearbook 1987, Table 1.3, pp.1-19, 1-21.

and non-cognitive tests designed to measure students' attitudes, motivation and aspirations (Psacharopoulos and Woodhall 1985). Others measure inputs into the educational machinery such as student–teacher ratios, student–teacher contact hours, availability and use of libraries, laboratory equipment, faculty research activity, teacher qualifications, measures of teaching ability and attitude, and other amorphous characteristics such as the learning environment. A positive relationship between inputs and quality of output is implied.

Apart from the obvious difficulties in administering external tests and making inferences about outcomes from inputs, there are other difficulties in defining and judging quality, such as the need to distinguish between a poorly taught, poorly administered but relevant curriculum, and a well-taught, well-administered but irrelevant one. In addition, the ability to get through a curriculum and the ability to learn may not be synonymous, and neither may be related to analytical ability or any other specific aspect of 'quality'.

Casual empiricism suggests that the average quality (in terms of cognitive and analytical ability) of Thai graduates at each level generally falls below educational objectives. This is especially so in rural areas, reflecting the low availability of educational inputs. In particular, expenditure on teaching materials, textbooks, and other education equipment is minimal, or even non-existent, in the small remote schools.

In a review of ten studies in developing countries, Hyneman et al. (1984) found a more consistently positive relationship between student achievement and the availability of books than any other input factor such as class size, teachers' training, or boarding facilities. In the Philippines, it was observed that scores in the first grade increased by 12 per cent on tests in mathematics, science and language after the ratio of students to books increased from 10:1 to 2:1 (Hyneman et al. 1984: 35).

In Thailand, the portion of recurrent expenditure for education spent on teaching materials or textbooks is very low. As in most developing countries, teachers' salaries absorb most educational expenditure. The one input that is not lacking in Thailand is teachers. The student–teacher ratio is quite low and class sizes range from 25 to 40, which is considered manageable. In the ASEAN region as a whole, the student–teacher ratio is low (Table 10.9), with figures rarely exceeding 30.

Table 10.9: Number of students per teacher in ASEAN countries, at various educational levels

	Primary		Secondary		Tertiary[a]	
	1975	1986	1975	(years in parentheses)	(years in parentheses)	
Brunei	19	17	19	11	2.5 (1980)	3.9 (1986)
Indonesia	29	28	··	15 (1985)	9.3 (1981)	13.0 (1984)
Malaysia	32	23	27	25 (1987)	10.4 (1980)	11.3 (1985)
Philippines	29	31	31	33 (1986)	24.2 (1975)	31.7 (1983)
Singapore	30	27	23	20 (1984)	15.6 (1975)	11.2 (1983)
Thailand	28	20	25	27 (1987)	14.4 (1975)	33.2 (1985)

[a] Tertiary does not include open universities.
Source: UNESCO, *Statistical Yearbook 1988*, Table 3.4, and calculated from Tables 3.5 and 3.7.

Despite the geographical imbalance, with some remote elementary schools having only one teacher for all classes, the situation has improved. The overall student–teacher ratio has declined steadily, and teachers' qualifications have also increased over time. In 1980, of all teachers in the training colleges in Thailand, 98 per cent had at least a bachelor's degree. In public secondary schools, 52 per cent had similar credentials and another 40 per cent had a diploma in education.

Whether the decline in student–teacher ratios or the rise in teachers' qualifications can be considered an achievement is a different matter. With widespread unemployment of university and teacher-training-college graduates, the favourable statistics may merely be a symptom of qualification escalation, or what has been called 'the diploma disease', unaccompanied by any significant increases in skill, ability or productivity. If this is the case, and education is reduced to a mainly unproductive screening device, then some of the resources spent in higher education might be better used elsewhere.

Whether higher teacher credentials improve the quality of teaching is still the subject of much debate. In developed countries, some studies cast doubt (Coleman 1966; Plowman 1967; Jencks 1972), suggesting that teacher attitude is more important than academic qualification in improving student achievement. There probably exists a threshold level beyond which teacher qualification ceases to be a major factor. Studies in developing countries provide some indication that trained teachers do improve student achievement levels (Husen et al. 1978).

With respect to student–teacher ratios, it is often argued that a reduction in student–teacher ratios would improve the quality of learning and that very small classes (15 students or less) can have an important positive effect on student achievement. However, while large class-sizes are obviously unwieldy and distracting, some reports argue that 'variation in the size of the class within a range of 20 to 40 makes little or no difference in average performance' (World Bank 1980). This is an area in which research is needed to identify where the upper threshold lies for each specific locality so that teacher recruitment can be optimized.

Thailand has placed great emphasis on teacher training, as articulated in the national development plans. It was seen not only as a natural prerequisite for education expansion, but later evolved by default into an outlet for unemployed high-school graduates who failed to gain admission into university. Today, the excess supply of teachers is obvious to even the casual observer. The government is the major employer and teachers' salaries already cut deeply into recurrent expenditure.

The difficulty with education policy is that it has to link up with the overall problem of national unemployment. Thus, while it may be argued that a further reduction in the student–teacher ratio is generally unwarranted, except in the remote areas, the unemployment of teachers remains a problem. This dilemma is typical of problems in the education sector today. A holistic approach to education planning is required because the piecemeal method characterizing past policy deals at best with specific problems while allowing underlying causes to persist.

Other measures of 'quality' and 'efficiency' most commonly used are repetition rates and drop-out rates at each school level The average percentage of repeaters at the primary and secondary levels for the ASEAN countries, presented in Table 10.10, shows considerable variation. At the primary level, an average 8 per cent of pupils repeat grades in Thailand, while only 1 per cent do so in Singapore. However, both repetition rates and drop-out rates are misleading indicators of 'waste' and 'inefficiency', for several reasons. First, if waste is define as use of educational resources not producing learning or enhancing ability, it is debatable whether dropping out before a specified cycle is completed implies that no knowledge has been gained before that time. Second, if repetition is considered wasteful because it allows fewer students to be admitted, this holds true only for the first level, and not others.

In addition, repetition rate may be influenced by a host of other factors. For example, the percentage of each cohort remaining after four years of primary school in Thailand in the 1960s was as low as 58 per cent. The percentage progressing from lower to upper secondary school during that period was even lower, at about 40 per cent. Before the standardized national school-leaving examination was abolished in 1976, the rate of progression from the penultimate year to the final year of high school was about 65 per cent. This was because the school's reputation rested on the percentage of students passing the national examination, and those deemed unprepared for this hurdle were retained in the penultimate year.

It was recognized that the examination system may have distorted the motive for learning because teacher and student became obsessed with examination scores. Together with the increasingly more diversified curriculum, this led to the abolition of the national school-leaving examinations, and the progression rate immediately jumped to 95 per cent. Any conclusion that internal efficiency had improved would be inappropriate if based on the lowered repetition ratio.

Table 10.10: Proportion of repeaters at the primary and secondary levels, ASEAN countries (per cent)

	Year	Percentage of repeaters	
		Primary	Secondary
Brunei	. .	. .	. .
Indonesia	1983	9.0	2.0
Malaysia	. .	. .	. .
Philippines	1982	2.0	. .
Singapore	1983	1.0	5.0
Thailand	1980	8.0	3.0

Source: UNESCO, Statistical Yearbook 1988.

Ultimately, the success of the education system depends on the students themselves. School achievement depends on the capacity of students to reap benefits from the facilities provided. Evidence indicates that poor children perform less well in tests of ability than those from more affluent segments of the population. It is well known that poor health affects attentiveness and motivation which in turn may increase absenteeism, induce apathy and harm a child's cognitive development. Several studies also show that a vibrant home environment is extremely important for intellectual stimulation and the motivation to learn. Programs to expand enrolment and cover wider segments of the socially and economically disadvantaged population will have to be undertaken in conjunction with other poverty-alleviating measures so that these initial handicaps can be counteracted and education made more effective.

Relevance

There are doubts in Thailand about the appropriateness of skill training at all levels, for differing reasons at each level. The curriculum that was used at the school level from 1954 into the 1960s had long been deemed unsuitable because of its focus on academic pursuits. This curriculum has been compared with a strait-jacket (Apichai 1987), forcing students to navigate to successive levels in a narrow, predetermined course. There was no flexibility in choice of subjects and standardized school-leaving examinations were administered by representatives of the central government, or the district authority along Western models of education. High-school graduates aspired to enrol in universities, partly because they were ill-equipped to find professional employment. High-school graduates also flocked to Bangkok, since the material learned in school had little connection with the rural working environment.

The curriculum has since been revised with vocational and professional studies gradually introduced. Purely academic schools were modified into what are now known as comprehensive schools. Flexibility in curriculum design at the local level meant that the centralized school-leaving examinations were no longer tenable. Each school is now in a position to design its own curriculum to suit local needs.

This system of diversified education is not working well. First, funds are too limited for the purchase of tools and equipment necessary for vocational education. Curriculum diversification involves higher cost because it requires new teachers and additional physical resources. With insufficient resources, the skills imparted are often inadequate to bring about significant differences in employment prospects.

Secondly, parents and pupils alike are often reluctant to aim for a vocational profession. Once the vocational stream is chosen, the chances of competing for admission to higher education are minimal. Social mobility is seen as dependent on academic education. Many students, forced to choose the vocational route because of failure to find placement in academic streams, are not motivated to take best advantage of the potential benefit that the vocational stream may offer. The benefits of vocational training also tend to be uncertain. There is no dependable empirical evidence to suggest that attitude towards work is improved among students who have gone through the diversified curriculum.

Another quirk in the system is that enrolment in higher education (four years instead of two, as in the vocational stream) allows military training to be undertaken once a week, with exemption from full-time military service. There is therefore an added incentive to stay in school and circumvent the military service requirement. This option attracts many students to the two open universities, as does the low level of fees charged at public universities.

The wastefulness of attending universities and colleges for reasons other than the aim of gainful, productive employment after graduation cannot be over-emphasized. Regular surveys of graduates conducted by the Ministry of University Affairs indicate that 30 to 40 per cent of graduates from government universities fail to find employment one year after graduation.

In 1983, the average waiting period before finding employment was 12 months for males and 14 months for females with first degrees; 13 months for males with master's degrees and for PhDs it was also as long as 12 months. Such long waiting periods were experienced by science graduates as well as those in arts and humanities. More detailed investigation by field of study reveals that the unemployment rate by cohort in the behavioural sciences, one year after graduation, can be as high as 45 per cent. The number of educated unemployed in 1986 was estimated at 200,000.

It is clear that the accommodating policies at the higher education level leave much to be desired in terms of the relevance of such education to the country's workforce needs. Even when productive pursuits are stressed, emphasis is placed more on employment-seeking than on entrepreneurship and innovative undertakings.

Workforce planning

The kind of workforce planning that attempts to identify future labour requirements—and thereby to design educational systems producing a labour force with the required skill attributes at the right time—has failed in Thailand. It has not been successful in avoiding and alleviating critical shortages and surpluses. The fixed relationship normally assumed between output and skill and the consequent matching of skill requirements and projections of output growth in the different sectors, ignores the impact of technological changes and the potentially vast possibilities for substitution between different kinds of labour and/or between labour and other productive inputs.

In addition, the assumed relationship between type of education received and type of occupation undertaken is often untenable. Also, workforce planning tends to focus on the formal wage sector and on higher levels of education or training, and most importantly, tends to suffer from wide margins of error (Psacharopoulos 1981). The resulting imbalance is clearly evident. The desirability of maintaining the current level of subsidy to higher education must be questioned.

With respect to the relevance of education for workforce requirements, the recent phenomenon of unemployment and long waiting periods before job placement among the educated raises further important questions. For example, what effect do long waiting periods and reduced prospects for employment have on the wage structure? Does it lead to compression of the wage structure, and a narrowing of wage differentials for different qualifications? Do declining job prospects encourage a change of attitude; do they reduce the prestige value of higher education? What role does post-school training play in increasing the access of the poorly educated to the higher-paying formal sector of the labour market? A dynamic picture is needed.

Financing of education

Since the 1970s, public spending on education in Thailand has fluctuated between 16 and 20 per cent of total government expenditure. Currently, the persistent shortfalls in tax collections and the increasing constraint on the size of public indebtedness at both the domestic and international level, make any increases in budgetary allocation for social expenditure highly improbable. In fact, it is even unlikely that current levels of subsidy would be maintained in real terms in the present situation of fiscal austerity.

The basic issues with respect to financing of education involve determining how much of the economy's total resources should be devoted to it, how much should be spent by government, and how much reliance should be placed on non-government sources of finance to meet the balance. To answer these questions, the providers, beneficiaries and sources of finance in the present system need to be identified. Providers include the Ministry of Education, other ministries and the private sector. The benefits of education and the characteristics of the recipients also need to be analysed to determine their willingness to pay and to deal with problems of equity.

The problem of how to pay for commodities such as education which contain public-good elements and which some consider as 'merit goods' in their own right is simple conceptually, but very complex at the operational level. At the conceptual level, the question is who should pay for the cost of providing services—the recipients of the services through pricing mechanisms (fees), the government through subsidies, or other funding sources such as private business, collective bodies and charitable organizations.

The basic economic principles are well known. Each good or service should ideally be priced so that the good is consumed where the marginal social cost is equal to the marginal social benefit. However, this criterion is difficult to apply directly, since marginal social costs and benefits cannot be easily observed. Nevertheless, one may proceed by first setting the price equal to marginal private cost and then adjusting this (upwards or downwards) by exploring the existence and size of externalities, public-good and merit-good elements, transactions costs, the administrative burden, the effect on services supplied, the difficulty in determining the level of individual consumption, and market failures in other sectors.

It is difficult to translate these general considerations into concrete financing strategies, but a financial masterplan and recommendations for its implementation are urgently needed. Apart from the magnitude and overall levels of spending, it is also necessary to resolve how public expenditure on education is to be allocated among the different levels of education and distributed between different kinds of educational inputs. Given the current fiscal constraints, cost-effective procedures are imperative.

The current level of public expenditure on education in the ASEAN countries is presented in Table 10.11. The proportion of government expenditure on education hovers around 2 to 4 per cent of GNP. Malaysia stands out with expenditure growing from 4.4 per cent of GNP in 1970 to 7.5 per cent in 1982 and 7.8 per cent in 1986. As a percentage of the government budget, Thailand diverges from the general pattern of falling expenditure, registering an increase from 17 per cent in 1970 to more than 20 per cent in 1986.

Much of the rising expenditure on education is non-discretionary. Teachers' salaries take up the major portion of recurrent expenditure on education (Table 10.12). In most developing countries teachers are government officials with lifetime employment and automatic annual promotion up the salary scale. Given this system of tenured employment, if current trends were to persist, teacher remuneration would soon absorb the entire current education budget.

Evidence abounds that teaching materials in general, and textbooks in particular, have an important effect on student achievement, but the realities of the situation must be taken into account. Because of the inability to terminate employment, a reallocation of resources towards education inputs other than teachers' salaries can be achieved only if a radical redeployment of personnel between different government departments is undertaken, or employment termination with severance pay becomes more acceptable. However, the problems with the las

Table 10.11: Public expenditure on education as a proportion of GNP and total government budget, ASEAN countries (per cent)

	Percentage of GNP			Percentage of total government budget		
	1970	1975	1980s	1970	1975	1986
Brunei	::	2.0	2.0 (1984)	::	12.2	9.6 (1982)
Indonesia	2.8	2.7	2.0 (1981)	::	13.1	9.3 (1981)
Malaysia	4.4	6.0	7.8 (1986)	17.7	19.3	16.3 (1985)
Philippines	2.6	1.9	1.7 (1986)	24.4	11.4	7.0 (1984)
Singapore	3.1	2.9	4.3 (1982)	11.7	8.6	9.6 (1982)
Thailand	3.5	3.6	3.9 (1985)	17.3	21.0	21.1 (1983)

Source: UNESCO, *Statistical Yearbook*, 1985 and 1988, Table 4.1.

Table 10.12: Distribution of public current expenditure on education by type of expenditure, ASEAN countries (per cent)

	Year	Teachers' salaries	Teaching materials	Subsidies not distributed
Brunei	1984	62.4[a]	2.5	· ·
Malaysia	1984	69.7	4.3	12.8
Philippines	1986	59.7	0.6	18.5
Singapore	1982	46.0	· ·	44.0
Thailand	1985	75.0	4.2	1.8

[a] Includes administrative staff.
Source: UNESCO, *Statistical Yearbook 1988*, Table 4.2

alternative are well known, and teachers' salaries are not high relative to other occupations. Turning to the distribution of expenditure by level of education, it can be seen from Table 10.13 that a disproportionate emphasis is placed on tertiary, relative to secondary education. In view of the abundant evidence that private returns from this level of education are high, continued subsidization seems highly questionable.

Public finance theory indicates that if there is reason to believe that individuals underestimate the returns from education and thus underinvest, thereby causing a loss of future welfare, then government intervention can be justified. Intervention in this case might only take the form of information provision, but if some of the positive returns to the individual spill over to the rest of the community, making social returns higher than the sum of individual returns, then government subsidy can be justified in order to induce students to obtain more education. Effectively, society would be sharing the costs with them. Such intervention is particularly important in a situation of imperfect capital markets. Even if individuals were equipped with perfect information about the returns to education, loans from the capital market cannot readily be obtained to finance education since the individual is unable to offer his or her own (expected future earnings as collateral.

Evidence from various studies (such as Psacharopoulos and Woodhall 1985) indicates clearly that the private returns to education exceed the social returns at all levels, and this i

Table 10.13: Distribution of public current expenditure on education by level of education, ASEAN countries (per cent)

	Year	Primary	Secondary	Tertiary
Brunei	1975	33.0	53.2	8.9
	1980	31.4	46.0	16.7
	1982	33.2	47.9	13.5
Malaysia	1980	35.0	34.0	12.4
	1982	33.6	34.0	14.0
	1986	38.2	37.6	14.4
Philippines	1976	65.7	6.7	22.4
	1982	60.0	19.1	20.1
	1986	61.8	12.7	20.4
Singapore	1976	38.1	34.3	17.6
	1980	35.8	41.1	17.1
	1982	34.3	34.4	26.4
Thailand	1975	62.5	16.2	11.1
	1983	60.2	21.1	13.8
	1985	58.4	21.1	13.2

Source: UNESCO, *Statistical Yearbook*, 1985 and 1988, Table 4.3.

particularly true for tertiary levels of education. The most important estimates of costs and rates of return at each level of education in Thailand are those of Blaug (1971). Other studies along the same lines, but differing in coverage and methodology, include works by Apichai (1976[T]), Supachai (1976[T]), Somjin (1977), Vacharee (1978[T]) and the National Education Council (1985). The most recent calculation of costs and rates of return at university level was undertaken by the National Education Council (1987). On the cost side alone, there have been several works such as those by Supaporn (1962[T]), Banchong (1965[T]), Kaew (1970[T]), Chuta and Chanida (1974[T]), Konthee (1975[T]), Lalita (1977[T]), and Pornlert (1982[T]). However, the coverage of these cost studies is limited, mostly being confined to specific fields and institutions.

The rate of return studies mirror the pattern found elsewhere. Private rates of return on investment in education exceed social rates at all levels. Blaug's study, based on a survey of Bangkok–Thonburi residents in 1970, found that the highest marginal social rates of return were for the lower primary level (primary 1–4), with progressively lower rates for successively higher levels of schooling. The highest social rate of 27 per cent was associated with completion of Primary 4, which at that time, was the statutory minimum schooling requirement in Thailand. The private rate, on the other hand, was found to be considerably higher. The private rate for completing Primary 4 was 49 per cent, almost double the social rate. As with social rates, private rates declined with each successive move up the educational ladder.

Blaug's estimates of the ratios of total private to total social costs, and of direct private to direct social costs (Table 10.14) also confirm the fact that, at least officially (i.e. disregarding rent-extracting solicitation of contributions), education is subsidized at all levels. More interesting is the large government subsidy to higher education, especially in comparison with the much smaller subsidy to the secondary (academic) level, where students actually paid 83 per cent of the direct costs.

The difference between total and direct costs, according to Blaug, is the earnings forgone while still in school. Thus, inclusion of this component of costs at the tertiary education level leads to the ratio of 0.7 in column (1). It is clear that, with the high rates of unemployment among the educated population at the present time, any current estimates of earnings forgone would have to be revised downwards considerably.

Preliminary findings by the NEC (1987) also show that the private rate of return to investment in university education is high, averaging about 18 per cent. On the other hand, the social rate of return to investment in university education is estimated

Table 10.14: Comparison of private and social costs at each level (per cent)

	Ratio of total private to total social costs (1)	Ratio of direct private to direct social costs (2
Primary	46	4
Secondary (academic)	95	8
Tertiary	70	1

Source: Adapted from Blaug (1971: 5–8).

to be only about 10 per cent, which compares unfavourably also with the social rate of return to other social investments such as irrigation, as well as the social rates to higher education in other developing countries. The NEC study also concluded that the contribution to society of university graduates was not significantly higher than that of high school graduates. On the cost side, it was found that the proportion of the total burden borne by the state is extremely high, at around 88 to 93 per cent, while the private contribution remains at 7 to 12 per cent.

In view of the inequality of access discussed earlier, and the high private returns, the efficiency of cost recovery through fees should be seriously considered, together with built-in mechanisms, such as scholarships and fee exemptions, and student loan schemes repayable from graduate incomes, to protect the truly needy. A great deal of information is required to calculate the appropriate level of fee increases. This information includes ability to pay, as well as the elasticities involved. Nevertheless, the system of education finance needs to be rationalized, so that the limited resources can be used more efficiently. Inappropriate pricing gives inappropriate signals to both providers and users.

Conclusions: educational reform

Like many countries, Thailand has expanded educational enrolment very rapidly over the past three decades, such that universal primary education has nearly been achieved. Education has increased the geographical mobility of workers by increasing their range of possible occupations and allowing them to take advantage of better earning opportunities. Nevertheless, problems of inequity, doubtful relevance, and demonstrated inefficiency pervade the education system. The benefits of education have not been equally distributed, and general dissatisfaction has contributed, on the one hand, to disillusionment with the education system and its perceived non-relevance, and on the other, to greater desires to complete even higher levels of education in the hope of capturing the benefits that apparently accrue to the highly educated few.

Unemployment among newly graduating high school leavers, as well as vocational school and college graduates, has been particularly serious in recent years. The expansion of educational opportunities has raised the level of educational attainment of the economically active population, but has not been accompanied by a parallel expansion in the capacity of the economy to absorb these graduates. The reason is that the type of education provided is generally ill-suited to labour market requirements.

In periods of austerity, budgetary allocation for social expenditure is not likely to be increased in real terms, and current levels of subsidy, if maintained, would considerably strain the country's fiscal capacity. Given its limited resources, the country faces a threefold dilemma. First, the relevance of the curriculum must be improved to avoid waste of resources. An important aspect of this policy problem is the choice between a more or less uniform curriculum and a more varied one. A curriculum that is deemed relevant to local needs may be seen as more appropriate, but such a curriculum is necessarily discriminating, and would thus deny students the opportunity to become more mobile both geographically and socially.

The debate over the introduction of productive work in the school curriculum is almost as old as the debate about the meaning of 'relevance'. Opinions about the virtues of such reform are as divergent today as they were a century ago. In recent years, many developing countries have introduced productive work into basic education. In a majority of cases, the official explanation is that such work increases the relevance of the curriculum. But a by-product is the possible sale of the products of this activity, and this could be a way to help finance recurrent costs and quality improvements. Thailand is currently experimenting with this system.

The second dilemma is to reconcile the need for both quality improvements and quantitative expansion. Given the social pressures to expand education, a reduction of unit costs must be achieved if enrolment is to be increased within a given budget. However, cost reduction may have detrimental effects on quality, unless the internal efficiency of education delivery is improved via reduction of wastage and organizational improvement. Various methods of cost recovery should also be explored. Contributions by private firms who use the output of the education system, alumni associations and 'goodwill' contributions by foundations and firms should be looked into as sources of finance. Package schemes involving graduate taxes, student loans, scholarships, and fee increases should also be explored. A general reallocation of resources between levels of education, as suggested by rate of return calculations, may be warranted. By cutting subsidies to higher education, public resources can be more efficiently shifted toward education at the lower levels.

The third dilemma is to determine the appropriate roles of the government and the private sectors, balancing the need to 'inform and protect' the public without undue restriction, and sharing the cost of education between public and private sectors, the latter including the individuals directly benefiting from the education system. Here also, recommendations differ by level of education, depending on the perceived external benefits to society as a whole that are generated by each type of education. Because controls and regulations are costly, the loosening of controls on private educational institutions, particularly at the higher levels, may also be a way to alleviate both equity and efficiency problems.

These dilemmas are interrelated. Inadequate provision is partly the result of large across-the-board subsidies and the limited resort to pricing mechanisms. The direct and implicit subsidy to university students is many times that of primary school students. Because of these subsidies, the private rate of return to higher education in particular greatly exceeds the social rate of return, generating excess demand for entry. Pupils are induced to take advantage of facilities that are heavily subsidized, and their decisions are divorced from the realities of the job market and the needs of the economy. When demand cannot be met, institutions resort to methods of rationing that reinforce existing inequities.

During progression up the education ladder, problems of social inequity are compounded as the disadvantaged groups are gradually weeded out. A very small percentage of the population is able to gain access to higher education, and since public tertiary institutions are more highly subsidized than lower-level schools, the benefits are confined to a small number of people who are already 'advantaged'.

The opportunity for the private sector to play a role in the education system is substantial, particularly in certain fields such as business administration where cost recovery through fees is feasible. Also, the division between public sector and private sector provision need not be clear-cut. A complete shifting of the burden to the private sector need not occur. Elements of private sector discipline and pricing can be incorporated into government-run activities, and private institutions can be subsidized if substantial external benefits to society are generated.

Appendix

Organizations/government offices with education-related roles in Thailand

Office of the Prime Minister

National Education Council
• Macro-level planning
• Overseeing formal system
• Overseeing non-formal educational system
• Analysis of education situation

National Youth Bureau
• Planning and coordination of non-formal education for youths
• Promotion and development of youth activities including recreational facilities

Ministry of Education

Office of the Under-Secretary
• Planning of non-tertiary and non-formal education
• Training of education administrators
• Promotion of teaching of science and technology
• Provision of education through radio services
• Overseeing the running of all provincial schools
• Coordination with SEAMES and UNESCO

Committee for Primary Education
• Planning at the primary level
• Running of district primary schools
• Records and statistics

Private Education Commission
- Control and evaluation of private schools
- Administration of grants and aid
- Maintenance of records and statistics on all private schools in Bangkok and in the provinces

Teachers' Committee
- Coordination of teachers

General Education Department
- Planning of secondary and special education
- Running of secondary schools and special projects
- Records and statistics

Physical Education Department
- Promotion of physical education and health

Technical Department
- Curriculum review and development
- Development of teaching aids and textbooks
- Education and occupational counselling

Teachers' Training Department
- Running and development of teachers' training colleges
- Teacher upgrading through correspondence courses and radio programs

Non-formal Education Department
- 'Integrated' education programs
- General and vocational education
- Radio programs and correspondence courses

Vocational Education Department
- Running of technical, vocational and agricultural colleges
- Professional development

Fine Arts Department
- Art education, libraries and archives

Teachers' Council (Khuru Sapha)

Ministry of University Affairs

Curriculum review and approval
Coordinates the running of the 12 government universities
Regulation of the 18 private universities and colleges

Ministry of Defence

- Military education and training
- Technical training, nurse training
- Training of high-level staff
- Military and strategic studies

Ministry of the Interior

- Police training, detective training, district officer training
- Various programs for staff training in management and technical skills
- Municipality schools
- Nursing schools
- Electronics training centres

Ministry of Finance

- Customs school

Ministry of Justice

- Law training programs

Ministry of Public Health

- Special programs in medical training, costing, and health economics

Ministry of Industry

- Handicraft training
- Special programs for cottage industries

II

Labour Markets

CHALONGPHOB SUSSANGKARN

The functioning of labour markets is central to the development process. This chapter reviews the operation of Thailand's labour markets and concentrates on two aspects of labour market performance: seasonality and segmentation. Unemployment in Thailand has two dimensions: in rural areas it is predominantly a seasonal phenomenon; in urban areas the unemployment problem is largely confined to better-educated groups. To understand this phenomenon the concept of labour market segmentation is applied to Thailand.

Together with a satisfactory growth performance, there has also been a rapid decline in the rate of Thailand's population growth—from over 3 per cent per year in the late 1960s to about 1.5 per cent in 1990. This has happened in spite of substantial declines in mortality rates, and is mainly the result of a rapid increase in contraceptive use, brought about in part by the highly successful National Family Planning Program. Real per capita GDP increased at around 4.3 per cent per year between 1970 and 1988.

In 1987, the labour force comprised about 28 million workers, of whom 54 per cent were male and 46 per cent female. For those of working age and not at school, male labour force participation is nearly universal, while that of females is also high by international standards, at about 82 per cent. As expected from the low rate of urbanization, most of the workforce is employed in agriculture. In 1987, the share of agricultural employment was around 65 per cent. This is extremely high when compared with the 16 per cent share of agriculture in GDP, and very high when compared with other countries with a similar share of agriculture in GDP.

Because of agriculture's importance for employment, seasonality is a central consideration in understanding employment
patterns. While some areas of the country, particularly the
Central Plains, are well irrigated and cultivation can easily take
place all year round, many areas, mainly in the North and
Northeast, still rely primarily on rain-fed agriculture. For these
areas, labour demand declines drastically during the dry season
months, and seasonal unemployment rates can be as high as
30–40 per cent of the labour force. This is a severe problem
for the rural labour force in the affected areas.

The implications of seasonal unemployment for the workings
of the labour market in Thailand have been debated extensively.
At one extreme it is suggested that most of these workers are
voluntarily unemployed, while at the other, it is claimed that
the problem indicates market failure, implying a need for
substantial government intervention in the form of job creation
programs. One goal of this chapter is to use a specially collected
set of national data on seasonal migration to explore this issue.
Seasonal migration is one important way in which the rural
labour force adjusts to the decline in agricultural labour demand
during the dry season, and a study of its pattern can give insight
into the desire for work during these months, and possible
impediments to labour market adjustments.

Apart from the employment problems stemming from the
seasonality of agricultural work, the general employment
situation in Thailand appears to be quite satisfactory. Overall,
open unemployment rates are very low, at around 1 per cent,
and while underemployment, in the form of few hours of
work, is higher, it is not severe. Nevertheless, demand–supply
mismatches at the middle to upper levels of education have
become an increasingly important problem. At the vocational
level, there are high unemployment rates; at the university level,
there is an excess supply of graduates in the humanities and
social sciences, while concurrently there are severe shortages
in the science and technology disciplines. This latter problem
of shortages in the science disciplines is recent. It dates from
1986 when growth rates of the industrial sectors accelerated
significantly due to rapid growth of manufactured exports,
which expanded at about 40 per cent per year from 1986
(TDRI/NESDB 1989).

While the urban problems of open unemployment of educated
people and shortages of workers both indicate a mismatching

of education supply and demand, this chapter focuses primarily on the educated open unemployment problem. The reason for this focus is that an analysis of the latter problem leads to insight into the structure and function of the labour market in Thailand. In the case of labour shortages, the basic labour market response is a rise in the relative wages of those skills that are in short supply. This is what one would expect from standard economic analysis, and there is no need to look at detailed structures of the labour market to understand it. In the case of open unemployment, however, wages do not appear to perform in an effective adjustment role, and the structure of the labour market needs to be analysed to understand the source of wage rigidities and the underlying reasons for persistent open unemployment. The paradigm of a segmented labour market, with a formal (or modern) sector co-existing alongside an informal (or traditional) sector, is used to explain the labour market structures in Thailand. An econometric analysis of labour market segmentation is presented, which indicates the factors influencing the ability to get into the formal sector, the wage differential between the two sectors, and the tendency to become openly unemployed.

The next section presents a brief overview of the labour market situation in Thailand, focusing on seasonality and labour market segmentation. The analysis then turns first to seasonal unemployment and seasonal migration and then to labour market segmentation and open unemployment.

Overview of Thailand's labour markets

The employment pattern by major production sectors for recent years is given in Table 11.1, specifying agriculture, industry and services, separately for the periods January–March and July–September. A feature of the data is the clear pattern of seasonal variation. The July–September period corresponds roughly to the peak cultivating seasons in most areas, while January–March is the dry season. We can see clearly that agricultural employment declines drastically between the two seasons. Industry and services employment increases slightly in the dry season. On average, agricultural employment declines by 4.5–6 million workers during the January–March period compared to the July–September period (except for the years

1981 and 1982 when the figures were 8 million). Employment in'industry and services increased by about 1 million workers in the dry season.

Table 11.2 gives the share of employment by major sectors (based on July–September figures). It can be seen that agricultural employment accounts for about two-thirds of total employment. Since 1977, the share of agriculture in total employment has been declining, from 73.6 per cent in 1977 to 64.5 per cent in 1987. The share of employment in agriculture is very high when compared with the share of value added from agriculture, implying substantial disparity between the value added per worker in agriculture and non-agriculture. In 1986, value added per worker in agriculture was one-tenth that of a worker outside agriculture.

While the share of employment in agriculture has fallen, the decline has been smaller than the decline in the share of value-added from agriculture. A major reason for this disparity has been the availability of new land and, increasingly, the introduction of successful new crops to replace paddy, such as cassava, maize and sugar. In the past, the rural population could only respond to population pressure by migrating to other rural areas to open up new land for cultivation.

In terms of cropping pattern, the importance of paddy has been declining, both in its share in agricultural GDP and also in cultivated area. In 1976, paddy accounted for 69 per cent of all cultivated land, declining to 64 per cent in 1983. Other tree crops and field crops, particularly the latter, have increased their share of the cultivated area accordingly. In terms of value added of the five major crops—paddy, cassava, rubber, sugar-cane and maize—the share of paddy declined from 76.3 per cent in 1972 to 51.2 per cent in 1986. Of the other crops, cassava showed the largest gain, increasing from 6.5 per cent to 18.5 per cent. Sugar more than doubled its share, from 3.2 per cent to 8.0 per cent. Rubber increased from 10 per cent to 16.8 per cent, and maize increased slightly from 4.0 per cent to 5.5 per cent. The types of crops are important for the distribution of labour demand throughout the year. This is particularly relevant to the issue of seasonal employment patterns. Table 11.3 shows the percentage of yearly labour requirements for two periods of the year in the Northeast (January–May and June–September).

Table 11.1: Employment by major sectors, 1977 to 1986[a] (number of workers)

	January-March				July-September			
	Agriculture	Industry	Services	Total	Agriculture	Industry	Services	Total
1977	9,841,199	2,428,177	3,831,754	16,101,130	15,012,786	1,760,950	3,626,516	20,400,252
1978	10,597,460	2,250,593	3,972,204	16,820,257	16,084,181	1,880,244	3,843,412	21,807,837
1979	9,796,872	2,896,196	4,242,172	16,935,240	15,161,841	2,228,103	3,987,839	21,377,783
1980[b]	:	:	:	:	16,092,129	2,322,839	4,265,863	22,680,831
1981	9,421,052	3,019,853	5,102,668	17,543,573	17,809,850	2,346,319	4,555,917	24,712,086
1982	9,790,624	3,305,928	5,519,624	18,616,176	17,428,853	2,680,079	5,260,335	25,369,267
1983	11,528,677	3,458,247	5,653,372	20,640,296	17,401,473	2,511,636	5,270,418	25,183,527
1984	13,398,676	3,318,997	5,602,838	22,320,511	18,130,356	2,767,493	5,101,085	25,998,934
1985	13,383,271	3,368,254	5,851,217	22,602,742	17,687,800	2,819,400	5,345,300	25,852,500
1986	13,606,100	3,693,200	6,181,400	23,480,700	17,836,400	2,823,400	6,030,800	26,690,600

Source: Labour Force Surveys 1977–1986, NSO.

[a] Until 1983, the National Statistical Office collected labour force data twice yearly so as to incorporate the important seasonal factors. Since 1983, data have been collected more frequently (usually three times a year).

[b] No data were collected in January–March because this was a census year.

Table 11.2: Shares of employment by major sectors, 1977 to 1987 (per cent)

Year	Agriculture	Industry	Services	Total
1977	73.6	8.6	17.8	100
1978	73.8	8.6	17.6	100
1979	70.9	10.4	18.7	100
1980	71.0	10.2	18.8	100
1981	72.1	9.5	18.4	100
1982	68.7	10.6	20.7	100
1983	69.1	10.0	20.9	100
1984	69.7	10.6	19.6	100
1985	68.4	10.9	20.7	100
1986	66.8	10.6	22.6	100
1987	64.5	11.7	23.8	100

Source: Labour Force Surveys, July–September, National Statistical Office.

Table 11.3: Share of labour use by cropping activities in the Northeast, 1985 (per cent)

Cropping activities	January–May	June–December
First non-glutinous rice	0.5	99.5
First glutinous rice	0.6	99.4
Second non-glutinous rice	100.0	—
Second glutinous rice	100.0	—
First maize crop	20.4	79.6
Second maize crop	—	100.0
Sorghum	—	100.0
First mungbean crop	100.0	—
Second mungbean crop	—	100.0
First soybean crop	100.0	—
Second soybean crop	—	100.0
First groundnut crop	100.0	—
Second groundnut crop	—	100.0
Kenaf	30.3	69.7
Cassava	39.3	60.7
Sugar-cane	70.9	29.1

Source: From data used in Yongyuth and Kanok (1985).

Seasonal unemployment

The seasonal cropping patterns lead to a variation in agricultural labour demand, as shown in Table 11.1. There is high seasonal unemployment during the dry season months of those who normally work in agriculture, and who are 'waiting' for the agricultural season. Table 11.4 gives the figures for seasonal unemployment from 1977 to 1985. These figures are based on the January–March rounds of the labour force surveys. Data were not collected for 1980 because it was a census year. These numbers have been adjusted to make them comparable across years (the Labour Force Survey underwent major changes in various unemployment definitions in 1983).

In relation to seasonal unemployment, the most controversial change in statistical definition was the inclusion as part of the employed workforce of own-account workers who would in earlier years have been regarded as seasonally unemployed. There are arguments both ways. Own-account workers in agriculture are mostly farm owners, and therefore, even with no work, they may stay to look after the farm. Nevertheless, those without work and in the labour force are essentially unemployed. In any case, the figures presented here use a definition consistent with the older one in order to be comparable. The table also gives the rate of seasonal unemployment (in relation to the labour force, which includes all those who are employed, underemployed, openly unemployed, and seasonally unemployed).

The data show that seasonal unemployment is a problem affecting some 4 million workers. The years 1981 and 1982, when the number was around 5.5 million, were exceptional. The seasonal unemployment rates were around 20 per cent, except for 1981–82. In the South seasonal unemployment tends to be less because rubber, the major crop, requires large inputs of labour during the dry season months. The Central region has around 400,000 seasonal unemployed, but this was less than 10 per cent of the labour force. Seasonal unemployment is most severe in the North and particularly the Northeast, affecting over 30 per cent of the workforce.

It is not surprising that there should be a large number of people seasonally unemployed. We saw above that the demand

Table 11.4: Seasonal unemployment numbers and rates, 1977 to 1985 (number of workers)

	North	Northeast	South	Central	Total
Labour Force Survey 1977 Round 1					
Seasonal unemployment	1,065,740	2,306,910	53,660	537,310	3,963,620
Seasonal rate (%)	24.51	30.32	2.34	13.78	21.84
Labour Force Survey 1978 Round 1					
Seasonal unemployment	863,930	2,673,870	38,850	445,410	4,022,060
Seasonal rate (%)	19.55	35.20	1.54	11.09	21.68
Labour Force Survey 1979 Round 1					
Seasonal unemployment	985,570	2,823,780	128,080	431,890	4,369,320
Seasonal rate (%)	21.60	36.18	5.38	10.86	23.34
Labour Force Survey 1981 Round 1					
Seasonal unemployment	1,497,200	3,274,970	48,440	749,980	5,570,590
Seasonal rate (%)	28.98	39.48	3.01	6.48	28.39
Labour Force Survey 1982 Round 1					
Seasonal unemployment	1,482,030	3,442,910	71,470	460,620	5,457,030
Seasonal rate (%)	27.35	40.13	2.57	9.75	25.38
Labour Force Survey 1983 Round 1					
Seasonal unemployment	992,420	2,775,220	75,320	573,810	4,416,770
Seasonal rate (%)	20.05	35.90	2.89	13.00	22.42
Labour Force Survey 1984 Round 1					
Seasonal unemployment	675,410	2,770,270	77,880	244,020	3,767,580
Seasonal rate (%)	12.79	33.26	2.87	5.37	18.05
Labour Force Survey 1985 Round 1					
Seasonal unemployment	946,680	2,771,820	121,390	348,620	4,188,510
Seasonal rate (%)	17.41	31.47	4.29	7.24	19.14

for labour in agriculture varies tremendously by season. The main problem is to interpret what seasonal unemployment means. Is it a problem? Does it signify some kind of market failure?

An influential study by Bertrand and Squire (1980) suggests that seasonal unemployment is not really a problem. Markets are thought to work fairly well in the rural areas, and if these unemployed really wanted work then wages would fall to absorb them. The seasonal unemployed are therefore considered to have voluntarily withdrawn from the labour force. During the cultivation season, when the demand for labour is particularly high, women and young children are drawn upon to help, and when the season is over they simply withdraw from the labour force, which explains the observed variation in employment between the wet and the dry season.

Table 11.5 shows the age and gender distribution of seasonal unemployment from the January–March 1985 survey. It can be seen that, ignoring the own-account workers where the mean age is quite high, most of the seasonally unemployed men are aged below 25. Almost 40 per cent are between the ages of 15 and 19. For women, the age distribution is less concentrated, and those below 25 make up about 54 per cent of the seasonal unemployed in contrast to the very high ratio of around 78 per cent for men.

It is important to note that because most of the rural population above the age of 15 are no longer at school, their presence as seasonally unemployed does not mean they can be regarded as having voluntarily withdrawn from the labour force. Other studies, such as Pasuk and Baker (1984), stress that there are many prime age males among the seasonally unemployed, and that information on job availability is a major constraint to finding jobs in the dry season. Although the labour market adjusts to some extent through a lower wage in the dry season relative to the wet season (as cited by Bertrand and Squire), this is insufficient to generate sufficient demand for labour to absorb those wanting work. One way rural workers adjust is to work off-farm in non-agricultural pursuits. It is estimated that about 15 per cent of those normally working in agriculture during the wet season find non-agricultural work in the same locality (based upon preliminary individual matching of data from various Labour Force Surveys, which

Table 11.5: Seasonal unemployment, 1985

	Number of workers			%		
	Own-account	Others	Total	Own-account	Others	Total
Males						
11–14	—	58,020	58,020	—	7.71	2.71
15–19	1,430	294,580	296,010	0.10	39.15	13.83
20–24	57,730	235,560	293,290	4.16	31.31	13.71
25–29	145,410	103,640	249,050	10.48	13.77	11.64
30–34	212,310	35,780	248,090	15.30	4.76	11.59
35–39	224,010	13,270	237,280	16.15	1.76	11.09
40–49	319,890	7,110	327,000	23.06	0.94	15.28
50–59	269,550	2,150	271,700	19.43	0.29	12.70
60+	156,960	2,310	159,270	11.31	0.31	7.44
Total	1,387,290	752,420	2,139,710	100	100	100
Females:						
11–14	—	56,530	56,530	—	3.28	2.76
15–19	3,170	400,120	403,290	0.97	23.23	19.68
20–24	11,820	301,150	312,970	3.62	17.48	15.28
25–29	36,200	218,930	255,130	11.10	12.71	12.45
30–34	38,420	181,640	220,060	11.78	10.54	10.74
35–39	27,030	151,680	178,710	8.29	8.80	8.72
40–49	86,640	217,440	304,000	26.56	12.62	14.84
50–59	94,980	147,360	242,340	29.12	8.55	11.83
60+	27,930	47,840	75,770	8.56	2.78	3.70
Total	326,190	1,722,690	2,048,800	100	100	100

normally uses the same sample frame for the January–March and July–September surveys).

Another form of adjustment, which is examined in more detail below, is seasonal migration. Because the various crops have different patterns of labour demand there is a demand for workers from elsewhere to help in particularly heavy periods. Sugar-cane plantations often recruit workers from other parts of the country to help during the heavy cutting season. Workers also move to find work outside agriculture. The study of seasonal migration below presents findings based on data that, for the first time, give the picture on seasonal migration for the whole kingdom.

While there have been a number of studies of seasonal migration for particular villages or areas (see Kosit and Sanchai 1985, for example), a complete picture for the country has not been available. The analysis below will also quantify the extent to which people are actively seeking work in the dry season. It shows that people actively seek jobs in the dry season. The main impediment, as stressed by some earlier studies on migration, is information on the availability of jobs (Fuller et al. 1983). The findings go against the view that seasonal migration is not really a problem because much of it is just a voluntary withdrawal from the labour force.

Open unemployment

The data on open unemployment in Thailand must be examined with care. First, the National Statistical Office has changed the definition of open unemployment a number of times in the past few years. Second, given any particular definition, there are more openly unemployed people during the dry season than in the peak agricultural season. This part of the discussion will abstract from the seasonal component by focusing on the peak agricultural season, and will draw on the data from the July–September rounds of the Labour Force Survey.

A major change has taken place since 1983 in the definition of open unemployment. Previously, the openly unemployed included those who did not work during the survey week, and who either looked for work in the survey week or would have looked for work if they were not ill or had thought that there was work available. In 1983, the definition was broadened to include those who did not look for work, but reported that they were available and willing to work. This change in the definition has been widely debated. The fact that someone says that he or she is available for work does not indicate the rate of remuneration they would accept. The person may have an unrealistically high expectation and may more appropriately be classified as voluntarily unemployed because the going market wage is too low.

The change in definition in 1983 reflected dissatisfaction with the very narrow concept of open unemployment used earlier. In a labour market which is not highly organized, such as in Thailand, a reference period of only one week looking for work is much too short. In developed countries, where the unemployed receive unemployment benefits and where there are well-developed labour exchanges, one can expect an unemployed individual to register at the labour exchange, and in effect 'look' for a job. Those who do not, and are willing to forgo unemployment benefits, can be regarded quite reasonably as being voluntarily unemployed.

The situation is very different in a country like Thailand, where the family is the prime source of finance during unemployment, and one does not have to register to get this assistance. Also, many people find jobs through friends or relatives. Thus, the idea that a person must be looking for a job in the survey week before being classified as openly unemployed is inappropriate. While 'willingness to work' is probably too vague to be useful, the 'correct' level of open unemployment probably lies between the levels of those actually looking for work in the survey week (or even in the past month) and those 'willing to work but who did not look for work'.

Table 11.6 shows the numbers of unemployed according to the two concepts of open unemployment for July–September 1984, broken down by municipal and non-municipal areas, and by educational levels. In total, 253,800 were unemployed according to the old definition of 'looking for work', and 353,500 did not look for work, but said they were available for work. Including both concepts yields an open unemployment figure of 607,300. The new definition increases the numbers regarded as openly unemployed by more than 100 per cent. It can be seen that the impact of this change in definition is much greater in the non-municipal areas. In municipal areas, those 'available for work' amount to about 35 per cent of those looking for work, but in non-municipal areas, there are twice as many looking for work.

In non-municipal areas, the extent of open unemployment of those with elementary education (or less) is most affected by the new definition. For those with at least secondary education, the 'available' group is about 45 per cent of the 'looking for work' group. For those with elementary education (or less), there are more than four and a half times as many people 'available' as 'looking for work'. In recent years, the problem of open unemployment has been one of educated open unemployment, so the change in definition will not matter in judging the extent of the problem. In looking at the trends, we rely on the old definition, as it is possible to get comparable figures for those unemployed 'looking for work' since 1983, but there are no figures for those 'available but not looking for work' for earlier years.

The recent trends in open unemployment (using the definition prior to 1983) during the peak agricultural season July–September are given in Table 11.7, broken down by educational levels. The table shows that the majority of the openly unemployed are educated only to primary level (or less). This is not surprising since 85–90 per cent of all workers in Thailand have only received primary education (or less). Table 11.8 shows the unemployment rates. It can be seen that the overall open unemployment rate—the ratio of the openly unemployed divided by the total workforce, which includes those with jobs and those who are unemployed—is only 1 per cent, with the rate for those with primary education or less being only 0.5 per cent. The highest open unemployment rate is experienced by those with vocational education, with a rate of 7.1 per cent in 1977 and about 10.8 per cent in 1986. The other groups have about the same rates of open unemployment of some 3–4 per cent.

Table 11.9 shows the rates of open unemployment in municipal and non-municipal areas (using the pre-1983 definition). First, it is clear that the open unemployment rate is much higher in the municipal areas and the total number of openly unemployed has increased rapidly. The average growth in total unemployment was 10.2 per cent per year from

Table 11.6: Numbers of unemployed who looked for work and those who did not look but were 'available' for work, 1984

| | Total | Level of education | | | | | |
		Primary and below	Secondary	Vocational	Teacher training	University	Unknown
Municipal							
Looked for work	106,000	35,600	24,500	34,300	2,600	8,900	100
Available	37,800	16,800	9,200	7,200	1,500	3,100	–
Total	143,800	52,400	33,700	41,500	4,100	12,000	100
Non-municipal							
Looked for work	147,800	59,700	23,300	46,000	14,700	3,500	600
Available	315,700	274,600	13,700	15,200	9,300	1,200	–
Total	463,500	334,300	37,000	61,200	24,000	4,700	600
Both areas							
Looked for work	255,500	95,300	47,800	80,300	17,300	12,400	700
Available	351,800	291,400	22,900	22,400	10,800	4,300	–
Total	607,300	386,700	70,700	102,700	28,100	16,700	700

Source: Labour Force Survey, July-September, 1984, NSO.

Table 11.7: Unemployed looking for work in survey week, 1977 to 1986

			Level of education			
	Primary and below	Secondary	Vocational	Teacher training	University	Total
1977	62,500	31,100	17,100	13,000	6,200	129,900
1978	52,600	37,200	17,500	15,000	6,900	129,300
1979	74,000	43,500	25,800	15,700	5,900	165,300
1980	90,400	37,900	28,000	12,300	6,700	176,900
1981	94,000	40,600	34,300	8,800	15,400	193,100
1982	181,700	50,800	57,400	12,100	13,600	315,900
1983	141,800	41,200	46,700	12,000	14,600	256,300
1984	95,300	47,800	80,300	17,300	12,400	253,100
1985	111,300	63,000	72,200	15,200	17,200	278,900
1986	130,600	69,200	107,500	21,800	20,500	349,600

Source: Labour Force Survey, July–September, NSO.

Table 11.8: Unemployment rates of those looking for work in survey week, 1977 to 1986 (per cent)

	Level of education				
	Primary and below	Secondary	Vocational	Teacher training	University	Total
1977	0.33	3.72	7.11	5.14	3.81	0.63
1978	0.26	3.86	7.02	5.07	3.69	0.59
1979	0.38	4.48	8.67	4.77	2.50	0.77
1980	0.43	3.57	8.74	3.43	2.65	0.77
1981	0.42	3.31	8.44	2.10	4.94	0.78
1982	0.79	3.70	11.91	2.31	3.92	1.23
1983	0.64	2.88	8.81	2.11	2.99	1.01
1984	0.43	3.19	12.65	3.19	2.78	0.97
1985	0.49	3.74	9.40	3.02	4.81	1.07
1986	0.57	3.53	10.84	3.94	4.55	1.29

Source: Labour Force Survey, July–September, NSO.

1977 to 1986. The percentage rates of growth by level of education were: primary and below 9.3; secondary 7.2; vocational 20.7; teacher 3.3; and university 14. From Tables 11.8 and 11.9, an upward trend can be seen in the rates of open unemployment, although these rates are still relatively small by industrial countries' standards. For those with primary education or below, with secondary education or with teacher training, the growth of their open unemployment has been slower than the growth of total unemployment. The number of unemployed with a university education has been increasing rapidly, especially in 1985 and 1986. This was in part because of a cutback in government employment and also because these years marked the bottom of a recession. The severest unemployment problem occurs with the group with vocational education. In 1986, the numbers of unemployed with vocational education was roughly equal to the total of the unemployed with secondary education, university education and teacher training.

Employment patterns

Table 11.10 sets out the employment structure by educational level between 1972 and 1984, together with the average growth rates and the shares. On average, total employment grew at a rate of 4.7 per cent per year between 1972 and 1977, and at 3.6 per cent per year between 1977 and 1984. In both periods, the growth rates of those with primary education and below were less than the average for the total labour force. However, for each of the other educational categories, the average growth rate was larger than that for the total labour force. Between 1972 and 1977, the two groups with the fastest rates of growth were those with vocational education and those with university education. The former grew on average 13.68 per cent per year, while the latter increased at 22.65 per cent per year. Those with teacher training grew at around 9.35 per cent per year, while those with secondary education grew at 6.61 per cent. In the period between 1977 and 1984, the pattern is still similar. Employment of university graduates still grew the fastest, but the rate slowed down, and is now similar to the vocational group, whose rate of growth was about the same as in the earlier period. Both the teachers and those with secondary

Table 11.9: Unemployment rates by area, 1977 to 1986 (per cent)

1. Municipal areas

	Level of education					
	Primary and below	Secondary	Vocational	Teacher training	University	Total
1977	1.32	3.17	7.60	4.54	4.18	2.26
1978	1.50	2.94	5.98	4.67	3.74	2.26
1979	1.76	4.24	9.10	3.92	2.84	2.76
1980	1.97	4.03	7.45	3.03	3.13	2.76
1981	1.93	3.33	7.25	2.75	4.42	2.79
1982	2.67	5.22	9.67	1.89	4.50	3.76
1983	1.86	3.19	7.59	2.48	3.77	2.75
1984	1.80	4.02	10.67	1.98	2.84	3.10
1985	1.84	4.70	7.18	2.01	4.24	3.10
1986	1.96	4.44	9.57	2.23	5.10	3.58

2. Non-municipal areas

	Primary and below	Secondary	Vocational	Teacher training	University	Total
			Level of education			
1977	0.22	4.32	6.05	5.42	1.89	0.39
1978	0.13	4.77	9.85	5.26	3.45	0.34
1979	0.22	4.69	7.87	5.15	1.41	0.45
1980	0.26	3.13	11.13	3.62	1.15	0.45
1981	0.27	3.29	10.31	1.87	7.11	0.48
1982	0.60	2.61	14.66	2.44	2.34	0.85
1983	0.52	2.67	10.19	2.00	1.57	0.74
1984	0.29	2.63	14.67	3.58	2.62	0.65
1985	0.31	3.10	12.97	3.45	7.38	0.68
1986	0.39	2.90	12.36	4.65	2.90	0.84

Source: Labour Force Survey, July–September, NSO.

education grew faster than before, the former at 12.6 per cent, compared with 9.35 per cent, and the latter at 8.8 per cent compared with 6.6 per cent.

As a result of the rapid increase in employment of all groups with more than primary education, the shares of these workers have increased. In 1972, just over 5 per cent of all workers had more than primary education, rising to over 12 per cent in 1984. Given that the educational pattern of employment has undergone rapid changes, it is useful to look at the pattern by sectors and work status, broken down by education. Table 11.11 gives such a breakdown for 1984 with total employment dissected along three dimensions:-

(i) Sectors: primary (agriculture and mining), industry and services.

Table 11.10: Trend of employment by education, 1972, 1977 and 1984 (number of persons)

	1972	1977	1984
Primary and below	15,208,310	18,884,500	22,839,226
Secondary	583,050	803,100	1,448,770
Vocational	115,260	218,800	554,562
Teacher	153,280	239,600	524,750
University	56,420	156,600	434,412
Total	16,116,320	20,302,600	25,998,934

Average growth rate per annum (%)		1972-77	1977-84
Primary and below		4.43	2.70
Secondary		6.61	8.80
Vocational		13.68	13.80
Teacher		9.35	12.60
University		22.65	15.80
Total		4.73	3.60

Share (%)	1972	1977	1984
Primary and below	94.37	93.02	87.85
Secondary	3.62	3.96	5.57
Vocational	0.72	1.08	2.13
Teacher	0.95	1.18	2.02
University	0.35	0.77	1.67
Total	100	100	100

Source: Labour Force Surveys, July-September, NSO.

(ii) Work Status: private (employees and employers), government (including state enterprises), and own-account workers (including unpaid family workers).

(iii) Education: those with primary education and below labelled 'primary' and those with secondary education and above labelled 'secondary'.

From the table, total employment in 1984 amounted to 26 million persons, of when 3 million had more than primary education, or 11.4 per cent of the total. Most were own-account (self-employed), making up 74.2 per cent. However, among the own-account workers, only 906,000 out of 19 million, or 4.7 per cent, had more than primary education. The most important source of employment for those with more than primary education was the government. The public sector (including state enterprises) employed 1.7 million persons, around 20 per cent of whom are in state enterprises, but the proportion with secondary education and above is extremely high, amounting to 73.7 per cent of the total. In contrast, the proportion of workers with secondary education and above employed by the private sector (excluding the own-account workers) is only 16.3 per cent. In total, of all the workers with secondary education and above in Thailand, 41.7 per cent are in the public sector.

Looking at the educational distribution across sectors of employment reveals the same story. The primary industries have a very low proportion of workers with more than primary education, because most of its workers are own-account. Industry draws 17.4 per cent of its workers from the group with more than primary education, and the figure for services is 38.3 per cent, which is much larger because many workers in services are employed by the government. It is possible to separate out government services from the rest, in which case the proportion of workers with secondary education or above in private services is 22.8 per cent. In government services, however, over 75 per cent of all workers have secondary education and above.

Table 11.11 reveals the predominant influence of the public sector on the employment prospects of those with middle to upper levels of education. It seems clear that the past high growth of educated labour supply was met mostly by an expansion in government employment. This is confirmed by Table 11.12 which shows that between 1977 and 1984 the public sector employees (including state enterprises) had the highest

Table 11.11: Employment by aggregate sectors and by education, 1984 (thousands of persons)

		Primary sector	Industry	Services	Total
Private	Primary[a]	1,785	1,484	946	4,215
	Secondary[b]	40	268	512	820
	Total	1,825	1,752	1,458	5,037
Government	Primary	24	60	356	441
	Secondary	5	110	1,119	1,235
	Total	30	171	1,475	1,676
Own-account	Primary	15,891	644	1,843	18,379
	Secondary	500	81	324	906
	Total	16,392	726	2,167	19,285
Total	Primary	17,701	2,189	3,145	23,036
	Secondary	546	460	1,955	2,962
	Total	18,247	2,650	5,101	25,998

a Primary refers to those with primary education and below.
b Secondary refers to those with secondary education or above.
Source: Labour Force Survey, July–September, NSO.

average rate of employment growth compared with the private sector and the own-account workers. Public sector employment growth expanded on average 9.5 per cent per year compared with total employment growth of 3.6 per cent per year. The own-account workers expanded by only 2.6 per cent per year, and the private sector by 6.8 per cent per year.

Such a situation, where the public sector plays a crucial role in the employment of the better educated, must be seen to be unhealthy. First, the dominant role of the public sector had educated employment creates a distortion in the relative remunerations among the educated, and between the educated and the less educated. Government wage structures are notoriously rigid and not particularly responsive to the dictates of supply and demand. It is likely that if the public sector does not absorb the bulk of the educated labour supply, the wage differential between the better educated and the less educated would change by much more than what we observe.

Table 11.13 shows the trends in relative wages over time by educational groups. It seems that the wages of those with vocational, teacher training, and university education, compared

Table 11.12: Employment by work status, 1977 to 1984 (thousands of persons)

	Government	Private	Own Account	Total
1977	944	3,074	16,380	20,400
1978	1,020	3,573	17,213	21,807
1979	1,132	3,834	16,410	21,377
1980	1,189	4,007	17,483	22,680
1981	1,390	4,300	19,021	24,712
1982	1,598	5,043	18,726	25,369
1983	1,780	4,724	18,678	25,183
1984	1,676	5,036	19,285	25,998

Average growth rate, 1977 to 1984 (%)

Private	6.8
Government	9.5
Own account	2.6
Total	3.6

Source: Labour Force Surveys, Round 2, NSO.

with those with primary education or below, hardly changed
between 1978 and 1984, although due to sampling errors there
are variations from year to year. If we look at the growth of
government employment by the same educational categories,
we find that over the period 1977–1984 public sector employment
grew fastest for university-educated workers, at an average
annual rate of 17 per cent, compared with growth at 9.5 per
cent in total government employment. The groups with
vocational and teacher training education also show very fast
public employment growth, at around 13 per cent per year.
Those with secondary education and below grew by much less,
at 5.8 per cent and 4.6 per cent per year, respectively. If this
is compared with the average growth of employment by
educational levels in Table 11.10 it can be seen that government
employment at the university and teacher training levels grew
faster than total employment (government and private) for these
groups. This is also true for those with primary education and
below. Employment for the group with vocational education
grew at a rate about 0.8 per cent less in the public sector than
for total employment. For those with secondary education,
however, public employment growth was much slower than
for total employment growth, 5.8 per cent per year for the public
sector, compared with 8.8 per cent for total employment.

What these data suggest is that the relatively slow public
employment growth for those with secondary education is an
important reason for the worsening wage differential for this

Table 11.13: Relative wages by education levels, 1978 to 1984 (Primary = 100)

Year	Primary and below	Secondary	Vocational	Teacher training	University
1978	100	151	171	176	281
1979	100	152	188	176	295
1980	100	150	183	184	307
1981	100	148	174	163	288
1982	100	148	187	191	280
1983	100	145	176	188	291
1984	100	136	172	172	269

Source: Labour Force Surveys, Round 2.

group compared with the others. For those with university education and teacher training, the rapid rate of increase in government employment helped keep the unemployment rate for these groups fairly stable or with a declining trend up until 1984 (see Table 11.8). This enabled these groups to maintain their wage differential with respect to the less educated groups over a period when there has been rapid change in the educational composition of the workforce. For those with vocational education, the rate of growth of public employment is slightly below that for total employment, and this led to a rapid rate of growth of open unemployment for this group. However, in terms of their wage differential with respect to those with elementary education or below, the trend is not clear, and appears to be relatively stable. That this remains the case, even though unemployment rates for the vocational group are the highest, is related to the way the labour market works, and the nature of segmentation in the market, which will be analysed in more detail below.

The fact that government employment helped to keep the wage differential for the educated groups relatively stable, except for those with secondary education, where government employment grew relatively slowly, probably contributed to a distortion in the returns to education for the various levels of education. The government itself pays a higher average wage than the private sector for all levels of education except at the university level (from Labour Force Survey data). Its high demand for the better educated group has also helped keep up the wages of these workers in the private sector. This becomes a vicious circle, because a distortion increasing the relative returns to education tends to increase the demand for education, which has to be met for political reasons. This generates further excess supply in the numbers of educated workers, which, if the Government continues to absorb them, perpetuates the distortion. Apart from this, the rigidities in government wage structures have also created shortages in key skilled areas, while there is a general excess supply of educated labour supply.

A second reason why the concentration of employment of the better educated in the government is not healthy is that it puts a tremendous pressure on the government budget. In 1986, almost half of all government revenues were spent on wages and salaries. For this reason, the government imposed an effective 2 per cent ceiling on civil service employment growth as from 1984. This was a major reduction in the growth of government employment, which had grown 10 per cent per year between 1977 and 1984. Given that the public sector is the major employer of the better educated, this obviously had an important impact on the employment prospects of the better educated.

Between 1984 and 1986, the numbers of educated unemployed rose quite sharply, particularly for those with university education, of whom 20,500 were openly unemployed in 1986 compared with 12,400 in 1984. In 1984, more than half of all university graduates were employed by the government, so the cutback was bound to affect this group severely. Also, 1985 and 1986 were recession years, with real GDP growth of 3.5 per cent and 4.7 per cent respectively, compared with an average real GDP growth of 6.2 per cent for the period 1980–1984. This meant that private employment demand also grew slowly in those years, and was insufficient to counteract the slower government employment growth. After 1986, the employment prospects of the better educated improved substantially due to the economic boom. There are labour shortages in the science and technology disciplines, but in disciplines not greatly in demand by the private sector, such as the humanities, there is still an excess supply.

This section has shown that the workforce in Thailand has undergone rapid changes towards higher levels of education. This is desirable, and makes for a workforce that is more amenable to skills-training that is necessary for economic development. However, the fact that the employment prospects of the better educated have been so intimately tied to the ability to obtain government employment is not desirable. Given the 2 per cent ceiling on government hiring, it falls on the private sector to absorb the supply of educated workers. The idea of labour market segmentation is relevant here. In a situation where labour markets work near to the competitive ideal, an excess supply of better educated workers, particularly those with vocational training, should lead to wage adjustments so that the supply can be absorbed. In a segmented labour market this need not be the case. Wages can remain well above the market clearing level, and demand for labour in the formal sector is rationed. If this is the case, then the better-educated group for whom there is insufficient demand in the formal sector will presumably have to content themselves with finding informal sector jobs. Otherwise, educated unemployment will remain.

The above has been a brief review of the employment issues in Thailand, as it relates to seasonality and segmentation. Both seasonal and educated open unemployment are likely to be important issues for Thailand for some time, the former because most of the labour force is still dependent on agriculture, the latter because of the current transition towards a more important role for the private sector to absorb the better-educated workers, and the mismatching of the skills that are produced in the educational system and those that are demanded by the private sector. To understand these problems, an appreciation of the way Thailand's labour markets operate is crucial.

Seasonal migration

Quantifying seasonal migration

By studying seasonal migration, one can learn how the rural labour force adjusts, or fails to adjust, to the decline in agricultural labour demand during the dry season. It is an important method for people in rural areas to supplement their income during this period. In 1984, data on seasonal migration from the rural areas were collected for the first time on a nation-wide basis. A joint World Bank/NSO/NESDB project added several questions to the July–September round of the 1984 Labour Force Survey. The additional questions concerned seasonal migration in the rural areas, and labour market segmentation in the urban areas.

The July–September period is when most of those temporarily migrating during the dry season should have already returned to their normal place of residence. The questions asked of respondents included the following: Did they live in the current village during January 1984 (i.e. the same village that they were currently living in during July–September 1984)? If so, did they move to work elsewhere between January and June? For those who moved, what was the reason for moving, where did they go, for how long, in which month, what kind of work did they do, how much were they paid, how did they find the job, did they obtain the job before moving, and how long did it take to find the job? For those who did not move, did they attempt to find work outside the village, if not, the reason why not, if they did, whether they got the job, and if so, why they did not move?

The overall picture is summarized in Tables 11.14 and 11.15 (the weights used for the individual observations correspond to the weights in the July–September survey). In total, nearly 30 million people lived in non-municipal areas during July–September of 1984. Of these, 98 per cent lived in the current village in January, and they can be classified in the following way. For these 29.4 million people, we separate out first those who did not move because either: (i) they had a job in the village, (ii) they did housework, (iii) they were studying, or (iv) they were too young or too old. In total, these amount to around 25 million or 81 per cent of those present in January 1984. The other 4 million are regarded as potential seasonal migrants. This may be an underestimate as those who work or do housework may also be potential movers.

Of the potential movers (potential seasonal migrants), 745,000 (18 per cent) actually moved to work (and to live) outside the village at some point during January–June 1984. Of those who did not move, about an equal number looked for a job outside the village. About half of these found a job but did not move, and a similar number could not find a job. Two and a half million people did not look for a job outside the village, although 35 per cent of these said the reason they did not look was because they did not know how to look for a job outside the village. Only 875,000 people (21 per cent) said that they simply did not want to move. The impression that emerges is that the rural population is quite active in trying to overcome the inevitable lack of employment in the dry season.

Looking at the variation by gender, the main difference is that women are less inclined to move, 12 per cent (200,000) of potential female movers, as compared with 23 per cent (545,000) for males. Of those who did not move, only 15 per cent of women tried to find an outside job compared with 27 per cent for men; 25 per cent of female potential movers said they did not want to move compared with 19 per cent for men. This pattern is to be expected, given that there are more risks involved for women in working and living away from home.

From the tables, one can also see the extent of seasonal inactivity. First, those who did housework, or were studying, or were too young or too old, can be regarded as not having been in the labour force. The seasonally inactive numbered 3.4 million and comprised 15 per cent of the total workforce. This hardly varies by gender, with the rate for males at 16 per cent and for females 14 per cent. These numbers cannot be directly compared with data on seasonal unemployment or seasonal inactivity derived from various January–March rounds of the Labour Force Surveys, because the latter are concerned only with work characteristics during the survey week, whereas the numbers here represent a picture over many months. The numbers can however be thought of as a lower estimate for seasonal inactivity when compared with the January–March labour force survey data. They confirm that seasonal inactivity is a widespread problem affecting millions of people.

Regional variations

The seasonal migration patterns show striking regional variations. There is a clear difference between the Northeast and elsewhere. First, in terms of absolute number, more seasonal migrants moved from the Northeast (288,000) than elsewhere. There were twice as many potential movers in the Northeast than in any other regions, but the ratio of the potential movers who actually moved was much lower in the Northeast (14 per cent) than elsewhere (21–23 per cent).

The results do not mean that people in the Northeast were potentially less active in seeking outside jobs than people in other regions. Table 11.16 provides various summary statistics on regional differences. The proportion of potential movers who actually looked for an outside job was lower in the Northeast (30 per cent) compared with elsewhere (around 42 per cent). Nevertheless, if one also includes those who would have looked if they knew how to do so, then the proportion in the Northeast becomes the highest (61 per cent). In the Northeast, 44 per cent of those who did not look for a job said they did not know how to look for a job outside the village. This compares with 27 per cent in the North, 24 per cent in the Central region, and only 5 per cent in the South. It is clear that an important constraint on seasonal migration is information, and that this problem is particularly severe for those in the Northeast.

Table 11.14: Work patterns during the dry season, 1984[a] (thousands of persons)

	Male	Female	Total
Total[b]	14,947	14,979	29,927
I Not in village	291	203	495
II In village[c]	14,655	14,776	29,431
1 Already got a job	9,504	8,957	18,462
2 Did housework	80	1,444	1,525
3 Studying	2,142	1,772	3,914
4 Too young or too old	529	869	1,398
5 Potential movers	2,399	1,732	4,131
5.1 Moved	544	200	744
5.1.1 No jobs available in the village	208	77	286
5.1.2 Jobs available but low income	100	26	127
5.1.3 Need additional income	156	67	223
5.1.4 New job is more secure	1	4	5
5.1.5 Others	77	24	102
5.2 Did not move	1,854	1,532	3,386
5.2.1 Looked for a job	508	226	734
5.2.1.1 Got that job	232	126	358
Reasons for not moving			
—Income did not compensate for the expenses	80	44	125
—Did not like the job	8	0	8
—Did not want to move	88	63	151
—Others	53	18	72
5.2.1.2 Did not get a job	275	100	376

5.2.2			
Did not look for a job	1,346	1,305	2,652
Reasons for not looking for a job			
—Did not want to move	354	369	723
—Did not know how to find a job	498	418	916
—Others	494	517	1,011

[a] Based on Additional Questions in Labour Force Survey, 1984 (Round 3)
[b] Total = I + II
[c] = 1+2+3+4+5

Source: Labour Force Survey, NSO.

Table 11.15: Distribution of work patterns during the dry season, 1984 (per cent)

	Male	Female	Total
Total[a]	100	100	100
I Not in village	1.95	1.36	1.66
II In village	98.05	98.64	98.34
Classification of persons in village[b]	100	100	100
1 Already got a job	64.85	60.62	62.73
2 Did housework	0.55	9.78	5.18
3 Studying	14.62	11.99	13.30
4 Too young or too old	3.61	5.88	4.75
5 No work in the area resided	16.37	11.72	14.04
Classification of potential movers	100	100	100
5.1 Moved[c]	22.69	11.56	18.02
Reasons for moving	100	100	100
5.1.1 No jobs available in village	38.25	38.87	38.42
5.1.2 Jobs available but low income	18.52	13.44	17.15
5.1.3 Need additional income	28.72	33.50	30.00
5.1.4 New job is more secure	0.21	2.11	0.72
5.1.5 Others	14.30	12.08	13.71
5.2 Did not move[d]	77.31	88.44	81.98
5.2.1 Looked for a job[e]	27.39	14.80	21.70
5.2.1.1 Got that job[f]	45.69		48.83

Reasons for not moving	100	100	100
—Income did not compensate the expenses	34.84	35.36	35.02
—Did not like the job	3.84	.00	2.48
—Did not want to move	38.18	49.95	42.33
—Others	23.15	14.69	20.16
5.2.1.2 Did not get a job[g]	54.31	44.15	51.17
5.2.2 Did not look for a job[h]	72.61	85.20	78.30
Reasons for not looking for a job	100	100	100
—Did not want to move	26.29	28.30	27.28
—Did not know how to find a job	37.02	32.04	34.57
—Others	36.69	39.66	38.15

a Total = I + II
b 1+2+3+4+5=100
c % of Item 5
d % of Item 5
e % of Item 5.2
f % of Item 5.2.1
g % of Item 5.2.1
h % of Item 5.2

Source: Labour Force Survey, NSO.

Without this constraint, those in the Northeast would be the most active in seeking outside jobs. The Northeast is the poorest region and the lack of information may be partly due to poor communications with the outside caused by inadequate infrastructure (roads, electricity, telephones).

Age and educational characteristics of migrants

It is obvious that seasonal migrants are not highly educated. No seasonal migrant with more than secondary education was found. While there may be some seasonal migration of the better-educated group (the results here are based on a 50 per cent sub-sample of the 1984 Labour Force Survey), it is clear that the numbers will be very small.

The age characteristics of migrants are given in Table 11.17. The data are quite illuminating. The group with the highest proportion of movers to potential movers is the 15–19 years age group (at 25 per cent), followed by 30–39 years (22 per cent), 40–59 years (16 per cent), 20–29 years (14 per cent), 11–14 years (14 per cent) and 60 and over (2 per cent). For males, the rates for the 30–39 and 15–19 group are almost equal, with that of the former being slightly higher. For females, the 15–19 age group has almost double the migration rate of those between 20 and 39, and the next highest group is those between 11 and 14, although the absolute number in this group is small because most children in this age group are still at school and are not considered potential movers.

The 15–19 years age group was most active in looking for outside work. The proportion of potential migrants in this age group who actually looked for work (including those who moved) was 45 per cent; the next largest group was the 30–39 age group at 40 per cent, and the lowest, excluding those over 60, was the 11–14 years age group. This ranking was the same for both males and females. The pattern is also fairly consistent across regions, with this pattern being the most pronounced in the North and the Northeast.

Finding seasonal migration jobs

Because seasonal migration is a temporary move to work elsewhere for a few weeks or months, the cost of moving and not finding a job is extremely high. It is therefore not surprising

... of seasonal labour usage by region, 1984 (per cent)

	North	Northeast	South	Central
Potential movers in labour force	16.5	23.0	7.9	17.8
Potential movers who moved	22.9	13.7	20.8	22.7
Potential movers who actually looked for job	40.6	30.1	42.5	42.9
Potential movers who looked or would have looked for job	56.6	60.7	45.1	56.5
Those who looked for a job who found one	87.0	67.9	59.8	77.3
Those who found a job by moving away	64.9	61.5	81.7	68.6
Labour force seasonally inactive	12.8	19.8	6.2	13.8
Those who did not know how to look for a job	26.9	43.7	4.5	23.8

Note: Data relate to both sexes.
Source: Labour Force Survey, July–September 1984, NSO .

Table 11.17: Ages of seasonal migrants and those who looked for a job, 1984 (per cent)

		Age (years)					
		11–14	15–19	20–29	30–39	40–59	over 60
Both sexes	Movers	13.8	24.9	14.3	22.3	16.3	1.9
	Looked for job	21.4	45.4	36.8	40.0	27.8	4.0
Male	Movers	13.7	28.4	17.5	28.6	23.9	2.7
	Looked for job	13.7	53.7	46.1	46.7	37.7	4.6
Female	Movers	14.0	19.5	10.2	10.9	7.7	0.9
	Looked for job	28.1	32.7	25.0	27.7	16.6	3.3

Source: Labour Force Survey, July–September 1984, NSO.

that most migrants have a job waiting for them before they move. In the South, around 50 per cent of all movers were already sure of a job before they moved. In the other regions, the proportion was over 60 per cent, with that in the North over 70 per cent. Of those who did not have a guaranteed job before they moved, most found a job within one week of moving. Thus, virtually all workers had to be sure of a job before they actually decided to move.

The implication of this is that the flow of information is a crucial factor in determining seasonal migration. To be sure of a job, one cannot just move to some destination based on the vague expectation of finding a job there. There must be prior contact either with potential employers, or with friends or relatives who can help in finding a job before the person actually moves. Some employers, especially those in agriculture who need workers at particular times of the year (e.g. sugar-cane planters) may have a contract with the workers, or an agent, beforehand, and many in the village will be hired as a team.

Econometric estimates of seasonal migration

To confirm the importance of information flows for seasonal migration, simple estimates were carried out on the determinants of seasonal migration. We start with a sub-sample of the potential mover population (which excludes those under 11 years and over 60 years old or those with more than secondary education because no one in this group moved). The dependent variable, whether an individual migrated seasonally or not, is equal to one if he or she did, and zero otherwise. The independent variables include dummies for region, for education and for relationship to household head. Also included are variables which capture information flows (to some extent). These are the number of other persons in the household who moved, and the number of other persons in the village who moved. The latter is entered as the ratio of other persons in the village who moved to the total number of persons in the village. A variable for the total size of the village is also entered to capture possible effects of village size on migration.

Generally, what these estimates confirm is that information is a prime determinant of seasonal migration. The more people there are who move from a particular village, the more information there is about job opportunity for those living in the village, and it becomes more probable that other individuals living in the village will also move. The availability of information is obviously dependent on access to communication networks. This may come through good infrastructural links with the outside (roads, electricity, telephones) as well as through information flows on job opportunities from friends or relatives or prior movers from the village. This, however, has an important implication. Over time, there is a built-in tendency for the disparities across villages in terms of access to seasonal migration to widen. Those villages that have very few or no seasonal migrants will probably continue on with very few seasonal migrants, because information on job opportunities does not flow in. Those with a tradition of seasonal migration will generate the information for others in the village so that over time more and more people move.

The statistical results can be summarized as follows.

- It seems clear that those who faced the drastic decline in the demand for labour during the dry season were quite active in seeking alternative employment, even away from the village. Many of them did so, and moved to work elsewhere. Many others said they did not know how to find a job.
- The most active group in moving was the 15–19 years age group. This is evidence against the notion that the young withdraw from the labour force during the dry season, and do not want to work.
- Information was a prime determinant of seasonal migration. If some people moved from a village, then others were likely to follow. The implication is that seasonal migration tends to be concentrated in villages; some villages have many who move, while others have hardly anybody moving.
- The target for government policy should be to improve the communication networks in the more remote villages and provide information on job opportunities. In some cases, this may need basic infrastructure development such as better roads, provision of electricity, and telephones. In other cases, more direct programs to supply information on labour demand may be sufficient. Villages suffering from seasonal inactivity and with a very small proportion of seasonal migrants should be the target for improved information on seasonal job opportunity.

- Given the clustering of movers within villages, there is a built-in tendency for the disparity across villages to increase over time. Therefore, there is a case for targeting job creation programs to the more closed, inward-looking villages.

Labour market segmentation

To understand open unemployment, it is necessary to understand the structure and operation of the labour market. The fact that a large number of people cannot obtain jobs signifies some form of market failure. The traditional view is that open unemployment stems from rigidity in wages, leading to a wage that is too high, and also a wage structure that does not reflect the relative marginal product of labour in different industries and occupations. This view would lead one to examine the reasons for wage rigidity, and identify policies that would make wage adjustments more indicative of demand and supply. The major cause of wage rigidity that has been identified and studied is the presence and strength of trade unions. By contrast, the Keynesian view plays down the importance of wage rigidity, and instead suggests that open unemployment depends on the level of effective demand in product markets. This latter view would suggest government stimulation of effective demand as the cure for unemployment.

With recent attempts to integrate Keynesian and neo-classical economics, it has become clear that the ideas underlying each school of thought are both relevant, rather than competing. Many new concepts have been introduced by economists, such as Search Unemployment, Segmented (or Dual) Labour Markets, Efficiency Wages, Implicit Contracts, and Job Ladders[1]. The segmented labour market model has in particular been applied in the context of LDCs, where one normally observes the existence of a well-organized (or modern) sector co-existing with more informal forms of work. This is also the case in Thailand, with the larger firms having somewhat rigid personnel structures and pay scales, while many smaller firms are unorganized.

In this section, we make use of data made available through the joint World Bank/NSO/NESDB project mentioned above to study the structure of labour market segmentation in Thailand. The analysis is closely related to the problem of educated open unemployment reviewed above.

The idea behind labour market segmentation is that there is a 'formal' sector and an 'informal' sector in the labour market. The key conceptual distinction is that, in the formal sector, wages do not completely respond to market forces, and some workers who want to work in the formal sector at the going wage cannot enter. In the informal sector, if a worker wants to enter then he or she can. If more people enter, the wage will fall.

There is a close relationship between segmentation and open unemployment. Because workers earn higher wages in the formal sector, this is their first preference. Those who cannot get in find themselves either in the informal sector or unemployed. Of course other factors are also relevant for the determination of open unemployment. For example, there may be friction in the labour market, so that workers need time to find a job, or there may be a lack of information, as in the seasonal migration case. However, in Thailand, it is unlikely that the problem of open unemployment is mainly a problem of frictional unemployment. One would expect frictional unemployment to be equally severe for workers at all educational levels, and as we have seen above, the educated group, particularly those with vocational education, is hardest hit by open unemployment. It is argued here that an important factor determining open unemployment, particularly for the educated group, is that they can earn a significant wage by getting into the formal sector.

One might ask why those who cannot get into the formal sector at a particular time do not work in the informal sector while waiting. Some do, but for many, especially those with relatively high levels of education, the types of work available in the informal sector are seen as low status. They expect that education will be rewarded, and in the past they were justified in this belief because the government had played the major role in providing jobs for the better educated. Also, they or their families are able to finance unemployment. Very few unemployed individuals must borrow to finance periods of unemployment. Of course, unemployment imposes hardships. It is wasteful, it can affect the individual's self-esteem, and, if the numbers become large, it can be politically untenable.

The structure of labour market segmentation

To analyse labour market segmentation, it is necessary to separate those workers working in the formal sector from those in the informal sector. Statistical proxies are required, but only a few indicators are available from the standard labour force survey. One important proxy is 'work-status'. A central distinction is whether the individual works for the government. Government work is regarded as part of the formal sector, because government wages and employment levels are essentially policy variables, and not determined by market forces.

For non-government workers, the majority are own-account workers and unpaid family workers. Most agricultural employment occurs in these groups. It is generally considered that these workers belong to the informal sector, i.e. that entry is fairly free. While this is probably accurate for most own-account and unpaid family workers, for certain occupations in this group, entry is far from easy, especially in the urban areas, for occupations requiring significant capital assets. Imperfections in the capital market can create major barriers to entry. Very little is known about this, however, and from some preliminary analyses of urban areas, the own-account workers turn out to be a mixture, partly formal and partly informal. Certainly entry is not easy, and it does not seem to be an attractive alternative for the better-educated workers.

Employers are really part of the formal labour market. Entry is difficult, but the barriers to entry arise not from labour market imperfections, but from the imperfections in the capital market. This group is a very small part of total employment (around 4 per cent in municipal areas, and about 0.6 per cent in non-municipal areas).

Private employees are the most numerous group in the municipal areas (43 per cent of total municipal employment). The situation for them is similar to that for the own-account and unpaid family workers in that, with the normally available information, it is difficult to separate out those in the formal sector from those in the informal sector. However, this group is important for the open unemployment problem. Future government employment cannot be expected to grow very fast. The private sector will have to play an increasingly important role in absorbing the better-educated workers. It will be the more attractive jobs in the private sector that become the real alternatives to government employment.[2] In the private sector, looking at the past trends in employment growth and structure of educated employment (Tables 11.11 and 11.12), employment of own-account workers has not been growing particularly fast, and this form of employment has a very small share of educated workers in the total.

Apart from the information on work status already discussed, the standard questions of the Labour Force Survey contain a few other pieces of information that could be used as reasonable proxies for determining the formal–informal split. The two that are available are the occupations and industries of the employees. Some occupations are those that can clearly be regarded as being part of the formal sector, for example doctors or lawyers. Similarly, employees in agriculture may be viewed as part of the informal sector.

Additional questions to the 1984 Labour Force Survey asked respondents living in municipal areas for details regarding their place of work, and their job or unemployment experience. These questions were restricted to respondents in municipal areas to minimize the cost of the survey, and because the open unemployment problem in rural areas is likely to spill over into the urban areas through migration. The questions yielded information on such variables as firm size, union activity and the types of contract, all relevant for the formal–informal distinction (Mazumdar 1981). The most important new variable is firm size. It is commonly regarded that large firms are part of the formal sector, with well-developed internal labour markets, firm–specific training, and many other features that modern theories of wage determination suggest may lead them to pay a wage above the market clearing level.

These data show the importance of Bangkok as a source of municipal employment accounting for 70 per cent of all private employment in municipal areas. Second is the Central region, with the Northeast the least important. Bangkok is also very important as the centre for the larger firms.

The role of the larger firms in the employment of the better educated is important for open unemployment. Larger firms tend to be the formal sector firms, and if their wage policy is unresponsive to the labour market situation, as hypothesized by the segmented labour market theories, then access to these firms is difficult. When the supply of the better educated exceeds the demand, these workers cannot hope that the formal sector will absorb all or most of the new entrants. It is thus necessary that they be willing to move to the informal sectors.

In general, there is a difference in wages between small and large firms for all the educational categories. The exception is those with university education, such as doctors and lawyers, who are concentrated in small firms. Even for the university educated, wages rise with firm size. Even controlling for education, firm size has an independent effect on wages. For the same level of education, working in a large firm pays better than in a small firm. This is similar to findings in other countries (Mazumdar 1981).

Other dimensions of the relationships between firm sizes and other variables can be summarized as follows:

- The workforce in larger firms tends to be more stable. They have a higher share of workers with long experience in the firm than smaller firms. In firms with five or fewer workers, only 24 per cent of the employees have worked for six or more years with the firm. This ratio is 37 per cent in firms with 50 or more employees.
- The entry point for migrants seems to be in the small firms. As they stay longer in the municipal areas, they move increasingly to larger firms. This may reflect upward mobility as they are assimilated into the area, and it may indicate that migrants who did not get good jobs in the larger firms tend not to remain long in the municipal areas.
- Firm size also correlates well with other possible indicators of being in the formal sector. Occupations which one would expect in the formal sector are mostly found in larger firms, the only exception being some professional occupations such as doctors and lawyers, who also work in the very small firms.
- Unionized firms are mostly large firms. Only 6.5 per cent of private employees in the municipal areas report that they belong to a firm with unions. However, over 20 per cent of workers in firms with 50 or more workers report that their firm is unionized. Over 80 per cent of all workers in unionized firms are in firms with 50 or more workers.
- Only 28 per cent of all employees report having some type of 'formal' contract with their employer. The larger the firm, the more likely it is to offer a contract to its workers.

- It seems that the three new proxies for segmentation (firm size, unionization, and the existence of a 'formal' contract with the firm) each have independent effects on wages. However, the impact of firm size on wages is much greater for those not in unionized firms and those who do not have a contract with their employer.
- Not all employees in large firms can be regarded as having formal sector employment. Large firms still employ significant proportions of their workforce on a daily basis, 23 per cent in firms with 50 or more workers, compared with 21 per cent in firms with five or fewer workers. For most workers under daily contract, there is really no stability of employment, something we would normally associate with formal sector employment. Also, for workers under daily contracts, the average wage scarcely changes across firm sizes, suggesting that they can best be regarded as part of the informal sector.

The formal sector represents 41 per cent of total private employment in the municipal areas. However, looking at the shares of employment by education, we can see that the government employs 24 per cent of workers with university education, compared with 17 per cent for the private formal sector. Similarly, for vocational education, the government employs 17 per cent, the private formal sector 15 per cent. The private formal sector employs a higher proportion of those with primary education or below (41 per cent compared with only 20 per cent in the government sector).

The structure of wage payments

The 1984 Labour Force Survey findings show a clear distinction between the formal and informal sectors. In the informal sector, education does not influence the wage. Thus, there is no return to education. The South, Central, and Bangkok regions all pay a higher informal wage than the North or the Northeast. Males receive higher informal sector wages (with females receiving about 64 per cent of the male wage). The relationship between age and wages is as expected, with a peak at around 39 years, followed by a decline. Experience in the firm also has a positive effect on wages. Migration status is only important for very new migrants. These tend to be paid less, but after a year or two their wages are indistinguishable statistically from those of other informal workers.

In the formal sector, there are high returns to education. Of non-migrant males of prime age (35 years old, with 10 years experience in the firm) in the private, formal sector in Bangkok (in 1984), those who completed primary education earned about 500 baht per month more than those with below primary education. Those with secondary education earned about 1,300 baht per month more than those with only primary education. Those with vocational education earned another 1,350 baht per month more than those with secondary education, and about 900 baht more than those with teacher training. Finally, those with university education earned 3,200 baht per month more than the vocational group. The government pays more than the private formal sector for all levels. In the formal sector, females receive about 83 per cent of the male wage, so there seems to be less discrimination than in the informal sector. Also, there appears to be no difference in the male–female differential between the private formal sector and the government sector. Wages are highest in Bangkok, followed by the Central and the Northeast, with the South and the North having the lowest.[3]

For the formal sector, migrants moving from a different province who have been in the area for less than five years tend to be paid less than the locals, whereas in the informal sector this is only true for 'one year migrants'. This may be because an important consideration for the formal sector is stability of employment, and migrants may move back to their original area after a short time with the firm.

In terms of the difference between the formal and informal sector, the most striking is the returns to education or lack of it in the informal sector.[4] This means that as the level of education rises, the return to be had from gaining access to the formal sector also rises sharply. Overall, for those with below primary education, the male wages in the formal sector were slightly above those in the informal sector, while the female wages were much higher. For Bangkok, the male differential between the private formal and informal sectors was only 30 baht per month for those with below primary level education. This rises to 547 baht for those with completed primary education, 1,883 baht for secondary education, 2,336 baht for teacher training, 3,232 baht for vocational education, and finally 6,253 baht for university graduates. For females in Bangkok, the private differential was 408 baht for below primary education, 848 baht for completed primary, 1,960 baht for secondary, 2,335 baht for teacher training, 3,082 baht for vocational, and 5,596 baht for university education.

Given these differentials, it is not surprising that those with better education are more likely to join the pool of unemployed rather than enter the informal sector. In the latter, they are not rewarded for their education, and there may be a stigma attached to working in the informal sector. Also, the better educated have a greater chance of eventually entering the formal sector.

Conclusions: employment prospects

This chapter has examined the issues of seasonal migration and labour market segmentation in order to clarify the operation of labour markets in Thailand. The seasonal migration issue is related to the operation of the rural labour market, particularly the way it adjusts to the decline in agricultural labour demand occurring in the dry season. The labour market segmentation issue concerns mainly the urban labour market and the problem of open unemployment.

These analyses are relevant for judging the future employment prospects in Thailand. The seasonal migration analysis showed that most of those made idle by low demand for labour in agriculture in the dry season would like to find work. This is particularly true for the relatively young age group who are hardest hit by seasonal unemployment. An important impediment is the lack of information on jobs available elsewhere. In the urban areas, the labour market exhibits sharp segmentation between the formal and informal sectors, with only the former offering high rewards to education. The formal labour market is therefore highly attractive to the better-educated workers. These workers are more likely to become openly unemployed than to work in the informal sector, should they not be able to enter the formal sector. Therefore, the demand for educated labour in the formal sector is crucial for determining the open unemployment prospects of the better educated.

In terms of dry season employment, the pattern and impediments to seasonal migration point to key roles for the government. Communication access and information flows could be improved, and government programs designed to help with rural employment should be targeted to the most remote, disadvantaged areas.

Regarding open unemployment, the private sector will have to play an increasing role in absorbing the better educated. This is a significant change from the past, where the government, in essence, produced educated workers for its own use. With more reliance on the private sector to absorb the better educated, the education system will need to be more flexible in producing the types of graduates demanded by the private sector (Myers and Chalongphob 1989). Thailand is currently experiencing shortages of scientific and technical workers, while there is excess supply of humanities graduates. The future employment prospects of the better-educated workforce will also depend on the continuation of the present economic boom. This is being led by rapid growth of manufactured exports, coming mostly from the formal sectors, which are major employers of the educated workers. If the current trend continues, the problem of educated unemployment should become less severe.

Notes to Chapter 11

[1] See for example Azariadis (1975), Bailey (1976), Gordon (1974), Leibenstein (1957), Doeringer and Piore (1971), Phelps (1970), Lippman and McCall (1979), Mazumdar (1979), Salop and Salop (1976), and Stiglitz (1974, 1976).

[2] With the economic boom of the late 1980s, formal private sector wages were fast outstripping government wages, and many began to refer to government employees as the 'new poor'.

[3] It is somewhat surprising that the Northeast has higher wages than the South or the Central. This may be due to the relatively small sample used in the estimation—only about 100 observations in the formal sector for each region outside Bangkok, but about 500 in Bangkok.

[4] This does not contradict earlier findings of the productivity effects of primary education in agriculture (see Lockheed, Jamison and Lau 1979), as I am here considering employees, and not the self-employed.

12

Poverty and Income Distribution

MEDHI KRONGKAEW

Although Thailand is a poor country, Thai scholars have only recently turned their attention to the problems of poverty. This chapter reviews the available statistical evidence on the incidence and nature of poverty in Thailand and the state of income distribution. Due to limited availability of data on this critical issue, the discussion necessarily concentrates on the period since the 1960s.

Previous studies

One statistical source dominates the study of income distribution and poverty in Thailand—the series of Socio-Economic Surveys (SES) conducted by the National Statistical Office (NSO). Virtually all serious analyses of income distribution and poverty in Thailand have used this source. Surveys have now been conducted in 1962–63 (when it was known as the Family Budget Survey), 1968–69, 1975–76, 1981, 1986, 1988 and 1990. In addition, a survey was conducted over the two-year period 1971–1973 but, because data for different parts of the country were collected during this period, they are not comparable.

Economic studies of the structure and incidence of poverty in Thailand were not undertaken in any systematic way until 1974, when the government of Prime Minister Sanya Dhammasak began to consider welfare-state policies for Thailand. Using the 1968–69 consumption patterns of households in Thailand to estimate the proportion of those households living in poverty, Medhi and Chintana (1975[T]) estimated the level of 'poverty incidence'. Using a different method, a second group studied the determination of an appropriate minimum wage for Thai workers (Trairong et al. 1975[T]). These two studies gave similar results as to where the poverty line should be drawn.

Oey (1979) then studied the economics of poverty in greater detail, using methods similar to those used by the second group of researchers above. Four important findings emerged:

- from the early 1960s to the mid-1970s, households throughout Thailand experienced a continuous increase in their real incomes, resulting in a steady decline in the incidence of poverty;
- average household income disparities between rural and urban areas narrowed over this period;
- the improvement in the status of households in rural areas came as a result of increased average farm commodity prices and the switch to new crops with high returns; and
- rural households earned a greater proportion of their household incomes from non-farm activities.

Oey's work was considered the definitive study of poverty at that time, but several researchers still questioned her data and methods of investigation. For example, Rizwanul Islam (1984) commented that use of the overall consumer price index in adjusting the poverty line for each year (rather than different price indices for different income classes) could overstate the past extent of poverty, because true price indices for the poor were likely to be larger than the measured index for an average family. The reason is that food prices in rural areas exceed urban prices for the same food items. This causes the appropriate price index for the poor to exceed the average price index because poor households tend to be concentrated in rural rather than urban areas, and also because food absorbs a higher proportion of the budget of the poor. Therefore, the reduction in present poverty levels could also be overstated. Islam claimed that even if poverty had been reduced, the inequality in income distribution could have increased. The distribution of income had not been mentioned by Oey, whose work focused on the incidence of poverty alone.

Medhi and Aphichart (1984) also criticized some of Oey's conclusions, arguing that the 1975–1976 Socio-Economic Survey of households understated the true incidence of poverty in that year, because interviews were repeated when income was found to be 'too low' in comparison with expenditure. This was done because recall of income was considered less reliable than recall of expenditures. In these repeat interviews, respondents were asked whether they may have forgotten any sources of income during the initial interview. If any were recalled, 'measured' income was duly increased, but no such follow-up questions were asked in relation to expenditure and follow-up interviews were not conducted at all for households whose recall of expenditures was 'too low' in relation to recalled income. The result was an upward bias in measured income, relative to expenditure, leading to a downward bias in the estimate of poverty incidence. In addition, 1975–76 was a good year for primary commodity prices and this led to an increase in farmers' income. As a result, since poverty is primarily a rural phenomenon, the actual incidence of poverty in that year was unusually low. It was not representative of the true incidence of poverty during the 1970s.

At the end of the 1970s, the available evidence on poverty and income distribution in Thailand was still insufficient and the true situation remained uncertain. The NSO conducted another Socio-Economic Survey in 1981. These new survey data were used by Enrique Rueda-Sabater et al. to write an unpublished report on the issues (World Bank 1985). The NSO conducted another survey for the whole country in 1986 and, while the official report was still under preparation, the original survey data were made available to the Thailand Development Research Institute (TDRI). Staff of TDRI had been making a preliminary study of the changes in poverty and income distribution since 1981. It is difficult to compare their results with the earlier studies. The changes they identified will therefore be discussed separately in this chapter, together with the results of the 1988 SES survey.

Changes in poverty incidence, 1975–76 and 1981

The details of how poverty is defined and how a poverty line is estimated for the purposes of this chapter are outlined in World Bank (1985). Once a poverty line is determined, the incidence of poverty, or the proportion of households or of the population whose incomes are below that designated poverty line, can be calculated from the SES data. By using such poverty-line estimates, poverty incidence rates in Thailand have been calculated for 1975–76 and 1981 and they are presented in Table 12.1.

From this it can be seen that the proportion of the poor in Thailand fell from 32 per cent in 1975–76 to 24 per cent in 1981. Both urban and rural areas experienced a reduction in poverty incidence. For example, the proportion of poor in urban areas fell from 21 per cent in 1975–76 to 16 per cent in 1981. This declining poverty incidence was more pronounced for the population of Bangkok, where only 4 per cent of the total population were considered poor in 1981, compared with 9 per

Table 12.1: Poverty incidence, 1975–76 and 1981[a] (per cent)

Subregion	Proportion of population 1975–76	Proportion in poverty 1981	Household adjusted incidence 1981[b]
Rural			
Upper North	41.3	30.0	40.4
Lower North	31.1	17.1	23.5
Upper Northeast	43.5	36.4	46.8
Lower Northeast	49.8	35.9	45.8
Central West	10.2	11.1	15.3
Central Middle	10.9	9.9	12.8
Central East	17.9	16.3	21.7
Upper South	27.3	22.4	30.6
Lower South	55.0	19.0	27.1
All rural	35.7	26.5	34.7
Urban			
Bangkok	8.9	3.9	6.5
Other urban	29.4	25.7	32.5
All urban	21.3	16.2	21.1
Whole Kingdom	31.7	23.9	31.3

[a] Incidence of poverty obtained by weighing households by number of household members.
[b] Adjusted for change in definition of household between 1975–76 and 1981.
Source: World Bank (1985).

cent in 1975-76. In rural areas, where the majority of the
population live, the incidence of poverty fell from 36 per cent
in 1975-76 to 27 per cent in 1981, but the reduction varied
between and within regions. The Lower South had the highest
fall in poverty incidence, from 55 per cent in 1975-76 to only
19 per cent in 1981. The Central West was the only subregion
where poverty incidence increased rather than declined. In the
Northeast, even with a steep fall in 1981, poverty incidence
was still the highest in the country, at 36 per cent of the
population.

It is significant that due to a change in definition of the
household between 1975-76 and 1981, the measured values of
average household size and therefore average income changed.
Unlike the 1975-76 survey, the 1981 SES treated extended
families as two or more households whenever there was one
or more married son or daughter whose income could be
separated from that of the older generation. This change makes
it difficult to compare the 1975-76 and 1981 data on poverty
incidence. The result of this change in definition was a significant
drop in average household size (from 5.5 to 4.2 persons) and
an increase in the number of households. When household sizes
are adjusted to approximate those shown in the 1980 population
census, the estimated level of poverty incidence increased across
the board, as shown in the last column of Table 12.1. When
allowance is made for this, it appears that the overall poverty
incidence had not changed much at all, with rural poverty
declining from 36 per cent to 35 per cent, and urban poverty
remaining stable at 21 per cent. For the whole kingdom,
measured poverty incidence decreased only marginally from
32 per cent to 31 per cent.

The 1981 study nevertheless showed conclusively that, over
the long term, poverty in Thailand was declining. In the twenty
years from 1962-63, when the first set of data on household
income and expenditure was available, it can be seen that the
proportion of people considered to be poor had steadily
decreased.[1]

The Relative Income Shortfall Index (Index R) and the Sen
Index (Index S)[2] can also be used to capture the extent of poverty
at the household level. Table 12.2 shows these additional
indicators of poverty for Thai households in 1975-76 and 1981.
It shows that poverty on a household basis is lower than on

a per capita or population basis, indicating that the size of poor families is larger than non-poor families. In 1981, the proportion of poor households was 19 per cent of total households, a reduction from 27 per cent in 1975-76. The direction of poverty reduction on a household basis was similar to that on a population basis across most areas.

When measured by Index *R*, the index for households in the urban areas is higher than in the rural areas (0.297 compared with 0.287). This indicates that urban poor households had a relatively larger income shortfall than their counterparts in rural areas. Although the incidence of poverty in urban areas was less than that in rural areas, those urban households who are poor are generally relatively worse-off than the poor in rural areas. The Northeast was highest in terms of relative income deprivation, having the highest income shortfall (*R*) among all rural households.

Index *S* represents the poverty incidence adjusted by the weight of income inequality among the poor groups. Therefore, the movement or direction of *S* and poverty incidence is generally the same. For instance, Bangkok households are shown to be the least poor, whereas Northeast households are shown to be the most poor.

Table 12.3 provides information on the distribution of poverty by occupations. Occupations were classified into six categories: farm operators; non-farm entrepreneurs; professional and technical positions; farm and general labourers; clerical, production and construction labourers; and economically inactive persons. The farm and general labourers category had the highest incidence of poverty, 29 per cent in 1981, virtually unchanged from 1975-76[3]. Next were farm operators with 26 per cent, which represented a reduction from the 1975-76 level of 38 per cent. As might be expected, the professional and technical group shown in Table 12.3 was the least poor, with a poverty incidence level in 1981 of only 1 per cent. The incidence of poverty levels for the remaining two categories (excluding the economically inactive group) appeared to be moderate at 12 and 9 per cent, respectively.

Table 12.2: Household poverty incidence, relative income shortfall and Sen index, 1975–76 and 1981

Subregion	Household poverty incidence (%)		Relative income shortfall[a]		Sen index[a]	
	1975–76	1981	1975–76	1981	1975–76	1981
Rural						
Upper North	36.0	24.6	0.275	0.264	0.139	0.099
Lower North	27.5	14.3	0.293	0.252	0.114	0.059
Upper Northeast	40.1	31.4	0.260	0.269	0.143	0.143
Lower Northeast	43.9	31.4	0.260	0.284	0.151	0.101
Central West	8.4	9.2	0.346	0.232	0.037	0.030
Central Middle	8.1	7.9	0.192	0.241	..[b]	..[b]
Central East	14.7	12.1	0.253	0.274	0.052	0.046
Upper South	22.6	17.8	0.273	0.237	0.090	0.059
Lower South	48.4	15.8	0.348	0.262	0.231	0.050
All rural	30.6	21.7	0.267	0.267	0.114	0.082
Urban						
Bangkok	7.1	2.9	0.241	0.283	0.024	0.012
Other urban	24.5	21.2	0.314	0.297	..[c]	..[c]
All urban	17.9	13.1	0.303	0.297	0.074	0.053
Whole Kingdom	27.0	19.4	..	..	..	..

[a] See chapter endnote 2 for definition.

[b] Since Gini coefficients for Central Middle including Changwats Samut Prakan, Non Thaburi and Pathua Thani are not available, the Sen indices are here presented separately: Central Middle, excluding Changwats Samut Prakan, Non Thaburi and Pathua Thani: 1975–76 = 0.163; 1981 = 0.062: Changwats Samut Prakan, Non Thaburi and Pathua Thani: 1975–76 = 0.134; 1981 = 0.024.

[c] The Sen indices, computed for urban areas by subregion, ranged from 0.036 for Upper South to 0.143 for Upper Northeast.

Source: World Bank (1985).

Table 12.3: Household poverty incidence by occupation, 1975–76 and 1981 (per cent)

Subregion	Farm operators		Non-farm entrepreneurs		Professional and technical		Farm and general labourers		Construction labourers		Clerical production and economically inactive	
	1975–76	1981	1975–76	1981	1975–76	1981	1975–76	1981	1975–76	1981	1975–76	1981
Upper North	45.1	32.7	17.1	16.4	3.3	—	34.5	24.9	13.1	11.0	16.1	11.8
Lower North	30.6	15.5	18.5	5.2	—	1.9	35.6	30.0	7.9	10.2	26.3	7.7
Upper Northeast	48.0	35.3	16.9	27.5	1.9	5.7	39.9	46.4	16.1	19.0	12.1	14.3
Lower Northeast	52.1	33.6	19.5	24.4	3.8	0.8	41.0	40.9	13.7	22.2	21.7	13.0
Central West	10.6	10.1	6.7	8.5	3.1	—	17.9	16.5	8.3	12.2	7.6	18.4
Central Middle[a]	13.9	13.9	9.8	6.0	1.3	1.9	19.2	27.8	4.6	8.0	9.8	11.7
Central East	18.8	20.6	0.6	7.8	—	—	18.7	22.0	4.3	8.8	8.2	13.1
Upper South	32.9	19.4	10.6	17.8	0.7	—	23.4	19.5	11.4	11.8	20.3	9.6
Lower South	62.2	19.8	24.6	8.7	—	—	26.3	24.1	23.9	13.5	47.5	5.2
Bangkok[b]	25.5	8.2	6.4	3.3	1.0	—	16.9	13.6	4.6	2.7	3.6	3.0
Whole Kingdom	38.4	26.0	12.8	11.5	1.6	1.1	28.6	29.0	8.8	8.7	15.8	10.4

[a] Excludes Changwats Non Thaburi, Pathua Thani and Samut Prakan.
[b] Includes Changwats Non Thaburi, Pathum Thani and Samut Prakan.
Source: World Bank (1985).

Changes in income distribution

In this section, attention is switched from poverty to income inequality. Three aspects of income inequality will be discussed: income disparities between regions; income disparities between urban and rural areas; and trends in income inequality in Thailand.

Regional disparities

Tables 12.4 and 12.5 indicate that major disparities exist in income levels between subregions. In Table 12.5 the national average per capita income index is given the value of 100, and in 1975–76 the subregion with the highest income index was Bangkok (with an index of 182), and the lowest was the Lower Northeast (with an index of 69). By 1981, the disparities had worsened, with the income index for Bangkok rising to 196, and those for the Upper Northeast and the Lower Northeast falling to 64 and 62, respectively. Between 1975–76 and 1981, the income indices improved in three subregions: Bangkok (182 to 196), the Lower North (92 to 104), and the Lower South (84 to 92). For all other subregions, the income indices declined, especially for the two Northeast subregions.

Disparities between urban and rural areas

Although it appears that the inter-regional differences in per capita personal income had increased between 1975–76 and 1981, the intra-regional disparities of per capita personal income between rural and urban areas appear to have decreased. Table 12.6 indicates that rural income as a percentage of urban income increased in all subregions except Central Middle and Upper South, which did not change in this period.

Characteristics and trends of income distribution

The most popular index used to measure inequality in income distribution is the Gini coefficient or Gini concentration ratio which has values between 0 and 1, corresponding to complete equality and complete inequality, respectively. Because the Gini

Table 12.4: Per capita household income, 1975–76 and 1981

Subregion	1975–76 per capita income (baht per year, current prices)	1981 per capita income (baht per year, current prices)	1975–76 to 1981 % growth (nominal) (%)	1975–76 to 1981 average annual growth (real)[a] (%)
Rural				
Upper North	3,939	7,156	135	7.6
Lower North	3,904	10,016	157	9.6
Upper Northeast	2,891	6,434	123	5.7
Lower Northeast	2,814	6,010	114	4.8
Central West	5,425	11,118	105	4.2
Central Middle	6,201	12,587	103	4.0
Central East	4,578	9,861	115	5.2
Upper South	4,140	9,075	119	5.9
Lower South	2,961	8,583	190	12.0
All rural	3,713	8,305	124	5.4[b]
Urban				
Bangkok	9,210	22,598	145	6.7
Other urban	7,138	14,545	104	3.5[b]
All urban	7,927	18,141	129	5.9[b]
Whole Kingdom	4,901	10,974	124	5.4

a Deflated by 1981 CPI (1976 = 100). Since rural price deflators are unavailable, urban regional price deflators have been used.
The 1981 price indices were:

North	162.8
Northeast	169.1
Central	167.2
South	164.4
Bangkok	176.8
Whole Kingdom	172.1

To the extent that rural prices have risen less rapidly than urban prices, it is likely that real rural growth rates have been underestimated.
b Using Whole Kingdom CPI, not weighted average.
Source: World Bank (1985).

Table 12.5: Subregional income disparities, 1975–76 and 1981

Subregion	1975–76 Index of per capita household income (Whole Kingdom = 100)	1981 Index of per capita household income (Whole Kingdom = 100)
Upper North	76.9	75.5
Lower North	91.8	104.2
Upper Northeast	69.2	64.0
Lower Northeast	69.6	62.4
Central West	125.2	110.7
Central Middle	131.5	117.2
Central East	100.9	96.1
Upper South	100.0	95.4
Lower South	84.4	91.9
Bangkok	182.2	195.9
Whole Kingdom	100.0	100.0

Source: World Bank (1985).

Table 12.6: Ratio of rural to urban household income per capita, 1975–76 and 1981 (per cent)

Subregion	1975–76	1981
Upper North	48.9	53.9
Lower North	49.1	56.4
Upper Northeast	46.6	58.3
Lower Northeast	42.4	43.0
Central West	66.2	73.4
Central Middle	74.0	73.4
Central East	62.3	78.2
Upper South	55.7	55.5
Lower South	38.7	53.0

Source: World Bank (1985).

coefficient is sensitive to changes around the mode of the distribution, the Theil Index and the Atkinson Index are also used. The Theil Index also has values ranging from 0 to 1, but its computation involves a special parameter, E, which reflects the degree of inequality aversion of the society or the government. In this study, E was assigned the value of 3, which denotes a strong aversion to inequality. This index is therefore very sensitive to changes in incomes of the poor.

Rueda-Sabater et al. (World Bank 1985) used both the 1975-76 SES and the 1981 SES to compute the three indices of income inequality (Table 12.7). All three show worsening trends of income inequality. For the whole Kingdom, the Gini coefficient for 1981 was estimated at 0.473, an increase (of inequality) from 0.451 in 1975-76. The other two indices show similar results: the Theil Index for 1981 worsened to 0.439 from 0.407 for 1975-76; and the Atkinson Index stood at 0.612 for 1981, an increase from 0.586 in 1975-76. When the income distribution by area is considered for 1975-76, it shows that in rural areas, where income has tended to be more evenly distributed, inequality had worsened by 1981. This indicates that increased income in the rural areas was concentrated more among upper income classes than lower income classes. The overall distribution of income in rural areas was still more equitable than in urban areas, except for urban Bangkok, which was the least inequitable subregion in both 1975-76 and 1981.

The overall distribution of income clearly worsened between 1975-76 and 1981. But was the distribution of income more or less equitable before 1975-76 compared with recent years? In an attempt to answer these questions, Somchai Jitsuchon analysed studies of earlier data on income distribution and made the necessary adjustments to make the inequality indices comparable over time (Somchai 1987). The longer term trends in income inequality in Thailand, indicated by Somchai's and earlier studies, are summarized in Table 12.8.

Table 12.8 is adapted from a similar table in Somchai's study. In it, one can see a series of inequality estimates relating to four periods, 1962-63, 1968-69, 1975-76 and 1981. Series (1) and (2) describe two alternative methods for calculating Gini coefficients, while series (3) to (5) describe three different methods for estimating the variance of log of incomes. The differences are described in Somchai's study and need not concern us here. The most interesting features of this table are the Gini coefficients, series (2), and the variance of log of income, series (3), which were adjusted by Somchai to make them comparable over time. The virtue of these estimates is that they clearly show the changes in income distribution over time.

Table 12.7: Inequality across households by location, based on household income per capita, 1975–76 and 1981

Subregion	Theil Index		Atkinson Index[a]		Gini	
	1975-76	1981	1975-76	1981	1975-76	1981
Urban						
Upper North	0.352	0.343	0.592	10.605	0.431	0.445
Lower North	0.574	0.451	0.646	0.641	0.494	0.478
Upper Northeast	0.414	0.353	0.590	0.563	0.470	0.448
Lower Northeast	0.356	0.406	0.655	0.624	0.444	0.466
Central West	0.355	0.310	0.530	0.604	0.436	0.408
Central Middle	0.360	0.372	0.583	0.585	0.421	0.454
Central East	0.361	0.375	0.518	0.696	0.419	0.467
Upper South	0.481	0.377	0.573	0.582	0.465	0.436
Lower South	0.384	0.404	0.587	0.607	0.464	0.463
Bangkok	0.336	0.386	0.527	0.547	0.397	0.389
Rural						
Upper North	0.249	0.291	0.451	0.513	0.344	0.398
Lower North	0.290	0.436	0.383	0.539	0.393	0.455
Upper Northeast	0.224	0.509	0.386	0.487	0.345	0.417
Lower Northeast	0.222	0.266	0.378	0.477	0.340	0.374
Central West	0.320	0.284	0.484	0.510	0.384	0.400
Central Middle	0.255	0.383	0.486	0.584	0.377	0.443
Central East	0.241	0.316	0.468	0.528	0.367	0.405
Upper South	0.291	0.362	0.574	0.528	0.392	0.431
Lower South	0.361	0.335	0.547	0.506	0.437	0.410
	0.275	0.274	0.459	0.511	0.379	0.389

Whole Kingdom	0.407	0.439	0.586	0.612	0.451	0.473
Urban	0.385	0.367	0.599	0.628	0.435	0.447
Rural	0.299	0.396	0.507	0.551	0.395	0.437

[a] The parameter E is set at 3.
Source: World Bank (1985).

Table 12.8: Trends of income inequality, 1962–63 and 1981

Year of study	Gini coefficients			Variance of log income	
	(1)	(2)	(3)	(4)	(5)
1962–63[a]	0.456	0.414	:	:	0.474
1968–69[b]	0.482	0.429	:	:	
1975–76[c]	:	0.439	0.436	0.581	0.618
1981[d]	:	0.446	0.451	0.661	0.658

[a] From Medhi Krongkaew, The Income Redistributional Effects of Taxes and Public Expenditures in Thailand: An Intertemporal Study, PhD dissertation, Michigan State University, 1975. Income unit: total household income

[b] From Pirom Chantaworn, The Decomposition Analysis of the Source of Income Inequality in Thailand, 1962–63 and 1968–69, Master's Thesis, University of the Philippines, 1975. Income unit: household income.

[c] Somchai Jitsuchon (1987), computed from SES 1975–76 data tapes. Income unit: total household income, unweighted.

[d] Somchai Jitsuchon (1987), computed from SES 1981 data tapes. Income unit: per capita household income, weighted by family size.

Source: Somchai Jitsuchon (1987: Table 6.2).

Taking the Gini coefficients, for example, in 1962–63 the Gini ratio was estimated at 0.414. Six years later, it had increased to 0.429. In 1975–76 and 1981, the income distribution worsened further to 0.439 and 0.446, respectively. Similar rising indices of income inequality can also be seen in the variance of income logarithms. Therefore, the trends were those of increasing inequalities. This finding is disturbing. It shows that the fruits of rapid economic development are not equally shared among the majority of the Thai population.

The distributional picture of Thai household incomes over this period is not encouraging, but it appears that although income distribution was worsening, it was happening more slowly.[4] Somchai predicted that, based on trends over the past 20 years, income inequality in Thailand will reach its peak by about 1991–92, if measured by Gini coefficient ratios, or about 1988–90, if measured by variance of the logarithms of income.[5]

Socio-economic characteristics of poor households in 1981

This section discusses some of the economic features of poor households in 1981. The poverty income level in 1981 was set at 3,454 baht per person per year for rural areas, and 5,151 baht per person per year for urban areas (which included municipal areas and sanitary districts). The following analysis will concentrate on two issues: income and its components, and other socio-economic characteristics of poor households.

Income and categories of income

Table 12.9 presents the 1981 average household per capita income of the poor, classified by urban/rural areas and by subregions. The average poor rural household had an average income of 2,533 baht per person per year, with households in the Northeast having the lowest average household incomes. It is notable that non-poor households in the rural Northeast still had lower incomes than non-poor households in other regions, confirming that the Northeast is the poorest region in Thailand.

Table 12.9: Average per capita income and subsistence indicator, 1981

Subregion	Average per capita household income (baht per year)		Subsistence indicator[a] (per cent)	
	Poor	**Non-poor**	**Poor**	**Non-poor**
Rural				
Upper North	2,539	8,660	33.3	19.8
Lower North	2,582	11,259	31.2	19.0
Upper Northeast	2,525	8,226	48.5	32.8
Lower Northeast	2,475	7,623	38.1	27.4
Central West	2,651	11,977	23.4	13.5
Central Middle	2,621	13,445	21.2	8.0
Central East	2,506	10,879	21.5	13.6
Upper South	2,634	20,471	28.0	17.5
Lower South	2,548	9,712	18.5	11.7
All rural	2,533	9,908	36.7	20.5
Urban				
Bangkok	3,695	23,165	3.2	1.1
Other urban	3,623	18,398	16.5	4.0
All urban	3,625	20,332	18.2	2.8
Whole Kingdom	2,734	12,955	33.0	15.3

[a] The value of home produced food as per cent of total household income.
Source: World Bank (1985).

The income differential between poor and non-poor is widest in Bangkok and is more pronounced in urban than rural areas. Of the rural households, those in the Central Middle region have the greatest income differential, and the income differential is lowest in the Northeast. Poor households depend more on home-produced food or food received free than non-poor households. This is demonstrated by the subsistence indicator computed from the ratio of the value of home-produced food to total household income. The subsistence indicators for both poor and non-poor households were highest in the Northeast. In the Upper Northeast, almost half the household income was attributable to home-produced food.

Table 12.10 shows the following five major categories of the sources of household income of the poor and non-poor:
(i) farm income, further subdivided into money income and income in kind;

(ii)   non-farm entrepreneurial income;
(iii) wages and salaries;
(iv) non-farm income in kind, which includes food and clothing provided by employers, or rent-free housing; and
(v)   other money receipts such as lottery winnings, life insurance money, and so on.

In rural areas the poor obtain a high proportion of their incomes in kind. If farm and non-farm income in kind are combined, they constitute about 60 per cent of total household income. Even for the rural non-poor, the income in kind proportion was as high as 40 per cent, which suggests that the production system and consumption patterns of a large segment of rural households are still outside the market system. The largest proportion of income in kind originated from farm activities, especially within poor groups in the Northeast. The ratios of income in kind to total household incomes were 49 and 38 per cent, respectively, for Upper and Lower Northeast. Next came the Upper North (34 per cent) and the Lower North (31 per cent). For other subregions the corresponding ratios were less than one-third. The non-poor exhibited a similar income pattern.

The opportunity to generate income outside the market system is greatest in rural areas, and the urban poor face greater hardship in acquiring the basic necessities of life. Among non-poor households, the proportionate contribution of income categories such as income from non-farm entrepreneurship, income from labour, and other money income, is normally greater than for the poor, where farm incomes predominate. Poverty is correlated with farm work more than any other occupation, except for the poor in Bangkok, who are mostly labourers.

Other socio-economic characteristics

Apart from differences in types and sources of income between poor and non-poor households, the two groups also differ in several socio-economic characteristics. Of these, family size, household dependency ratio, age of head, gender of head, education level of head, occupation of head, employment status of head, and household migration pattern are now considered.

Family size
Table 12.10 shows that poor families were larger than non-poor families in every location (urban/rural, regional and subregional). In 1981, the average family size of poor households was 5.5 persons compared with 4.2 persons for non-poor households. Both poor and non-poor urban families are more likely to have a smaller household size than rural families.

Household dependency ratio
The dependency ratio is defined as the ratio of dependants in a family to total family members. Surprisingly, this ratio is lower for the poor than the non-poor. One possible explanation is that this dependency ratio takes on different meanings between those households whose heads were wage and salary earners, and those farm operators' households whose family members are likely to be unpaid family workers. The dependency ratio should be looked upon as an indicator of the degree of family labour force participation, rather than as an indicator of the ability to earn income.

Age of head
In rural areas, the non-poor heads of households are likely to be older than the poor heads. This reflects the life-cycle effect where a young, newly established family is more likely to face hardship than an old established family. The younger generation also has less opportunity to own land, or owns less land, thereby reducing expected returns from farming.

Gender of household head
The 1981 data showed that except in Bangkok, there were proportionately more households with female heads in the non-poor than in the poor groups. This contrasts with the 1975–76 situation where households headed by females were likely to be poorer than those headed by males.

Education of household head
Table 12.11 shows that heads of households having little or no formal education are more likely to be poor, and the non-poor heads are likely to have more years of schooling. Although education level may not be the most important variable

Table 12.10: Composition of household per capita income, 1981 (per cent)

| Subregion | Farm income | | Poor households | | | |
	Money	In kind	Non-farm entrepreneurial	Wages and salaries	Other money receipts[a]	Non-farm income in kind
Rural						
Upper North	18.4	33.9	5.9	12.7	1.4	27.7
Lower North	27.0	31.4	0.7	16.1	1.9	22.9
Upper Northeast	18.0	48.6	2.7	8.2	3.0	19.5
Lower Northeast	19.8	38.1	3.0	14.7	3.4	21.0
Central West	12.4	24.2	3.8	23.5	4.1	32.0
Central Middle	10.9	21.2	2.8	23.2	7.9	34.0
Central East	26.4	21.5	1.3	25.8	0.8	24.2
Upper South	26.0	28.3	7.6	14.6	2.8	20.7
Lower South	25.0	18.5	5.9	13.9	3.5	25.2
All rural	20.1	36.7	3.5	13.9	3.0	22.8
Urban						
Bangkok	1.7	3.2	24.7	46.4	8.4	15.6
Other urban	16.0	19.9	14.0	20.0	6.6	23.5
All urban	14.8	18.2	14.8	22.4	6.7	23.1
Whole Kingdom	19.1	33.3	5.6	15.5	3.6	22.9

Rural						
Upper North	25.4	20.6	9.6	10.7	4.3	21.4
Lower North	39.3	19.8	4.8	14.4	6.3	15.4
Upper Northeast	37.9	33.2	4.9	10.2	6.2	17.6
Lower Northeast	30.7	27.8	3.5	13.7	6.3	10.0
Central West	32.4	14.1	7.9	18.1	6.2	21.3
Central Middle	19.8	8.0	9.8	31.4	8.5	22.5
Central East	35.3	13.9	8.8	16.7	5.9	19.4
Upper South	30.1	17.6	8.2	18.1	6.5	19.5
Lower South	27.7	11.9	11.3	26.0	4.8	18.3
All rural	30.1	20.5	6.8	16.9	6.8	18.9
Urban						
Bangkok	0.2	1.1	21.3	49.4	9.2	18.8
Other urban	8.3	4.0	23.4	36.2	9.6	18.5
All urban	5.0	2.9	22.2	41.6	9.5	18.8
Whole Kingdom	22.8	15.3	11.3	24.1	7.5	19.0

[a] Calculated as a residual.

Source: World Bank (1985)

Table 12.11: Comparison of poor and non-poor households by age, education and gender of head, family size and dependency ratio, 1981

Subregion	Average age of household head		Percentage of households with female head		Average size of household		Dependency ratio		Average no. of years in formal education	
	Poor	Non-poor	Poor	Non-poor	Poor	Non-poor	Poor	Non-poor	Poor	Non-poor
Rural										
Upper North	44.4	43.9	4.1	12.3	5.0	3.8	0.39	0.55	2.4	3.4
Lower North	43.6	43.6	16.7	20.6	5.2	4.2	0.37	0.49	2.8	3.6
Upper Northeast	42.3	45.5	15.4	19.4	6.0	4.8	0.27	0.40	3.4	4.0
Lower Northeast	41.9	46.3	15.8	19.4	5.8	4.7	0.31	0.43	3.4	3.9
Central West	48.6	47.3	11.1	18.1	5.4	4.4	0.44	0.50	2.7	3.7
Central Middle	49.2	46.8	17.6	22.4	5.3	4.2	0.39	0.53	2.8	4.3
Central East	43.8	49.3	7.7	23.0	6.1	4.3	0.28	0.49	3.0	3.4
Upper South	43.5	46.9	11.4	18.5	5.7	4.3	0.32	0.50	3.0	4.2
Lower South	44.3	44.2	13.0	20.3	5.2	4.1	0.44	0.56	1.5	3.0
All rural	43.3	45.9	13.6	19.8	5.7	4.4	0.33	0.48	3.1	3.8
Urban										
Bangkok	41.7	41.6	36.9	24.3	5.6	4.1	0.35	0.55	3.4	7.0
Other urban	46.3	43.8	18.3	24.0	5.2	3.9	0.39	0.55	3.0	6.4
All urban	45.9	42.9	19.9	24.2	5.2	4.0	0.39	0.55	3.2	6.7
Whole Kingdom	43.9	45.1	16.1	22.1	5.5	4.2	0.34	0.50	3.1	4.7

Source: World Bank (1985).

explaining poverty, education makes a clear difference when it comes to earning capacity.

Occupation of household head
Table 12.12 divides poor and non-poor households into seven occupational groups: farm operators primarily owning land; farm operators primarily renting land; fishing and forestry; non-farm entrepreneurs; professional, technical and managerial; labourers and employees; and economically inactive. From these data, household heads who are farm operators are more likely to be poor than those who are not.

Employment status of heads and household members
It can be seen from Table 12.13 that poor families had a greater proportion of unpaid family workers in the households than non-poor (38 per cent compared with 24 per cent). An explanation for the greater proportion of poor household members wanting more work is that either there was an excess supply of labour or they received lower returns from their labour. The 1981 SES data show that unemployment in every subregion in Thailand (except Bangkok) was very low. Underemployment was also indicated to be quite low throughout the country.

Household migration
From Table 12.14 it can be seen that poor families tended to move around less than non-poor families. It would seem that migration is perceived as a successful means of escaping poverty. Indeed, families whose members embarked on frequent migrations tended to stay above the poverty line.

Changes in poverty and income distribution since 1981

Since 1981, the NSO has conducted a series of SES surveys— in 1986, 1988 and 1990. The 1986 survey showed Thai households and the general population to be in a depressed state. Farm prices in 1986, especially paddy prices, were the lowest of recent times, resulting in reduced income and earnings in most rural

Table 12.12: Socio-economic characteristics of all households, 1981 (per cent of all households)

Subregion	Farm operator primarily owning land				Farm operator primarily renting land	
	less than 2 rai[a]	2–9 rai	10–39 rai	more than 40 rai	19 rai	more than 20 rai
Rural						
Upper North	0.7	31.9	13.4	0.2	11.9	0.8
Lower North	0.2	8.6	30.3	16.6	5.6	8.0
Upper Northeast	0.4	16.2	48.9	7.6	1.7	1.1
Lower Northeast	0.7	13.9	48.6	6.4	2.7	1.3
Central West	2.1	11.0	27.7	7.9	6.2	7.2
Central Middle	0.6	4.0	8.6	4.6	5.9	9.6
Central East	0.6	7.2	22.1	11.8	4.4	14.3
Upper South	0.6	18.5	32.9	3.0	3.6	0.2
Lower South	2.1	24.7	15.7	1.4	8.9	0.7
All rural	0.7	15.3	32.6	7.1	4.9	3.9
Urban						
Bangkok	0.1	0.2	—	—	0.1	—
Other urban	0.4	4.0	9.6	2.1	2.6	2.4
All urban	0.3	2.3	5.4	1.2	1.5	1.4
Whole Kingdom	0.6	11.8	25.2	5.5	4.0	3.2
Poor	0.8	21.4	32.2	2.7	7.6	2.9
Non-poor	0.5	9.4	23.5	6.1	3.1	3.3

Subregion	Fishing and forestry	Non-farm entrepreneur	Professional technical and managerial	Labourers and employees	Economically inactive	Total
Rural						
Upper North	1.2	12.9	1.3	20.2	5.4	100
Lower North	1.9	4.9	1.7	15.3	6.9	100
Upper Northeast	1.1	5.0	3.0	10.0	5.2	100
Lower Northeast	1.6	3.4	2.4	14.7	4.2	100
Central West	1.0	9.6	4.4	18.8	4.1	100
Central Middle	1.6	12.3	4.6	37.2	10.8	100
Central East	3.1	10.0	0.9	21.2	4.4	100
Upper South	4.9	10.1	3.6	17.0	5.5	100
Lower South	—	12.3	4.8	27.4	2.0	100
All rural	1.9	7.7	2.8	17.5	5.7	100
Urban						
Bangkok	0.1	26.5	9.2	55.7	8.1	100
Other urban	2.1	26.8	11.6	28.4	10.0	100
All urban	1.2	26.6	10.5	40.5	9.2	100
Whole Kingdom	1.7	12.8	4.9	23.8	6.7	100
Poor	2.1	7.5	0.3	18.9	3.5	100
Non-poor	1.6	14.1	6.0	24.9	7.4	100

a One rai = 1,600 square metres = 0.16 hectares = 0.4 acres

Source: World Bank (1985).

Table 12.13: Employment status of the potential labour force, 1981[a] (per cent)

Subregion	Economically inactive		Unpaid family worker		Wanting more work		Unemployed		Average hours worked per week	
	Poor	Non-poor	Poor	Non-poor	Poor	Non-poor	Poor	Non-poor	Poor	Non-poor
Rural										
Upper North	24.1	21.8	43.5	33.9	17.9	19.0	—	—	57.7	56.7
Lower North	19.4	18.1	47.5	43.9	12.6	7.0	0.6	0.1	63.6	61.8
Upper Northeast	21.5	21.0	47.8	47.0	32.2	23.3	0.4	0.1	57.3	57.8
Lower Northeast	22.2	20.8	44.6	44.2	31.2	22.9	—	—	63.2	62.2
Central West	30.2	21.1	37.5	40.8	16.7	13.7	—	0.1	62.5	56.6
Central Middle	30.9	28.6	33.7	25.3	14.0	10.5	0.5	0.7	54.1	52.5
Central East	25.3	20.9	42.5	39.6	7.1	12.7	—	0.1	51.9	54.2
Upper South	29.0	25.2	38.3	34.4	3.2	4.6	—	—	54.0	52.0
Lower South	30.0	24.5	28.6	25.1	5.3	5.3	—	—	51.7	48.0
All rural	23.8	23.2	43.6	37.0	22.6	14.1	0.2	0.2	58.8	56.6
Urban										
Bangkok	33.9	42.0	10.0	7.9	3.0	2.9	3.5	1.3	49.2	49.6
Other urban	22.8	35.6	31.1	16.5	19.6	7.7	0.6	0.5	56.3	53.9
All urban	23.8	38.3	29.1	12.9	18.0	5.5	0.9	0.8	55.8	52.3
Whole Kingdom	27.9	31.1	37.7	24.3	20.8	9.2	0.5	0.6	57.7	54.6

[a] Potential labour force = population of 11 years and older.
Source: World Bank (1985).

Table 12.14: Household mobility, 1981 (per cent)

Subregion	Always lived in same district[a]		Lived in district over 10 years		Lived in district less than 10 years		Working away from home[b]	
	Poor	Non-poor	Poor	Non-poor	Poor	Non-poor	Poor	Non-poor
Rural								
Upper North	73.5	69.4	17.7	19.0	0.8	11.6	3.4	4.7
Lower North	50.0	45.8	31.1	38.3	18.9	16.0	4.8	7.9
Upper Northeast	66.8	60.7	21.0	28.7	12.2	10.5	1.7	3.7
Lower Northeast	61.8	66.8	28.9	23.6	9.2	9.6	4.3	4.3
Central West	51.8	72.8	29.6	20.8	18.5	7.2	9.3	4.7
Central Middle	69.5	58.2	19.4	27.2	11.1	14.6	2.3	2.5
Central East	64.1	67.4	28.2	25.2	7.7	7.4	1.4	1.8
Upper South	69.3	72.4	25.0	14.6	5.7	13.1	2.2	5.9
Lower South	69.6	69.9	21.7	17.1	8.7	13.0	7.1	4.7
All rural	65.1	62.3	24.1	25.6	10.8	12.1	3.1	4.2
Urban								
Bangkok	18.5	15.7	53.8	42.0	27.7	42.3	5.4	3.3
Other urban	57.8	42.5	29.1	31.5	13.1	26.0	3.9	4.5
All urban	54.4	31.6	31.2	35.8	14.4	32.6	4.0	4.0
Whole Kingdom	60.8	46.0	26.9	31.0	12.3	23.0	3.5	4.1

a Percentage of households.
b Percentage of population.
Source: World Bank (1985).

areas in Thailand. Thailand's recession was in part a consequence of the world recession of the early 1980s, which reached its trough around 1985–86. By 1987, the situation in Thailand was improving and by 1988, the Thai economy had attained a previously unanticipated GDP growth rate of 11 per cent. The survey of 1986, though unlikely to give a true picture of regular patterns and trends of poverty and income distribution in Thailand, is still the most recent useful source of information on household and individual income.

While the 1986 SES data were being processed by the NSO, its data were made available to the Thailand Development Research Institute (TDRI). The result was a report on poverty and income distribution in Thailand in 1986 by Suganya and Somchai (1988). The following discussion draws upon the results presented in that study.

Change in average income

Since the data processing and classification by Suganya and Somchai are different from those of the World Bank (1985), any comparison is difficult and this is why their findings were not incorporated into the analyses of poverty and income distribution in the earlier sections of this chapter. This section adopts the classification and presentation of Suganya and Somchai's study without attempting to make them comparable to the earlier parts of this chapter. On this basis, the change in average income of Thai individuals is presented in Table 12.15. The results are classified into five categories: by the whole kingdom, by region, by sector of production, by quintile group, and by poverty status.

The following discussion relates to nominal incomes per capita. To interpret the results it should be noted that Thailand's average annual rate of (CPI) inflation over the 1981–86 period was 2.8 per cent. For the whole kingdom, from 1981 to 1986, average individual income increased from 8,916 to 10,022 baht per person per year (an average annual increase of about 2.4 per cent). This rate of growth is low, and there is considerable regional variation. In the North, average individual income increased by 1.5 per cent per year, slightly higher than the South at 1.4 per cent. People of the Northeast had, on average, virtually

Table 12.15: Average incomes, 1981 and 1986

	Income per capita, (baht per year)[a]		Annual growth[b] (%)
	1981	**1986**	**1981–86**
Whole Kingdom	8,916	10,022	2.4
Region			
North	8,270	8,927	1.5
Northeast	5,848	5,860	—
Centre	9,994	11,161	2.2
South	8,754	9,407	1.4
Bangkok - City	19,920	25,404	5.0
Bangkok - Suburb	16,920	22,404	5.8
Bangkok - Fringe	11,239	14,988	5.9
Sector of production			
Inactive	13,056	14,484	2.1
Agriculture	6,032	5,768	-0.9
Non-agriculture	13,056	15,744	2.6
Quintile group			
Poorest quintile	2,412	2,280	-1.1
Second quintile	4,055	3,941	-0.6
Third quintile	5,963	6,058	0.3
Fourth quintile	9,197	9,955	1.6
Richest quintile	22,944	27,864	4.0
Poverty status			
Poor	2,686	2,810	0.9
Non-poor	10,956	13,284	3.9

[a] Current prices.
[b] These data relate to nominal (money) incomes. To interpret them it should be noted that Thailand's average annual rate of (CPI) inflation from 1981 to 1986 was 2.8 per cent.
Source: Adapted from Suganya and Somchai (1988).

the same income in 1986 as in 1981, whereas income increased by about 2.2 per cent per year in the Central Region. The most dramatic change was the increase in the average income of those living in Bangkok, where the annual growth rate ranged from 5.0 to 5.9 per cent. The concentration of income growth in the Greater Bangkok area is beyond doubt.

When the data were classified by sector of production, a disturbing picture emerged. Agricultural income actually declined, even in nominal terms, from 6,032 baht in 1981 to 5,788 baht in 1986 (a negative rate of 0.9 per cent per year), while income of the non-agricultural sector grew faster (at 2.6 per cent) than the national growth rate of 2.4 per cent. When the change of income is organized by quintile group; the lowest quintile experienced a reduction in total income between 1981 and 1986, as did the second quintile. It appears that, overall, growth was almost entirely induced by growth of income in the richest quintile. When the population is classified into poor and non-poor, both groups experienced an average income increase, but the proportional increase by the non-poor was much larger than the poor.

The economic adversity in 1986 was fully reflected in the reduction of absolute income for about half the population. These people were mainly farmers or those who worked in agricultural sectors in the North, Northeast, and the South. The people of Bangkok and, to a lesser extent, the Central Region still enjoyed positive income growth.

Changes in poverty incidence

Given that the absolute income of about half of the population had fallen during 1986, it is not surprising that the incidence of poverty, calculated from the 1986 SES, increased from the level of 1981.[6] Suganya and Somchai presented estimates of poverty incidence in Thailand for both 1986 and 1981 and these are given in Table 12.16.

It is apparent from this that the overall incidence of poverty for the whole kingdom had increased from 23 per cent in 1981 to 30 per cent in 1986. Although this was a large increase, two qualifications should be mentioned. First, 1986 was an unusually bad year. Second, the poverty incidence for 1981 was understated relative to later years because of the change in definition of households. If the incidence figure for 1981 was adjusted upward, and that for 1986 downward to, say, 25–26 per cent, it may well be the case that the overall incidence of poverty did not change between 1981 and 1986.

While it is not unreasonable to make this optimistic interpretation of the results it must still be considered

Table 12.16: Poverty incidence, 1981 and 1986 (per cent)

Region and location	1981[a]	1986
North	21.5	25.5
Villages	23.3	27.7
Sanitary districts	16.2	20.2
Municipal areas	8.0	6.9
Northeast	35.9	48.2
Villages	37.9	50.5
Sanitary districts	20.8	33.3
Municipal areas	18.0	18.7
Central	13.6	15.6
Villages	14.2	17.4
Sanitary districts	11.6	11.4
Municipal areas	11.7	8.9
South	20.4	27.2
Villages	22.2	31.2
Sanitary districts	6.8	8.1
Municipal areas	15.2	8.6
Bangkok	3.9	3.5
City core	3.7	3.1
Suburbs	2.6	2.5
Fringes	9.2	8.8
Whole Kingdom	23.0	29.5

[a] The incidence figures given by Suganya and Somchai (1988) for 1981 are generally lower than those given by World Bank (1985) and presented in this paper. This was probably because the World Bank researchers had made several household size and income adjustments, which tended to correct the upward bias of the original income positions. No attempt is made to reconcile these differences, but readers are alerted to them.

Source: Suganya and Somchai (1988).

undesirable for poverty incidence to remain unchanged after many years of positive overall economic growth. The situation in the Northeast is of special concern. The unadjusted figures show a noticeable rise in poverty incidence and no amount of adjustment can change the fact that the Northeast was the largest sufferer of the recession years. Clearly, 1986 was the year of the urban dwellers. The people of Bangkok experienced a reduction in their already low poverty incidence, as did the people of all other municipal areas, except the Northeast.

Changes in income distribution

With the rural population becoming worse off and the urban population better off, the distribution of income must have worsened. Suganya and Somchai adopted a convenient way to present their findings about trends in Thai income distribution by showing the income share of five quintile groups and, as a means of confirming the trends, by including summary indices of Gini coefficients and variance of log of income. These statistics are summarized in Table 12.17.

The income share of the four lowest quintiles fell continuously from 50.7 per cent to 44.4 per cent between 1975–76 and 1986, with the lowest quintile suffering the most with its income share falling from 6.1 to 5.4 to 4.6 per cent, respectively for 1975–76, 1981 and 1986. By contrast, the income share of the top quintile increased from 49.3 to 55.6 per cent for the corresponding periods.

Poverty and income distribution in 1988

In 1988, the NSO conducted another socio-economic survey of the whole Kingdom. The results, which became available in early 1990, showed that by 1988 the incidence of poverty had in general continued to decline relative to the recorded incidence in 1981 and 1986. Nevertheless, the relative income distribution

Table 12.17: Distribution of incomes, 1975–76, 1981 and 1986 (per cent)

Quintile group	1975–76	1981	1986
Poorest quintile	6.1	5.4	4.6
Second quintile	9.7	9.1	7.9
Third quintile	14.0	13.4	12.1
Fourth quintile	21.0	20.6	19.9
Richest quintile	49.3	51.5	55.6
Total share	100.0	100.0	100.0
Gini coefficients	0.426	0.453	0.500
Variance of log of income	0.530	0.602	0.737

Source: Suganya and Somchai (1988).

had continued to worsen. A study based on these data (Medhi, Pranee and Suphat 1991) compared the incidence of poverty in 1981 and 1988, and also the Gini coefficients and other indicators of income inequality for the same periods. These comparisons are shown in Tables 12.18 and 12.19.

Table 12.18 summarizes poverty incidence in 1981 and 1988 using a different locational classification from the one used elsewhere in this chapter. The table uses a classification previously used by Suganya and Somchai (1988), and its use here makes it possible to compare the 1988 results with those for earlier years. Suganya and Somchai treated sanitary districts as rural areas (SD-rural) in contrast with Medhi et al. who treated them as urban areas (SD-urban), and the urban poverty cut-off income was used to identify the poor there. The 1988 figures show the difference in these two treatments. Based on the SD-rural concept (column 2 of the table), the incidence of poverty across the whole kingdom had declined from 23 per cent in 1981 to 21.2 per cent in 1988, a proportionate reduction of some 8.1 per cent. However, when the SD-urban concept was used (column 3), poverty incidence in the whole Kingdom was estimated at 22.8 per cent, showing only a marginal poverty reduction. The rank-order of regions by poverty incidence remained unchanged. That is, the Northeast still remained the poorest region, followed by the North, the South, the Central Region and Bangkok in that order.

The distribution of income had worsened by 1988 as shown in Table 12.19. The overall Gini coefficient (based on population income share) increased to 0.479, compared with 0.453 in 1981. The quintile classification shown in Table 12.19 also clearly indicated that the income distribution must have been more unequal, as each of the four poorest quintiles (or 80 per cent of the total population ranking from the poorest upward) had a lower income share in 1988 compared with 1981, whereas the top or richest quintile increased its income share from 35.4 per cent to 37.8 per cent over the same period.

Conclusions: widening inequality

This chapter has discussed the available evidence on the state of poverty and income distribution of the Thai population in 1975–76, 1981, 1986 and 1988. The important findings are:

Table 12.18: Poverty incidence, 1981 and 1988 (per cent)

Region	1981[a]	1988[a]	1988[b]
North	21.5	20.0	22.3
Municipal	8.0	10.5	10.5
Sanitary	16.2	15.1	36.4
Village	23.3	21.6	21.6
Northeast	35.9	34.6	36.3
Municipal	18.0	18.6	18.6
Sanitary	20.8	18.6	41.8
Village	37.9	36.8	36.8
Central	13.6	12.9	14.8
Municipal	11.7	7.7	7.7
Sanitary	11.6	5.9	18.7
Village	14.2	15.0	15.0
South	20.4	19.4	20.5
Municipal	15.2	10.8	10.8
Sanitary	6.8	10.2	25.7
Village	22.2	21.7	21.7
Bangkok and greater areas	3.9	3.5	4.1
City Centre	3.7	2.7	2.7
Surrounding provinces	—	6.6	9.6
Whole Kingdom	23.0	21.2	22.8
Municipal	7.5	6.1	6.1
Sanitary	13.5	12.2	29.6
Village	27.3	26.3	26.3

[a] Applying the rural poverty line to sanitary districts. In 1981 the line was 3,454 baht per capita per year, and in 1988 it was 4,076 baht.
[b] Applying the urban poverty line to sanitary districts. In 1981 the line was 5,151 baht and in 1988 it was 6,203 baht.
Source: Medhi et al. (1991).

- *Increase in incomes.* Between 1975–76 and 1981, real incomes in most occupational groupings and most regions increased rapidly. Even in rural areas, the rate of increase of real income was as high as that in urban areas. There is reason to believe that the general increase in household income was not an increase in permanent income, because savings increased more than proportionately. From 1975–76 to 1981, farm prices improved continuously, giving rise to unusually high earnings. At the same time, levels of household expenditure increased at a slower rate than increases in income. The

Table 12.19: Income shares by quintile group and Gini coefficient, 1981 and 1988

Quintile	Income shares	Income shares	Consumption shares
	1981	1988	1988
Lowest 20%	5.41	4.50	5.90
Second 20%	9.10	8.09	9.23
Third 20%	13.38	12.27	13.14
Fourth 20%	20.64	20.26	20.16
Top 20%	51.47	54.88	51.56
Top 10%	35.44	37.76	34.93
Gini coefficient	0.453	0.479	0.433

Source: Medhi et al. (1991).

population of Bangkok benefited most compared with other regions, especially the Northeast. Between 1981 and 1985, crop prices declined steadily, reaching their lowest point in 1986. The income survey in 1986 showed that about half the population experienced an absolute decline in total income. Improving economic conditions in the late 1980s reversed this decline.

- *The fall in poverty incidence.* Poverty incidence declined as a result of the increase in real income for most sections of the population. From 1975–76 to 1981, the proportion of poor people fell from 32 per cent to 24 per cent. The proportion of poor households fell similarly. The poor were still clustered in the rural areas, especially the Northeast, whereas Bangkok and the Central Region were the regions with the smallest percentage of poor. This incidence was shown to have increased in 1986, but data for 1988 suggested that this had been temporary. The fall in poverty incidence can be expected to continue in the future.

- *The worsening pattern of income distribution.* Although the incidence of poverty has clearly declined, the pattern of income distribution has remained inequitable. The divergence in standards of living between urban and rural areas appears to have increased. The populations of Bangkok and the Central Region continue to reap the benefits of development, whereas those in the rural areas struggle behind.

• *Influence of socio-economic factors.* Factors such as size of family, occupation of household heads and location of residence, play important parts in influencing the relative welfare positions of people. Education of the family head makes a significant difference, except in rural areas, where the effect is small.

If Thailand continues along the same development path of the past 20 years, the incidence of poverty can be expected to continue its downward trend. However, the unequal income distribution will remain a problem. Whether this will receive adequate attention from the government depends on decision-makers' perceptions. If it is thought that continuing growth-oriented policies will bring benefits that will 'trickle down' sufficiently to obviate any need to rectify income inequality, the government will maintain its current policy stance. However, if it recognizes the possibility of social unrest within the present, but long-established, situation of income inequality, the government will be more anxious at least to appear to be taking action.

Notes to Chapter 12

[1] The poverty incidence for the whole Kingdom in 1962/63 and 1968/69 was 57 and 39 per cent, respectively. For more detail, see World Bank (1980).

[2] The relative income shortfall index (R) is computed from $R = (Y^*-Y_p)/Y^*$ where Y^* is the poverty line, and Y_p is the average income of the poor. The Sen Index (S) is computed from $S = F(Y^*)[1-Y_p(1-G_p)]$ where $F(Y^*)$ is the head-count ratio or the proportion of household or population in poverty, and G_p is the Gini coefficient of inequality among the poor. It will be noticed that S incorporates indicators of incidence and severity of poverty, and an index of income inequality among the poor.

[3] The implication of this finding is rather serious. If the trend continues, it would mean that these people are either being made landless or finding too little land on which to work.

[4] This seems to contradict the conclusion made by the present author (Medhi 1985) where it was stated that the worsening trends were increasing at an increasing rate. After checking the consistency of the data and income concepts, it seems that Somchai's analysis is more correct. His results will be followed here.

⁵ Prediction is carried out through the use of equations that regress inequality indices against changes in time.

⁶ For 1986, the poverty-line incomes for rural and urban populations were 3,828 and 5,834 baht per person per year, respectively.

Thai Language Bibliography

Ammar Siamwalla (ed.), 1990. *Credit in Rural Thailand*, Bangkok, Thailand Development Research Institute.

——, Chirmsak Pinthong and V. Thosanguan, 1981. 'Agricultural marketing and pricing policy in Thailand', Research Paper for National Economic and Social Development Board (NESDB), Bangkok.

—— and Viroj Na Ranong, 1990. *Factbook on Rice*, Bangkok, Thailand Development Research Institute.

Amnuey Saengnoree, 1984. *Comparative Analysis of Market Structure, Economies of Scale and Profit Behavior of Thai Commercial Banks and Finance and Security Companies*, Bangkok, King Mongkut Institute of Technology.

Apichai Puntasen, 1976. 'Education in Thailand' in Narongchai Akrasanee and Rangsan Thanapornpun (eds), *Rak Muang Thai*, Bangkok, Thailand Social Sciences Association: 226–255.

Asjana Watananukij, 1985. Foreign debt of public enterprises. Seminar paper on Foreign Debt Crisis of the Thai Government, 11–12 February, Faculty of Economics, Thammasat University, Bangkok.

Banchong Thongkoom, 1965. An Analysis of the Cost of Producing Graduates from the Faculty of Education, Chulalongkorn University, MA Thesis, Chulalongkorn University.

Bandid Nijathaworn and Madee Weerakitpanich, 1987. 'Economic fluctuations and stability of the commercial banking system', Symposium paper, The Stability of Financial Institutions, Thammasat University, Bangkok.

Bhanupong Nidhiprabha and Atchana Wattananukit, 1987. 'Assets holding behavior and the stability of Thai commercial banks', Symposium paper, The Stability of Financial Institutions, Thammasat University, Bangkok.

Chaiyong Pativintranond, 1984. Lending Behavior of Commercial Banks in Thailand, MA Thesis, Thammasat University, Bangkok.

Chesada Loohawenchit, 1984. Public enterprises in the Thai economy, Seminar paper, Thai Public Enterprises: Past, Present and Future, 26–27 January, Bangkok.

——, (n.d.). State enterprises and their impact on the government budget, Thammasat University, Bangkok (mimeo).

Chirmsak Pinthong, 1984. 'Distribution of benefit of government rice procurement policy in 1982/1983', *Thammasat University Journal*, 13(2):166–187.

—— and Pranee Tinakorn, 1982. *Evaluation of the Government's Rice Procurement Policy 1980/81*, Bangkok, Faculty of Economics, Thammasat University, Research Series No.49.

Chuta Chatragupta and Chanida Silpa-Anan, 1974. Report on the cost per student based on budgetary and extra-budgetary allocation, Chulalongkorn University, Experimental Document Printing Project.

Direk Patamasiriwat and Pairoj Benjamanon, 1982. 'Concentration and mobility of commercial banking system in Thailand', *Journal of National Institute of Development Administration*, 22(2):278–304.

—— and Supaporn Prompongsri, 1983. *Commercial Bank Borrowing Behavior in Thailand: 1977–1980*, Bangkok, National Institute of Development and Administration.

Institute of Science and Technology Research in Thailand, 1982. *Study on Thailand Tourists Potentials*, Bangkok.

Inthapanya Watdhithep and Jumlong Atikul, 1985. 'Economic Impact of Tourism in Thailand', Tourism Authority of Thailand, Bangkok (mimeo).

Kaew Roongdang, 1970. 'Investment in education in Thailand', *National Journal of Education*, 4(8):51–67.

Konthee Soongsathitanond, 1975. Private Costs of Graduate Students in Chulalongkorn University, MA Thesis, Chulalongkorn University.

Krirkkiat Phipatseritham, 1982. *The Distribution of Ownership in Thai Big Business*, Bangkok, Thammasat University Press.

——1987. 'Financial centralization and the setting of economic policies', Symposium paper, The Stability of Financial Institutions, Thammasat University, Bangkok.

Lalita Rueksamran, 1977. *Private Costs of Ramkamhaeng University Students*, Bangkok, Ramkamhaeng University.

Martin, Will and Warr, Peter G., 1990. 'Explaining agriculture's declining share of Thai national income', *Chulalongkorn Journal of Economics*, 2(2):178–224.

Medhi Krongkaew and Chintana Chernsiri, 1975. 'The determination of the poverty level in Thailand', *Thammasat University Journal*, 5(1):48–68.

Nampech Sintavee, 1979. Market Structure and Performance of the Thai Commercial Banking System and its Impact on the Economy, MA Thesis, Chulalongkorn University.

Naris Chaiyasoot, Varakorn Samakoses and Cheunruthai Pornpatrakul, 1987. 'Structure and problems of financial institutions in the Thai economy', symposium paper, The Stability of Financial Institutions, Thammasat University, Bangkok.

Narongchai Akrasanee and Rangsan Thanapornpun (eds), 1976. *Rak Muang Thai*, Bangkok, Thailand Social Science Association: 105–121.

Nimit Nontapanthawat, 1976. 'Foreign borrowing of commercial banks in Thailand' in Narongchai Akrasanee and Rangsan Thanapornpun (eds), *Rak Muang Thai*, Bangkok, Thailand Social Science Association: 123–164.

Nimitr Aswaraksa, 1978. The Opportunity of Continuation to Upper Secondary Level, Classified by Types of School, Personal Status and Class Performance of Students in the South, MA Thesis, Srinakharinwirot University.

Nipon Poapongsakorn, 1981. Policy and effect of the control of tuition fees and subsidy to private schools. Research Report to the Social Project Division, National Economic and Social Development Board, Bangkok.

——1987. 'Is BAAC trying to gain profit from farmers like commercial banks?', *Matichon*, 10 (January 19–20): 6,7,14.

Nipon Theerakamolkit, 1984. 'The liquid asset holding behavior of commercial banks in Thailand', *Monthly Economic Report*, June:43–62.

Nitida Prayong, 1987. Socio-economic Changes Resulting from Tourism: a Case Study at Samui Island, Suratthani Province, MA Thesis, Mahidol University.

Nongluck Prasert, 1973. The Relationship between Scholastic Achievement at Secondary Education Level and the University Entrance Examination: a Case of Students of Demonstration School, MA Thesis, Chulalongkorn University.

Nopporn Ruengsakul, 1986. *Commercial Banking Path*, Bangkok, Thammasat University Press.

——, et al. (eds), 1987. *Money and Banking and Implementation of National Economic Policies*, Bangkok, Chulalongkorn University Press.

Paisan Chaimonkol, 1976. *Public Enterprises*, Bangkok, Thai Watana Panich.

Pannee Bualek, 1986. *An Analysis of Thai Commercial Bank Capitalists: B.E. 2475–2516*, Bangkok, Chulalongkorn University.

Penpimol Koosiriwichien, 1983. An Analysis of Factors besides Talent that Affect Achievement in Mathematics, MA Thesis, Srinakharinwirot University.

Pipat Thai-aree, 1986. *Policy and Process of Privatization: the Cases of the United Kingdom and Thailand*, Bangkok, Chulalongkorn University.

Pornlert Uampuang, 1982. Private Costs of Silpakorn University Students, MA Thesis, Chulalongkorn University.

Ruengwit Sawekkomate, 1981. Factors Determining Foreign Borrowing of Commercial Banks, MA Thesis, Thammasat University.

Saeng Sanguanruang, Somsak Tambunlertchai and Nit Sammapan, 1977. *A Study of Small and Medium Scale Industries in Thailand*, Bangkok, National Institute of Development Administration.

Sataporn Jinachitra, 1987. 'Efficiency, Stability, Supervision of the Financial Institutions' in Nopporn Ruengsakul et al. (eds), *Money and Banking and Implementation of Economic Policies*, Bangkok, Chulalongkorn University Press:143–157.

Sirilaksana Khoman, 1988. 'The burden of expenditure on higher education in Thailand and the role of the private sector' in Nipon Poapongsakorn and Rangsan Thanapornpun (eds), *The Economy: On the Path of Peace and Social Justice*, Bangkok, Thammasat University Press.

Somchai Ratanakomut, 1986. *Study for Tourism Plan during the Sixth National Economic and Social Development Plan B.E. 2530–2534*, Bangkok, Chulalongkorn University.

Sunee Busayawit, 1978. A Comparison of Costs of Sugarcane Cutting by Means of Labor and by Means of Machines: with special reference to the Western region of Thailand, MA Thesis, Thammasat University.

Supachai Panichpakdi, 1976. 'The changing rates of return on investments in education' in Narongchai Akrasenee and Rangsan Thanapornpun (eds), *Rak Muang Thai*, Bangkok, Thailand Social Science Association:189–225.

Supang Chantavanich, 1979. 'Equality of opportunity of continuation to secondary education', *Journal of National Education*, 14(1):15–32.

Supaporn Pornnapa, 1962. An Analysis of Private Costs of Students in the Faculty of Education, Chulalongkorn University, MA Thesis, Chulalongkorn University.

Supote Chunanunthatham, 1978. 'The binding of the exchange rate between Thai baht and US dollar', paper presented at Current Economic Situation and Policy Analysis of Thailand, economics symposium, Faculty of Economics, Thammasat University, Bangkok.

Tarisa Derethinan, 1987. 'The development of Thai financial institutions' in Nopporn Ruengsakul et al. (eds), *Money and Banking and Implementation of National Economic Policies*, Bangkok, Chulalongkorn University Press:123–141.

Thailand, Bank of Thailand, various issues. *Monthly Economic Report*, Bangkok.

——, Department of Labour, 1986. *Thai Workers Abroad,* Bangkok.

——, Ministry of Education, 1984. 'National private schools commission', document used in the training course in Accounting Practices for Private School, Rayong, 2-4 May.

——, National Economic and Social Development Board. *Tourism Plan During the Period of Fifth National Development Plan 2525-2529 B.E.,* Bangkok.

——,——, *Tourism Plan During the Period of Sixth National Development Plan 2530-2534 B.E.,* Bangkok.

——,——, 1990. *Summary: Direction of Development Under the Frame of the Seventh Plan (1992-1996),* Bangkok.

——,——and Thailand Development Research Institute, 1989. 'The structure of the labour market and estimates of labour market situation during the 7th plan period', paper prepared for the project on Promotion of Analysis and Consideration of Population Consequences of Development Planning and Policy in Thailand, Bangkok.

——, National Education Council, 1984. *Report on the Evaluation of Educational Management and Performance of the Fifth National Educational Development Plan (1982-1986),* Bangkok.

——, Tourism Authority of Thailand, 1986, 1987. *Summary of Marketing Activity Plan,* Bangkok, Tourism Authority of Thailand.

Thailand Development Research Institute, 1986. Land Tenure Policy (Land Rights and Land Titling), *Land Tenure Policy,* Vol. 5, Bangkok, Thailand Development Research Institute.

——, 1987. The impact of high business tax rates on tax evasion of industrial entrepreneurs and on fiscal status of the government. Submitted to the Association of Thai Industries, Bangkok.

The Environmental Social Science Project, 1986. *Social and Cultural Impact of Tourism: A Case Study of Chiangmai,* Faculty of Social Science and Humanities, Mahidol University, Bangkok.

Thienchay Kiranandana, 1988. 'Education: crucial factors in human resource development in Thailand' in Nipon Poapongsakorn and Rangsan Thanapornpun (eds), *Thai Economy: On the Path of Peace and Social Justice,* Bangkok, Thammasat University Press:505-52.

Trairong Suwankiri et al., 1975. 'The determination of minimum wages in Thailand and their economic impact', *Thammasat University Journal,* 5(1):2-47.

Vacharee Vilasdechnond, 1979. Rate of Return to Investments in Vocational Education, MA Thesis, Chulalongkorn University.

Vares Oupatiga, 1986. *Roles of Financial Institutions in Thailand in Savings Mobilization and Credit Allocation,* Bangkok, Faculty of Economics, Thammasat University.

Vuthiphong Priebjrivat, 1987. 'Public human resources management under fiscal constraints', *Journal of Finance*, 3(16):51-71.

Yokporn Tantisavetrat, 1986. Factors Affecting the Thai Commercial Banks' Operations, MA Thesis, Thammasat University, Bangkok.

English Language Bibliography

Allan, F., 1933. 'Capital and the growth of knowledge', *Economic Journal*, 43 (September):379–389.

——, 1939. 'Primary, secondary and tertiary production', *Economic Record*, 15 (June):24–38.

Ammar Siamwalla, 1978. 'Farmers and middlemen: aspects of agricultural marketing in Thailand', *Economic Bulletin for Asia and Pacific*, 29(1):38–50.

—— and Suthad Setboonsarng, 1989. *Trade, Exchange Rate and Agricultural Pricing Policies in Thailand: Comparative Studies on the Agricultural Pricing Policy*, Washington DC, World Bank.

—— and Prayong Nettayarak, 1990. 'Estimating the Cost of Subsidies for Agricultural Credit', Bangkok, Thailand Development Research Institute (mimeo).

Anat Arbhabhirama, Dhira Phantumvanit, Elkington, J. and Phaitoon Ingkasuwan (eds), 1988. *Thailand Natural Resources Profile*, Bangkok, Thailand Development Research Institute.

Ando, A., Marshall, E.B. and Irwin, F., 1985. *The Structure and Reform of the U.S. Tax System*, Cambridge, The MIT Press.

Apichai Puntasen, 1987. 'Internationalization of higher education: a case of innovative destruction', *Discussion Paper* 94. Faculty of Economics, Thammasat University.

Armatonoff, G.L., 1965. *State Owned Enterprises of Thailand*, Bangkok, Agency for International Development, USOM to Thailand.

Azariadis, C., 1975. 'Implicit contracts and underemployment equilibria', *Journal of Political Economy*, 83(6):1183–1202.

Bailey, M.N., 1976. 'Wages and employment under uncertain demand', *Review of Economic Studies*, 33(1):25–66.

Barker, R., Herdt, R.W. and Rose, B., 1985. *The Rice Economy of Asia*, Washington DC, Resources for the Future.

Beltz, P.A. and McCormack, B.P., 1982. 'The origins of the banking industry in Thailand', *Thai-American Business*, 14(6):7–11.

Bertrand, T.J. and Squire, L., 1980. 'The relevance of the dual economy model: a case study of Thailand', *Oxford Economic Papers*, 32(3):480–511.

Bhagwati, J., 1984a. 'Splintering and disembodiment of services and developing nations', *The World Economy*, 7(2):133–144.

——1984b. 'Why are services cheaper in the poor countries?', *Economics Journal*, 94 (June):279–284.

——, 1987. 'Trade in services and the multilateral trade negotiations', *The World Bank Economic Review*, 1(4):549–569.

Blaug, M., 1971. The rate of return to investment in education in Thailand, Bangkok, National Council (mimeo).

Block, P., Sirilaksana Chutikul and Nipon Poapongsakorn, 1986. *Public sector employment in Thailand: civil service and state enterprises*, Background Paper for World Bank Economic Report on Thailand.

Business in Thailand, 1972. *Return on Investment in Thai Bank*, Bangkok.

Caldwell, J.C., 1967. 'The demographic structure' in T.H. Silcock (ed.), *Thailand: Social and Economic Studies in Development*, Canberra, Australian National University Press:27–64.

Caves, R.E., 1970. 'Uncertainty, market structure and performance: Galbraith as conventional wisdom' in J.W. Markham and G.F. Papanek (eds), *Industrial Organization and Economic Development*, Boston, Houghton Mifflin:283–302.

Chaipat Sahasakul, 1987. *Features of the Tax System in Thailand*, Bangkok, Thailand Development Research Institute.

——, Thongpakda Nattapong and Kraisoraphong Keokam, 1989. *Lessons from the World Bank's Experience of Structural Adjustment Loans (SALs): A Case Study of Thailand*, Bangkok, Thailand Development Research Institute.

Chaiyawat Wibulswasdi, 1984. 'Formulation and implementation of monetary policy: a study of Thailand monetary experience during 1983 and 1984', Paper for the 15th SEANZA Central Banking Course, Kathmandu.

Chalongphob Sussangkarn, 1983. 'Government employment and alternative labor market closures in an economy-wide setting: application to Thailand', paper for the SIAMII conference on CGE Frameworks and Analyses for Thailand, Pattaya.

——, 1986. Labour market segmentation and the prospects for open unemployment, Thailand Development Research Institute (mimeo).

——, 1987. 'The Thai labour market: a study of seasonality and segmentation', paper prepared for the International Conference on Thai Studies, 3–6 July, Australian National University, Canberra.

——, 1988a. 'Production structures, labour markets and human capital investments: issues of balance for Thailand', *Paper Series* No.46. Tokyo, Nihon University Population Research Institute.

——, 1988b. 'Elementary education in the Thai economy and role for non-formal education', paper for the Ministry of Education Seminar on Alternative Education for Primary School Learners, July, Nakorn Pratom.

——, T. Ashakul and Myers, C., 1986. 'Human resources management', paper for Thailand Development Research Institute's Year-End Conference, Pattaya.

——, Direk Patamasiriwat, Teera Ashakul and Kobchai Chimkul, 1988. 'The long-term view on growth and income distribution', paper for the IDRI Year-End Conference, December, Bangkok.

——and Yongyuth Chalamwong, 1989. 'Thailand's economic dynamism: human resource contributions and constraints', paper prepared for the Nihon University's International Symposium on Sources of Economic Dynamism in the Asia and Pacific Region: A Human Resource Approach, 20–23 November, Tokyo.

Chaudhri, D.P. and Dasgupta, A.K., 1985. *Agriculture and the Development Process*, London, Croom Helm Publishers.

Chesada Loohawenchit, n.d. State enterprises and their impact on the government budget, Bangkok (mimeo).

Chirmsak Pinthong, 1977. A Price Analysis of the Thai Rice Marketing System, PhD Thesis, Stanford University.

Clark, C., 1957. *The Conditions of Economic Progress*, London, Macmillan.

Clem, T., 1984. *Tourism, the Environment, International Trade and Public Economics*, Kuala Lumpur and Canberra, ASEAN-Australia Joint Research Project, Economic Papers No.6.

Coleman, J.S., 1966. *Equality of Educational Opportunity*, Washington DC, US Government Printing Office.

C. Pongtanakorn, Chalongphob Sussangkarn, Kanok Katikarn and Yongyuth Chalamwong, 1987. 'A study of the impact of agricultural product price changes on labour absorption in Thai agriculture: a non-linear programming approach', paper for the Thailand Development Research Institute's Macroeconomic Research Conference, 17–18 October, Cha-am.

De Kadt, Emmanuel, 1979. *Tourism Passport to Development*, London, Oxford University Press.

Direk Patamasiriwat and Suewattana Sakeddao, 1990. 'Sources of Growth of Agricultural Production 1965–1985: Analysis Based on TDRI Model', *Warasarn Settasat*, Thammasat, 8(1):43–69.

Doeringer, P.B. and Piore, M.J., 1971. *International Labor Markets and Manpower Analysis*, Massachusetts, Heath Lexington.

Driscoll, M.J. and Lahiri, A.K., 1983. 'Income velocity of money in agricultural developing economies', *Review of Economics and Statistics*, 65(3):393–401.

Emery, R.F., 1970. *The Financial Institutions of Southeast Asia: A Country-by-Country Study*, New York, Praeger Publishers.

Enrique, R.S. *et al.*, 1985. Thailand: poverty review, East Asian and Pacific Division, World Bank (mimeo).

Feder, G., Tongroj Onchan, Yongyuth Chalamwong and Chira Hongladarom, 1988. *Land Policies and Farm Productivity in Thailand*, Baltimore, Johns Hopkins University Press.

Fields, G.S., 1980. Education and income distribution in developing countries: a review of the literature, World Bank (mimeo).

Friedman, M., 1968. 'The role of monetary policy', *American Economic Review*, 58(1):1–17.

Fuchs, V.R. (ed.), 1969. *Production and Productivity in the Service Industries*, New York, Columbia University Press for NBER.

Fuller, T.D., Prathet Kamnuansilpa, Lightfoot, P. and Samakhom Rathanamongkolmas, 1983. *Migration and Development in Thailand*, Bangkok, The Social Science Association of Thailand.

Galbraith, J.K., 1967. *The New Industrial State*, Boston, Houghton Mifflin.

Goldfeld, S.M., 1966. *Commercial Bank Behavior and Economic Activity*, Amsterdam, North Holland Publishing Company.

——and Chandler, L., 1986. *The Economics of Money and Banking*, New York, Harper & Row.

Goldsmith, R.W., 1969. *Financial Structure and Development*, New Haven, Yale University Press.

Gordon, D.F., 1974. 'A neo-classical theory of Keynesian unemployment', *Economic Inquiry*, 12:431–459.

Haddad, W.D., 1978. 'Educational effects of class size', *World Bank Staff Paper*, No.280, Washington DC, World Bank.

——, 1979. 'Sample selection bias as specification error', *Econometrica*, 47(1):153-61.

Hewison, Kevin, 1989. *Bankers and Bureaucrats: Capital and the Role of the State in Thailand*, Yale Centre for International and Area Studies, Monograph Series 34, Yale University, New Haven, Connecticut.

Hicks, J.R., 1935. 'Annual survey of economic theory: the theory of monopoly', *Econometrica*, 3 (January):1–20.

Hill, T.P., 1977. 'On goods and services', *Review of Income and Wealth*, 23(4):315–338.

Husen, T., Saha, L.J. and Noonan, R., 1978. 'Teacher training and student achievement in less developed countries', *World Bank Staff Working Paper*, No.310, Washington DC, World Bank.

Hyneman, S.P., Farrell, J.P. and Sepulveda-Stuardo, M.A., 1984. 'Textbooks and achievement: what we know', *World Bank Staff Working Paper*, No.298, Washington DC, World Bank.

Industrial Management Corporation, 1984. *A Study of Fiscal Implications of Investment Incentives and Promotion Efficiency*, Bangkok.

——, 1985. *Industrial Restructuring Study for the NESDB*, Bangkok.

Ingram, J.C., 1971. *Economic Change in Thailand: 1850–1970*, Stanford, Stanford University Press.

International Bank for Reconstruction and Development, 1959. *A Public Development Program for Thailand*, Baltimore, Johns Hopkins Press.

International Labour Office, Asian Regional Team for Employment Promotion, 1984. *Employment Issues in Thailand's Sixth Plan*, Bangkok, ILO.

Inthapanya Wutdhithep and Jumlong Atikul, 1988. 'Urban self-employment in Bangkok', a report for the National Economic and Social Development Board of Thailand, New Delhi.

Jamison, D.T. and Lau, L.J., 1982. *Farmer Education and Farm Efficiency*, Baltimore, Johns Hopkins University Press.

Japan, 1985. Report on Japanese Overseas Air Travellers 18th Survey, Tokyo.

Jencks, C., 1972. *Inequality: A Reassessment of the Effect of Family and Schooling in America*, New York, Basic Books.

Jimenez, E., Marlaine, L. and Nongnuch Wattanawaha, 1987. *The Relative Effectiveness of Private and Public Schools in Enhancing Achievement: the Case of Thailand*, Washington DC, World Bank.

Jones, L.P., 1975. *Public Enterprise and Economic Development: the Korean Case*, Seoul, Korean Development Institute.

——, (ed.), 1982. *Public Enterprise in Less Developed Countries*, Cambridge, Cambridge University Press.

Juanjai Ajanant, Supote Chunanuntatham and Sorrayuth Meenaphant, 1986. *Trade and Industrialization of Thailand*, Social Science Association of Thailand.

Katz, L.F., 1986. 'Efficient wage theories: a partial evaluation', National Bureau of Economic Research, Working Paper 1906.

Kosit Panpiemras and Somchai Krusuansombat, 1985. 'Seasonal migration and employment in Thailand' in T. Panayotou (ed.), *Food Policy Analysis in Thailand*, Bangkok, Agricultural Development Council:303–341.

Kraiyudht Dhiratayakinant, 1987. 'Privatization: an analysis of the concept and its implementation in Thailand', Bangkok, Thailand Development Research Institute (mimeo).

——, 1989. Privatization of public enterprises: the case of Thailand. A research report commissioned by Asian and Pacific Development Centre, March, Kuala Lumpur.

Krueger, A.O., Schiff, M. and Valdes, A., 1988. 'Measuring the impact of sector-specific and economy-wide policies on agricultural incentives in LDCs', *World Bank Economic Review*, 2(3):255–271.

Kumpa, L., 1985. The Economics of Production and Industrial Trade of Thai Maize, MADE Thesis, Australian National University.

Kuznets, S., 1966. *Modern Economic Growth: Role, Structure and Spread*, New Haven and London, Yale University Press.

——, 1971. *Economic Growth of Nations*, Cambridge, Harvard University Press.

Lee, S.Y. and Jao, Y., 1982. *Financial Structures and Monetary Policies in Southeast Asia*, Hong Kong, Macmillan Press.

Leff, N. and Sato Kazuo, 1980. 'Macroeconomic adjustment in developing countries: instability, short-run growth and external dependency', *Review of Economics and Statistics*, 62(2):170–179.

Leibenstein, H., 1957. *Economic Backwardness and Economic Growth*, New York, Wiley.

Lippman, S.A. and McCall, J.J. (eds), 1979. *Studies in the Economics of Search*, New York, North Holland.

Lockheed, M., Jamison, D. and Lau, L., 1979. 'Farmer education and farm efficiency: a survey', *Economic Development and Cultural Change*, 27(1):26–45.

Mabry, Bevars D., 1984. 'The development of labor institutions in Thailand', Southeast Asia Program, *Drake Paper*, No.112, Cornell University, Ithaca, New York.

Maddala, G.S., 1983. *Limited-dependent and Qualitative Variables in Econometrics*, Cambridge, Cambridge University Press.

Markham, J.W. and Pananek, G.F. (eds), 1970. *Industrial Organization and Economic Development*, Boston, Houghton Mifflin.

Mathana Phananiramai and Mason, A., 1988. 'Enrolment and educational cost in Thailand', paper for Demographic and Economic Forecast for Thailand, 2–3 July,

Mazumdar, D., 1979. 'Paradigms in the study of urban labor markets in LDCs: a reassessment in the light of an empirical survey in Bombay City', *World Bank Staff Working Paper*, No.366, Washington DC, World Bank.

——, 1981. *The Urban Labor Market and Income Distribution*, London, Oxford University Press.

Medhi Krongkaew, 1985. 'Agricultural development, rural poverty, and income distribution in Thailand', *The Developing Economies*, 23(4):325–346.

——and Aphichart Chamrasrithirong, 1984. Poverty in the northeast: a study of low-income households in the northeastern region of Thailand. A research report submitted to the Council for Asian Manpower Studies, April, Manila.

——, Pranee Tinakorn and Suphat Suphachalasai, 1991, 'Priority Issue and Policy Measure to Alleviate Rural Poverty: the case of Thailand', Economic Development Resources Center, Asian Development Bank, Manila.

Meltzer, A.H., 1987. 'Limits of short-run stabilization policy', *Economic Inquiry*, January:1-14.

Mishkin, F.S., 1976. 'Illiquidity, consumer durable expenditure, and monetary policy', *American Economic Review*, 66(4):642-54.

Modigliani, F., 1977. 'The monetarist controversy or, should we forsake stabilization policies?', *American Economic Review*, 67(2):1-19.

Moerman, M., 1968. *Agricultural Change and Peasant Choice in a Thai Village*, Berkeley, California, University of California Press.

Muangchai Tajaroensuk, 1975. 'Educational planning in Thailand: status and organization', *Bulletin of the UNESCO Regional Office for Education in Asia*, June (16):128-140.

Muscat, R., 1966. *Development Strategy in Thailand*, New York, Praeger Publishers.

Myers, C.N., 1986. 'Quality of human resources in human resources management', paper for IDRI Year-End Conference, December, Bangkok.

—— and Chalongphob Sussangkarn, 1989. 'Economic transformation and flexibility of the education system', paper for Human Resource Problems and Policies, 24-25 February, Hua-Hin.

Nalinee Homasawin, 1984. A Regional Analysis of Financial Structure in Thailand: growth and distribution, MA Thesis, Thammasat University.

Narongchai Akrasanee, 1973. The Manufacturing Sector in Thailand: a study of growth, import substitution, and effective protection, 1960-1969, PhD Thesis, Johns Hopkins University.

——, 1977. *The Structure of Effective Protection in Thailand: A Study of Industrial and Trade Policies in the early 1970s*, Report prepared for the Ministry of Finance, the National Economic and Social Development Board of the Government of Thailand, and the International Bank for Reconstruction and Development, Washington, DC.

——, 1983. *Rural Off-farm Employment in Thailand: Summary and Synthesis of the Rural Off-farm Assessment Project*, Bangkok, Industrial Management Consultants.

Nimit Nontapanthawat, 1978, 'Financial capital flows and portfolio behavior of Thai commercial banks', Bangkok, Faculty of Economics, Thammasat University, Research Report Series No.5.

Nongnuch Wattanawaha, 1986. A Study of Equity in Mathematics Teaching and Learning in Lower Secondary School in Thailand, PhD dissertation, University of Illinois.

Oey Meesook, 1979. 'Income, consumption and poverty in Thailand, 1962/63 to 1975/76', *World Bank Staff Working Paper*, No.364, Washington DC, World Bank.

Pairote Wongwuttiwat, 1975. The Structure of Differential Incentives in the Manufacturing Sector: a study of Thailand's experience, 1945-1974, MA Thesis, Thammasat University.

Paitoon Wiboonchutikula, Rachain Chintayarangsan and Nattapong Thongpakde, 1989. *Trade in Manufactured Goods and Mineral Products*, The 1989 TDRI Year-End Conference, Thailand Development Research Institute.

Pasuk Phongpaichit, 1980. *Economic and Social Transformation of Thailand 1957–1976*, Bangkok, Chulalongkorn University, Social Science Research Institute.

——, 1982. *From Peasant Girls to Bangkok Masseuses*, Geneva, International Labour Office.

——, 1986. General employment situation in Thailand. Background Paper for World Bank Economic Report on Thailand, Bangkok.

—— and Baker, C.J., 1984. Bertrand's choice and seasonal unemployment reconsidered, Bangkok, Chulalongkorn University (mimeo).

Phelps, E.S., 1970. *Microeconomic Foundations of Employment and Inflation Theory*, New York, W.W. Norton.

Phitsanes Jessadachatr, 1977. A History of Sugar Policies in Thailand: 1937–75, MA Thesis, Thammasat University.

Plowman, C., 1967. *Children and Their Primary Schools*, London, Her Majesty's Stationery Office.

Poirier, D.J. and Melino, A., 1978. 'A note on the interpretation of regression coefficients within a class of truncated distributions', *Econometrica*, 46(5):1207–1209.

Poonsin Ingavala, 1989. 'Privatization in Thailand: slow progress amidst much opposition', *Asean Economic Bulletin*, March.

Prakarn Aphasih, 1982. Estimation of Manufactured Export Supply Model in Thailand, MA Thesis, Thammasat University.

Prasan Boonserm, 1973. Liquidity and Lending: the Volume of Bank Credit in Thailand, MA Thesis, Thammasat University.

Prateep Sondysuvan (ed.), 1975. *Finance, Trade and Economic Development in Thailand*, Bangkok, Sompong Press.

Prayuth Thongtheppairot, 1972. 'Return on investment in Thai Bank', *Business in Thailand*, 3(8):19–20.

Psacharopoulos, G., 1981. 'Return to education: an updated international comparison', *Comparative Education*, 17(3):321–341.

——and Woodhall, M., 1985. *Education for Development: analysis of investment choices*, New York, Oxford University Press.

Riddle, D.I., 1987. *Service-led Growth: The Role of the Service Sector in World Development*, New York, Praeger.

Riggs, F.W., 1966. *Thailand: The Modernization of a Bureaucratic Policy*, Honolulu, East–West Center Press.

Rizwanul, I., 1984. 'Poverty, income distribution and growth in rural Thailand' in A.R. Khan and E. Lee (eds), *Poverty in Rural Asia*, Bangkok, International Labour Office Asian Regional Team for Employment Promotion:205–229.

Robinson, D., Yangho Bycon and Ranjit Teja, with Wanda Tseng, 1991. *Thailand: Adjusting to Success, Current Policy Issues*, International Monetary Fund Occasional Paper No. 85, Washington.

Rozenthal, A.A., 1970. *Finance and Development in Thailand*, New York, Praeger Publishers.

Sabolo, Y., 1975. *The Service Industries*, Geneva, International Labour Office.

Sadab Attasara, Somchai Wudhiprecha and Surat Silpa-Anan, 1974. *Educational Administration in Thailand*, Bulletin of the UNESCO Regional Office for Education in Asia, 15:179-202.

Salop, J. and Salop, S., 1976. 'Self-selection and turnover in the labor market', *Quarterly Journal of Economics*, 90(4):619-627.

Sa-Ngob Pannarugsa, 1975. 'Profitability of commercial banks in Thailand' in Prateep Sondysuvan (ed.), *Finance, Trade and Economic Development in Thailand*, Bangkok, Sompong Press:79-91.

Sataporn Jinachitra, 1974. *A Portfolio Adjustment Model of Commercial Banks in Thailand*, Bangkok, Bank of Thailand.

Schlossstein, Steven, 1991. *Asia's New Little Dragons: the dynamic emergence of Indonesia, Thailand, and Malaysia*, Illinois, Contemporary Books Inc.

Shiskin, J., 1971. *Signals of recession and recovery*, New York, NBER, Occasional Paper No. 77.

Silcock, T.H. (ed.), 1967. *Thailand: Social and Economic Studies in Development*, Canberra, Australian National University Press.

——, 1970. *The Economic Development of Thai Agriculture*, Canberra, Australian National University Press.

Singapore, Singapore Tourist Promotion Board, 1985. *Survey of Overseas Visitors to Singapore*.

Sirichai Leelakitkul, 1982. Risk, Market Power and Profitability: a Case Study of Thai Commercial Banks, MA Thesis, Thammasat University.

Sirilaksana Chutikul, 1986. *Malnourished Children: An Economic Approach to the Causes and Consequence in Northeastern Thailand*, Paper Series, No.93, East-West Center, Honolulu.

——, 1987. 'The economics of education subsidies and the effect of fee increases: a case study', *Discussion Paper 93*, Faculty of Economics, Thammasat University.

——, 1988. 'The education sector in Thailand: problems, policy dilemmas, and the role of the government', *Discussion Paper 95*, Faculty of Economics, Thammasat University.

Skully, M.T., 1984. *Financial Institutions and Markets in Southeast Asia*, London, Macmillan Press.

Somchai Jitsuchon, 1987. Sources and Trend of Income Inequality: Thailand 1975/76 and 1981, MA Thesis, Thammasat University.

Somchai Ratanakomut, 1987. 'Tourism industry in Thailand', paper prepared for the International Conference on Thai Studies, 3–6 July, Canberra.

Somjin Plengkhum, 1977. A Cost-Benefit Analysis of Nonformal Education, MA Thesis, Thammasat University.

Somkid Saengpetch, 1972. Commercial Bank Borrowing Behavior in Thailand: 1962–1970, MA Thesis, Thammasat University.

Sompop Manarungsan, 1989. *Economic Development of Thailand, 1850–1950*, Bangkok, Chulalongkorn University.

Somsak Tambunlertchai, 1977. *Japanese and American Investment in Thailand's Manufacturing Industries*, Tokyo, Institute of Developing Economies.

——, 1984. 'Manufactured exports and employment in Thailand' in V.D. Pitou and V. Harmen (eds), *Export-Oriented Industrialization and Employment: Policies and Response*, Amsterdam, Vriji University De Boelelann:102–121.

——and Chesada Lohawenchit, 1981. 'Labour-intensive and small-scale manufacturing industries in Thailand' in A. Rashid (ed.), *The Development of Labour Intensive Industry in ASEAN Countries*, Geneva, International Labour Organization:175–227.

——and McGovern, I., 1984. 'An overview of the role of multinational corporations in the development of Thailand' in Nongyao Chaiseri and Chira Hongladarom (eds), The *Role of Multinational Corporations in Thailand*, Bangkok, Thammasat University Press:71–108.

——and Yamazawa, I., 1983. *Manufactured Export Promotion: The Case of Thailand*, Tokyo, Institute of Developing Economies Joint Research, Program Series No.38.

Stanback, T.M. Jr. et al., 1981. *Services: The New Economy*, New Jersey, Rowman and Allanheld.

Stiglitz, J.E., 1974. 'Alternative theories of wage determination and unemployment in LDCs: the turnover model', *Quarterly Journal of Economics*, 88(2): 194–227.

——, 1976. 'The efficient wage hypothesis, surplus labour and the distribution of income in LDCs', *Oxford Economic Papers*, 28(2):185–207.

Suehiro, Akira, 1985. *Capital Accumulation and Industrial Development in Thailand*, Bangkok, Chulalongkorn University Social Research Institute.

——, 1989, *Capital Accumulation in Thailand: 1855–1985*, Centre for East Asian Cultural Studies, Tokyo.

Suganya Hutaserani and Somchai Jitsuchon, 1988. 'Thailand's income distribution and poverty profile and their current situations', paper for the 1988 IDRI Year-End Conference, Thailand.

Sukanya Nitungkorn, 1988. 'The problems of secondary education expansion in Thailand', *Journal of Southeast Asian Studies*, 26(1):24–41.

——and Chitra Vutisart, 1980. The distribution flow of education in the formal school system in Thailand: an analysis of factors affecting scholastic achievement of students of different levels of education. Faculty of Economics, Thammasat University (mimeo).

Sungsidh Piriyarangsan, 1983. *Thai Bureaucratic Capitalism 1932–1960*, Bangkok, Chulalongkorn University, Social Research Institute.

Supachai Panichpakdi, 1981. *Issues in Banking and Finance in Thailand: 1975–1980*, Bangkok, Marketing Media.

——, 1985. *Financial Development in Thailand and Other Developing Countries*, Bangkok, Marketing Media.

Supoj Rojpibulstit, 1976. Bank Competition in Thailand, MA Thesis, Thammasat University.

Suthad Setboonsarng, Boonjit Titapiwatanakun and Somnuk Tubpun, 1989. *Competitiveness of Animal Feed and Livestock Production in Thailand*, Bangkok, Thailand Development Research Institute.

——, Sarun Wattanutchariya and Banlu Puthigom, 1988. 'Seed Industry in Thailand: Structure, Conduct and Performance', *Research Report* No.32., Tilburg, The Netherlands, Development Research Institute, Tilburg University.

Suwat Patanapaikul, 1983. 'The service industry: golden opportunities for business in present-day Thailand', *Journal of Economics and Business Administration*, 10(3):5–29.

Tan, E. and Wannasiri Naiyavitit, 1984. 'The distribution flow of education in the formal school system: an analysis on distribution of education attainment', *Journal of the National Research Council of Thailand*, 16(2):19–43.

Thailand, Bank of Thailand, 1979. *Statistical Bulletin*, Bangkok.

——, ——, 1986. *Financial Institutions in Thailand*, Bangkok.

——, Department of Labour, 1986. *Thai Workers Abroad*, Bangkok.

——, Ministry of Education, 1985. *Ministerial Regulation Regarding Subsidy to Private School Teachers*, Bangkok.

——, ——, (various years). *Education Statistics*, Bangkok.

——, (various years). *Survey of Employment of University Graduates*, Bangkok.

——, Ministry of University Affairs, 1987. *Report on the Joint Higher Education Entrance Examination, Academic Year 1983*, Bangkok, Paabpim Press.

——, National Economic and Social Development Board, 1983. *Summary of the Financial Situation and Operation of 60 Public Enterprises During* the First Two Years of the Fifth Development Plan (B.E. 2525 and 2526), Bangkok (mimeo).

——, ——, 1975, 1980. *Input-Output Table of Thailand*, Bangkok.

——, ——, various issues. *National Economic and Social Development Plan*, Bangkok.

——, ——, various issues. *National Income of Thailand*, Bangkok.

——, National Education Council, 1985. *Cost and Investments in Private Universities and Colleges*, Bangkok.

——, ——, 1986. 'Determination of targets and budgetary allocation according to the Sixth Education Plan', Bangkok (mimeo).

——, ——, 1987. 'Cost and contribution of higher education', Bangkok, draft report.

——, National Statistical Office, 1977 and 1983. *The Children and Youth Survey*, Bangkok.

——, ——, 1984. Unpublished worksheets for the number of students and teachers.

——, ——, various issues. *Labour Force Survey, Round 2 (July-September)*, Bangkok.

——, ——, various years. *Report of Students and Teachers*, Bangkok.

——, Tourism Authority of Thailand, 1984, 1985, 1986, 1987. *Annual Statistical Report on Tourism in Thailand*, Bangkok.

Thailand Development Research Institute and National Economic and Social Development Board (TDRI/NESDB), 1989. *S&T Manpower Situation: An Update*, Bangkok, Human Resources and Social Development Program and Human Resources Planning Division.

Thammanoon Pongsrikul and Somchai Ratanakomut, 1989. 'Thailand in the international community', paper for the 1989 IDRI Year-End Conference, 16-17 December, Chonburi.

Thwatchai Yongkittikul, Phaithoon Wiboonchutikula and Somchai Meenaphant, 1989. 'The Role of Services in the Development of the Economies of the ESCAP Region: The Case of Thailand', report submitted to ESCAP, Thailand Development Research Institute, Bangkok.

Tobin, J., 1978. 'Monetary policy and the economy: the transmission mechanism', *Southern Economic Journal*, 44(3-4):421-431.

Trairong Suwankiri, 1970. The Structure of Protection and Import Substitutions in Thailand, MA Thesis, University of the Philippines.

Trescott, P.B., 1971. *Thailand's Monetary Experience: The Economics of Stability*, New York, Praeger Publishers.

Udom Kerdpibul, 1983. The market structure and competition of the wholesale trade in Bangkok, Kasetsart University, Bangkok (mimeo).

United Nations Educational Scientific and Cultural Organization, 1985, 1986, 1987, 1988. *Statistical Yearbook*, Bangkok, UNESCO.

Usher, D., 1967. 'The Thai rice trade' in T.H. Silcock (ed.), *Thailand: Social and Economic Studies in Development*, Canberra, Australian National University Press:206–230.

Virabongsa Ramangkura, 1975. 'A macroeconomic model for Thailand: a classical approach' in Prateep Sondysuvan (ed.), *Finance, Trade and Economic Development in Thailand*, Bangkok, Sompong Press:209–221.

Vongphakdi, J.M., 1982. Financial Development in Thailand and the Role of Central Banks, MA Thesis, University of New England.

Vuthiphong Priebjrivat, 1987a. *Consolidated Public Sector Finance in Thailand: A Management Approach*, Bangkok, Thailand Development Research Institute.

——, 1987b, *Financial Picture of the Thai Public Sector*, Bangkok, Thailand Development Research Institute.

Wanee Choikiatkul, 1983. 'The role of the service industry in reducing the process of economic development', Paper for the Annual Seminar for 1983, 17–18 February, Faculty of Economics, Thammasat University, Bangkok.

Warr, Peter G. and Bandid Nijathaworn, 1987. 'Thai economic performance: Some Thai perspectives', *Asian-Pacific Economic Literature*, vol.1, 60–74. Reprinted [in Chinese] in *Jingjixue Yicong (Economic Translations)*, vol.10. (1988), 59–66.

Wilson, D.A., 1960. *Politics in Thailand*, New York, Cornell University Press.

World Bank, 1959. *A Public Development Program for Thailand*, Baltimore, Johns Hopkins Press.

——, 1980. *Income Growth and Poverty Alleviation*, A World Bank Country Study, Washington DC, World Bank.

——, 1982. *Industrial Sector Background Report Vol. 1: The Main Report*, Washington DC, World Bank.

——, 1984. *Thailand: Managing Public Resources for Structural Adjustment*, Washington DC, World Bank.

——, 1985, *Thailand: poverty review*, East Asian and Pacific Division, mimeo, Washington DC, World Bank.

——, 1986. *Thailand: Growth with Stability: A Challenge for the Sixth Plan Period: A Country Economic Report Vol. 2: the Main Report*, Washington DC, World Bank.

——, 1988. *World Development Report*, Washington DC, World Bank.

Wright, Joseph J., 1991. *The Balancing Act: A History of Modern Thailand*, Bangkok, Asia Books.

Wyatt, David K., 1984. *Thailand: A Short History*. New Haven, Connecticut, Yale University Press.

Index